Emerging Trends and Innovations in Financial Services:

A Futurology Perspective

Muhammad Ali
Taylor's University, Malaysia

Syed Ali Raza
Iqra University, Pakistan

Chin-Hong Puah
Universiti Malaysia Sarawak, Malaysia

IGI Global
Scientific Publishing
Publishing Tomorrow's Research Today

Vice President of Editorial Melissa Wagner
Director of Acquisitions Mikaela Felty
Director of Book Development Jocelynn Hessler
Production Manager Mike Brehm
Cover Design Jose Rosado

Published in the United States of America by
IGI Global Scientific Publishing
701 East Chocolate Avenue
Hershey, PA, 17033, USA
Tel: 717-533-8845
Fax: 717-533-7115
Website: https://www.igi-global.com E-mail: cust@igi-global.com

Library of Congress Cataloging-in-Publication Data

Names: Ali, Muhammad, 1986- editor. | Raza, Syed Ali, 1985- editor. | Puah, Chin-Hong, editor.
Title: Emerging trends and innovations in financial services : a futurology perspective / edited by Muhammad Ali, Syed Ali Raza, Chin-Hong Puah.
Description: Hershey, PA : IGI Global, [2026] | Includes bibliographical references and index. | Summary: "This book's main goal is to present a futuristic study of the technological advancements that are revolutionizing the financial services industry"-- Provided by publisher.
Identifiers: LCCN 2024048733 (print) | LCCN 2024048734 (ebook) | ISBN 9798369371602 (hardcover) | ISBN 9798369371619 (paperback) | ISBN 9798369371626 (ebook)
Subjects: LCSH: Financial services industry--Technological innovations. | Finance--Technological innovations.
Classification: LCC HG173 .E543 2025 (print) | LCC HG173 (ebook) | DDC 332.10285--dc23
LC record available at https://lccn.loc.gov/2024048733
LC ebook record available at https://lccn.loc.gov/2024048734

British Cataloguing in Publication Data
A Cataloguing in Publication record for this book is available from the British Library.

Table of Contents

Detailed Table of Contents

also highlighted the theoretical points that are associated with the literature in order to make work relevant to academics, research and policy-making.

This paper discusses development of mobile wallets and impact on fintech in India. Section begins with brief history of digital payment systems in India. It covers pioneers and leading players today like Paytm, PhonePe and Google Pay. Additionally, roles of government support, increased smartphone penetration regulatory guidelines and development of Unified Payments Interface (UPI) are examined. Literature is gathered regarding technology adoption models, trust and consumer behavior related to digital payments. The discussion in this book chapter is extended to show that mobile wallets are now moving beyond payments to include savings and investment propositions, thereby contributing to financial inclusion. The chapter concludes with some possible implications for understanding the evolution of mobile wallets in the context of transitioning to a cashless economy and the transformations in consumer behavior, as well as potential gains and difficulties in the future.

The world is continuously moving towards digitization. In fact, every activity from routine-based activities to professional activities is now performed in a digitized way. Similar is the case of financial transactions that were initiated through physical exchange and now are mostly transformed into digitized platforms. Among these platforms, one of the most progressive ones is mobile wallets. Mobile wallets are different from mobile banking and now associated with casual and everyday activities of life. However, there are some challenges associated with the mass acceptance and usage of mobile wallets. Especially from developing sides of the world, the growth of mobile wallets is getting limited just because of associated threats and problems. Therefore, this chapter is designed specifically with reference to the developing sides of the world in order to shed light on the importance of mobile banking as well as factors that are limiting the use of mobile banking.

Preface

In the past decade, the financial services industry has undergone a profound transformation, driven by unprecedented technological innovation, the global push for sustainability, and evolving consumer expectations. From artificial intelligence and blockchain to mobile wallets and quantum computing, the contours of financial ecosystems are being redrawn in real time. This edited volume, *Emerging Trends and Innovations in Financial Services: A Futurology Perspective*, seeks to capture this ongoing evolution and offer critical insights into where the industry is heading. Through a curated selection of research and applied studies, this book explores the fusion of finance, technology, and behavioral change in shaping the future of financial systems globally.

We, the editors, have collaborated with a diverse and interdisciplinary group of scholars and practitioners from across Asia, reflecting a shared urgency to document and analyze the rapid changes transforming financial services in emerging economies and beyond. The chapters featured in this volume reflect an impressive range of perspectives—delving into themes such as Islamic FinTech, privacy and trust, post-COVID behavioral shifts, AI and blockchain innovation, sustainability, and immersive technologies like VR/AR. Each contribution was selected for its ability to illuminate both practical applications and theoretical implications in our fast-evolving financial landscape.

This book is not merely an observation of what *is* but a deliberate reflection on what *could be*. It represents a collective effort to think futuristically—beyond current disruptions—towards the structural, ethical, and technological trajectories likely to define financial systems in the years ahead. As such, this volume is especially suited for academics, policymakers, fintech professionals, and institutional stakeholders who seek to understand and contribute to the next chapter in financial innovation.

CHAPTER OVERVIEW

Chapter 1: A New Revolution: Fin-Tech & Islamic Banking. Concepts, Uses, and Drawbacks in the Light of Archival Data

This chapter explores the dynamic relationship between financial technology (FinTech) and Islamic banking, focusing on the context of Pakistan. It provides a descriptive analysis based on archival data to assess how FinTech is shaping practices, opportunities, and limitations within the Islamic banking sector. The discussion sheds light on the limited academic attention to this intersection in emerging economies and emphasizes its relevance for stakeholders in academia, finance, and policy.

Chapter 2: Importance of Privacy Protection in Fin-Tech Operations

This chapter addresses the critical issue of privacy protection in FinTech operations, with particular attention to consumer trust. It emphasizes the growing need for research in this area and presents theoretical perspectives to support policy and academic discourse. By highlighting privacy concerns as a barrier to adoption, the chapter underscores the importance of integrating secure data practices into FinTech ecosystems to promote user confidence.

Chapter 3: Fostering FinTech Through Mobile Wallets: An Indian Scenario

This chapter examines the evolution of mobile wallets in India and their growing role in the FinTech landscape. It traces the development of major platforms like Paytm and Google Pay, analyzes government initiatives such as UPI, and reviews relevant literature on user trust and behavior. The discussion reveals how mobile wallets are expanding beyond payments to offer broader financial services, contributing to financial inclusion and the shift toward a cashless economy.

Chapter 4: Mobile Wallets: A Detailed Perspective with Reference to the Developing Countries

Focusing on developing countries, this chapter investigates the growing but uneven adoption of mobile wallets. It distinguishes mobile wallets from traditional banking and explores their role in daily transactions. The authors analyze key challenges—such as security concerns and infrastructure limitations—that hinder widespread adoption, offering insights into the necessary conditions for growth in underserved regions.

Chapter 5: Behavioral Finance in Post-COVID-19 World

This chapter explores how the COVID-19 pandemic has reshaped financial decision-making through the lens of behavioral finance. It investigates the psychological and emotional factors influencing investors during crises and highlights gaps in the literature, particularly in the Asian context. The chapter calls for broader geographic representation in behavioral finance studies and offers valuable insights into investor psychology in volatile times.

Chapter 6: The Future of Behavioral Finance: Challenges and Opportunities in the Era of Digital Transformation

This conceptual chapter examines the evolving relationship between digital technologies—such as AI, blockchain, and big data—and behavioral finance. It considers how generational shifts and digital tools are influencing investment behavior and decision-making. By highlighting both opportunities and complexities, the chapter provides a roadmap for future research and organizational adaptation in a digitally transforming financial landscape.

Chapter 7: Navigating Sustainability in Digital Financial Services: Transforming the Future

This chapter investigates how digital financial services intersect with sustainability goals, including SDGs and ESG principles. Through a systematic review, the authors identify key themes in the literature and offer strategic insights for integrating sustainability into financial innovation. The analysis positions green finance as a critical area for development, emphasizing its potential to align financial growth with ethical and environmental objectives.

Chapter 8: Artificial Intelligence and the Future of Financial Decision-Making

Focusing on AI's role in financial services, this chapter categorizes its applications across six domains: data analysis, risk assessment, automation, trading, personalization, and security. It provides a conceptual overview of how AI technologies are reshaping financial decision-making processes and enhancing strategic outcomes for both individuals and institutions.

Chapter 9: The Future of Personal Finance: Artificial Intelligence, Machine Learning, and Big Data

This chapter explores how AI, machine learning, and big data are revolutionizing personal finance. It details how these technologies empower individuals to make smarter financial choices, optimize investments, and manage risks. The discussion integrates existing literature and practical insights, offering recommendations for consumers and financial institutions on navigating this data-driven landscape.

Chapter 10: Revolutionizing Financial Services with AI and Blockchain: Pioneering Innovations for a Digital Future

This chapter analyzes the transformative potential of AI and blockchain in redefining financial services. It highlights innovations such as smart contracts, fraud detection, and personalized services, supported by real-world case studies. The authors discuss the strategic opportunities and implementation challenges, offering a forward-looking perspective on how these technologies are reshaping financial ecosystems.

Chapter 11: Smart Contracts in AI-Driven Decentralized Finance: Navigating Emerging Technologies and Market Dynamics

Examining the use of smart contracts within decentralized finance (DeFi), this chapter highlights both their advantages—efficiency and transparency—and vulnerabilities, especially in security. It emphasizes the role of AI in mitigating risks and calls for standardized frameworks to support wider adoption. The chapter provides a critical perspective on how smart contracts may transform industries and regulatory environments.

Chapter 12: Robotic Process Automation (RPA): A Catalyst for Innovation in Financial Services

This chapter explores how Robotic Process Automation (RPA) is driving innovation in finance by automating routine processes and improving operational efficiency. It offers implementation strategies, ROI considerations, and real-world examples such as DBS Bank. The discussion extends to future trends, including integration with IoT and cybersecurity, showcasing RPA's growing importance in digital transformation.

Chapter 13: Quantum Computing: Transforming the Landscape of Financial Markets

Focusing on the emerging capabilities of quantum computing, this chapter examines its potential applications in financial markets, including risk management, portfolio optimization, and derivative pricing. It outlines how quantum technology may address problems beyond the scope of classical computing and anticipates its growing role in financial analytics and strategic modeling.

Chapter 14: Virtual Reality and Augmented Reality in Financial Services

This chapter explores the application of virtual and augmented reality technologies in financial services. It analyzes how immersive technologies are enhancing activities like risk analysis, portfolio visualization, and virtual bidding. Drawing from existing literature, the chapter highlights AR/VR's potential to modernize client interactions and offers insights for financial professionals and technology developers.

The future of financial services is neither linear nor predictable. As emerging technologies continue to challenge existing systems and introduce new paradigms, the need for ongoing research, ethical scrutiny, and agile policy frameworks becomes more pressing than ever. This volume serves not as a conclusion but as an invitation—to think critically, act responsibly, and innovate boldly within a rapidly shifting financial environment. The complexities explored throughout these chapters remind us that transformation in finance is not only technological—it is fundamentally human, social, and institutional.

We, as editors, recognize that the questions raised in this book will continue to evolve. FinTech, AI, decentralized systems, and sustainability are not endpoints, but dynamic forces that will require ongoing re-examination. As scholars, regulators, industry leaders, and educators, we must be prepared to engage in this work not just as observers, but as active participants in shaping financial systems that are inclusive, secure, and future-ready. Our hope is that this volume encourages such engagement—grounded in knowledge, guided by foresight, and motivated by purpose.

In closing, we express our sincere gratitude to all contributors who brought their insight and expertise to this endeavor. We also extend our thanks to the readers, whose curiosity and commitment to understanding financial innovation fuel the relevance of work like this. As we look ahead, may this book serve as a foundation for meaningful discourse, informed experimentation, and collaborative progress in the ever-expanding world of financial services.

Muhammad Ali

Taylor's University, Malaysia

Syed Ali Raza
Iqra University, Pakistan

Chin-Hong Puah
Universiti Malaysia Sarawak, Malaysia

Chapter 1
A New Revolution:
Fin-Tech and Islamic Banking – Concepts, Uses, and Drawbacks in the Light of Archival Data

Muhammad Faisal Sultan
Khadim Ali Shah Bukhari Institute of Technology, Pakistan

Muhammad Nawaz Tunio
https://orcid.org/0000-0003-1376-5371
University of Sufism and Modern Languages, Pakistan

Imamuddin
Institute of Business Management, Pakistan

ABSTRACT

The chapter has two folds as it is written to highlight the impact of Fin-Tech on Islamic Banking and vice versa. However, the main concern is the impact of FinTech on Islamic Banks in Pakistan. The reason to select the area of Islamic banking is the growing field and relating it with FinTech is one of the recent trends in the financial industry. However, a lack of research concern has been observed in emerging countries like Pakistan. Thus, this chapter has been developed purposively to reflect the importance of the relationship of Fin-Tech with the Islamic Banking sector in a holistic manner. The purpose of this study is descriptive and the content analysis method has been used to assess archival data. The entire chapter has highly important for a diverse set of stakeholders from the field of academia, research, Islamic Banking, etc.

DOI: 10.4018/979-8-3693-7160-2.ch001

BACKGROUND

Financial Industry has changed a lot. In fact, with the passage of time, the industry came so far across from book-keeping. In fact recently we are observing central national banks & complex asset markets etc. These developments were mainly formulated in the last one and a half decades when we observed technological integration in every aspect of the financial industry. In fact, the PWC report of 2016 highlighted that more than 50% of the banks were using Fin-Tech services to optimize their performance. Similarly, most emerging economies are trying to link themselves with FinTech in order to decrease the existence of unbanked people (Saba et al., 2019). Although the element (i.e., Fin-Tech) on which the relationship as well as the chapter is focused has its roots in the eighteenth century where the early development was initiated in 1866 (Alshater et al., 2022). The collaboration of financial institutions and banks actually resulted in the formulation of a win-win situation in which both entities may earn & grow through the strengths of each other (Saba et al., 2019).

Phases of FinTech Development

FinTech development is based upon three phases i.e., The initial phase (1866-1967); The Second Phase (1967-2008) & Third phase (2008-Onwards). The prominent examples of the first phase of FinTech are the Trans-Atlantic cable system and telegraph mechanism. Similarly, major examples of the second phase of FinTeh development are the online banking mechanism and Automatic Teller Machines (ATMs). Lastly, the common examples of the third and recent phase of FinTech are the use of High-Tech by companies to generate new landscapes of competitive edge for financial institutions (Alshater et al., 2022).

INTRODUCTION

Fin-Tech in Islamic Banking Industry

The growth of the financial sector is getting excessive due to the integration of FinTech with financial products. The use of Fin-Tech also resulted in steep challenges for traditional financial institutions due to the products offered due to the integration of Fin-Tech. Some of the common examples of hurdles for traditional financial institutions is the launch of blockchain technology which is the base of crypto-currencies (Hasan et al., 2020).

Fin-Tech & Islamic Banking Industry of Pakistan

Pakistan is one of the recent charms for Fin-Tech companies and services due to the prevalence of the economy as a cash-based economy with around 85% of the population is still unbanked. However, the country also has a major population in the firm of youth that is inclined towards the use of mobile phones, and internet usage is also getting higher day after the other (Ahmad et al., 2021). Other than these launches of Fin-Tech is also creating some major issues for Islamic Banking but according to research hand there are some of the factors that may pose challenges and hindrances for the Fin-tech based products in the Islamic banking industry (Hasan et al., 2020). Therefore, the impact of the association between Islamic Banks and Fin-Tech might go either way and therefore there is a need for focused research work to comprehend effectively the impact of the association between Fin-Tech and Islamic Banks (Ahmad et al., 2021)

Major Breakthrough of Fin-Tech and Islamic Banks in Pakistan

Fin-Tech was not popular and widely used in Islamic Banking operations till 2015. However, the progress became substantive in 2016 which ultimately resulted in breakthrough development by virtue of which Meezan Bank Limited and Ufone formulate U-paisa as the example of the first Islamic branchless banking solution (Saba et al., 2019). The partnership enabled inhabitants of Pakistan to pay bills, receive online payments, and another form of banking facilities with the least effort and time. Then in 2017, Meezan Bank Limited joined hands with (PMEX) Pakistan Mercantile Exchange Limited to formulate the first-ever Murabaha transaction (Saba et al., 2019).

The aim of the venture is to develop Islamic money and capital markets and for this purpose, Meezan Bank provided Shariah technical services to PMEX after getting accepted by the State Bank of Pakistan first ever online Murabaha transaction was conducted between Meezan Bank and Dubai Islamic Bank. After these one of the other remarkable collaborations was made between Dubai Islamic Bank Limited & Zing to provide branchless banking facilities to unbanked customers (Saba et al., 2019).

STATEMENT OF PROBLEM AND GRAY AREA

The estimated worth of the Islamic Finance industry is around $ 3 Trillion and from these figures, one may estimate what is the capability of Islamic FinTech. How far it may take to the area of Islamic Banking? Perhaps the area is already at boom.

Hence, studying this area is a vibrant field of research as Islamic FinTech has the capability to push Islamic Banking Industry to new peaks although in order to do so there is also a need to make FinTech in line with Shariah objectives. On the other side, there are very few studies that are related to this area which is forcing researchers to have a go in this field (Alshater et al., 2022). On the other side, everyone has their own assumptions and level of understanding regarding the association of FinTech with Islamic Banking (Ali et al., 2019). In fact, very few qualitative studies like Alshater et al (2022); Rabbani et al (2020), and Saba et al (2019) etc exists under this vein. Hence difficult to assume the result of the association is still not clear and hence there is a need of clarifying and understand relate concepts, challenges, opportunities and issues more clearly (Ali et al., 2019).

SCOPE OF FIN-TECH FOR THE ISLAMIC BANKING SECTOR

Previously it has been embarked by several studies that the use of FinTech by Islamic financial institutions will be beneficial for financial inclusion, decrease poverty, and increase in reach of financial institutions. Although recent studies also highlighted that cooperation and integration of FinTech are also beneficial for the health as well as the market share of Islamic Financial Institutions. In fact, a similar has been proved amid COVID-19 when the use of FinTech assists the stability of the Islamic Banking industry, causing a decrease in the cost of services and a surge in profitability. Hence overall use of FinTech was significantly important for the increase in the efficiency level of the Islamic Banking Industry (Alshater et al., 2022). In fact, Fin-Tech also has the ability to retain customers, and similar has been proved by the study of Baber (2020) on the bases of primary data collected from the customers of the Islamic Banking sector of Malaysia. Thus, legitimate to quote FinTech is one of the fastest-growing industries and has the ability to produce highly significant results when it gets associated with the Islamic Banking industry

Hurdles and Challenges Associated with Fin-Tech in Islamic Banking

Other than the benefits and prospects of Fin-Tech for the Islamic banking industry & vice-versa there are some hurdles and challenges for Fin-Tech services providers as indicated by Hasan et al (2020). On the other side, Iskandar et al (2022) revealed that challenges that may threaten the association of FinTech and the Islamic Banking industry can be classified into internal as well as external challenges.

Although the severity of internal challenges likes Staffing, Sharia compliance, and the need for investment, etc are the major forms of issues. Therefore, Islamic financial institutions are required to pay serious attention to these hurdles and challenges in order to outwit the weaknesses of both partners (Ali et al., 2019)

Continuous Monitoring: Continuous monitoring of processes is mandatory after the implementation of blockchain technology needs continuous and improved monitoring of complex working relationships between agents and key stakeholders. Improved and continuous monitoring is mandatory due to strict vigilance from governmental agencies to protect against any harm caused by electronic transactions (Hasan et al., 2020).

Designing of Islamic Products: Islamic Financial Institutions are also required to develop & monitor the perception of their offerings in the minds of the customers. This is required in order to simplify the current and upcoming products in order to decrease the level of confusion in the minds of the customers (Ali et al., 2019).

Testing of New Technology: Islamic Banking industry also needs to test new technologies like Blockchain, Big Data, Robo Advisors, etc. These forms of technologies are already getting testing by traditional financial institutions. Therefore, to compete effectively with traditional financial institutions and to simplify Islamic Financial products there is a need to test new technologies in an optimal way (Ali et al., 2019). The study of Iskandar et al (2022), also reflected the same from Indonesian Islamic Banking Sector and revealed that current practices of the Islamic Banking Industry in Indonesian include testing of new technologies in order to provide sustainability to the growth of the Islamic Banking industry

Lack of Stakeholders Understanding: There is also a lacking of the proper and desired level of understanding of Fin-Tech operations. This lacking is mainly due to the under-developed eco-system of several Fin-Tech-based infrastructures and therefore causing serious hindrances in market capitalization and growth (Hasan et al., 2020).

Noncompliance with Shariah: One of the major limiting factors for Fin-Tech services like crypto-currencies and others is non-compliance with Shariah. Therefore, Fin-Tech services require systematic development of standards that must also be approved by Shariah principles to create a positive picture of offerings and technology in the minds of the customers. A similar case has been indicated previously by Saba et al (2019) that the perception associated with technology is neutral but it may become problematic if the use of technology goes against Shariah (Hasan et al., 2020).

Security and Privacy: Security and Privacy are also one of the major prevailing challenges for Fin-Tech services in the Islamic Banking Industry (Hasan et al., 2020). Similar was indicated by the study of Iskandar et al (2022) that the top-notch challenge from the external environment is data security and privacy. Hence there is a need for serious focus on the resolution of this problem.

Staffing challenges: Islamic Financial Institutions also need to have the right person at the right place at the right time in order to oversee & assess the requirement of the recent era. Moreover, the right staffing is also the prerequisite for effective digital transformation and also for attaining adequate competitive advantage through using FinTech (Ali et al., 2019).

METHODOLOGY

The study is one of the qualitative investigations that is based on content analysis (Creswell & Creswell, 2017). Therefore it is based on archival contents published in well-known scholarly research journals and books. Hence according to Saunders et al (2007), the philosophy of research used to compile the chapter is epistemology as the aim of writing the chapter is to increase the knowledge base associated with the association of Islamic Banks and FinTech.

Similarly, the philosophical stance for relating the research approach with methodological choices is Post-Positivism and the research approach was deductive (Saunders et al., 2015). Both of the claims are looking optimal as the initiation point of the study is the gray area associated with the application of Fin-Tech and Islamic Banks and through marching onwards the study combines several studies to enhance end-user knowledge. Other than these parameters the methodological choice for compiling this study is mono-method and the time horizon is cross-sectional (Saunders et al., 2015).

Case Study of the Indonesian Islamic Banking Sector

A study by Iskandar et al (2022) indicated that the association of FinTech and the Islamic Banking industry might be threatened by internal as well as external factors. Hence the solution must also be developed to handle internal as well as external issues. However, the Islamic Banking Industry of Indonesia must be accompanied by effective strategies to provide effective IT system solutions, resolve the need for effective staffing and increase Islamic Financing. Although data security issues due to collaboration with FinTech may also threaten the progress of the Islamic Banking industry. Thus, there is a need for effective strategy development that may make the Islamic Banking industry flourish over a long period of time. A similar case has been indicated by Iqbal et al (2022) that the relationship of FinTech with the Islamic Banking sector of Indonesia is one of the greatest opportunities. In fact, digitized products of Islamic Banking are the need of the post-pandemic era. Although lack of consumer knowledge to handle advanced-level technology, mobile phones, and digitized products may hinder the growth of the financial industry. Therefore, Islamic Banks must try to increase their association with stakeholders like National Sharia Council and Islamic Economic Community, etc. in order to make increase the Islamic financial literacy of consumers.

CONCLUSION

The association between FinTeh and the Islamic banking industry is phenomenal for societal as well as industrial growth. In fact, the association has many benefits that may be further classified as consumer, industrial, and societal benefits.

However, the significance is also accompanied by severe and tough challenges that need to be monitored and encountered by the Islamic finance industry in order to capitalize upon the set of opportunities coming towards them in an adequate manner. Therefore the major focus of the study is to present the challenges that are presented by prior studies in order to make researchers, academicians, intrapreneurs and entrepreneurs focus on these hindrances and limitations in desired & appropriate way.

REFERENCES

Ahmad, A., Sohail, A., & Hussain, A. (2021). Emergence of financial technology in Islamic banking industry and its influence on bank performance in covid-19 scenario: A case of developing economy. *Gomal University Journal of Research, 37*(1), 97–109. DOI: 10.51380/gujr-37-01-09

Ali, H., Abdullah, R., & Zaini, M. Z. (2019). Fintech and its potential impact on Islamic banking and finance industry: A case study of Brunei Darussalam and Malaysia. [IJIEF]. *International Journal of Islamic Economics and Finance, 2*(1), 73–108. DOI: 10.18196/ijief.2116

Alshater, M. M., Saba, I., Supriani, I., & Rabbani, M. R. (2022). Fintech in islamic finance literature: A review. *Heliyon, 8*(9), 8. DOI: 10.1016/j.heliyon.2022.e10385 PMID: 36060472

Baber, H. (2020). FinTech, crowdfunding and customer retention in Islamic banks. *Vision (Basel), 24*(3), 260–268. DOI: 10.1177/0972262919869765

Creswell, J. W., & Creswell, J. D. (2017). *Research design: Qualitative, quantitative, and mixed methods approaches*. Sage publications.

Hasan, R., Hassan, M. K., & Aliyu, S. (2020). Fintech and Islamic finance: Literature review and research agenda. [IJIEF]. *International Journal of Islamic Economics and Finance, 3*(1), 75–94. DOI: 10.18196/ijief.2122

Iqbal, M., Sumantri, R., & Khoirunnisa, R. (2022). Acceleration of Financial Technology Growth in Islamic Banks as an Existence Effort to Face the Pandemic of COVID-19. *Al-Masraf: Jurnal Lembaga Keuangan dan Perbankan, 7*(2), 21-31

Iskandar, R. D. M., Maryanti, T., Jayaprawira, A. R., & Sari, S. N. (2022). Indonesian islamic banking fintech model strategy: Anp method. [ATT]. *Aptisi Transactions on Technopreneurship, 4*(2), 142–152. DOI: 10.34306/att.v4i2.257

Rabbani, M. R., Abdulla, Y., Basahr, A., Khan, S., & Moh'd Ali, M. A. (2020, November). Embracing of Fintech in Islamic Finance in the post COVID era. In *2020 international conference on decision aid sciences and application (DASA)* (pp. 1230-1234). IEEE DOI: 10.1109/DASA51403.2020.9317196

Saba, I., Kouser, R., & Chaudhry, I. S. (2019). FinTech and Islamic finance-challenges and opportunities. *Review of Economics and Development Studies, 5*(4), 581–890. DOI: 10.26710/reads.v5i4.887

Saunders, M., Lewis, P., & Thornhill, A. (2007). Research methods. *Business Students 4th edition Pearson Education Limited, England, 6*(3), 1-268

Saunders, M. N. K., Lewis, P., Thornhill, A., & Bristow, A. (2015). *Understanding research philosophies and approaches: Research methods for business students*. Pearson.

Chapter 2
Importance of Privacy Protection in Fin-Tech Operations

Muhammad Faisal Sultan
Khadim Ali Shah Bukhari Institute of Technology, Pakistan

Aamir Firoz Shamsi
Bahria University, Karachi, Pakistan

Kashif Mehmood
Usman Institute of Technology, Pakistan

ABSTRACT

Privacy Protection is one of the major issues in using Fin-Tech and related services. However, there is a lack of studies that focus intensively on privacy protection in Fin-Tech operations. Especially there is a need for studies that may not only highlight the need for further research work but will also indicate the reason behind the importance of privacy protection. Hence this chapter is developed to highlight the concern with reference to Fin-Tech. A special focus has been given to privacy protection with reference to the consumer as addressing of this issue in an adequate manner will resolve trust issues and make users inclined toward Fin-Tech. Therefore, the study also highlighted the theoretical points that are associated with the literature in order to make work relevant to academics, research and policy-making.

DOI: 10.4018/979-8-3693-7160-2.ch002

INTRODUCTION

Fin-Tech is the abbreviation of Financial Technology is the classification of the wide range of operations that are associated with the enhancement of service quality through applying information technology. Recent developments in the field of Fin-Tech are very advanced as these technologies are empowered with multiple technologies e.g., big data, mobile networks, cloud computing, and data analytics systems etc (Gai et al., 2017). Hence Fin-Tech is not only limited to financial technology but it is also termed as an example of entrepreneurship, new industry, startup, product, and even a threat. Therefore, Fin-Tech can easily be described as the set of organizations or platforms that use sophisticated technologies to optimize the pace of transactions & ease out lengthy procedures. Research in the areas of Fin-Tech initiated from evaluation of Fin-Tech, i.e., the use of machines & financial instruments as well as on ethical and social outcomes of using technology (Suryono et al., 2020).However, the large stream of data in this vein is associated with user adoption of technologically integrated financial services and user perception (Suryono et al., 2020). Fin-Tech companies usually store plenty of personally identifiable information (PPI) that is required to be protected in order to boost the level of customer trust. Therefore, data privacy is a major concern for Fin-Tech companies and data breach has much wider consequences for these forms of firms. In fact, the statement is valid as the data breach for Fin-Tech companies affected a large set of users and consequently produced a drastic impact on stakeholders (Hernández et al., 2019).

Hence the Fin-Tech providers are rendering full efforts to prevent data from malicious activities and attacks by hackers. Therefore, strict policies and governance are required to protect users from theft of information and assets (Kang, 2018).

GRAY AREA AND NEED OF RESEARCH

Recent developments in the arena of Fin-Tech are innovative and have been supported by the latest technologies. However, there emergence of the latest technologies is not free from issues of security and privacy (Gai et al., 2017). Similar points have been highlighted by Suryono et al (2020) that privacy and security are the premier issues in the development and growth of Fin-Tech. However, studies could not provide a thorough illustration of the Fin-Tech model and process that may satisfy customers' concerns associated with data security and data privacy, etc. Therefore, studies are demanding better and innovative theories as well as pragmatic Fin-Tech models that may trigger the Fin-Tech adoption process (Stewart & Jürjens, 2018). Similar indications were provided by Suryono et al (2020) that there is a need to devise better mechanisms and processes to optimize security and privacy in the use of Fin-Tech. However, findings are insisting upon improvement of financial technology that may also incorporate rules and regulations related to operations in different countries, etc.

THEORETICAL IMPLICATIONS

Studies indicated various theories for illuminating the use of technology that may also bring some threats and issues for individual use of mobile-related technologies. Initially, researchers used the theory of reasoned action (Ajzan, 1980 & Fishbein & Ajzen, 1975);then moved towards the technology acceptance model, i.e., TAM (Davis, 1989 & Venkatesh & Davis, 2000) and at last the theory that is connected to use of mobile technologies is Unified theory of acceptance and use of technology, i.e., UTAUT (Venkatesh et al., 2003). TRA proposed by Ajzan, (1980) highlighted that behaviors and subjective standards are the main indicators of one's willingness to use technology. Later TAM was introduced by Davis (1989) as one of the most distinguished and important models for studying technology acceptance in the history of literature. Initially, studies using TAM were conducted to uncover the acceptance ratio of computers. TAM includes perceived usefulness (U), ease of use (E), behavior, and usage are the major components of the theory that influences one's intention to use new technology (Stewart & Jürjens, 2018). However, Khalilzadeh et al. (2017) indicated that the UTAUT theory may also be effectively related to the latest technologies like computerized products, cell phones, etc. The study also indicated that one of the major variables in the UTAUT theory is attitude and therefore the presence of attitude in the construct may create issues for reliability in the research model.

However, the use of theory is subjective and discussion is the primary element. Hence the discussion of all the relevant theories is required and mandatory for thorough and better understanding.

LITERATURE REVIEW

Trust is one of the important aspects associated with user-acceptance of innovative technologies. Similar is the case of Fin-tech in which trust is the major factor associated with the use of the technology. In fact, users of mobile applications are exposed to multiple threats. Thus, the importance of trust is highly significant for the use of Fin-Tech (Aldboush & Ferdous, 2023 & Stewart & Jürjens, 2018). Therefore, it is legitimate to believe privacy protection is one of the prime aspects of financial security & preserving data associated with private information is a major issue for any advanced technology. A similar is true for new financial services e.g., cyber security thus formulation of an effective strategy for customer privacy protection is mandatory. Moreover, use of the electronic approaches for detecting financial fraud is also perceived as the prime factor for Fin-Tech. Previously statistical data helped firms in the detection of fraudulent activities (Gai et al., 2017). However, with the increase in digitization, it is very difficult to gauge real-time deception activities (Gai et al., 2017). However, recent techniques of protection available with Fin-Tech providers are not adequate or effective. Thus, there is a need to improve strategy for security and privacy, especially in the wake of the era of technologies (Hernández et al., 2019). Literature highlighted following points that may cause that are associated with ethical and privacy concerns of using Fin-Tech

Ethical and Privacy Issues in Using Fin-Tech

Discussion on ethical points in the arena of Fin-Tech is based on the integration of AI, Big Data, and privacy. The main issues are bias, discrimination, privacy, transparency, justice, ownership, and control.

Fairness

Fairness is required to make ethical and indiscriminate outcomes. Complete data would always result in discrimination that may produce negative impact on individuals (Aldboush & Ferdous, 2023).

Transparency

According to studies for effective design and implementation of Fin-Tech, the transparency of data in terms of data collection, data processing, and data analysis is mandatory. Following these protocols would also produce a positive impact on the individuals (Aldboush & Ferdous, 2023).

Data Protection

Data Protection is also a mandatory aspect of Fin-Tech usage. Hence, there is a need for strict compliance of laws of data protection and regulations (Aldboush & Ferdous, 2023).

COMPLEX ASSOCIATION BETWEEN FIN-TECH AND CUSTOMER'S TRUST

Trust is mandatory for the use of fain-Tech. According to studies, data security and privacy are the major elements that foster customer's trust and increase the adoption rate of Fin-Tech. In recent times studies observed a significant surge in the issues associated with customer trust. The major reasons reported are vulnerabilities of online banking and an increase in the rate of data breaches. Hence, according to research, there is a need for steep focus on customer trust to foster the adoption of Fin-Tech (Aldboush & Ferdous, 2023).

RECENT TRENDS IN PRIVACY & PROTECTION OF FIN-TECH OPERATIONS

Previously researchers recommended the use of cloud computing in Fin-Tech applications to add a thorough and advanced layer of protection for the users of Fin-Tech. According to researchers, Fin-Tech data needs multiple layers of security i.e., transmission, transaction, and system output. Thus, security at all levels seems mandatory for smooth Fin-Tech operations. The development of effective security measures will enable the company to deal with predictable as well as unpredictable risks and threats. One of the technologies that may aid a firm in the enhancement of security and privacy protocols is the implementation of cloud computing which is efficient in protecting from internal and external attacks and threats. Thus, cloud computing is perceived as one of the most important tools to protect data privacy and protection in recent times (Hernández et al., 2019).

Machine Learning (ML) was also introduced to analyze the tradeoff between data security and data usage. Adding a further layer to security, one of the methods i.e., the K-means clustering algorithm was also implemented to separate highly sensitive data coming from multi-party clustering scenarios through the ML approach. Researchers also proposed Privacy Preserving Location Based Services which is a much better option than location-based services. Privacy-Preserving Location Based Services filters redundant encrypted records in a blind way. However, the use of advanced methods of Fin-Tech also raises concerns for safety and privacy (Mehrban et al., 2020). Therefore, Aldboush and Ferdous (2023) reflected that the use of artificial intelligence (AI) tools along with the Internet of Things (IoT) may lead to severe issues of security and privacy. This may happen due to the reliance of AI on incomplete data sets.

Therefore, companies must adhere to all the pertaining laws and regulations. Therefore, further studies must be conducted to understand the approach that may substantiate the impact of security and privacy. However, if the Fin-Tech companies are using outsourced cloud services then the Fin-Tech firm needs to have effective service level agreements with their outsourced partners especially for outsourced cloud-services (Stewart & Jürjens, 2018). Thus, the significance of the Service Level Agreement (SLA) is much wider for Fin-Tech providers in order to take necessary actions and corrective actions that may be taken by the Fin-Tech company or outsourced cloud service providers (Stewart & Jürjens, 2018).

METHODOLOGY, PURPOSE OF RESEARCH AND SIGNIFICANCE

Purpose of this chapter is to highlight the relevance of privacy protection in the Fin-Tech ecosystem to induce usage. Hence the chapter is based on the collection of points from different sources to highlight the need for research, theoretical interlining, and relevant literature. Hence the overall purpose of the chapter is to increase the knowledge of researchers, students, and academicians. Thus, the philosophy of research indulged in this chapter is an epistemology which is the philosophy of knowledge (Saunders et al., 2007). The philosophical stance that is required to relate the philosophy of research with the research approach and research approach (Saunders et al., 2015) is the best stance to use with secondary-data (Syed & McLean, 2021). The research strategy is archival and the time horizon is cross-sectional (Saunders et al., 2007)

IMPLICATIONS & STRATEGIES

Mitigation of customer trust is one of the prime issues in the adoption of Fin-Tech. Hence, corporations are focusing on multiple alternatives to optimize customer's trust. Among these strategies, one is corporate digital responsibility commonly termed as CDR that is used to emphasize ethical data usage and technological innovations. The benefits of CDR implementation in the organization increased customer satisfaction, digital trust, reputation, and financial performance of the firm. Other than CDR companies may also comply with laws of data protection in the country to assure data privacy and security. General Data Protection Regulations (GDPR) implemented in European countries make organizations achieve consent of individuals in an explicit manner explicitly achieve consent of individuals to make information transparent through applying efficient security measures for data security and privacy (Aldboush & Ferdous, 2023)

CONCLUSION AND DISCUSSION

The use of Fin-Tech is much important for financial inclusion and reduction of poverty. It also has several other benefits to the economy and society although use of Fin-tech is impaired with multiple threats. Thus, companies are always required to ensure an advanced level of data privacy and security to optimize the level of customer trust. Although enhancement of trust has become much more difficult in the recent era of technologies and the growth of technologies like AI and big data are fostering issues of data privacy and security. Therefore, companies are required to implement advanced technologies that have advanced levels of data security and privacy protocols than cloud computing and outsourcing.

FUTURE DIRECTIONS FOR RESEARCH

The addition of AI and big data into the ecosystem of Fin-Tech operations resulted in numerous benefits for service providers e.g., reduction of cost and increased operational efficiency. However, this may also lead to concerns associated with privacy and security. Hence policymakers must develop effective standards, policies, and guidelines to ensure an ethical and responsible Fin-Tech ecosystem. The continuous evolution of technology is not only causing recent studies to be outdated but also not free from limitations and subjectivity. Thus, continuous and focused research is always required in the field of technology like Fin-Tech (Aldboush & Ferdous, 2023).

REFERENCES

Ajzen, I. (1980). *Understanding attitudes and predicting social behavior*. Prentice Hall.

Aldboush, H. H., & Ferdous, M. (2023). Building trust in fintech: An analysis of ethical and privacy considerations in the intersection of big data, AI, and customer trust. *International Journal of Financial Studies, 11*(3), 90. DOI: 10.3390/ijfs11030090

Davis, F. D. (1989). Perceived usefulness, perceived ease of use, and user acceptance of information technology. *Management Information Systems Quarterly, 13*(3), 319–340. DOI: 10.2307/249008

Fishbein, M., & Ajzen, I. (1977). *Belief, attitude, intention, and behavior: An introduction to theory and research*. Addison-Wesley.

Gai, K., Qiu, M., Sun, X., & Zhao, H. (2017). Security and privacy issues: A survey on FinTech. In *Smart Computing and Communication: First International Conference, SmartCom 2016, Shenzhen, China, December 17-19, 2016* [Springer International Publishing]. *Proceedings, 1*, 236–247.

Hernández, E., Öztürk, M., Sittón, I., & Rodríguez, S. (2019). Data protection on FinTech platforms. In Highlights of Practical Applications of Survivable Agents and Multi-Agent Systems. The PAAMS Collection: International Workshops of PAAMS 2019, Ávila, Spain, June 26–28, 2019 [Springer International Publishing]. *Proceedings, 17*, 223–233.

Kang, J. (2018). Mobile payment in Fintech environment: trends, security challenges, and services. *Human-centric Computing and Information sciences, 8*(1), 1-16

Mehrban, S., Nadeem, M. W., Hussain, M., Ahmed, M. M., Hakeem, O., Saqib, S., & Khan, M. A. (2020). Towards secure FinTech: A survey, taxonomy, and open research challenges. *IEEE Access : Practical Innovations, Open Solutions, 8*, 23391–23406. DOI: 10.1109/ACCESS.2020.2970430

Saunders, M., Lewis, P., & Thornhill, A. (2007). *Research methods. Business Students* (4th ed.). Pearson Education Limited.

Saunders, M. N., Lewis, P., Thornhill, A., & Bristow, A. (2015). Understanding research philosophy and approaches to theory development. In Saunders, M. N. K., Lewis, P., & Thornhill, A. (Eds.), *Research Methods for Business Students* (pp. 122–161). Pearson Education.

Stewart, H., & Jürjens, J. (2018). Data security and consumer trust in FinTech innovation in Germany. *Information and Computer Security*, *26*(1), 109–128. DOI: 10.1108/ICS-06-2017-0039

Suryono, R. R., Budi, I., & Purwandari, B. (2020). Challenges and trends of financial technology (Fintech): A systematic literature review. *Information (Basel)*, *11*(12), 590. DOI: 10.3390/info11120590

Syed, M., & McLean, K. C. (2021). Disentangling paradigm and method can help bring qualitative research to post-positivist psychology and address the generalizability crisis. Behavioral &amp. *Brain Sciences*, *45*, 58–60. DOI: 10.1017/S0140525X21000431 PMID: 35139943

Venkatesh, V., & Davis, F. D. (2000). A theoretical extension of the technology acceptance model: Four longitudinal field studies. *Management Science*, *46*(2), 186–204. DOI: 10.1287/mnsc.46.2.186.11926

Venkatesh, V., Morris, M. G., Davis, G. B., & Davis, F. D. (2003). User acceptance of information technology: Toward a unified view. *Management Information Systems Quarterly*, *27*(3), 425–478. DOI: 10.2307/30036540

Chapter 3
Fostering FinTech Through Mobile Wallets:
An Indian Scenario

R. Arunachalam
https://orcid.org/0000-0001-8848-0659
SASTRA University, India

R. Amudha
SASTRA University, India

ABSTRACT

This paper discusses development of mobile wallets and impact on fintech in India. Section begins with brief history of digital payment systems in India. It covers pioneers and leading players today like Paytm, PhonePe and Google Pay. Additionally, roles of government support, increased smartphone penetration regulatory guidelines and development of Unified Payments Interface (UPI) are examined. Literature is gathered regarding technology adoption models, trust and consumer behavior related to digital payments. The discussion in this book chapter is extended to show that mobile wallets are now moving beyond payments to include savings and investment propositions, thereby contributing to financial inclusion. The chapter concludes with some possible implications for understanding the evolution of mobile wallets in the context of transitioning to a cashless economy and the transformations in consumer behavior, as well as potential gains and difficulties in the future.

DOI: 10.4018/979-8-3693-7160-2.ch003

INTRODUCTION

Sustainability is a comprehensive framework that addresses the long-term balance between environmental protection, social well-being and economic growth. Traditionally, sustainability is viewed through three distinct dimensions: the environmental aspect, which emphasises the conservation of natural resources and reducing carbon footprints; the social aspect, which focuses on inclusivity, community empowerment, and equitable growth; and the economic aspect, which is concerned with fostering stable, long term growth while responsibly managing resources.

Digital Financial Services (DFS) refers to any financial services delivered or accessed through digital channels, including mobile payments, digital wallets, online banking, and other innovative financial technologies that streamline transactions and enhance financial inclusion. In the context of India, DFS has played a pivotal role in reshaping the financial ecosystem by providing convenient, secure, and accessible payment options, which in turn support broader sustainability objectives.

Integrating DFS with sustainability frameworks, the study observes a transformative impact on the financial industry and society. Using mobile wallets and digital payment systems increases transaction efficiency and transparency. It contributes to environmental sustainability by reducing the dependence on cash and lowering the environmental costs associated with printing and transporting money.

In India, mobile wallets (or) e-wallets usage has grown to be an innovative factor in redefining the financial ecosystem, which has promoted economic growth. These digital platforms have changed transactions by enabling individuals and businesses to save, send, and receive money electronically. Mobile wallets, which offer a practical, safe, and easily accessible payment option, have simplified financial inclusion and improved transactional transparency.

On November 8, 2016, the Indian government took the historic and bold step of demonetising all 500 and 1,000 banknotes. This move led to an unexpected and severe cash shortage, costing around 86% of the country's currency. While the initiative's stated goals were to remove black money (unaccounted money) and counterfeit notes (used for illegal transactions), it had a broad impact that extended beyond those and acted as an incentive for the growth of digital payment possibilities in India.

In the Deloitte report on FinTech in India, the landscape of FinTech was classified into twenty segments across six significant areas of financial services. These segments were very close to the insights from the Deloitte global research study on "Future of Financial Services" in collaboration with the World Economic Forum, bringing emerging innovations for structuring the financial services sector to light.

The FinTech landscape includes several key segments contributing to digitising and improving financial services. In the Credit segment, peer-to-peer lending, crowdfunding, and marketplace loan solutions emerged, revolutionising access to capital by connecting borrowers with institutional and non-institutional lenders. Moreover, online lenders and credit scoring platforms incorporated alternative scoring methods and digital channels into more efficient acquisition processes.

The Payments segment concentrated on facilitating seamless fund transfers through different services: mobile wallets or M-wallets, prepaid payment instruments or PPIs, merchant payment solutions and international remittances. These services supported various transactions: person-to-person or P2P, person-to-merchant or P2M, and government-to-person or G2P payments.

In Investment Management, robo-advisors, discount brokers and online financial advisory services use technology to deliver personalised wealth management solutions: algorithm-driven investment strategies.

Personal Finance Management has tools to manage taxes, track spending, and plan finances, which assist individuals in monitoring and controlling their financial profiles, such as investment portfolios, credit scores, and spending habits.

In Bank Tech, big data and blockchain were responsible for customer onboarding. They allowed for the creation of comprehensive risk profiles by analysing various data points, an innovative substitute for the typical underwriting ways that tended to leave out individuals without much credit history to show.

The Insurtech segment brought to market such innovations as insurance aggregators and insurance models, which were very much designed for small businesses. The Internet of Things (IoT) and wearables added to these developments by providing more tailored insurance products with coverage criteria dependent on real-time information. These sectors demonstrate how fintech is changing the financial services industry, making it more accessible, efficient, and tailored to individual needs than ever before.

Mobile Wallet History in India

A mobile wallet, which is also the term for a digital wallet or, in other words, an e-wallet, is a software-based system that stores the user's payment information and enables mobile devices for transactions. The mobile wallet is gaining market traction in India, changing how people make payments. Digital wallets were not new to Indian users; the concept of mobile wallets started in India in 2004. The first mobile wallet, Oxigen Wallet, was launched in July 2004. Despite its early introduction, the Oxigen wallet failed to gain significant usage among Indian users. Following Oxigen Wallet, in 2006, the Yes Bank partnered with Times Group, launched a mobile wallet, and named it "Wallet365.com". This platform also struggled to gain Indian users and did not achieve the desired success in the Indian financial market.

In 2009, the Mobikwik e-wallet was introduced; with this launch, the digital landscape in India experienced a profound change. Mobikwik became a successful mobile wallet among Indian users. Another reason for Mobikwik's success was its acceptance by merchants across various business domains in the country. Mobikwik sets the stage for other major players to enter the expanding digital wallet market.

Other market players inspired Mobikwik's success with digital wallets, and numerous service providers were introduced to mobile wallets. Followed by Mobikwik, industry giants such as Paytm, Google Pay (erstwhile Tez), Amazon Pay, and Airtel Money entered the Indian mobile wallet market. These mobile application platforms were operated with advanced technologies and secure payment gateways to offer a convenient and secure way for users to conduct transactions digitally. In addition, they also offered cashback and coupons, which attracted more users to onboard their services.

The demonetisation of currency notes in 2016 provided the perfect opportunity to grow the mobile wallet business in India. Individuals and businesses were forced to explore alternative payment methods as there was a shortage of physical cash, making mobile wallets emerge as a viable solution. In 2018, e-wallets had become widely used by almost 8% of the Indian population. Individuals and businesses started using mobile wallets for regular and day-to-day transactions and accepted this as an effective alternative to physical cash. This transformation indicated the unprecedented change in the nation's payment system towards cashless transactions.

MOBILE WALLETS IN INDIA

Paytm

One of India's biggest digital payment stories is the launch of Paytm by Vijay Shekhar Sharma. Originally a mobile recharge platform of One97 Communications, it has become a digital wallet and created a financial services ecosystem. Paytm's first big move was to launch its mobile wallet. It gained popularity because of its simple user interface and fast transactions. Paytm exploited the large smartphone market in India and saw a need for digital payment solutions, especially after demonetisation in 2016 when people went digital due to a cash crunch. Paytm grew because of its marketing and partnerships with other companies.

The platform has many services, such as mobile recharges, bill payments, and ticket bookings. These services were for different types of customers. Paytm invested in technology and infrastructure to develop technology that could do seamless and secure transactions and build customer trust. The availability of various financial services like insurance and mutual funds marked Paytm's journey from a digital wallet to a fintech company. This growth is backed by access to different revenue streams and an expanded financial ecosystem.

Paytm's success is not just about adapting to market and consumer behaviour but also about being innovative. The company adopts new payment methods and technologies, learns new skills, and documents its integrated products and services. It has become India's leading electronic payment method and a significant player in a cashless economy.

PhonePe

PhonePe was founded in December 2015 by Sameer Nigam, Rahul Chari and Burzin Engineer. It is one of the leading digital payments platforms in India. The company was one of the first to enter the rapidly growing fintech space in the country and offers a seamless and secure way to do digital transactions. PhonePe's launch was closely tied to the Indian government's push towards a cashless economy post-demonetisation in November 2016.

Built on the Unified Payments Interface (UPI) system developed by the National Payments Corporation of India (NPCI), PhonePe quickly gained popularity because of its simple interface and wide acceptance across various sectors. Users can make instant money transfers, pay utility bills, recharge mobile phones, and make payments at online and offline merchants. One of the key reasons for PhonePe's success is its focus on innovation and customer-centric solutions. Over the years, the platform has added insurance, mutual funds, gold investments and many other financial services to cater to various customer needs. The company has also made strategic partnerships and acquisitions to strengthen its position in the market and expand its service offerings.

Today, PhonePe has millions of users and processes billions of transactions every year, making it one of the most trusted and widely used digital payment platforms in India. Its journey from a startup to a leader is a testament to the power of fintech in India and the country's shift towards digitalisation and financial inclusion.

Google Pay

Google Pay has been a massive success in India since it launched. It got millions of users across the country in no time. It grew faster than many local players in the digital payment space. The app's success is because of its simple and user-friendly design. It made digital payments accessible to a large number of users. Google Pay allows transactions between banks to happen seamlessly. Users could send money to anyone with a bank account, whether the bank was the same or not. The application also allowed quick business payments, leading to merchants' adoption. The company's aggressive marketing strategy played a significant role in its growth. Google offered cashback and rewards to early adopters and encouraged users to try and stick to the application. Word-of-mouth recommendations further fueled its popularity among friends and family groups.

Google Pay has had a considerable impact on India's digital economy. It has accelerated the move from cash to digital. Many small businesses now accept digital payments, which results in financial inclusion. The app has also triggered innovation in fintech and for consumers. Within two years of launch, Google Pay processed billions of transactions. It captured a significant share of the UPI payment space. The app has over 100 million users, competing with established players. Google Pay is not limited to urban areas. It has reached smaller towns and rural areas. It has brought digital financial services to the unbanked and has become part of the Digital India initiative.

Amazon Pay

Amazon Pay, the digital payment system developed by Amazon to complement the increasing demand for online marketplaces, launched in India in 2017. It is part of Amazon's holding company strategy to boost its ecosystem and facilitate easy customer payment solutions. Amazon Pay uses the Amazon brand to tap into the comfort and trust that users have in it as a platform for carrying out various kinds of financial transactions. Its service offering started by making payments more manageable; it integrates with bill payments and mobile recharges and is available online and offline to merchants. The strategy was to give users a reason to make it part of their daily life. The service works on the UPI system built by the NPCI, resulting in fast and secure transactions. Like Apple Pay, one of Amazon Pay's best features is how well it plugs into the larger Amazon ecosystem, letting users use their existing Amazon account to make purchases on other sites.

Amazon Pay offers other businesses, such as digital lending and insurance, which have further widened its portfolio. The company has partnered strategically with several merchants and service providers to increase its penetration and provide end-to-end payment solutions. Amazon Pay is a strong player in India's digital payments space. It has grown along with the growth of digital payment adoption in India and validates the role of global majors in shaping India's fintech landscape.

Bharat Interface for Money (BHIM)

A transformative digital payment application, Bharat Interface for Money (BHIM), was developed by NPCI and launched in December 2016 - a flagship initiative to drive digital transactions and financial inclusion in India, supported by the UPI system. The simplifying objective of BHIM is to make digital payments easy and fast for users by letting them send and receive money, pay bills, and make purchases with their smartphones. BHIM uses a phone number as a payment address, allowing users to easily remember and share it with others to enable transactions with added convenience.

BHIM has been developed as a simple and easy-to-use application that will work on UPI-enabled devices, thereby facilitating a digital payment mechanism for those sections of society that are currently not digitally connected/equipped. BHIM is India's statement about adopting technology to make financial services more accessible and efficient as users leverage the digital highway. It has been a major driver in India's adoption of digital payments. The growth is evidenced in user numbers an the volume of transactions processed through BHIM.

PayZapp

Launched by HDFC Bank, PayZapp stands as a versatile digital payment solution for consumers to manage their finances on the go, securely and conveniently. It was introduced in 2015 to meet the growing needs of digital payment solutions within an evolving fintech framework in India. PayZapp is a single payment app for shopping, travel, entertainment, and other payments that enables users to pay securely from one interface. Among the many offers, one notable feature of the app is its integration with SmartBuy, HDFC Bank's exclusive e-commerce portal with offers on cashback and discounts spread across categories.

PayZapp supports several payment modes, including credit and debit cards and UPI and enables multiple payment transaction methods that are possible through HDFC Bank's safe and secure payment infrastructure. HDFC Bank, a reputable private sector bank in India, provides support and a sense of trust to small and large transactions made by the user in PayZapp. The features of PayZapp make it an attractive financial services app, and it includes a feature called "SmartHub", which enables users to connect all their accounts and cards for financial activities, increasing the ease and flexibility of making financial transactions daily. PayZapp now also offers services like wallets and mobile recharges to attract different kinds of users. HDFC Bank offers this service interface for free, and over the years, it has proved popular with its existing banking customers and a broader set of users in India.

MobiKwik

MobiKwik, founded in 2009 by Bipin Preet Singh and Upasana Taku, is one of India's pioneering digital payment platforms. Initially launched as a mobile recharge and bill payment service, MobiKwik evolved into a comprehensive digital wallet and financial services application that caters to the growing demand for cashless transactions in the country. MobiKwik was one of the first movers in India's digital wallet market. It leveraged this early advantage to build a strong customer base. Over time, the company introduced many new features, including UPI payments, credit card bill payments and microloans. Thus, it became a versatile financial service application for users.

MobiKwik formed online and offline partnerships with merchants, ensuring seamless transactions for various products and services. It has concentrated on financial inclusion and is making it easier for the underserved segment of the population to access financial services, including financial products such as small loans and insurance products. These financial services products offered by MobiKwik are directly available through the application, thus further promoting digital financial literacy and improving accessibility to financial services in India.

Freecharge

Freecharge, founded in 2010 by Kunal Shah and Sandeep Tandon, is one of India's early entrants into the digital payment ecosystem. Launched as a platform for mobile recharges and bill payments, Freecharge quickly gained popularity due to its innovative approach of offering discounts and cashback rewards on transactions. Such strategies resonated strongly with the tech-savvy youth of India. The platform was designed to provide a simple, fast and secure way for users to recharge their mobile phones; it also facilitated the payment of utility bills. FreeCharge relied on a value proposition that provided the customer with rewards for every transaction. The company's success in attracting millions of users made it a notable player in India's emerging fintech landscape.

In 2015, Freecharge was acquired by Snapdeal, one of India's largest e-commerce platforms. This landmark acquisition highlighted the growing importance of digital payments in the country's online retail sector and allowed Freecharge to expand its services. It integrated with Snapdeal's ecosystem and allowed users to pay for goods and services directly through the Freecharge wallet. Following the acquisition, Freecharge added features like UPI-based payments, peer-to-peer money transfers and integration with various online and offline merchants. Freecharge has expanded its scope to offer financial services like digital credit, insurance, and investment products to provide its users with a full range of financial services.

JioPay

Jio Pay, launched by Reliance Jio, is a digital payment platform aiming to realise Digital India's vision by providing millions of users with seamless and secure financial solutions. Jio Pay is part of Reliance Jio's grand strategy to build an integrated digital ecosystem. This ecosystem caters to the financial needs of India's rapidly growing smartphone users. Jio Pay is built on UPI infrastructure developed by NPCI. It allows users to make instant payments. Users can also transfer money and pay bills directly using smartphones. The platform is integrated into the MyJio application. This integration offers a convenient and accessible digital payment solution to Jio's mobile subscribers. It follows the trend of offering comprehensive digital services within one app to improve user convenience.

The distinct features of Jio Pay are security and simplicity, and it uses advanced encryption and security protocols to ensure that all transactions are safe and protected. The User-friendly interface of Jio Pay ensures that even users unfamiliar with the technology can efficiently process digital payments. One of the significant strengths of the Jio Pay platform is its integrated connection to various services by Jio, such as JioMart, JioSaavn and JioFiber. Users can effortlessly pay for various products and services within the Jio ecosystem using Jio Pay, which various online and offline merchants accept. Jio Pay has gradually expanded use beyond basic financial transactions by including features such as mobile recharges and DTH payments. This expansion increases the range of service options available for users.

Axis Pay

Axis Pay, launched by Axis Bank, is a digital payment application designed to facilitate seamless and secure transactions using the UPI system. In 2016, Axis Pay was developed as part of Axis Bank's strategy to hold a rapidly growing digital payments ecosystem in India. It allows customers to conveniently access and manage their finances from their smartphones. Axis Pay is primarily based on UPI, allowing users to connect their bank accounts and make instant money transfers without sharing personal bank details. With the simple Virtual Payment Address (VPA), users can send and receive money, pay bills, and purchase at any online or offline merchant. The application was designed with the user in mind; it is user-friendly to ensure anyone can navigate and use it regardless of digital payment experience.

Axis Pay integrates with various Axis Bank services, allowing users to access their bank accounts, check their balances, make payments and view transactions directly in the application. This integration with other bank services supports Axis Bank's holistic digital banking experience and caters to tech-savvy customers. Axis Pay aims to increase digital adoption and promote digital literacy with UPI. The bank has run campaigns and initiatives to promote the UPI among its customer base, offering cashback and rewards to users. This initiative ensures a larger market share of people using digital payments.

One of the key components of Axis Bank's digital banking offering is Axis Pay, which aligns with the push for a cashless economy in India. It is important to note that traditional banks can innovate with fintech. Traditional financial institutions can adapt and innovate to meet the needs of their customers in the digital age.

THE SUCCESS OF DIGITAL WALLET SERVICES IN INDIA

Government Support

The Indian government's support has significantly helped mobile wallets succeed in India. The Digital India program started in 2015 and aimed to make India more digital. This program created good conditions for growing digital payment systems like mobile wallets. The 2016 demonetisation was a big push for mobile wallet use. People needed other ways to pay when the government removed high-value currency notes. Many Indians turned to digital payment options. Mobile wallets have become a handy solution for many.

The government did more than create a need. It taught people digital skills, especially in rural areas. These efforts helped more people understand digital finance and mobile wallets. The government also gave rewards for using digital payments. These rewards included tax benefits and cashback offers. The Reserve Bank of India (RBI) made rules that helped mobile wallets grow safely. The RBI's guidelines covered user verification, spending limits, and how different wallets work together. These rules made users and companies feel more confident about mobile wallets.

The Jan Dhan Yojana program started in 2014 and has helped mobile wallets grow. This program brought many unbanked Indians into the banking system. It created a significant new market for digital financial services, including mobile wallets. The Aadhaar system, which gives each person a unique ID, also played a significant role. Aadhaar made it easier for mobile wallet companies to add new users. It helped them follow the rules while growing their customer base.

The government's support for the Unified Payments Interface (UPI) through the BHIM app showed its commitment to digital payments. UPI sometimes competed with mobile wallets, but it also helped them. It made it easier to add money to wallets and got more people to use digital payments. The government also encouraged new ideas in financial technology. It created unique environments where mobile wallet companies could try new features safely. This approach helped companies improve their services.

The Indian government's efforts addressed many challenges. These challenges included a lack of awareness, limited bank access, and unclear rules. By solving these problems, the government helped mobile wallets succeed in India. India is still working towards using less cash. The government's continued support remains important. The success of mobile wallets shows how good government programs can change a country's digital future.

Penetration of Smartphones, Technology and Infrastructure

India's mobile wallet success is closely connected to its growing technology and widespread smartphone use. These two factors have grown the base for mobile wallets, bringing digital payments to millions of Indians. Smartphones play a key role in this tech change. India has seen a massive rise in smartphone use, becoming the world's second-largest smartphone market. Many local and foreign companies offer smartphones at low prices and provide smart devices to many people, including those with less money and those in rural areas.

The smartphone increase has turned millions of Indians into possible mobile wallet users. These devices are the primary way people use mobile wallet apps. They provide the tools needed for digital transactions. The touchscreen, camera for scanning codes, and security features on most smartphones help mobile wallet services work well. However, smartphones alone were insufficient; India's internet also had to improve. Launching 4G networks nationwide was a big step in making 4G connections faster and more reliable than older networks, making it easier for people to trust using their phones for monetary transactions.

India's telecom service provider companies have also competed hard, which led to much cheaper data costs. Now, many people can always afford to stay connected to the internet. The new 5G networks will make connections even faster and more stable. Behind the scenes, cloud computing and data centres in India have grown. This growth has helped mobile wallet companies handle millions of transactions safely and quickly. More local data centres have sped up processing. They have also helped companies follow rules about keeping data in India.

Standard APIs (Application Programming Interfaces) have also been important. APIs help mobile wallets, banks, and shops collaborate smoothly to create a well-connected digital payment system. Better security tech has built trust in mobile wallets. Encryption keeps user data and transaction information safe. Tokenisation added security to financial transactions by replacing sensitive data with unique symbols. Using fingerprints and face scans for security has made mobile wallets safer and easier.

The tech backbone extends to shops; many businesses now use digital payment systems. QR code payments have become popular, which makes it easy for all kinds of businesses to accept mobile wallet payments. It has increased the usefulness of mobile wallets for everyday purchases. India's strong tech base and high smartphone use have created the perfect setting for mobile wallets to succeed. These factors have provided hardware, internet access, and backend support. They have changed mobile wallets from a small service to a primary payment method. As tech keeps improving, it will shape the future of mobile wallets and digital payments in India.

The Unified Payments Interface (UPI)

The National Payments Corporation of India (NPCI) created the Unified Payments Interface (UPI), which has changed how digital payments are made in India. The July 2024 Unified Payments Interface (UPI) transaction data highlights the significance of digital payments in India. The total value of UPI transactions for the month reached 20.64 lakh crore, demonstrating the widespread use of NPCI's initiative. UPI works well with mobile wallet services. This payment option allows instant money transfers between bank accounts using mobile phones. People can send money using a virtual payment address (VPA) without sharing complete bank details. It marks a big step in India's move towards a cashless economy.

Mobile wallet companies see UPI as both a challenge and an opportunity. UPI competes with traditional wallet services by allowing direct bank transfers. However, it also gives wallets a chance to improve their services. UPI has made it easier to add money to mobile wallets. Before UPI, people used net banking or cards to load their wallets. Now, they can transfer money from their bank to their wallet quickly. This ease of use has made more people adopt mobile wallets.

UPI has also made different payment systems work together better. The NPCI wants mobile wallets to connect through UPI. Now, users can move money between different wallets, making mobile wallets more valuable in the digital economy. No cost (or) less cost on using UPI transactions has encouraged more people to use digital payments. Mobile wallet services have become more popular as more people use digital money.

UPI has helped small shops accept digital payments. The QR code payment option in UPI is simple to use. As more shops started taking UPI payments, they also began accepting mobile wallets. Many wallets now include UPI features. Mobile wallet providers have started offering new services because of UPI. They want to stand out in the market. Many wallets let users pay bills, invest money, and get small loans. Wallets have changed from simple payment tools to complete financial service platforms.

Other countries have noticed UPI's success. This global interest has shown that India's digital payment methods, including mobile wallets, are outstanding. UPI has changed how mobile wallets work. It has made transactions easier and expanded what wallets can do. UPI has helped connect different payment systems. It has also encouraged shops to accept digital payments. These changes have pushed mobile wallet companies to create new services. UPI will likely shape how mobile wallets and digital payments work in India.

MOBILE WALLETS LEGAL FRAMEWORK IN INDIA

Payment and Settlement Systems Act, 2007

The Payment and Settlement Systems Act, 2007 (PSS) governs India's e-wallets and other digital payment systems. This landmark legislation was enacted to regulate and supervise the country's payment systems and establish the Reserve Bank of India (RBI) as the authority for that purpose.

The PSS Act provides a comprehensive framework for regulating and overseeing payment systems, including e-wallets facilitating digital transactions. Digital wallet operators must obtain an RBI license before starting their operations in India. The RBI can set conditions, revoke licenses and issue directions to ensure proper service to the users.

The Act also grants the RBI the ability to regulate and supervise payment systems. These include the RBI to:

- Determine standards for the functioning of payment systems
- Call for returns, documents, and other information from service providers
- Access any service provider payment system and their books of accounts
- Enter and inspect any premises where a mobile wallet service is operated
- Carry out audits and inspections of mobile wallet service providers

These clauses will allow RBI to properly check e-wallet activities to ensure that all service providers follow the rules and protect users' interests. The PSS Act introduces a Payments and Settlement Systems Committee, which the RBI Governor heads. This committee plays an important role in setting policies related to payment systems, including those affecting mobile wallets.

The Act also discusses the finality of settlements, which is necessary to operate payment systems efficiently. In particular, it states that settlements carried out according to the rules and procedures of a payment system cannot be unsettled or reversed, thus giving assurance and guarantee to e-wallet platform transactions.

In the payment sector, the PSS Act authorises RBI to make appropriate rules and regulations to safeguard the customers of payment systems, resulting in drafting various guidelines and directives aimed at the safety and reliability of e-wallet services. The Act also provides penalties and punishments for non-compliance. These penalties vary from fines to imprisonment, and they work as an imposing tool against the violations and security of e-wallets within the regulatory framework.

Since its enactment, the Payment and Settlement Systems Act has been an essential means of influencing the development and reshaping of digital payments in India, including mobile wallet services. It has given grounds for the RBI to release such things as the Master Direction on Prepaid Payment Instruments as well as guidelines and regulations.

The Payment and Settlement Systems Act, 2007 is the fundamental law in India on e-wallets. It has proved to be a key player by setting up a firm regulatory network and making the RBI the central authority, resulting in improved e-wallet services. Even in the ever-changing digital payment environment, the PSS Act remains a key pillar in maintaining the integrity and stability of digital wallet services in India.

Master Direction on Issuance and Operation of Prepaid Payment Instruments (PPIs)

The Master Direction on Issuance and Operation of Prepaid Payment Instruments (PPIs) is a comprehensive framework for the service of digital wallets and other prepaid payment systems in India. These directions were first introduced in October 2017 by the Reserve Bank of India and have been updated periodically. This master direction elaborates on the provisions of the Payment and Settlement Systems Act 2007 and provides detailed guidelines for e-wallets.

Under these directions, e-wallets fall under the category of PPIs, which are defined as instruments that enable the purchase of goods and services, including financial services, remittance facilities and the like, against the value stored on such instruments. The Master Direction categorises PPIs into Closed, Semi-closed, and Open System PPIs. Most e-wallets are Semi-closed System PPIs that can be used for goods and services, including financial services, at a group of clearly identified merchant locations or establishments with a specific contract with the issuer to accept these payment instruments.

One of the key aspects of the Master Direction is the eligibility criteria for PPI issuers. It states that only banks and non-bank entities registered under the Companies Act, 1956/2013 can issue PPIs in India with specific approval from the RBI, which ensures that only legitimate and financially sound entities can operate e-wallet services.

The Master Direction also specifies strict capital requirements for non-bank PPI issuers. As per the latest guidelines, they need a minimum positive net worth of 15 crore at the time of application, which should increase to 25 crore within the third financial year of getting authorisation. These guidelines ensure that e-wallet providers have sufficient financial resources to operate and protect consumer interests.

Another important aspect of the Master Direction is the Know Your Customer (KYC) norms for PPI users. It has a tiered KYC approach with different levels of KYC requirements for different transaction limits. These regulatory requirements balance security with ease of access, allowing quick user onboarding and necessary safeguards against fraud and money laundering.

The Master Direction also talks about interoperability among PPIs. It mandates that all KYC-compliant PPIs should be interoperable, allowing users to transfer funds between different e-wallets and bank accounts through a Unified Payments Interface (UPI). This regulatory direction has increased the utility and acceptance of e-wallets.

Security and risk management is an important part of the Master Direction. PPI issuers need robust information and data security infrastructure and systems to prevent and detect fraud, which includes transaction limits, velocity checks, and real-time fraud monitoring.

Data Protection Laws

Data protection laws are integral to the legal framework governing e-wallets in India, as e-wallets handle financial and personal information. Though India does not have a comprehensive data protection law, several existing laws and regulations address data protection aspects of e-wallets.

The primary law governing data protection in India is the Information Technology Act, 2000 (IT Act) and the Information Technology (Reasonable Security Practices and Procedures and Sensitive Personal Data or Information) Rules, 2011 (SPDI Rules), framed under it. These laws have implications for e-wallet providers regarding how they collect, process, store, and protect user data.

Under the IT Act and SPDI Rules, e-wallet providers are considered "body corporates" dealing with sensitive personal data or information (SPDI). SPDI is defined in the SPDI Rules to include passwords, financial information such as bank account, credit card, debit card or other payment instrument details and any other information classified as sensitive under the rules.

The SPDI Rules require e-wallet providers to obtain consent from users before collecting, using or storing their sensitive personal data. The user can provide this consent by agreeing to use digital wallet terms and conditions. The law mandates that digital wallet companies have a privacy policy and make it easily accessible to users.

The SPDI Rules state that sensitive personal data should only be collected for a lawful purpose connected with the organisation's function. This data can be retained only for as long as necessary and should be used only for the purpose for which it was collected.

Regarding data security, the IT Act and SPDI Rules clarify that e-wallet providers should adopt and maintain reasonable security practices and procedures, including documented information security programmes and policies with managerial, technical, operational and physical security controls as per the protected information. IT Act also provides penalties in case of negligence in implementing and maintaining reasonable security practices, which results in wrongful loss or gain to any person; this results in a big responsibility on e-wallet providers to ensure data protection measures.

Besides the IT Act and SPDI Rules, e-wallet providers must also comply with data protection guidelines issued by sectoral regulators. For example, the Reserve Bank of India (RBI) has issued guidelines on information security, electronic banking, technology risk management and cyber security for banks and financial institutions, which apply to e-wallet providers.

As the country moves towards a more robust data protection regime, e-wallet providers must keep updated with changing regulations and improve their data protection practices. In future, India is expected to have a comprehensive data protection law. The Personal Data Protection Bill, which is under consideration, proposes to set up a Data Protection Authority and impose strict obligations on data fiduciaries (which would include e-wallet providers) on data processing, data localisation and user rights.

FEATURES AND BENEFITS OF MOBILE WALLETS

Digital Transactions

The digital wallet helps users carry out money-related transactions without using physical money, including but not limited to payment for groceries, dining and travelling. The shift from cash to digital transactions simplifies payment processes and reduces the handling of physical money.

Bank Integration

Most of the mobile wallets are integrated into users' bank accounts. A digital wallet seamlessly manages different bank accounts through debit cards and Unified Payments Interface (UPI) in a single application. This integration helps users quickly transfer funds for their transactions.

Quick Response (QR) Code Payments

In most places, QR code payments simplify the payment process. It allows the user to scan a merchant's QR code to complete transactions quickly. This autogenerated QR code eliminates the need to manually enter the payment amount, minimising the risk of entering an incorrect amount.

Recharges and Bill Payments

The mobile wallets ease the settling of mobility bill expenses as mobile phone recharges, utility bill payments (electricity, water, and gas), and services such as DTH (Direct-to-Home television) and broadband. This mobile wallet feature helps users save much time.

Peer-to-Peer Transfers

Mobile wallets allow convenient peer-to-peer (P2P) transactions through which people can instantly send money to friends and family. This choice also eliminates the need for physical or traditional bank transfers.

Rewards and Offers

Many mobile wallets offer cashback, discounts, and reward points to attract customers to use them more often. These perks can involve percentages of cashback on purchases made and discounts with specific retailers.

Security Features

Mobile wallets incorporate security measures to protect the user's data and transactions. The security measures are encryption, biometric authentication (fingerprint or facial recognition), and two-factor authentication (2FA), which increase safety and prevent fraud.

User-Friendly Interface

Mobile wallets created with simplicity in mind present users with interfaces that are very easy to follow, thus making users have an easy time navigating. Considering the interface design, enabling accessibility is almost sure, even for people not much into technology.

Tracking and Budgeting

Many mobile wallets have features for tracking expenses and budgeting. Users can see their transaction history, categorise expenses, and set financial goals, which helps them manage their finances better.

Integration with E-Commerce

Integration with e-commerce sites allows users to check out their purchases using a mobile wallet. This arrangement is powered by different payment system providers among other payment gateways, so as a result, the process of financial transactions on the web is hassle-free and secure.

Literature Review

The development of digital technologies at a high level has redefined the field of finances, especially in emerging markets like India. Mobile payment and money transfer companies developed from financial technology have provided new access to financial services and have changed consumer habits.

Determinants of Behavioral Intention in Digital Payment Systems

Hasan et al. (2024) conducted surveys to examine the determinants of behavioural intention to use digital payment systems, particularly the M-Wallet concept, by the Indian youth. The primary findings reveal that values and trust, the main categories, along with compatibility and influence, are the determinants of behavioural intention. Trust and compatibility are the major factors affecting the intention of the user to adopt M-wallets. The research suggests that M-wallet companies should focus on these factors to increase the adoption rates of users and provide secure services.

Kumar et al. (2023) assess the presence of two factors, namely, perceived financial cost and perceived risk, as predictors of trust, which affect the acceptance of mobile banking services in India. The study extends the Unified Theory of Acceptance and Use of Technology (UTAUT). It indicates that performance expectancy, effort expectancy, social influence, and perceived financial cost are significant predictors of behavioural intentions. Besides that, perceived risk and trust are moderating variables directly affected by behavioural intention, allowing insight into factors responsible for the adopted mobile banking technology.

Upadhyay et al. (2022) studied the insight of the meta-Unified Theory of Acceptance and Use of Technology (meta-UTAUT) model, including perceived severity and self-efficacy as external variables influencing emerging issues about the digital finance environment during the pandemic. The study's potential is that the facilitating conditions and self-efficacy- the two factors that show positive relationships with attitude and effort expectancy – are excluded or included as successful in creating the effect of attitude to intention. Social influence does not have a direct effect.

Esawe (2022) has provided insight into the UTAUT model by connecting how mobile self-efficacy, perceived enjoyment, and satisfaction affect the e-wallet context. It is found that mobile self-efficacy significantly affects perceived enjoyment, which further influences satisfaction, effort expectancy, and performance expectancy. Performance expectancy, social influence, and satisfaction directly influence purchase intention, while effort expectancy and facilitating conditions do not. This expanded framework gives a more in-depth insight into the elements that drive e-wallet adoption and usage in developing countries.

Chawla and Joshi (2020) examine the mediating factor of perceived usefulness, trust, and attitude toward clients' intention to take to mobile electronic wallets in India. With the help of data from the 744 respondents and the application of structural equation modelling, the examination discovered that the effects of perceived usefulness and trust on users' feelings and dedication to the mobile wallet are of utmost significance. The discovery is a remarkable one concerned with an entity's respect, which is regarded as the utilisation of gadgets. Considering the existence of several mediators reveals the exquisite prospects of mobile wallets in the Indian consumer market.

Shankar and Datta (2018) explored the mobile payment adoption decision factors for a given TAM framework, with user-centred constructs as an auxiliary constitution. The study obtained SEMs to analyse the data gathered from 381 m-payment potential users. The experience demonstrates that the adoption intention of m-payment is influenced by four issues: perceived usefulness, ease of use, trust, and self-efficacy.

Role of Trust, Compatibility, and Risk in Technology Adoption

Dawood et al. (2021) highlight the role of Mobile Perceived Trust (MPT) in adopting FinTech innovations. The study emphasises that MPT is a mediator affecting consumers' intention and adoption of FinTech services via mobile technology. Despite its importance, few studies have explored MPT's mediation effects, with most research treating trust as an independent variable. The systematic literature review conducted by Dawood et al. (2021) underscores the need for more research on MPT's mediation effects to understand its role in FinTech adoption better.

Chawla and Joshi (2021) examine the degree of awareness and its antecedents concerning mobile wallets. The study reveals that 69% of respondents are highly aware of mobile wallets, with gender, occupation, and income significantly impacting awareness levels. Awareness levels, perceived usefulness, trust, security, and lifestyle compatibility strongly predict attitudes towards mobile wallets. The logistic model developed in the study has a predictive ability of 89.11%, providing a robust framework for understanding user behaviours and attitudes related to mobile wallets.

Siew Bee and Yan Ying (2021) investigate the determinants of e-wallet adoption in Malaysia, focusing on perceived ease of use, usefulness, risk, social influence, and government support. The study finds that social influence significantly affects e-wallet adoption, particularly among younger users whom their reference groups influence. The findings suggest that increasing e-wallet adoption can drive the growth of the digital economy in Malaysia and support the transition towards a cashless society.

Kapur et al. (2019) used a different approach, using the Bass model to study the adoption pattern of the BHIM, a UPI-based mobile payment application. The study employs regression analysis to estimate the model parameters and finds that the coefficient of imitation has a more significant effect than the coefficient of innovation. The study suggests that social influence and peer usage play a more critical role in adopting the BHIM application than individual innovativeness. The study provides a mathematical perspective on adoption patterns, offering practical implications for practitioners and suggesting future research directions using extended versions of the Bass model.

Chaurasia et al. (2019) explored the intention to use mobile payments (M-payments) by integrating the motivational model with awareness about the demonetisation policy. The study surveyed 362 M-payment users and employed partial least squares for data analysis. The findings confirm that extrinsic motivation and awareness about the demonetisation policy positively influence the intention to use M-payments. The study finds a positive relationship between intrinsic and extrinsic motivation and a positive moderation effect of awareness about the demonetisation policy on the extrinsic motivation-behavioural intention relationship. However, the hypothesised moderating effect of awareness on the intrinsic motivation-behavioural intention relationship is not supported. These results underscore the raising awareness about government policies to enhance M-payment adoption.

Leadership, Innovations, and Financial Inclusion in FinTech

According to the study done by Baba et al. (2023), different and creative kinds of management led by creativity and innovation were treated as the only success factor in the Indian financial services advantages of the adoption of FinTech. This research suggests that perceived ease of use (PEOU) and perceived usefulness are the primary mediators that are crucial in the relationship between leadership and FinTech adoption. The study firmly focused on user-friendly technology and innovative leadership in this regard. It also indicates that the prospects for the FinTech sector in the country are excellent, as it can not only be a significant employer but also a part of the digital revolution in India.

Asif et al. (2023) wrote about FinTech and digital financial services' effect on financial inclusion in India. The study demonstrates that the money-sending companies' use of mobile money in small or developing markets has illuminated the path towards developing countries. FinTech startups have played an important part in such a development through inclusive financial systems. They have explicitly set people experiencing poverty as those who need them most. It is also necessary to meet the unbanked people's needs with related financial services and to pave a conductive way for FinTech companies. The study reflects the leaders' attitude to innovate. It captures the data and aims to address policy implications such as integrating the more significant part of the population into the national financial system.

Regarding the change in the financial sector driven by technological innovations, Anifa et al. (2022) address this issue; they claim that embracing the digital revolution makes it a great leader in the financial services sector. The study shows the fast spread of financial technologies all over the world. However, fintechs' excellence in this field is because they are the said technologies that have a distributional effect, which is inclusive and rare. It stresses that, for the financial industry, not only is the legal framework important, but the occurrence of innovation in the finance sector is also a must to succeed in the future.

Mobile Payment Services and Consumer Behavior

Neelam and Bhattacharya (2023) stress the importance of mobile payment applications in uplifting the financial standard of the poor residents of Pune, Maharashtra. Strict conditions that lead to the inclusion of the application are performance expectancy, economic benefit, convenience, technical conditions, hedonic motivation, and social influence. The study underscores security, ease of use, and technical requirements as ICT devices that must be mitigated to improve user acceptance. The study also reports that women frequently use mobile payment apps, thus showing a more significant role than men in technology.

Purba et al. (2021) surveyed the use of digital payment systems in Indonesia during the COVID-19 pandemic, highlighting the partnerships between technology companies and online transportation services collaboration. A clear majority of the younger generation is using digital technology applications. The study reveals that the most important reason is the convenience, comfort, and effectiveness of the systems as technology factors, especially among the millennial generation's representatives in the transportation industry. Implementing digital technology applications connected to the internet, big data, and smart mobile phones has aroused people's curiosity to adopt them. The conclusions drawn from the research are that the pandemic has caused a surge in the use of digital payment systems.

Vinayamoorthi and Manickam (2020) studied the consumer usage of digital wallets in Bangalore, India. This research remarks that the speed of mobile wallet adoption is the primary reason people like them. The study also delves into customer ideas, likes, and mobile wallet usage, showing that mobile wallet payment system users are usually good with this technology and are grateful for the advantages they carry.

The Evolution of Fintech: Mobile Payments, Sustainability, and Key Success Factors

Hopalı et al. (2022) summarise that mobile wallets are an environmental benefit in terms of service delivery sustainability by eliminating cash from the payment process. The study classified 128 articles published between 2012 and 2022 according to relevance. It concluded that mobile wallets provide cashless transactions, cost-efficient services, and traceable options, which are all related to the sustainability of the service. According to the comprehensive review, mobile wallets can be offered as environmental traceability, customer lifetime value and security, serving as a key driver to creating a more sustainable payment ecosystem.

Błach and Klimontowicz (2021) investigate the factors that lead to the sustainable success of the PayTech system in the mobile payment market through the case study of BLIK in Poland. The study mentions important factors for the entry and expansion of mobile wallets, such as the number of entrants and acceptants, the scope of transactions, and the number of users who use BLIK for daily transactions. The research emphasises the ease of accessing information and its role in the successful PayTech Innovation.

Kumar et al. (2020) build on the traditional TAM with subjective norms, personal innovativeness, trust, and self-efficacy as additional constructs. This research grounded the construct and conducted a data analysis using 203 potential future users of mobile banking to test the proposed model. Structural equation modelling (SEM) evidence confirms that perceived usefulness, perceived ease of use, subjective norms, personal innovativeness, trust, and self-efficacy significantly impact the intention to accept mobile banking. This universal strategy is not only helpful to the banks and the mobile service companies but also serves as a vital tool for them in their quest to design effective marketing strategies.

Mobile Wallets and Investments: An Indian Scenario

In India, retail investors can access many financial services through mobile wallet applications beyond payment platforms. India is going digital, and these innovative solutions are changing how users manage their money using mobile applications. In a country where a large population is underbanked, mobile wallets have filled the gap by providing a convenient and accessible way for people to save and grow their wealth. These digital solutions have lowered barriers for retail investors by incorporating savings and investment options into e-wallet platforms. So, even people with limited financial resources can develop the habit of setting aside money for their future goals.

Indian mobile wallet companies have partnered with established financial institutions and investment firms to offer a broader range of products and services, including mutual funds, fixed deposits, and digital gold - all accessible directly from users' mobile phones. This shift has made investing more democratic, helping people previously excluded from traditional financial services due to geographical barriers, administrative hurdles, or lack of financial literacy.

The user-friendly interface and simple mobile wallet application design have made investing more straightforward to understand with clear explanations, visual aids and real-time tracking of portfolios; these platforms have made investing more accessible and transparent for the investor. Mobile wallets also offer personalised recommendations, allowing users to make informed decisions based on their risk profile and financial goals.

Mobile wallets have also enabled micro-savings programs, which allow users to round up their daily transactions and automatically deposit the balance into savings accounts or investment instruments. This program is helpful for people with irregular or low income as it helps them to develop a savings habit without affecting their daily expenses.

Mobile wallets have enabled financial inclusion by providing formal financial services to underserved communities – women, rural populations and marginalised groups. These digital solutions have given individuals control over their financial lives and contributed to the country's overall economic growth and stability by providing a secure and convenient platform for savings and investments.

As India goes digital, savings and investment in mobile wallets will only get more integrated. With rising internet penetration, growing digital literacy, and supportive regulations, digital wallets can transform many individuals' financial habits. They can foster a culture of savings and long-term wealth creation. By leveraging technology and strategic partnerships, mobile wallets can reshape India's financial landscape, drive economic growth, and support the country's development goals.

CONCLUSION

This book chapter covered a mixed digital payment adoption path along individual, technological, and societal fields. Trust, user experience, and ease of use are the most important determinants of adopting digital payment systems enhanced by technology that is both easy to use and compatible. Along with this, indirect social connections and government support have significantly impacted user usage, thus supporting the initial migration. The study illustrates the relevance of inventive leadership and consumer-centred technologies in advancing FinTech and improving financial user access.

Mobile wallets in India are a game changer and a path to financial inclusion, economic empowerment, and sustainable growth. By addressing existing challenges and fostering a collaborative ecosystem, India can unlock the full potential of mobile wallets and get numerous benefits for its citizens. This technology covers the way for a more inclusive, prosperous and transparent financial future and a cashless digital economy. Government policies like demonetisation are key factors for technology adoption. This study highlights the possibilities of online payment systems to reform financial services for underserved people and calls for constant research and policy moves to help this become a reality.

REFERENCES

Anifa, M., Ramakrishnan, S., Joghee, S., Kabiraj, S., & Bishnoi, M. M. (2022). Fintech Innovations in the Financial Service Industry. *Journal of Risk and Financial Management, 15*(7), 287. Advance online publication. DOI: 10.3390/jrfm15070287

Asif, M., Khan, M. N., Tiwari, S., Wani, S. K., & Alam, F. (2023). The Impact of Fintech and Digital Financial Services on Financial Inclusion in India. *Journal of Risk and Financial Management, 16*(2), 122. Advance online publication. DOI: 10.3390/jrfm16020122

Baba, M. A., Haq, Z. U., Dawood, M., & Aashish, K. (2023). FinTech Adoption of Financial Services Industry: Exploring the Impact of Creative and Innovative Leadership. *Journal of Risk and Financial Management, 16*(10), 453. Advance online publication. DOI: 10.3390/jrfm16100453

Błach, J., & Klimontowicz, M. (2021). The Determinants of PayTech's Success in the Mobile Payment Market – The Case of BLIK. *Journal of Risk and Financial Management, 14*(9), 422. Advance online publication. DOI: 10.3390/jrfm14090422

Chaurasia, S. S., Verma, S., & Singh, V. (2019). *Exploring the intention to use M-payment in India. Transforming Government: People*. Process and Policy., DOI: 10.1108/TG-09-2018-0060

Chawla, D., & Joshi, H. (2020). Role of Mediator in Examining the Influence of Antecedents of Mobile Wallet Adoption on Attitude and Intention. *Global Business Review, 24*(4), 609–625. DOI: 10.1177/0972150920924506

Chawla, D., & Joshi, H. (2021). *Degree of Awareness and the Antecedents of the Digital Media Platform: The Case of Mobile Wallets*. FIIB Business Review., DOI: 10.1177/23197145211023413

Dawood, H. M., Liew, C. Y., & Lau, T. (2021). Mobile perceived trust mediation on the intention and adoption of FinTech innovations using mobile technology: A systematic literature review. F1000Research, 10. https://doi.org/DOI: 10.12688/f1000research.74656.2

Esawe, A. T. (2022). Understanding mobile e-wallet consumers' intentions and user behavior. *Spanish Journal of Marketing - ESIC, 26*(3), 363–384. Advance online publication. DOI: 10.1108/SJME-05-2022-0105

Hasan, A., Sikarwar, P., Mishra, A., Raghuwanshi, S., Singhal, A., Joshi, A., Singh, P. R., & Dixit, A. (2024). Determinants of Behavioral Intention to Use Digital Payment among Indian Youngsters. *Journal of Risk and Financial Management*, *17*(2), 87. Advance online publication. DOI: 10.3390/jrfm17020087

Hopalı, E., Vayvay, Ö., Kalender, Z. T., Turhan, D., & Aysuna, C. (2022). How Do Mobile Wallets Improve Sustainability in Payment Services? A Comprehensive Literature Review. *Sustainability (Basel)*, *14*(24), 16541. Advance online publication. DOI: 10.3390/su142416541

Kapur, P. K., Sharma, H., Tandon, A., & Aggarwal, A. G. (2019). *Studying BHIM App Adoption using Bass Model: An Indian Perspective*. International Journal of Mathematical, Engineering and Management Sciences., DOI: 10.33889/IJMEMS.2020.5.1.011

Kumar, A., Dhingra, S., Batra, V., & Purohit, H. K. (2020). A Framework of Mobile Banking Adoption in India. *Journal of Open Innovation*, *6*(2), 40. Advance online publication. DOI: 10.3390/joitmc6020040

Kumar, R., Singh, R., Kumar, K., Khan, S., & Corvello, V. (2023). How Does Perceived Risk and Trust Affect Mobile Banking Adoption? Empirical Evidence from India. *Sustainability (Basel)*, *15*(5), 4053. Advance online publication. DOI: 10.3390/su15054053

Neelam, K., & Bhattacharya, S. (2023). *The Role of Mobile Payment Apps in Inclusive Financial Growth. Australasian Accounting*. Business and Finance Journal., DOI: 10.14453/aabfj.v17i1.02

Purba, J. T., Samuel, S., & Budiono, S. (2021). *Collaboration of digital payment usage decision in COVID-19 pandemic situation: Evidence from Indonesia*. International Journal of Data and Network Science., DOI: 10.5267/j.ijdns.2021.8.012

Shankar, A., & Datta, B. K. (2018). Factors Affecting Mobile Payment Adoption Intention: An Indian Perspective. *Global Business Review*, *19*(3_suppl), S72–S89. DOI: 10.1177/0972150918757870

Siew Bee, T., & Ying, Y. K. (2021). An examination of determinants for e-wallet adoption in Malaysia: a combined approach. F1000Research. https://doi.org/DOI: 10.12688/f1000research.73402.1

Upadhyay, N., Upadhyay, S., Abed, S. S., & Dwivedi, Y. K. (2022). Consumer adoption of mobile payment services during COVID-19: Extending meta-UTAUT with perceived severity and self-efficacy. *International Journal of Bank Marketing*, *40*(5), 960–991. Advance online publication. DOI: 10.1108/IJBM-06-2021-0262

Vinayamoorthi, G., & Manickam, T. (2020). Consumer's Adoption of Digital Wallets With Special Reference to Bangalore City. *Management Science*, *8*(2), 108–113. DOI: 10.34293/management.v8i2.3429

Chapter 4
Mobile Wallets:
A Detailed Perspective With Reference to the Developing Countries

Muhammad Faisal Sultan
Khadim Ali Shah Bukhari Institute of Technology, Pakistan

Abdul Kabeer Kazi
https://orcid.org/0000-0001-9860-2891
Baqai Medical University, Pakistan

Muhammad Asim Rafique
National University of Modern Languages, Pakistan

ABSTRACT

The world is continuously moving towards digitization. In fact, every activity from routine-based activities to professional activities is now performed in a digitized way. Similar is the case of financial transactions that were initiated through physical exchange and now are mostly transformed into digitized platforms. Among these platforms, one of the most progressive ones is mobile wallets. Mobile wallets are different from mobile banking and now associated with casual and everyday activities of life. However, there are some challenges associated with the mass acceptance and usage of mobile wallets. Especially from developing sides of the world, the growth of mobile wallets is getting limited just because of associated threats and problems. Therefore, this chapter is designed specifically with reference to the developing sides of the world in order to shed light on the importance of mobile banking as well as factors that are limiting the use of mobile banking.

DOI: 10.4018/979-8-3693-7160-2.ch004

BACKGROUND

Virtual payments are one of the latest and well-known technologies that have replaced physical currency in multiple forms of transactions (Mumtaza et al., 2020). Actually, demonetization is the main factor that makes users prefer e-payments which ultimately enhances the ratio of cashless transactions. Cashless transactions need the use of plastic money e.g., debit cards and credit cards, etc., or digitized modes e.g., mobile wallets and bet banking etc. These initiatives are pushing revolutionizing the economy and pushing it towards digitization. However, effective government initiatives are mandatory for enhancing the digitization of systems, processes as well as the entire economy (Sarika & Vasantha, 2019).

In fact, there are several advantages of virtual payments that give it a significant edge over the use of physical currency. Among these advantages most significant are ease of conducting transactions, Effective and efficient tracing of money, Reduction in the burden of currency printing lesser chances of money laundering, etc are most prominent. There are several examples of virtual payments e.g., online transfers, credit cards, mobile banking, and mobile wallets etc (Mumtaza et al., 2020). However, the use of m-wallets has increased significantly; especially amid the pandemic use of mobile wallet provide users with a safe and touch-free mechanism. The mechanism makes users motivated to use mobile wallets. Thus in Asian countries like India, we have evidence significant increase in the usage rate. However, the overall adoption of m-wallet is not very promising. Therefore, m-wallet companies tried to enhance research activities in order to understand the reason that may attract consumers to the technology (Kapoor et al., 2022)

Mobile Wallets

These are equivalent to the physical wallets that we mostly carry with us. The platform enables users to keep money digitally. The only requirement is to open an account with a mobile service provider after which money can be credited into the account through using technologies like debit cards, credit cards, online transactions, or even through from an account in the form of cash (Vijai, 2019).

There are two major differences between online transaction and mobile wallet i.e., mobile wallets are hassle-free and does not require the customer to enter PIN or card details for every transaction. Moreover, the mobile wallet does not charge any fees for the transaction. On the other side, people are confused in differentiating mobile wallets from mobile banking but in actuality, mobile banking is a much broader concept (Vijai, 2019). Studies highlighted that mobile banking is only limited to the transactions that are limited to online transactions made by banks. However, mobile wallets or mobile payments are generic and are made by service providers that exist as telecom companies (Iman, 2018). In fact, through using mobile wallets we use mobile phones for making transactions and payments for any sort of need. Thus the use of mobile wallets causes significant reduction in the demand for physical cash (Vijai, 2019). Therefore, using mobile payments companies may reach the unbanked population that lies at the bottom of the pyramid (Iman, 2018).

INTRODUCTION

The use of credit cards is the most well-known and dominant form of virtual payments. In fact, 95% of virtual transactions conducted in the United States of America are based on credit cards (Mumtaza et al., 2020). However, the dawn of the 20th century resulted in the use of advanced technologies like 3G and 4G which along with the increased use of cellular phones makes people more inclined towards the use of mobile wallets (Chuhan et al., 2017).

However, the use of credit cards also has some limitations, and therefore in recent times one of the new technologies termed as a mobile wallet is gaining popularity. It is very rare and only used in a few countries for very limited purposes like mobile games, movie tickets, and online content. However, the use of mobile wallets is unique and completely digitized based on digital cards, digital receipts digital coupons, etc. Hence it is optimal to believe that the use and application of digital wallets are more advantageous in comparison to any other cashless system. On the other hand, there are various threats that are threatening the use of mobile wallets such as IT crimes and difficulties in differentiating criminals and business groups that are trying to lure the advantages of new technologies (Mumtaza et al., 2020).

Similar sort of indications are also prompted by Ayoola (2013) and Cisar (2003) who indicated that the use of cashless and mobile transactions was unable to reduce corruption. In fact, the use of cashless systems may only shift corruption and related activities from one person or group to another without reducing the percentage of criminal activities (Mumtaza et al., 2020).

GRAY AREAS AND PURPOSE OF THE STUDY

The global economy might be geared up by combining innovation and technology. On the other side, South-Asian countries have massive potential to push their economies through entrepreneurial efforts and new doors. Among these steps, one of the most dominant is the introduction of mobile payments that are getting popular in various South-Asian countries like Pakistan, India Sri Lanka, etc. On the other side mobile Banking is also raising revenue by reducing the informal economy, aiding in financial inclusion, and producing a positive impact on the economic conditions of the country (Latif & Ozcan, 2019).

However, access to internet facilities is still much different in developed and developing sides of the world. Developing sides does not have still do not have proper access to internet services. However, digitization of the economy causes an increase in opportunities as well as challenges for developed as well as developing sides of the world (Hoffmann et al., 2018). On the other side, the use of mobile payments also has some threats and issues for the developing world where the lack of IT infrastructure, legislative protection, consumer unawareness, and differences in consumer skills etc are hindering in way of growth of mobile payments (Huang et al., 2020). Hence the awareness & attention of consumers as well as policy makers is mandatory for pushing the acceptance, use, and significance of the technology to the required extent. Hence, this chapter is developed to shed light on mobile payments, the type of mobile wallets, theories associated with consumer preferences, limiting factors as well as some future implications of mobile wallets. In fact, the chapter is also associated with multiple case studies from developing sides of the world in order to make users relate the contents as well as practical implications, challenges, and threats to the growth of mobile payments.

THEORETICAL UNDERPINNING

Previously Technology Acceptance Model (TAM) and Unified Theory of Acceptance and Use of Technology (UTAUT) were used to discuss and elaborate on an individual's intention toward using and adopting new technologies. In fact, initial studies related to the mobile wallet were also inclined towards the use of TAM & UTAUT. However, these theories have some limitations as their major concern is towards the application of new technologies and techniques within organizational domain and hence mainly associated with employees. Hence in order to relate mobile wallets with individual perspectives and behavior studies initiated the use of the Stimulus-Organism-Response (S-O-R) model to explain the use of mobile wallets (Kapoor et al., 2022)

LITERATURE REVIEW

In recent times electronic wallets have become popular in several developing and developed countries. In fact, developing Asian countries like China, Hong Kong, and Taiwan are becoming prominent in the list of countries using mobile wallets. Around 50% of Chinese inhabitants are regular users of mobile wallets. Hong

Kong and Taiwan are a bit slower in the race of mobile wallet adoption (Mumtaza et al., 2020): Similar is the case of India where the market size of mobile wallets is increasing day after another. In fact, studies expected that it may reach up to $ 6.6 Billion by 2020. Hence it is a massive opportunity for mobile wallet providers which are trying to provide attractive packages and offers to prospective customers. Thus, the surge in the use of mobile wallets has been observed in various activities like mobile recharge, bill payments, ticket booking, banking transactions, and payment of utility bills, etc. Moreover, leading telecom companies like Vodafone, Airtel, and Paytm after getting permits for payment bank licenses may take the growth in mobile wallet use to new hives. In fact, mobile wallets may take multiple types for the increase in customer convenience and market penetration (Chuhan et al., 2017; Vijai, 2019).

a) **Open Wallet:** The type of wallet is open for all sorts of transactions i.e., digitized and physical which permits users to transfer funds to accounts as well as to peers electronically and also aids in withdrawing and submitting funds physically (Chuhan et al., 2017).
b) **Semi-Open Wallet:** It is a form of electronic wallet that permits users to load money to specific applications associated with specific companies (Chuhan et al., 2017).
c) **Close Wallets:** This form of e-wallets is popular in the field of e-commerce. Several companies use these forms of wallets for conducting smooth transactions. In this form of e-wallet, a minimum amount is reserved with the merchant to safeguard against of return or cancellation of products (Chuhan et al., 2017).
d) **Semi-Closed Wallets:** The most popular type of mobile wallet is semi-closed wallets. Using this form of wallet does not allow users to withdraw funds and it may only be used for purchase from business markets. It allows users to purchase from listed merchants authentically through an account registered with their name (Chuhan et al., 2017).

CHALLENGES IN THE ADAPTATION OF CASHLESS SYSTEMS IN THE DEVELOPING WORLD

There are several reasons for the lack of electronic currency adoption. However, different countries have different reasons for less adoption of Internet banking or cashless systems. Although in South Asia one of the major reasons for the lack of adoption is the lower rate of SMART-Phone adoption the premier reason for the lack of use is the mass presence of unbanked people. Therefore it is not appropriate to use any particular country(s) as the benchmark or base for any assessment (Mumtaza et al., 2020). Some of the studies like Iman (2018) also indicated some hurdles and factors that are limiting the growth of mobile payments in the developing world.

a) **Restrictions and Regulations:** Developing countries of the world have several factors that are limiting the growth of mobile payments. Among these one of the most detrimental factors is the requirement of banks to play a major role in the ecosystem. In fact, without the inclusion of a bank, the eco-system of mobile payments cannot work effectively. Hence the growth in mobile payments is much slower as compared to the pace of technological growth (Iman, 2018).
b) **Rear Collaborations:** Collaborations are mandatory between telecom service providers and banks. Although most of the banks do not have specific & specialized mechanisms to deal with mobile payments. Similar is the case of India where mobile service providers are facing severe difficulties in collaborating with banks which affected negatively the eco-system as well as consumers. In fact, it takes five years to make M-PESA collaborate with commercial banks. Therefore, the lack of collaborations is actually causing roadblocks and hindering the way of growth mobile payments (Iman, 2018).
c) **Security Development:** Developing countries do not have proper IT infrastructure which may also prevent the growth of mobile payments. In fact, the severity of cybercrimes is found to be directly associated with a lack of IT infrastructure. Other than these point developing countries also does not have proper legal framework and enforcement mechanism. Moreover, consumers from the developing world are also fully aware of cybercrimes and also pay less attention to these sorts of activities. Hence in combination, these forms of security issues are hindering the growth of mobile payments (Iman, 2018).
d) **Under-Developed Eco-System:** There are several shortcomings that exist in developing countries e.g., lack of features in cellular phones, insufficient infrastructure, issues of telecom networks, etc. The lack and absence of these elements are actually making the ecosystem inefficient. Hence legitimate to declare the ecosystem as under developed ecosystem (Iman, 2018). Other than these issues studies like Mumtaza (2020) have also discussed some factors that are equally responsible for limiting the growth of mobile payments.
e) Less than fifty percent rate of literacy
f) Lesser internet users
g) Internet banking or cashless systems are a source of attraction for only literate people
h) Additional fees associated with the use of online systems of payments
i) People prefer to use physical currency as most people are not connected to banks

RESEARCH DESIGN

The purpose of this chapter is mainly to discuss and elaborate on the use of mobile wallets in developing sides of the world. Hence for its formulation, different elements have been collected from different sources.

Hence readers will have a detailed understanding of mobile payments in the developing world in consistent with pertaining issues. Therefore, the actual significance of the chapter is to make academicians, students, scholars, and policy-making understand the implications, scope, and challenges that are pertaining to mobile payment. This objective actually coincides with Saunders et al (2007) which use research onion as the concept for devising research methodology for scholarly work and mention epistemology as the philosophy of knowledge. However, as per Saunders et al (2015), there is a need for a philosophical stance to relate the philosophy of research with the research approach and research methods and techniques. Although the stances provided by Saunders et al (2015) are not suited best for qualitative research compilation through secondary data. Hence this study uses the philosophical stance that has been developed by Syed and McLean (2021) known as constructivism and usually used to relate and co-integrate parts of already published work. Hence, the research strategy is archival as the study is actually based upon previously published and authentic work that is also indexed in Google Scholar. Therefore, according to the concept of research onion by Saunders et al (2007) and Saunders et al (2015), the strategy used in the research is archival. It also clarified that the time horizon for the development of this study is cross-sectional (Saunders et al., 2015 & Sekaran & Bougie, 2016).

Case Study 01 "Use of Mobile Wallets in Pakistan amid COVID-19 Pandemic"

Mobile wallets are getting popular in developed as well as developing sides of the world. Similar is the case of Pakistan where the total number of mobile wallet accounts reached up to 47 million in 2019. However, after the government imposed restrictions on unregistered accounts the tally fell to 36 million in 2019.However, the outbreak of COVID-19 resulted in a significant surge in the use of mobile wallets as in April 2020 the number of registered mobile wallets again reached 47 million with almost 195,000 agents working across Pakistan. In fact, the restriction on movement and lockdown significantly increased the number of mobile wallet users as the user tally reached up to 52 million during COVID-19. Adding to the figures studies also indicated that by June 2022 the number of mobile wallet users reached 87 million with cash value of 2183408 million and thousand agents (Latif & Ozcan, 2022).

However, most people are using this technology only for payments of bills, person-to-person transfers, and mobile top-ups. However, during the pandemic, the technology was also used to transfer funds like salaries, and pensions as well as funds to needy and deserving who are suffering from disaster. In fact, analysis of data through the inferential statistics reflected that there is a causal relationship between mobile wallets and the GDP of Pakistan as an increase in the use of mobile wallets produces a positive impact on the GDP of the country (Latif & Ozcan, 2022).

Case Study 02 "Challenges and Threats to the Use of Mobile Wallets"

An increase in the use of mobile banking increases the probability of entrepreneurship and also fosters individual income through using online mediums. In fact, the use of mobile banking is also very important for financial inclusion. However, there are some drawbacks and limiting factors that we must also understand especially with respect to developing countries like China. Among these points, one of the major drawbacks is digital inequality which is actually the inequality of underserved communities with respect to information, communication technologies, access, use, and skills, etc. Moreover, the use of financial technologies like mobile wallets is also creating complexities of financial regulations. Therefore, consumer protection and safety is the major concern for these companies and diminishes firms' motivation to provide the best quality of services. Other than this issue inappropriate banking model in developing economies with a highly concentrated market structure is one of the major limiting factors for the growth of mobile payments. Therefore, there is a genuine need for a better banking model in order to leverage the financial risk of new businesses (Huang et al., 2020).

FUTURE IMPLICATIONS

The evolution of mobile technologies and electronic fund transfer cannot be stopped as it is associated with the evaluation of technology. Therefore, the speed of evolution is the same as that of technology. It is moving very fast and has recently touched the ultimate heights of the paradigm from e-payments to payments through the scanning of quick response (QR) codes.

Even in developed and technologically sound payments transfers are associated with face scans that provide ultimate safety and security to customers. In short advancement of technology is affecting consumer behavior positively and makes customers more inclined towards making electronic transactions with comfort, ease, and convenience as the transactions are just a touch away through using mobile (Soegoto et al., 2021).

CONCLUSION AND DISCUSSIONS

This chapter provides a detailed discussion of mobile payments their use and their significance concerning emerging markets in South Asia. Hence the chapter is extremely beneficial for knowledge as well as policy making etc. Through this chapter, it is clear that mobile payments are extremely beneficial for the economic aspects of the country. However, it may lead to issues of consumer safety and legislation as in developing countries consumers are not well-informed about the technology and its use which may affect the penetration of the technology. Supplemented with weak IT infrastructure and improper legislative reforms there is a chance of an increase in digital crimes that may not only produce negative impacts on individuals and organizations but may also produce drastic impacts on the country's economy and well-being.

REFERENCES

Ayoola, T. (2013). The effect of cashless policy of government on corruption in Nigeria. *International Review of Management and Business Research, 2*(3), 682–690.

Chauhan, M., Shingari, I., & Shingari, I. (2017). Future of e-wallets: A perspective from under graduates. *International Journal of Advanced Research in Computer Science and Software Engineering, 7*(8), 146. DOI: 10.23956/ijarcsse.v7i8.42

Cisar, O.(2003). Strategies for using information technologies for curbing public-sector corruption: The case of the Czech Republic (CR). Budapest: Open society institute

Hoffmann, J., Bakhoum, M., & Beneke, F. (2018). Digital markets, mobile payments systems and development–Competition policy implications in developing countries in light of the EU experience. *Max Planck Institute for Innovation & Competition Research Paper*, (18-13)

Huang, Y., Wang, X., & Wang, X. (2020). Mobile payment in China: Practice and its effects. *Asian Economic Papers, 19*(3), 1–18. DOI: 10.1162/asep_a_00779

Iman, N. (2018). Is mobile payment still relevant in the fintech era? *Electronic Commerce Research and Applications, 30*, 72–82. DOI: 10.1016/j.elerap.2018.05.009

Kapoor, A., Sindwani, R., Goel, M., & Shankar, A. (2022). Mobile wallet adoption intention amid COVID-19 pandemic outbreak: A novel conceptual framework. *Computers & Industrial Engineering, 172*, 108646. DOI: 10.1016/j.cie.2022.108646 PMID: 36118531

Latif, M. N., & Ozcan, R. FIN-TECH adoption in Pakistan: mobile wallet service (MWS) over GDP causality evidence for pre and post COVID-19. Journal of Research & Reviews in Social Sciences Pakistan, 6 (1), 1999-2011

Mumtaza, Q. M. H., Nabillah, S. I., Amaliya, S., Rosabella, Y., & Hammad, J. A. (2020). Worldwide mobile wallet: A futuristic cashless system. *Bulletin of Social Informatics Theory and Application, 4*(2), 70–75. DOI: 10.31763/businta.v4i2.204

Sarika, P., & Vasantha, S. (2019). Impact of mobile wallets on cashless transaction. *Int. J. Recent Technol. Eng, 7*(6), 1164–1171.

Saunders, M., Lewis, P. & Thornhill, A. (2007). Research methods. Business Students 4th edition Pearson Education Limited, England, 1-268.

Saunders, M. N., Lewis, P., Thornhill, A., & Bristow, A. (2015). Understanding research philosophy and approaches to theory development. In: Saunders, Mark N. K.; Lewis, Philip and Thornhill, Adrian eds. Research Methods for Business Students. Harlow: Pearson Education, 122–161

Soegoto, E. S., Purna, S., & Sumitra, T. P. (2021). Mobile Payment Technology for Future Transaction. *Jurnal Ilmiah Sistem Informasi, 1*(2), 86–92. DOI: 10.46306/sm.v1i2.11

Syed, M., & McLean, K. C. (2021). Disentangling paradigm and method can help bring qualitative research to post-positivist psychology and address the generalizability crisis. *Behavioral and Brain Sciences, 45*, 58–60. DOI: 10.1017/S0140525X21000431 PMID: 35139943

Vijai, C. (2019). Mobile wallet and its future in India. *Journal of Emerging Technologies and Innovative Research, 6*(5), 574–580.

Chapter 5
Behavioral Finance in Post-COVID-19 World

Bushra Qamar
https://orcid.org/0000-0002-3992-5129
Iqra University, North Karachi, Pakistan

ABSTRACT

COVID-19 pandemic, historically substantial worldwide disaster, has elevated the complexity of human behavior to the fore of financial markets and decision-making. The study investigates a convergence of behavioral finance and post-COVID-19, offering insight into how individuals' psychological biases and emotional responses have influenced how they make investments, market dynamics, and economic outcomes. The study constructs a robust theoretical framework for researchers and academicians through a rigorous demonstration of extant literature on behavior biases. As a result, it can be concluded that this area of behavioral finance remains underdeveloped and requires the attention of researchers globally. Furthermore, a significant number of studies are conducted in American, European, and African regions, but are almost non-existent in Asian markets. This study adds to existing knowledge and provides investors with insights into psychological biases that may affect investment decisions. Additionally, other factors may also influence how investors make decision-making.

1. INTRODUCTION

With over 100 million cases, COVID-19 has claimed the lives of over 2 million individuals globally. This is one of the most devastating pandemics in recent memory, costing not only human deaths with billions of dollars to worldwide economies (Ramphul et al., 2021). In many economies, both financial and labor sectors faced

DOI: 10.4018/979-8-3693-7160-2.ch005

substantial contractions and upheavals. Virus was assumed a China-specific disease at start of 2020, and outside people did not consider it a severe warning. After virus was swiftly identified as a pandemic on March 11, 2020 individuals were overcome with fear and anxiety (Sohrabi et al., 2020; WHO, 2020). Ramelli and Wagner, (2020) state investors throughout world first avoided equities with China exposure, and as disease spread, markets considered economic ramifications of these problems on corporations.

In first half of 2020, there was one of most devastating stock market crashes in history. The virus that caused the crash was born in Wuhan, China. In December 2019, Wuhan reported its first COVID-19 case. Initially, it was believed that this virus would spread globally without causing death. Numerous economic activities have to be put on hold as a result of virus' quick global spread and ensuing panic (Ganie et al., 2022). To stop the virus from spreading, many nations imposed strict lockdowns and stopped all major economic activities. These actions were ultimately negatively appraised by financial markets, which led to inevitable market turmoil in March 2020. During pandemic, Sweden, for example, enforced very few social restrictions (Gupta, 2023). Conversely, numerous other countries imposed severe restrictions, including social isolation and complete lockdowns. Similarly, stock markets around world witnessed varied degrees of fall in response to COVID-19, with some markets losing more than 30% (Mazur et al., 2021; Chowdhury et al., 2022). One question arises here is what are those factors affecting the behavior of investors while investing?

In context of behavioral finance behavior of investors in making investments is considered an important sub area to explore how they predict, perceive, study, and review decision-making process (Jan et al., 2022). A majority of finance scholars regard investor rationality and market efficiency as the fundamental beliefs for enlightening financial theories. Markets are believed to be constructed to maximize perceived advantage, and investors are always assumed to make rational judgments. Contrarily, several scholars have shown in recent years that conventional financial theories fall short of capturing investors' irrational behavior while making investment decisions (Huang et al., 2018). According to Thaler and Ganser (2015), investors' behaviors are often irrational due to a variety of behavioral biases that they are subject to in everyday life. Various studies of behavioral finance in the literature analyzed and discovered that psychological factors affect the decisions of investors making investments (Ahmed et al., 2022). As opposed to conventional financial assumptions, which presume investors are always rational, behavioral finance takes into account and theoretically demonstrates, when choosing an investment, investors are sometimes rational rather being irrational. Furthermore, the current global pandemic highlights need to identify aspects that influence investor behavior in evaluating investment decision-making (Jan et al., 2022). According to behavioral finance theory, thorough knowledge regarding behavioral psychology assists in analyzing inconsistencies in stock market and investing decisions. Furthermore, knowing psychology of investors when making investment decisions helps investors deal with behavioral biases and transform these into advantageous profits encouraging to continue investing (Boda & Sunitha, 2018).

Stock market influences investors' decisions greatly, which simultaneously raises the effectiveness of corporate governance (Samuel, 1996). There are many misconceptions about stock market investments since some investors merely want to seize control of the company and become the sole owner, while others are more interested in dividends and still others only invest for capital gains (Croushore, 2007). To hold designated places on the board of directors, investors typically need to own a predetermined amount of shares in the company (Aziz & Khan, 2016). This allows them to actively participate in important decision-making processes even in uncertain and risky scenarios. According to traditional financial theories like the Theory of the Efficient Market investors can easily get accurate information about a variety of investment opportunities and have it presented in a reasonable and practicable way. Stock markets frequently exhibit uncertainty, and investors band together in response to similar moves performed by others, basing their investment plans purely on the choices and activities of other modern investors (Fernandez et al., 2006; Sabir et al., 2019).

The study's purpose is to look into psychological and emotional behavioral elements that influence investors' decisions to invest in stock market in light of the post-COVID-19 situation. To explain psychological effects of investing, this study integrates an examination of psychological and emotional elements of market volatility with a focus on investor rationality. Traditional finance holds as investors are sensible and normal while making stock market investment decisions, they are less likely to participate in figure manipulation and risk-return trade-offs. Efficient market model states investors should evaluate all pertinent data and make impartial, unbiased investing decisions. Psychologists, in comparison with economists, favored illogical behavior in individuals. Investors are not always as rational as they seem (Babajide & Adetiloye, 2012; Bashir et al., 2013). As a result, behavioral finance can investigate and explain the differences in investor behavior. Kengatharan and Kengatharan, (2014) state Behavioral finance studies effect of psychological factors on experts, individuals, investors, portfolio managers, and experts. It makes an effort to comprehend how mental blunders and emotional factors affect investor conduct. Additionally, it looks at why investors act irrationally when compared to how people would assume they would. Researchers have highlighted different psychological factors influencing investors' decisions while making stock market investments in literature on behavioral finance. The proliferation of COVID-19 influences all facets of life, especially public health. Sustainability of financial and global stock markets has various significant ramifications (Guo et al., 2020; Ali, 2020). Investors, on the other hand, are part of a social setup impacts their enthusiasm, feelings, sentiments, and glumness about future stock values (Wang et al., 2023). As a result, in this study, we will examine how behavioral finance has evolved in post-COVID-19 period, highlighting key findings and consequences.

2. LITERATURE REVIEW

2.1 Behavioral Finance

Behavioral finance looks into how psychological influences affect the actions and results of market players, with a focus on decisions made by individual investors. Furthermore, it looks into how investors make decisions depending on specific facts, as well as the impact these decisions have on their biases as well as opinions (Antony, 2020). Behavioral finance can fill in the gaps left by rational models in describing specific financial occurrences, providing a more in-depth explanation of the phenomenon. Thus, behavioral finance may be utilized to obtain a better knowledge of the financial world, such as corporate finance, stock market purchases, and consumption habits, as well as how different investors' biases impact those behaviors (Barberis & Thaler, 2002). Following a review of the behavioral finance literature over the previous two decades, Subrahmanyam (2008) concluded traditional finance has had little impact on understanding issues such as the reason why investors trade in goods, how they operate and select their portfolios, and why stock returns vary across stocks for reasons other than risk. Because of this, behavioral finance is now being used to address issues which traditional finance and its models cannot, which is very advantageous for investors to understand because it enables them to acquire an in-depth knowledge of financial phenomena along with how their own beliefs and actions may be influenced. He also identifies behavioral finance as an interesting new topic with several transformative implications for both individual investors and CEOs. Therefore, the industry offers not only potential benefits to individual investors but also considerable opportunities for top business executives and others working in the financial sector to expand their understanding of the world of finance. Behavioral finance is important in understanding unexpected and massive market increases since financial bubbles are frequently the result of investor biases caused due to emotions affecting decisions (Hirvonen, 2021). These distorted emotions frequently lead inefficient and irrational financial decisions, which can result in market disasters. Furthermore, knowing the flaws in human judgment is critical to understanding financial inconsistencies and bubbles. These financial irregularities have a disastrous effect on the financial markets' health. According to Kapoor and Prosad (2017), it is critical to have a more in-depth investigation of behavioral finance because anomaly prevention is achievable when investors know their psychological and behavioral constraints.

2.2 Investors

According to Ozkan and Ozkan (2020), the investing process is hard since each investor is a unique sort of person with varied emotional processes, personality features, and mental flaws. Investors often possess behavioral biases for investment probability and tend to make decisions on basis of their emotions and feelings, even when thoughts do not have any hard data to support investment decisions, so making decisions regarding the purchase or sale of different stocks requires a great deal than just analyzing numbers. Baker and Ricciardi (2014) classified them as cognitive biases and emotional biases. Cognitive biases are personality traits that cause investors to make decisions and engage in actions that may lead to erroneous conclusions. Emotional biases are financial judgments made using feelings and emotions. According to association between personality traits and psychological biases, Individuals have different ways of thinking, access to information from various sources, and emotional responses, so one investor may view a given investment opportunity, such as a manufacturing culture stock or a corporate bond, entirely differently from an individual having different beliefs and personality traits. Knowing one's personality features and implementing decisions depending on one's financial risk tolerance might provide one a considerable edge in the competitive financial markets (Kubilay and Bayrakdaroglu, 2016). The fact that only certain investors are concerned about their prejudiced tendencies and may change their investing selections by considering the biases into consideration may thus have a big positive impact. People have varied biases due to certain personality features. This is why evaluating and understanding the investor's biases can be highly important when aiming for higher earnings and overall better performance with investing. Shepherd et al. (2015) addressed importance of understanding individuals', financial experts', and traders' cognitive processes and emotional issues, emphasizing behavior of investors might notify investors with regard to these biases and even allow them to optimize their decision-making progress as identifying investments, products, and strategies. As a result, understanding how investors act and biases may help consumers and financial advisors make better investment decisions, as well as judgments in other aspects of investing such as planning and purchasing.

2.3 Behavioral Finance Biases and Their Concepts

Behavioral Finance integrates market phenomena and individual investor behavior to apply knowledge gained from financial theories and psychological field (Chia et al., 2023; Utama, 2023). According to Zahera and Bansal (2018), investor behavior is thus incorporated as a component of behavioral finance to explore implications of the structured financial market inside psychological decision-making process. Furthermore, behavioral aspects influencing investor decision-making are divided into four categories: (1) prospect theory, (2) herding effect (3) market considerations, and (4) heuristic theory. Every theory in the group reflects the general picture demonstrating that behavioral aspects significantly influence investors' decisions, particularly those made in stock market. Thus, no matter type of stock market (frontier, emergent, or developed), these four theories can be used to understand and recognize behavior of institutional and individual investors participating in secured trading (Ngoc, 2014).

2.3.1 Heuristic Theory

To define Heuristic Theory (Ritter, 2003) rule of thumb is a phenomenon tends to make decision-making simpler and easier, especially in complicated circumstances and under uncertain conditions. Theory includes a process of lowering such complexities through probability of assessment and vital judgments to forecast values (Kahneman & Tversky, 1979). Heuristic effects are advantageous, particularly when time is restricted (Waweru et al., 2008; Riaz et al., 2020). Some studies attempted to demonstrate heuristic effects frequently lead to biases (Siraji, 2019). It is widely accepted that Kahneman and Tversky (1979), often regarded as the first writers on the subject, investigated three other critical aspects, known as availability bias, anchoring, and representativeness, including them in heuristic theory. Waweru et al. (2008) incorporated two additional elements, Overconfidence and Gamblers fallacy, into the heuristic framework.

Overconfidence is strongly considered to increase tenacity, mental capacity, resolve, and risk tolerance. To be more precise, it aids in fostering professional effectiveness and performance in addition to improving others' perceptions and skills to promote individuals more quickly and for longer periods (Quddoos et al., 2020). The preceding projections can be regarded understated, for instance, when an investor wishes to overestimate his capacity to acquire the necessary knowledge to get thoroughly acquainted with the material at hand. Therefore, a person is very accurately described as an overconfident investor when they tend to exaggerate precision and accuracy of their informative signals rather than relying on publicly available informative signals (Daniel et al., 1998). Overconfident investors are persons who believe their decisions are better than they are (Trivers, 1991). Overconfidence is a word used in psychological literature and current finance theories to describe the conduct of persons. Further studies revealed overconfidence in human behavior is a primary contributing factor that leads to extraordinary overtrading in the financial market by investors. Barber and Odean (2001) contributed to the research increased trading volume might be due to overconfidence among investors and that investors frequently regret their prior judgments and conclusions since they were incomparable with those of others.

2.3.2 Prospect Theory

Prospect Theory was originally proposed by Kahneman and Tversky (1979), who stated Individuals have an irrational tendency to be less inclined to gamble with profits than with losses. However, Tvede (1999) disagreed with proposed theory since it frequently exhibits typical human behavior when investors are almost ready to deal with risks, uncertainty, and insecurity. The majority of individuals are probable to choose facts and, as a result, place greater trust in outcomes that seem more assured. Investors like to take risks and struggle with finances, whereas those who make earnings and gain benefits are typically exposed to potential dangers. Humans are only risk averse in situations where they stand to gain (Kishore, 2004), don't consistently adapt to risk aversion, and plan to take risks even when they fail. People respond differently to dependence on structured decisions, whether in terms of profits or losses (Riaz et al., 2020). There are two techniques that investors can employ when making decisions. The first is known as Prospect Theory, and second is known as Expected Utility Theory (EUT), both of which are regarded from different perspectives and suitable points of view. According to Filbeck et al. (2005), the former provides insight into investors' subjective decision-making, whereas the latter emphasizes reasonable and typical expectations. There are several notable areas in which the EUT and the Prospect theory diverge.

First, whereas value maximization is referred to be a utility in EUT, it is a pure value in Prospect theory (Plous, 1993). Prospect theory, wealth maximization is described as precise values taking place among revenues and expenses, but in EUT, it is often referred to as a final wealth position. Additionally, according to Meng & Weng (2018), wealth function is often concave, with profits being less steep and losses being steeper and convex. Rashata (2022) points out although wealth functions regarding losses may be steeper and larger than wealth functions for profits, their values are equal. The significance of variance between EUT and prospect theory led to several noteworthy and astounding findings. EUT regulates analysis and results of risky decision-making since it is a standard model of rational decisions and a persuasive model of economic behaviors. Since this explanation could not explain why individuals tended to be more drawn toward insurance and less attracted toward gambling, detractors severely contested it. People often give less weight to outputs with uncertainty and probability than to outcomes that are clear and secure, and they are more likely to act differently under the same conditions, whether there are benefits or losses (Illiashenko, 2017).

According to Prospect Theory a person's decision-making process is influenced by their mental state, which includes (i) regret aversion (iii) mental accounting, and (ii) loss aversion (Waweru et al., 2003). When people encounter equivalent quantities of gains and losses, they might feel varying degrees of mental shocks and penalties, which is referred to as loss aversion (Barberis & Huang, 2001). There is strong evidence to suggest that people are more worried and unsettled by the possibility of losses than by the possibility of gains (Barberis & Thaler, 2002). Moreover, any losses endured following sufficient victories are less excruciating than losses experienced following defeats (Barberis & Huang, 2001). According to Lehenkari and Perttunen (2004), historical returns, whether positive or negative, often operate as a source of support for declining trends in trading factors and capital investment losses. Investors therefore seem to be more vulnerable to loss aversion. The risk-aversion trait, which is considered to be typical investor behavior, tends to result in detrimental effects on their wealth and influences any poor judgments they make (Odean, 1998).

2.3.3 Market Factors

Market elements are often excluded from behavioral determinants because they are regarded as external factors that influence behavior of investors. DeBondt and Thaler (1995) suggested that behavioral finance has a significant effect on financial markets if its perspectives are correct and precise, investors may exhibit the following characteristics: some sort of reaction to price changes or even updates; past trends projected into future; focus on popular stocks; ignorance of key elements of underlying stocks; and seasonal price cycles. These market factors influence decision-making process of stock market investors. Other market factors identified by Waweru et al. (2008) and Sochi (2018) that influence investor decision-making include price changes, over-reaction to price change, reliable data for market conditions, buyer preferences, basic features of underlying stocks, and prior trends common to stock markets. Fluctuations in stock price, market information, and underlying stock fundamentals are often due to main factors causing over-under reactions to price shifts.

According to experimental validation, modifications have a far greater influence on decision-making behaviors of investors (Han et al., 2009; Waheed et al., 2020).

Most studies, such as DeBondt and Thaler (1985), attempted to persuade price change news to cause overreaction in investors. However, Lai (2001) and Rashata (2022) observed under-reaction in identical price change news, which had an incredible impact on their activities. Investors gradually contemplate employing several alternative trading tactics to make a good investment. Waweru et al. (2008) concluded that sound market strategy knowledge significantly influences investor choice, causing consumers to be attracted toward the most well-liked lucrative stocks and other alluring profitable endeavors. Barber and Odean (2001) emphasized that investors have a strong and significant familiarity with successful stock market activities, where their behavior are rapidly diverted, without having knowledge of investments will provide high performance and reliable outcomes in the future. Odean (1998) conducted research and created impressive data to show many investors trade excessively as a result of overconfidence and only depend on stock quality, market knowledge, and markets when making prior investment decisions. He went on to say that, in general, investors prefer to acquire stocks that have seen significant price movements in last two years than sell those that have seen no price changes. Waweru et al. (2008) found fluctuations in stock prices had great effect on behavior of investors with time.

2.3.4 Herding Effect

Herding, as the name indicates, affects financial markets by recognizing investors' tendency to follow trader movements and trail after them (Roy et al., 2023). Since there is a stronger reliance on community knowledge over information from other sources, many practitioners often wish to look at the existence of herding factors. It can result in unstable and unpredictable price changes for assets based on fundamental values (Riaz et al., 2020). As a result, many chances for beneficial investments may be missed, potentially having negative long-term effects. Similarly, scholars have focused particularly on herding effects due to their potential to have an impact on asset pricing theories and tie stock price fluctuations to risk and return models (Tan et al., 2008; Rashata, 2022).

According to Bakar and Yi (2016), under the herding theory, investors make decisions about selling or purchasing shares in security markets, together with the masses' decisions. Conversely, educated and trustworthy investors do not intend to follow trends because it causes markets to work smoothly. Herding produces some degree of crisis in inefficient markets, as evidenced by speculative bubbles (Caparrelli et al., 2004). To be more specific, Herding investors generally acted similarly to early investors having limited knowledge about backgrounds and relying on one another for safety, support, and intelligence. Additionally, they made an effort to support idea that when stock prices fluctuate, investors may attracted by effects of a herding tendency and will behave similarly to other investors. According to a separate finding Waweru et al. (2008), investors might be making poor judgments because they are basing their decisions on inaccurate estimates of stock returns during market fluctuations. Because the finest stock selection is determined by their choices.

Investors who follow the herd frequently choose well-performing equities in recent times, but selling the prior lost stock is preferred by logical investors because it provides tax deferral. Conversely, behavioral investors like to sell their prior successful shares to make up for losses from stock trading decisions. (Chen et al., 2007). Previous patterns of inequities that had an impact on investors' decision-making behavior at specific levels have been widely investigated (Waweru et al. 2008). As a result, before making any investment decision, investors carefully conceptualize past trends using technical approaches. Several other factors influence investors' herding behavior, such as investment volume, overconfidence, and so on. According to herding theory, trustworthy investors trust more reserved information in investing decisions and appear less concerned with their actions.

Investors who invest with greater numbers of money typically want to follow in the footsteps of other investors to minimize risks. The herding feature is preferred by different sorts and types of investors. Individual investors have a greater propensity than other types of investors to follow the lead of other investors when making investment decisions (Goodfellow et al., 2009). Herding theory helps investors develop aversion attitude toward regretting prior decisions, despite attempts to argue that decisions of selling and buying significantly influenced by other investor decisions (Riaz et al., 2020). Similar findings apply to institutional investors as they vary from individual investors in other decisions. This assertion was made in opposition to the preceding claim made above, according to which individual investors are more aware of herd behavior than other types of investors.

2.4 Behavioral Finance in the Stock Market

Efficient market hypothesis (EMH) addresses stock prices effectively and reflect all currently available information in market having high levels of liquidity (Ţiţan, 2015). A number of studies discovered long-term historical occurrences in the securities markets defy the efficient market hypothesis and cannot be well reflected in theories based on perfect investor rationality. (Singh, 2012; Blankespoor et al., 2020; Aljifri, 2023). According to Kamoune and Ibenrissoul (2022), EMH assumes that while setting stock prices, market players examine both present and future external and internal elements. When analyzing stock market, behavioral finance claims markets aren't always efficient. The impact of psychological and societal influences on stock purchases and sales may now be studied. As a result, practicing behavioral finance biases in the stock market and other trading marketplaces is something that may be done frequently. Major market irregularities like bubbles and protracted recessions have also been better understood using behavioral finance theory. (Shefrin & Statman, 2011; Jain et al., 2022). Even if they are not EMH members, behavioral finance developments are significant to investors and portfolio managers. These outlines might be utilized to assess market price fluctuations and movements to assist in speculating and decision-making.

2.5 Market Dynamics in a Post-COVID-19

Market dynamics relate towards changes and shifts that have happened in financial markets and economic activity accordingly of COVID-19 pandemic. According to Wójcik and Ioannou (2020) these dynamics significantly influence many aspects of global economy and financial systems.

2.5.1 Volatility and Uncertainty

The world after COVID-19 has been marked by increased financial volatility and unpredictability. The early shock of the epidemic caused extreme market volatility, with quick falls followed by a surprising recovery. Investors have had to manage a climate where virus, economic recovery, and government policy uncertainties are all still relatively high (Notteboom et al., 2021).

2.5.2 Remote Work and Technology

The pandemic boosted the acceptance of remote employment and technology. Soto-Acosta (2020) claimed companies in the technology and digital sectors expanded significantly, altering market dynamics. Furthermore, the transition toward digital platforms and e-commerce has influenced consumer behavior in developed sectors

2.5.3 Government Interventions

To reduce the economic impact of the epidemic, central banks and governments around the world undertook extraordinary monetary and fiscal policies. These interventions, such as stimulus packages and interest rate changes, have had a wide-ranging impact on financial markets, impacting interest rates, inflation, and asset prices (Tian et al., 2022).

2.5.4 Sectorial Shifts

The epidemic has altered industry dynamics. While certain businesses failed, such as travel and hospitality, others thrived, such as healthcare, technology, and e-commerce. Adams et al. (2021) stated Investors and firms have had to alter their strategies to fit with these shifting sectorial patterns.

2.5.5 Supply Chain Disruptions

Global supply chains were made vulnerable by the pandemic. Supply chain disruptions impacted industries reliant on international commerce, resulting in supply shortages and influencing market dynamics (Miroudot, 2020; Xu et al., 2021).

2.5.6 Sustainability and ESG Investing

Decisions on investment and sustainability are becoming more and more influenced by environmental, social, and governance (ESG) considerations. Therefore, investors are increasingly incorporating sustainability and responsible investing criteria into their portfolios in response to changing market dynamics driven by societal and environmental concerns (Shehab, 2021).

2.5.7 Geopolitical Factors

Market dynamics have been influenced by geopolitical concerns and trade conflicts. The epidemic has intensified existing geopolitical tensions while also posing new hurdles to global trade and investment (Wang et al., 2022; Luo & Van Assche, 2023).

2.58 Low-Interest Rates

Interest rates are all-time low due to Central Bank's attempts to contribute to economic recovery. This has made an impact on bond yields, asset valuations, and investment strategies, resulting in yield-seeking behavior and greater risk-taking in financial markets (Song & Zhou, 2020).

2.59 Digital Currencies and Fin-Tech

Fin-tech advancements and digital currency have gained more attention. Governments and central banks are investigating the possibility of central bank digital currencies (CBDCs), and fin-tech firms are disrupting traditional financial services, transforming the financial market environment (Ward & Rochemont, 2019; Srivastava, 2021).

3. CONCLUSION

One of most contagious infections in recorded history, the coronavirus (COVID-19), spread quickly around globe, affecting thousands of people by the year 2020. Disasters not only resulted in a significant number of fatalities, but they also spread chaos, panic, and commercial disruption all over the world. Therefore, this research aimed to determine how psychological biases affected individual investors' decisions regarding their investments after the COVID-19 epidemic. Although this comprehensive study of the literature is insufficient to investigate all elements of behavioral biases, thus, only some of the identified biases have been examined. Individual decisions to invest in financial market, particularly in equity greatly influenced by the diversity of rewards that each individual expects from owning a specific stock. At this point, it's critical to pinpoint them at the micro level and analyze their impact on both the individual and institutional levels. Degree of variance determined by financial competence, aptitude, and knowledge. If an investor detects these biases early in the investment process, it will be easier to make better investment decisions and will tend toward a market portfolio, as suggested by Fama (1960) in the efficient market hypothesis. It is also proposed that studying individual investor behavior could assist in explaining stock market irregularities. Finally, thinking about behavior can lead to several strategies that individual investors should use while investing in financial market. Findings of current study may be useful to stock financiers and other investors as they make investing decisions. The findings should contribute to body literature of behavioral finance since it recognized significance of prospect theory in revealing interaction among psychological elements and individual investor investment decisions in single model. Ultimately, study provides an innovative approach to the study of factors that influence decisions regarding investments in wake of COVID-19 epidemic.

3.1 Practical Implications

This research will benefit financial professionals, policymakers, and economic institutions, in developing better stock market strategies and making sound decisions regarding investments. The study also recognized significance of different behaviors having a significant influence on investing decisions of investors in stock market after COVID-19. Moreover, findings of research help stock market practitioners and regulators understand significance of different biases in investing decisions.

The investor's capacity to access information is essential for making educated and logical investing decisions. To make substantial stock market investment decisions, it is crucial to have legislation that effectively addresses the availability of information to investors.

REFERENCES

Adams, K. M., Choe, J., Mostafanezhad, M., & Phi, G. T. (2021). (Post-) pandemic tourism resiliency: Southeast Asian lives and livelihoods in limbo. *Tourism Geographies, 23*(4), 915–936. DOI: 10.1080/14616688.2021.1916584

Ahmed, M. A., Khattak, M. S., & Anwar, M. (2022). Personality traits and entrepreneurial intention: The mediating role of risk aversion. *Journal of Public Affairs, 22*(1), e2275. DOI: 10.1002/pa.2275

Ali, F., Khurram, M. U., & Jiang, Y. (2021). The five-factor asset pricing model tests and profitability and investment premiums: Evidence from Pakistan. *Emerging Markets Finance & Trade, 57*(9), 2651–2673. DOI: 10.1080/1540496X.2019.1650738

Aljifri, R. (2023). Investor psychology in the stock market: An empirical study of the impact of overconfidence on firm valuation. *Borsa Istanbul Review, 23*(1), 93–112. DOI: 10.1016/j.bir.2022.09.010

Antony, A. (2020). Behavioral finance and portfolio management: Review of theory and literature. *Journal of Public Affairs, 20*(2), e1996. DOI: 10.1002/pa.1996

Aziz, B., & Khan, A. (2016). Behavioral factors influencing individual investor's investment decision and performance, Evidence from Pakistan Stock Exchange. *International journal of research in finance and marketing, 6*(7), 74-86.

Babajide, A. A., & Adetiloye, K. A. (2012). Investorsâ€™ Behavioural Biases and the Security Market: An Empirical Study of the Nigerian Security Market. *Accounting and Finance Research, 1*(1), 219–219. DOI: 10.5430/afr.v1n1p219

Bakar, S., & Yi, A. N. C. (2016). The impact of psychological factors on investors' decision making in Malaysian stock market: A case of Klang Valley and Pahang. *Procedia Economics and Finance, 35*, 319–328. DOI: 10.1016/S2212-5671(16)00040-X

Baker, H. K., & Ricciardi, V. (2014). How biases affect investor behavior. *The European Financial Review*, •••, 7–10.

Barber, B. M., & Odean, T. (2001). Boys will be boys: Gender, overconfidence, and common stock investment. *The Quarterly Journal of Economics, 116*(1), 261–292. DOI: 10.1162/003355301556400

Barberis, N., & Huang, M. (2001). Mental Accounting, Loss Aversion, and Individual Stock Returns. *The Journal of Finance, 56*(4), 1247–1292. DOI: 10.1111/0022-1082.00367

Barberis, N., Thaler, R., Constantinides, G. M., Harris, M., & Stulz, R. (2003). *Handbook of the Economics of Finance. A Survey of Behavioral Finance (1052-1090)*. Elsevier Science BV.

Barberis, N., & Thaler, R. H. (2002). A Survey of Behavioral Finance. SSRN Electronesearch, 15 (1), 55-72. DOI: 10.2139/ssrn.327880

Bashir, T., Azam, N., Butt, A. A., Javed, A., & Tanvir, A. (2013). Are behavioral biases influenced by demographic characteristics & personality traits? Evidence from Pakistan. *European Scientific Journal*, *9*(29).

Blankespoor, E., deHaan, E., & Marinovic, I. (2020). Disclosure processing costs, investors' information choice, and equity market outcomes: A review. *Journal of Accounting and Economics*, *70*(2-3), 101344. DOI: 10.1016/j.jacceco.2020.101344

Boda, J. R., & Sunitha, G. (2018). Investor's psychology in investment decision making: A behavioral finance approach. *International Journal of Pure and Applied Mathematics*, *119*(7), 1253–1261.

Caparrelli, F., D'Arcangelis, A. M., & Cassuto, A. (2004). Herding in the Italian stock market: A case of behavioral finance. *Journal of Behavioral Finance*, *5*(4), 222–230. DOI: 10.1207/s15427579jpfm0504_5

Chen, G., Kim, K. A., Nofsinger, J. R., & Rui, O. M. (2007). Trading performance, disposition effect, overconfidence, representativeness bias, and experience of emerging market investors. *Journal of Behavioral Decision Making*, *20*(4), 425–451. DOI: 10.1002/bdm.561

Chia, W. T., Koh, K. F., Ng, W. K., & Yap, Z. H. (2023). *The linkage between behavioral factors and investment intention among youth in Malaysia* (Doctoral dissertation, UTAR).

Chowdhury, E. K., Khan, I. I., & Dhar, B. K. (2022). Catastrophic impact of Covid-19 on the global stock markets and economic activities. *Business and Society Review*, *127*(2), 437–460. DOI: 10.1111/basr.12219

Croushore, D. (2007). Money and banking: a policy-oriented approach.

Daniel, K., Hirshleifer, D., & Subrahmanyam, A. (1998). Investor psychology and security market under-and overreactions. *the Journal of Finance, 53*(6), 1839-1885.

De Bondt, W. F., & Thaler, R. H. (1995). Financial decision-making in markets and firms: A behavioral perspective. *Handbooks in Operations Research and Management Science*, *9*, 385–410. DOI: 10.1016/S0927-0507(05)80057-X

Fama, E. F. (1960). Efficient market hypothesis. *Diss. Ph.D. Thesis, Ph. D. dissertation*.

Fernandez, V. (2006). The impact of major global events on volatility shifts: Evidence from the Asian crisis and 9/11. *Economic Systems, 30*(1), 79–97. DOI: 10.1016/j.ecosys.2005.09.004

Filbeck, G., Hatfield, P., & Horvath, P. (2005). Risk aversion and personality type. *Journal of Behavioral Finance, 6*(4), 170–180. DOI: 10.1207/s15427579jpfm0604_1

Ganie, I. R., Wani, T. A., & Yadav, M. P. (2022). Impact of COVID-19 outbreak on the stock market: An evidence from select economies. *Business Perspectives and Research*, •••, 22785337211073635. DOI: 10.1177/22785337211073635

Goodfellow, C., Bohl, M. T., & Gebka, B. (2009). Together we invest? Individual and institutional investors' trading behaviour in Poland. *International Review of Financial Analysis, 18*(4), 212–221. DOI: 10.1016/j.irfa.2009.03.002

Guo, M., Kuai, Y., & Liu, X. (2020). Stock market response to environmental policies: Evidence from heavily polluting firms in China. *Economic Modelling, 86*, 306–316. DOI: 10.1016/j.econmod.2019.09.028

Gupta, N. (2023). Volatility Response to "Black Swan Event" of COVID-19 in Asian Stock Market: An Empirical Study Using EGARCH Model. *International Journal of Engineering and Management Research*, •••, 13.

Han, H., Hsu, L. T. J., & Lee, J. S. (2009). Empirical investigation of the roles of attitudes toward green behaviors, overall image, gender, and age in hotel customers' eco-friendly decision-making process. *International Journal of Hospitality Management, 28*(4), 519–528. DOI: 10.1016/j.ijhm.2009.02.004

Hirvonen, T. (2021). Behavioural finance in financial crises: the case of Covid-19.

Huang, W., & Zheng, Y. (2020). COVID-19: Structural changes in the relationship between investor sentiment and crude oil futures price. *Energy Research Letters, 1*(2).

Illiashenko, P. (2017). Behavioral finance: History and foundations. *Visnyk of the National Bank of Ukraine*, (239), 28–54. DOI: 10.26531/vnbu2017.239.028

Jain, A., Agrawal, S., Goswami, S., Banga, S., Kumar, S., & Singh, N. (2020). Behavioural Finance Effect on Stock Price Trends During Covid-19 Pandemic. *Management Dynamics, 20*(2), 6.

Jan, N., Jain, V., Li, Z., Sattar, J., & Tongkachok, K. (2022). Post-COVID-19 investor psychology and individual investment decision: A moderating role of information availability. *Frontiers in Psychology, 13*, 846088. DOI: 10.3389/fpsyg.2022.846088 PMID: 36248582

Kahneman, D., & Tversky, A. (1979). On the interpretation of intuitive probability: A reply to Jonathan Cohen.

Kamoune, A., & Ibenrissoul, N. (2022). Traditional versus Behavioral Finance Theory. *International Journal of Accounting, Finance, Auditing, Management and Economics, 3*(2-1), 282-294.

Kapoor, S., & Prosad, J. M. (2017). Behavioural finance: A review. *Procedia Computer Science*, *122*, 50–54. DOI: 10.1016/j.procs.2017.11.340

Kengatharan, L., & Kengatharan, N. (2014). The influence of behavioral factors in making investment decisions and performance: Study on investors of Colombo Stock Exchange, Sri Lanka. *Asian Journal of Finance & Accounting*, *6*(1), 1. DOI: 10.5296/ajfa.v6i1.4893

Kishore, R. (2004). Theory of behavioural finance and its application to property market: A change in paradigm. *Australian Property Journal*, *38*(2), 105–110.

Kubilay, B., & Bayrakdaroglu, A. (2016). An empirical research on investor biases in financial decision-making, financial risk tolerance and financial personality. *International Journal of Financial Research*, *7*(2), 171–182. DOI: 10.5430/ijfr.v7n2p171

Lai, M. M., Low, K. L. T., & Lai, M. L. (2001). Are Malaysian investors rational? *The Journal of Psychology and Financial Markets*, *2*(4), 210–215. DOI: 10.1207/S15327760JPFM0204_5

Lehenkari, M., & Perttunen, J. (2004). Holding onto the losers: Finish evidence. *Journal of Behavioral Finance*, *5*(2), 116–126. DOI: 10.1207/s15427579jpfm0502_5

Luo, Y., & Van Assche, A. (2023). The rise of techno-geopolitical uncertainty: Implications of the United States CHIPS and Science Act. *Journal of International Business Studies*, *54*(8), 1–18. DOI: 10.1057/s41267-023-00620-3 PMID: 37359753

Mazur, M., Dang, M., & Vega, M. (2021). COVID-19 and the march 2020 stock market crash. Evidence from S&P1500. *Finance Research Letters*, *38*, 101690. DOI: 10.1016/j.frl.2020.101690 PMID: 32837377

Meng, J., & Weng, X. (2018). Can prospect theory explain the disposition effect? A new perspective on reference points. *Management Science*, *64*(7), 3331–3351. DOI: 10.1287/mnsc.2016.2711

Miroudot, S. (2020). Reshaping the policy debate on the implications of COVID-19 for global supply chains. *Journal of International Business Policy*, *3*(4), 430–442. DOI: 10.1057/s42214-020-00074-6

Ngoc, L. T. B. (2014). Behavior pattern of individual investors in stock market. *International Journal of Business and Management*, *9*(1), 1–16.

Notteboom, T., Pallis, T., & Rodrigue, J. P. (2021). Disruptions and resilience in global container shipping and ports: The COVID-19 pandemic versus the 2008–2009 financial crisis. *Maritime Economics & Logistics*, *23*(2), 179–210. DOI: 10.1057/s41278-020-00180-5

Oberlechner, T., & Osler, C. L. (2008). Overconfidence in currency markets. *Available atSSRN* 1108787.

Odean, T. (1998). Are investors reluctant to realize their losses? *The Journal of Finance*, *53*(5), 1775–1798. DOI: 10.1111/0022-1082.00072

Ozkan, M., & Ozkan, O. (2020). Financial evaluation of mental accounting.

Plous, S. (1993). *The psychology of judgment and decision making*. Mcgraw-Hill Book Company.

Quddoos, M. U., Rafique, A., Kalim, U., & Sheikh, M. R. (2020). Impact of behavioral biases on investment performance in Pakistan: The moderating role of financial literacy. *Journal of Accounting and Finance in Emerging Economies*, *6*(4), 1199–1205. DOI: 10.26710/jafee.v6i4.1512

Ramelli, S., & Wagner, A. (2020). What the stock market tells us about the consequences of COVID-19. *Mitigating the COVID Economic Crisis: Act Fast and Do Whatever, 63*.

Ramphul, K., Ramphul, Y., Park, Y., Lohana, P., Dhillon, B. K., & Sombans, S. (2021). A comprehensive review and update on severe acute respiratory syndrome coronavirus 2 (SARS-CoV-2) and Coronavirus disease 2019 (COVID-19): What do we know now in 2021? *Archives of Medical Sciences. Atherosclerotic Diseases*, *6*(1), 5–13. DOI: 10.5114/amsad.2021.105065 PMID: 34027207

Rashata, H. (2022). Investors' Behavior in the Pakistan Financial Market during the COVID-19 Pandemic. *Available atSSRN* 4013498. DOI: 10.2139/ssrn.4013498

Rashata, H. (2022). Investors' Behavior in the Pakistan Financial Market during the COVID-19 Pandemic. *Available atSSRN* 4013498. DOI: 10.2139/ssrn.4013498

Riaz, S., Ahmed, R., Parkash, R., & Ahmad, M. J. (2020). Determinants of stock market investors' behavior in COVID-19: A study on the Pakistan Stock Exchange.

Ritter, J. R. (2003). Behavioral finance. *Pacific-Basin Finance Journal*, *11*(4), 429–437. DOI: 10.1016/S0927-538X(03)00048-9

Roy, S., Arefin, S. R., & Mallik, A. (2023). How Volatility and Herding of the Stock Markets in the Oceania Region Influence Investors and Policymakers: A Sector-Wise Exploration in Pre and Post-COVID Period. *International Journal of Economics and Finance, 15*(1), 24. DOI: 10.5539/ijef.v15n1p24

Sabir, S. A., Mohammad, H. B., & Shahar, H. B. K. (2019). The role of overconfidence and past investment experience in herding behaviour with a moderating effect of financial literacy: Evidence from Pakistan stock exchange. *Asian Economic and Financial Review, 9*(4), 480–490. DOI: 10.18488/journal.aefr.2019.94.480.490

Samuel, D. (1996). Investigation of ancient Egyptian baking and brewing methods by correlative microscopy. *Science, 273*(5274), 488–490. DOI: 10.1126/science.273.5274.488 PMID: 8662535

Shefrin, H., & Statman, M. (2011). Behavioral finance in the financial crisis: market efficiency, Minsky, and Keynes. *Santa Clara University, November.*

Shehab, A. R. (2021). Environmental, social and governance (ESG) considerations in real estate investments. Impact of environmental performance disclosure, activities and score on financial performance of SIIQ.

Shepherd, D. A., Williams, T. A., & Patzelt, H. (2015). Thinking about entrepreneurial decision making: Review and research agenda. *Journal of Management, 41*(1), 11–46. DOI: 10.1177/0149206314541153

Singh, S. (2012). Investor irrationality and self-defeating behavior: Insights from behavioral finance. *Journal of Global Business Management, 8*(1), 116.

Siraji, M. (2019). Heuristics bias and investment performance: Does age matter? evidence from Colombo stock exchange. *Asian Journal of Economics. Business and Accounting, 12*(4), 1–14.

Sochi, M. H. (2018). Behavioral factors influencing investment decision of the retail investors of Dhaka stock exchange: An empirical study. *Cost and Management, 46*(1), 20–29.

Sohrabi, C., Alsafi, Z., O'neill, N., Khan, M., Kerwan, A., Al-Jabir, A., Iosifidis, C., & Agha, R. (2020). World Health Organization declares global emergency: A review of the 2019 novel coronavirus (COVID-19). *International Journal of Surgery, 76*, 71–76. DOI: 10.1016/j.ijsu.2020.02.034 PMID: 32112977

Song, L., & Zhou, Y. (2020). The COVID-19 pandemic and its impact on the global economy: What does it take to turn crisis into opportunity? *China & World Economy, 28*(4), 1–25. DOI: 10.1111/cwe.12349

Soto-Acosta, P. (2020). COVID-19 pandemic: Shifting digital transformation to a high-speed gear. *Information Systems Management, 37*(4), 260–266. DOI: 10.1080/10580530.2020.1814461

Srivastava, D. A. (2021). Central banking, financial stability and Macro-Prudential policy. *CAB Calling, 44*(1&2).

Subrahmanyam, A. (2008). Behavioural finance: A review and synthesis. *European Financial Management, 14*(1), 12–29. DOI: 10.1111/j.1468-036X.2007.00415.x

Tan, L., Chiang, T. C., Mason, J. R., & Nelling, E. (2008). Herding behavior in Chinese stock markets: An examination of A and B shares. *Pacific-Basin Finance Journal, 16*(1-2), 61–77. DOI: 10.1016/j.pacfin.2007.04.004

Thaler, R. H. (2015). *Misbehaving: The making of behavioral economics.* WW Norton & Company.

Tian, J., Yu, L., Xue, R., Zhuang, S., & Shan, Y. (2022). Global low-carbon energy transition in the post-COVID-19 era. *Applied Energy, 307*, 118205. DOI: 10.1016/j.apenergy.2021.118205 PMID: 34840400

Ţiţan, A. G. (2015). The efficient market hypothesis: Review of specialized literature and empirical research. *Procedia Economics and Finance, 32*, 442–449. DOI: 10.1016/S2212-5671(15)01416-1

Trivers, R. (1991). Deceit^ ind Self-Deception The Relationship between Communication and Consciousness.

Tvede, L. (1999). *The psychology of finance*. Wiley.

Utama, A. N. B. (2023). Analysis of the Development of Financial Management Theory to Support Financial Research.

Waheed, H., Ahmed, Z., Saleem, Q., Din, S. M. U., & Ahmed, B. (2020). The mediating role of risk perception in the relationship between financial literacy and investment decision. *International Journal of Innovation. Creativity and Change, 14*(4), 112–131.

Wang, J., Cui, M., & Chang, L. (2023). Evaluating economic recovery by measuring the COVID-19 spillover impact on business practices: Evidence from Asian markets intermediaries. *Economic Change and Restructuring, 56*(3), 1–22. DOI: 10.1007/s10644-023-09482-z

Wang, K. H., Kan, J. M., Jiang, C. F., & Su, C. W. (2022). Is geopolitical risk powerful enough to affect carbon dioxide emissions? Evidence from China. *Sustainability (Basel), 14*(13), 7867. DOI: 10.3390/su14137867

Ward, O., & Rochemont, S. (2019). Understanding central bank digital currencies (CBDC). *Institute and Faculty of Actuaries*, 1-52.

Waweru, N. M., Munyoki, E., & Uliana, E. (2008). The effects of behavioural factors in investment decision-making: a survey of institutional investors operating at the Nairobi Stock Exchange. *International Journal of business and emerging markets, 1*(1), 24-41.

Wójcik, D., & Ioannou, S. (2020). COVID-19 and finance: Market developments so far and potential impacts on the financial sector and centres. *Tijdschrift voor Economische en Sociale Geografie, 111*(3), 387–400. DOI: 10.1111/tesg.12434 PMID: 32836484

World Health Organization. (2020). World health statistics 2020.

Xu, Z., Elomri, A., Kerbache, L., & El Omri, A. (2020). Impacts of COVID-19 on global supply chains: Facts and perspectives. *IEEE Engineering Management Review, 48*(3), 153–166. DOI: 10.1109/EMR.2020.3018420

Zahera, S. A., & Bansal, R. (2018). Do investors exhibit behavioral biases in investment decision making? A systematic review. *Qualitative Research in Financial Markets, 10*(2), 210–251. DOI: 10.1108/QRFM-04-2017-0028

Chapter 6
The Future of Behavioral Finance:
Challenges and Opportunities in the Era of Digital Transformation

Rija Anwar
https://orcid.org/0009-0006-7297-9619
Iqra University, Pakistan

ABSTRACT

The digital transformation has changed the society and industries through digital technologies which cause the number of challenges and opportunities. These digital technologies include a broad range of technologies and innovation such as artificial intelligence, big data analytics, cloud computing, blockchain, and the Internet of Things. The application of aforesaid digital technologies re-forming the investors' behavior towards trading and making investment decisions. Therefore, this paper investigates the complex link between digital transformation and behavioral finance, discovering the challenges and opportunities in an ever-evolving technological setting. Technological advancement and demographic shifts suggest that the adaptation of digital change by distinct age groups and their behavioral impacts towards financial decision-making are crucial. This conceptual paper examines the effects of these elements and provide vision regarding organizations' navigation at this multifaceted environment to prosper in the future.

DOI: 10.4018/979-8-3693-7160-2.ch006

1. INTRODUCTION

Behavioral finance is a discipline of behavioral economics. It was developed as a response to the drawbacks of conventional theories of finance, specifically the Efficient Market Hypothesis (EMH) and rational choice theory. These theories reflect that investors are well aware of all pertinent information and act rationally on that information (Hill, 2018). However, behavioral finance illustrates that individuals may not make decisions based on a rational inquiry of all the available information[1] and financial markets are not always perfectly efficient. It recognizes that investor behavior can be influenced by psychological biases, such as overconfidence, herding behavior, and loss aversion. Psychological factors and biases can serve as a valuable source for elucidating numerous kinds of market anomalies, including those detected in the stock market, such as the rise and fall in stock prices. Behavioral finance proposes that psychological factors and biases influence the behaviors of investors and financial practitioners while making key financial decisions[2]. In recent years, behavioral finance has attained more recognition and importance. As the world is experiencing a swift digital transformation, behavioral finance is also developing gradually.

Digital transformation can be defined as a process that aims to improve an entity by activating significant changes to its properties through combinations of information, computing, communication, and connectivity technologies (Vial, 2019). Digital transformation encompasses the profound changes taking place in society and industries using digital technologies (Agarwal et al. 2010; Majchrzak et al. 2016). At the industrial level, it refers to an array of technological innovations and evolution to novel business frameworks and revenue series comprising three vigorous pillars such as automation, upgraded manufacturing procedures, and production enhancement[3]. At the societal level, it alters the methods of people's interaction and living their lives (Margiono, 2021). The industrial level contains a number of digital transformation activities such as; the incorporation of the Internet of Things which was adopted by industries in order to garner actual data from some procedures and tools; automation via robotics and artificial intelligence (AI) are established across industries; industries use cloud computing facilities to store and process data; adoption of advanced analytics and machine learning algorithms, cyber security actions to guard sensitive data, supply chain optimization, use of chatbot and virtual aid to progress customer services. Whereas, digital transformation at the societal level includes online government services for tax filing, licenses, and voting to update administrative procedures; education and remote learning which was developed during COVID-19; e-commerce and online payments system; development of smart cities where data and technology are used to enhance traffic stream; decrease energy consumption, and advance public services; lastly, digital platforms to ease communication and sharing the information. In both industrial and societal settings, digital transformation is an enduring process, determined by technological innovation. It needs to adapt to change, accept new opportunities, and deal with emerging challenges to connect the full power of digital technologies. Therefore, this study examines the manifold challenges and opportunities that the digital era presents to behavioral finance, and it provides insights into its successful future forecasts.

2. BEHAVIORAL FINANCE AND DIGITAL TRANSFORMATION

Recently, finance has become more collaborative with new-generation data science and artificial intelligence (DSAI) techniques (Dunis et al., 2016; Arslanian & Fischer, 2019; Hilpisch, 2020; Qi & Xiao, 2018; Cao et al., 2021). The Data Science and Artificial Intelligence (DSAI) techniques contain an extensive series of tools and techniques used to abstract deep insights from data and construct intelligent systems. These techniques are essential for various contemporary applications and are used in numerous industries. For example; finance, marketing, supply chain, logistics, utilities, manufacturing, retail, and healthcare (Dwivedi et al., 2019; Bredt, 2019; Safdar et al.,2020; Ben-Israel et al., 2020). Moreover, the application of these techniques is shaping the investors' behavior towards trading and making investment decisions. It encompasses a broad range of technologies and innovations, including artificial intelligence, big data analytics, cloud computing, blockchain, and the Internet of Things. These technologies are changing the way businesses operate, interact with customers, and compete in the market.

2.1 Internet of Things

The Internet of Things (IoT) describes the network of physical devices, applications, automobiles, and other tangible and visible entities that are implanted with software, sensors, and network connections that enable them to gather and share data (He et al., 2014; Pretz, 2013). According to Yilmaz and Hazar (2019), IoT holds substantial potential for use in the financial sector. IoT including mobile banking, crowd-based finance, M-banking, virtual currency, cybercrime, high-frequency trading firms, big data, and IT analytics have a direct impact on financial services (Khanboubi et al., 2019). The IoT-founded Efficient Data Visualization Framework (IoT-EDVF) was established to fortify the risk of leaks, evaluate manifold data sources, and screen data quality for business intellect in corporate finance (Shao et al., 2022). The study of Tang et al. (2018) inferred that IoT adopters demonstrate better performances regarding return on assets, return on equity, inventory turnover, labor productivity, asset employment, collection efficacy, and leverage. Additionally, the authors confer that IoT-adopted firms have greater financial performance and increasing market value. The connection between IoT and behavioral finance is interesting since IoT technology can provide real-time facts on customer behavior and choices. Financial institutions can utilize this data to examine and anticipate the financial decision-making of individuals considering their emotional biases. This can result in more personalized and effectual financial services and products that line up with the unique behavior of investors.

2.2 Cloud Computing

Cloud computing is one of the IoT technologies (Tang et al., 2018), which refers to the transfer of distinct services via the Internet. These resources contain tools and applications such as data storage, databases, servers, software, and networking. Cloud-based storage saves the data to a remote database instead of a patented hard drive or local storage drive. When an electronic device reaches the web, it reaches the data and the software programs to function it. Cloud computing is famous among individuals and businesses due to cost-saving benefits, upturn productivity, promptness and efficiency, enactment, and safety[4]. At present time, businesses use a broad spectrum of cloud-based software specifically for enterprise resource planning (ERP), customer relationship management (CRM), accounting, and commerce (Dandapani, 2017).

Sorescu and Spanjol (2008) illustrate that technological innovations can influence firms' risk and return in a different way. So risk and return as diverse dimensions of shareholder value produce a rough perception regarding the performance implications of transferring to cloud computing. Nezami et al. (2022) suggested that shifting to the cloud raises shareholder wealth by plummeting idiosyncratic risk. Moreover, cloud computing has renovated the investment setting by giving investors better access to data, analytical instruments, scalability, and cost savings. It has also prepared for more refined and data-driven investment strategies with enlightening teamwork and safety. Investors who hold cloud technology can experience augmented efficacy and determination in the financial markets. Though cloud computing has ensured the greater accessibility and efficiency of financial information, it has also commenced new challenges regarding behavioral biases. Investors should be watchful of these biases and account for employing cloud-based instruments and platforms to improve perceptions of their behavior and make highly well-versed decisions. Additionally, they can influence technology to offset biases through data-driven examination and automated strategies provided by robo-advisors and algorithmic trading methods.

2.3 Blockchain

A blockchain is a decentralized database or ledger spread out across a network's multiple nodes. They are eminent for their vital function in cryptocurrency mechanisms because they uphold a safe and distributed record of transactions, but they are not restricted to cryptocurrency mechanisms[5]. Chen et al. (2019) advocate a cryptocurrency-specific lexicon that assists in quantifying investors' emotions and estimating the returns of the cryptocurrency market. Results reveal that investor sentiment positively forecasts surplus CRIX (cryptocurrency index) returns without notable signs of return reversal. Aloosh and Ouzan (2020) stated that the cryptocurrency market's participants seem to be performing irrationally. The study displays that the cryptocurrency market has a substantial price bias, which supports that investors answer to news in a different way based on the price levels. Eventually, the authors prove that cryptocurrencies at low prices are highly volatile than their costly counterparts.

Blockchain-based cryptocurrencies have had an insightful influence on behavioral finance by presenting novel dynamics in investor behavior. The constancy and transparency of blockchain technology can reduce information asymmetry and influence investors' observance and faith in financial markets. Cryptocurrencies, mainly manifest high volatility, resulting in a rise in emotional responses, speculative trading, and herd behavior exhibiting usual behavioral biases. Additionally, the interminable cryptocurrency markets have increased the fear of missing out (FOMO) and loss aversion biases because investors constantly observe price movements. Güler (2021) inferred that Bitcoin investors exhibit FOMO behavior when they experience fear of loss while unnoticing the profitable investments or trading opportunities. Moreover, the ability of blockchain to allow smart indentures and decentralized finance (DeFi) applications leads to mechanization and eliminates the role of intermediaries, possibly plummeting biases arising from overconfidence in financial experts. Generally, blockchain and cryptocurrencies have equally worsened and alleviated certain behavioral biases, emphasizing the multifaceted interaction between human psychology and technology in financial decision-making.

2.4 Machine Learning

As an emotional presence in human beings displays dissimilar hopes, fears, and objectives, humans are unable to perform sound, particularly while making fact-based decisions, specifically if those decisions contain their connections. In these scenarios, if the machine makes those decisions on the basis of the facts erudite from real data, it will be benefitted to the people (De Prado, 2018). Ghoddusi et al. (2019) defined machine learning as a collection of data science frameworks, which can erudite from data and progress their performance with the passage of time and experience. Indeed, machine learning is the drawing out of knowledge rooted in data and can be employed to forecast or produce novel information. Additionally, machine learning has several uses in the domain of finance. A few sectors have already applied data processing, for instance, bankruptcy prediction, detection of money laundering, decisions regarding loans, master card approval, examination of the stock, and else can be detected through it. Moreover, the financial statement fraud can be detected by employing data mining techniques (Königstorfer & Thalmann, 2020).

Huang et al. (2015) stated that machine learning techniques including profound learning and collaborative approaches have improved the predictive model accurateness in behavioral finance. These models have the potential to recognize patterns and irregularities in financial data that could not be detected by applying conventional statistical methods. Furthermore, sentiment analysis, supported by natural language processing (Tetlock, 2007), has given crucial perceptions of market sentiment, while providing a huge comprehension of behavioral biases and psychological elements navigating investment decisions (Daniel et al., 1998). These high-tech developments have opened the way for the development of more refined algorithmic trading approaches, robo-advisory platforms, and portfolio optimization instruments (Brodie et al., 2009), and all of them are modified to distinct investor profiles. In addition, the incorporation of machine learning has widened the possibility of behavioral finance investigation, permitting for the complete examination of theories and hypotheses within the arena (Baker et al., 2019). Generally, this transformative attribute of machine learning has navigated better decision-making and upgraded risk-controlling strategies in financial markets.

2.5 Artificial Intelligence

Artificial Intelligence (AI) in the financial market and other finance sectors is used for estimation purposes, bankruptcy forecast, investment decision-making, credit rating, and fraud detection. Financial investors are mainly intent on bankruptcy predictions by using machine learning to surge the predictive ability, and decision-making on the basis of AI. AI based decision making has the potential to perform better where decisions are highly precise (Bisht et al., 2022). Additionally, AI-driven trading algorithms have the ability to adapt the fluctuating market settings and bend trading strategies as per the market circumstances. These algorithms can use behavioral biases including herding behavior, over-reaction, and loss aversion which are vital constituents of behavioral finance theory. By including these biases in trading frameworks, AI is able to expand trading strategies and possibly increase investment performance (Lo, 2017). The study of Bhatia et al. (2020); Königstorfer and Thalmann (2020a, 2020b) also stated that AI has been broadly employed to illustrate behavioral biases.

2.6 Big Data

Big data refers to large and diverse data that is garnered, arranged, and analyzed with the help of certain instruments. Big data and analytics assist a number of financial sectors. For instance; banks use big data and analytics to collect and evaluate data to acutely understand customer behavior. These acute understandings can further be used to boost their services, increase customer satisfaction, and make decisions on the basis of data to assist both the bank and its customers. (Bisht et al., 2022).

When a company has to collect vast data, big data platforms such as Spark, Apache Hadoop, and else can assist in cutting costs. These technologies support businesses in searching for more effective methods to perform operations. Businesses can collect data from a range of sources by applying real-time in-memory analytics and can do sentiment analysis by using Big Data techniques. It enables businesses to fulfill client prospects (Bisht et al., 2022).

Moreover, big data also influences behavioral finance. One important effect of big data on behavioral finance is the capability to identify and evaluate behavioral biases on a higher scale (Barberis & Thaler, 2003). In addition, big data has made the accessibility and analysis of financial information and analysis easier for people (Lo, 2017). Retail investors are now able to get access to large data and research, letting them make more well-versed decisions and possibly avoid common behavioral drawbacks. This augmented transparency can endorse financial literacy and add to more rational and less biased investment behavior.

2.7 Metaverse and Digital Twin

Metaverse is a recently developed digital asset that is based on blockchain. Metaverse is the term that refers to a substitute virtual environment where individuals can generate programs, interconnect with one another, and purchase, vend, and distribute products and services through avatars (virtual illustrations) of themselves. Undeniably, the Metaverse can perform better because emergent inventive technologies comprising Artificial Intelligence, the IoT, Big Data, and Digital Twins can offer rich datasets and fundamental reckoning of individual behavior. There are some questions covering ethical, social, human, and cultural grounds connected to the Metaverse effect such as the influence of the Metaverse on interconnection among individuals (Allam et al., 2022; Bisht et al., 2022). In addition, the need to focus on high customer satisfaction through online channels is becoming vital for each additional year because of substantial consumer moves toward retrieving financial services by desktop devices or mobiles. Financial institutions are engaged with other organizations to gather data regarding customers' interaction with online services to cultivate a customer and management relationship and give solutions that would substitute the constraint of appointing sustenance workforces. This will provide key information regarding the usage of third-party data to fully use it and make replications using the cybernetic platform, and to generate virtual assistants that can support customers with their complications (Bisht et al., 2022).

Metaverse can also impact behavioral finance by modifying the conventional investment setting. In the Metaverse, investors can allocate their funds to digital assets like digital art, virtual real estate, and digital currencies such as cryptocurrencies. These digital assets may have actual economic value, and investors' behaviors in the Metaverse can reflect their actual financial decision-making practices. For example, investors may divulge herd behavior in the Metaverse, which was determined by social inspiration and the fear of missing out (FOMO), which are firm behavioral biases in conventional finance (Barberis & Thaler, 2003). Additionally, investors can generate a Digital Twin of their investment portfolio and evaluate diverse investment strategies, assist them in mitigating cognitive biases, and make better rational decisions regarding investments. Additionally, the availability and easy trading of virtual assets in the Metaverse may cause impulsive choices and speculative bubbles, which are usual behavioral drawbacks in conventional financial markets (Shiller, 2015).

2.8 Robo-Advisors

Robo-advisors refer to digitally controlled online portfolio management facilities with limited human support (Ferri, 2014). After the 2008 Global Financial Crisis, the prime generation of robo-advisors emerged which was principally designed for allocation and rebalancing of portfolio. (Phoon & Koh, 2018). Usually, robo-advisors have resemblances, which incorporate a questionnaire procedure together with numerous investment elucidations (Hougan, 2015; Bhatnagar, 2016; Phoon & Koh, 2018). In robo-advisors, there is a model of portfolio allocation that contains exchange-traded funds (ETFs) or mutual funds (Bhatnagar, 2016; Uhl & Rohner, 2018). Consistent with Phoon and Koh (2018) the robo-advisor also provides standard investing methods, for instance, mean-variance optimization. Moreover, Black Rock which is a top investment management firm, is employing robo-advisors for algorithmic trading (Tokic, 2018) shows that in investment management firms, robo-advisors are being used. Robo-advisors lessen investors' biases while executing risk analysis and outlining the investors. Conversely, as per the study of Bhatia et al. (2020), robo-advisory platforms cannot perform risk analysis perfectly for retail investors.

2.9 Artificial Neural Networks (ANNs)

Artificial Neural Networks (ANNs) are computing modeling instruments that are emerging and widely accepted in many departments for modeling complicated practical problems. ANNs help in performing numerous tasks such as subjective data-based decision-making, estimating future outcomes, and resolving several practical issues. These networks have turn into vital in several areas and industries for a few years (Bahrammirzaee, 2010).

Moreover, these networks are very useful digital tools in the realm of behavioral finance, where they assist in identifying the way psychological biases affect financial decision-making and the behavior of the market. ANNs has the ability to forecast investor behavior, evaluate risk, examine sentiment in recorded data, identify market irregularities, improve portfolios, manage risk, and also provide assistance in fraud revealing. ANNs incorporate behavioral visions into financial models for getting a deep thought of the difficulties of financial markets and offer insights for traders, investors, and risk managers search for making more well-versed decisions.

2.10 Social Media and Behavioral Finance

Nowadays accessibility to large amounts of data is increasingly available to investors. This employs not merely examining data from social media but also from investing and trading in financial markets. Social media analytics enable investors to make decisions regarding what to invest in and when to invest in. Likewise, social media analytics can be utilized to influence the behavior of investors and traders on the basis of social media information (Barros et al., 2021). The existing literature demonstrates that the influences of conventional media or news quality is examined as the occurrence of negative arguments (Tetlock et al., 2008; Tetlock, 2011). In contrast to conventional media sources, social media is a two-way communication platform, and social media sentiment is crucial for examining the optimistic and negative commentaries on stocks. Social media offers the opportunity to gather direct data regarding these human elements at the aggregate level (Duz Tan & Tas, 2021).

3. AGE DEMOGRAPHICS, BEHAVIORAL FINANCE, AND DIGITAL TRANSFORMATION

Generation views and behavior play an important role in the adoption of digital transformation. The interaction among technology, age, and finance is an intricate and emerging dynamic. Age demographics have a significant impact on the strategies that organizations use in the digital transformation process. The generations from

Baby Boomers to Generation Z, show different choices, attitudes, and behaviors in the adoption of technology which influences businesses to modify their digital assistance accordingly. Baby Boomers who were born between the period 1946 to 1964, have less tendency to accept and apply new technologies. They mainly prefer frontal interactions and outdated working approaches. They mostly look for human support for making crucial financial decisions and may benefit from easy-to-use interfaces and digital skills development. Conversely, Generation X was born between the time of 1965 and 1980. They are primary adopters of technology, do not hesitate using E banking and financial applications, and are worth the digital solutions that can save time and ease difficult tasks while ordering safety and confidentiality. Millennials were the generation, born between the years 1981 and 1996. They are digital nations who willingly use mobile banking, fintech applications, and robo-advisors, supposing tailored and Omni channel proficiencies and ready to explore novel financial products and services. Finally, Generation Z birth from the year 1997 ahead, are real digital nations, choosing mobile-first banking and immediate payment options, and rigorous to transparency and social accountability from financial institutions. They are greatly dependent upon social media and colleague referrals for making their financial decisions. Identifying these generational dissimilarities is principal for financial institutions intending to effectively navigate the digital transformation setting. Financial institutions need to section their customer base and modify digital solutions to encounter the particular requirements and preferences of individual generations. This needs a profound understanding of customer behavior, customer experience design, and operative communication plans (Tapscott, 2010; Mitchell, 2023).

4. CHALLENGES AND OPPORTUNITIES FOR BEHAVIORAL FINANCE DURING DIGITAL TRANSFORMATION

Existing literature epitomizes that digital transformation has significantly impacted the financial industry, introducing new challenges and opportunities in the context of behavioral finance. One prominent challenge is the growth of algorithmic trading. These trading algorithms are determined by multifaceted mathematical frameworks that can perform thousands of trades every second. Though they render liquidity to markets, they can also augment market volatility and intensify the effect of behavioral biases. For example, in severe market events, algorithmic trading may cause flash crashes, where asset prices plunge in a few minutes followed by a rapid recovery. The anxiety and fright curtailed by such kinds of events can be worsened by cognitive biases, instigating more unpredictability in the market. Furthermore, the digital era has evident the dawn of social media platforms and online mediums as powerful means of financial data and views. These platforms can be nurtured for herding attitudes and speculative concepts that can activate absurd trading activities. The GameStop trading frenzy was an extremely eminent event that occurred at the commencement of 2021 (Hasso et al. 2022) and illustrated that online societies can upset conventional financial markets. A mutual irrationality determined by collective closed-mindedness and information dissemination through social media platforms causes unusual stock price volatility.

One more challenge is the rapid market dealings in the digital age. High-frequency trading (HFT) systems perform trades at a fast speed (O'hara, 2015). Businesses or investors use HFT when they evaluate significant data to make crucial decisions regarding trades or investments within the space of a few seconds. HFT facilitates ample amounts of trades in a very short time and watchdog on market ups and downs (Chen, 2021). It also recognizes arbitrage opportunities. In this highly rapid setting, investors can respond thoughtlessly to fluctuations in the market, determined by emotional biases such as terror and self-indulgence (Shefrin, 2016). This quick decision-making can cause substantial financial losses. Even though the digital age encounters challenges, it also renders opportunities for behavioral finance to flourish.

Robo-advisors and AI-driven financial apps are among the most noteworthy opportunities that exist in the domain of technologically driven financial services. Robo-advisors and AI-driven financial apps offer personalized financial direction to people through automation and artificial intelligence, and consequently, more people can get benefit from these technological services, irrespective of their financial background or proficiency. The aforementioned technological instruments influence data analytics and behavioral visions to offer investors personalized investment approaches. Moreover, these technological advancements assist investors in order to make highly well-versed decisions and alleviate their cognitive biases in light of their rare financial objectives, behavioral biases, and risk tolerance.

Samuel (2017) focused on Machine Learning and behavioral finance and illustrated that Machine learning algorithms can examine the data to spot irrational behavior patterns. For instance, one can recognize illustrations of panic selling or extreme hopefulness in financial markets. Equipped with the data, financial institutions can improve predictive models to stabilize behavioral biases in actuality. Investors are provided timely notices or intrusions by these models which plummet the influence of behavioral biases on their decision-making. In addition, the future of Behavioral Finance seems hopeful but multifaceted. It will probably develop into a more interdisciplinary arena, incorporating visions from machine learning and data science. For example, progress in brain imaging technology can provide deeper perceptions of the audiovisual origin of financial decision-making. Researchers are able to gain a deep understanding of the roots of cognitive biases by studying individual behavior while making financial decisions.

Moreover, researchers and practitioners are discovering the perspective of AI and machine learning in Behavioral Finance. Progressive AI models may not only identify behavioral biases but also offer modified interventions to alleviate them. These interventions may assort from behavioral encouragement in trading apps to modified financial instruction programs. By vigorously addressing the psychological elements that affect decision-making, these AI-driven keys have the capability to improve investor revenues and stimulate further rational financial behavior. Behavioral Finance will also play an essential part in addressing ethical issues emerging from AI usage in finance. The effect of algorithms on investment choices increases the guarantee of transparency and ethical behavior in the digital financial ecosystem. In line with Kamila and Jasrotia (2023), Munoko et al. (2020), Carter et al. (2020), and Desouza et al. (2020), AI system creators should consider the interests of all stakeholders when applying responsible reasoning in the development procedure. This discourse declares that the ethical issues that arise in a technology-centered society are properly addressed, assuming that the progression of AI has the ability to aggravate a broad spectrum of ethical concerns (Kamila & Jasrotia, 2023; Kooli, 2023a, 2023b; Gill, 2021).

5. CONCLUSION, PRACTICAL IMPLICATIONS, AND FUTURE RECOMMENDATIONS

5.1 Conclusion

Behavioral Finance remains a crucial field in order to have deep insight into human psychological effects on financial decisions. In the rapid transformation of digital finance, it is needed to admit the challenges and seize the opportunities presented by the digital age. Implementing technology-based solutions, for instance, AI-driven interventions, and robo-advisors may assist investors in order to make rational investment decisions and alleviate cognitive biases. In the course of advancement, achieving an equilibrium between technological power usage for healthier decision-making and protection counter to the possible downsides of irrationality augmented by the digital domain will be important to the sustained growth and significance of Behavioral Finance.

Digital transformation is redesigning the business setting, and considering the interaction between behavioral finance and age demographics which is vital for organizations intended to prosper in this novel age. As dissimilar generations hold technology at wavering rates, businesses necessarily modify their digital contributions to satisfy different choices and needs.

Behavioral finance provides valuable understanding in order to identify the way individuals make financial decisions in the digital era. By identifying and dealing with cognitive biases and emotional retorts, financial institutions can cultivate more real financial products and services. Still, they must perform uprightly, safeguarding transparency and data safety.

To cope with the challenges and grasp the chances offered by digital transformation, organizations must invest in digital presence, training, and ground-breaking solutions. Behavioral nudges, customization, and fintech alliance are significant strategies to determine investors' engagement and achievement in the quickly developing digital setting.

As digital transformation endures modification and continuous changes in demographics, organizations that highlight the need to understand behavioral finance and age demographics will perform better in order to fulfill the ever-changing requirements of their investors and flourish in the forthcoming time.

5.2 Practical Implications

The practical insinuations of given recommendations are substantial. Firstly, the organizations must be flexible in order to parallel with the technological advancement and to deal with the preferences of different generations. This flexibility can result in a competitive edge in a developing market. Customization at some extent not merely improves customer satisfaction but also determine devotion and commitment, possibly increasing revenue. Incorporating behavioral finance values aids in developing trust among customers by administering them to greatly up-to-date financial decisions, which can decrease risks for both financial institutions and customers. Arranging digital skills development training proves an assurance of inclusivity and accountable digital alteration. Associations with fintech innovators nurture revolution and swiftness, letting organizations sustain with the newest trends and technologies. Ethical data develops trust and decreases governing risks. Lastly, a customer-centric strategy improves user knowledge, growing customer retention and enhancing customer satisfaction. These practical implications may improve competitiveness, enhance customer associations, and maintain growth for organizations in the digital era.

5.3 Future Recommendation

The research on behavioral finance in the setting of digital transformation can be conducted by focusing on the complicated relationship of human psychology with digital financial ecosystems. Studies into the influence of digital performances on financial well-being, the ethical measurements of digital nudging, and the neuroscientific foundations of digital financial decisions will possibly produce valuable insights. Moreover, discovering the ability of machine learning to enhance organizations' or financial institutions' predictive skills about investor behavior in the financial markets, together with multicultural studies will aid in forming the future setting of financial services. These research possibilities are not merely deepening the insights into behavioral biases in the digital transformation era but also preparing the ground for more operational and accountable digital financial implements and services, promoting both people and organizations equally.

REFERENCES

Agarwal, R., Gao, G., DesRoches, C., & Jha, A. K. (2010). Research commentary—The digital transformation of healthcare: Current status and the road ahead. *Information Systems Research, 21*(4), 796–809. DOI: 10.1287/isre.1100.0327

Allam, Z., Sharifi, A., Bibri, S. E., Jones, D. S., & Krogstie, J. (2022). The metaverse as a virtual form of smart cities: Opportunities and challenges for environmental, economic, and social sustainability in urban futures. *Smart Cities, 5*(3), 771–801. DOI: 10.3390/smartcities5030040

Aloosh, A., & Ouzan, S. (2020). The psychology of cryptocurrency prices. *Finance Research Letters, 33*, 101192. DOI: 10.1016/j.frl.2019.05.010

Arslanian, H., & Fischer, F. (2019). *The future of finance: The impact of FinTech, AI, and crypto on financial services*. Springer. DOI: 10.1007/978-3-030-14533-0

Badakhshan, E., & Ball, P. (2023). Applying digital twins for inventory and cash management in supply chains under physical and financial disruptions. *International Journal of Production Research, 61*(15), 5094–5116. DOI: 10.1080/00207543.2022.2093682

Bahrammirzaee, A. (2010). A comparative survey of artificial intelligence applications in finance: Artificial neural networks, expert system and hybrid intelligent systems. *Neural Computing & Applications, 19*(8), 1165–1195. DOI: 10.1007/s00521-010-0362-z

Baker, M., Bradley, B., & Wurgler, J. (2011). Benchmarks as limits to arbitrage: Understanding the low-volatility anomaly. *Financial Analysts Journal, 67*(1), 40–54. DOI: 10.2469/faj.v67.n1.4

Barberis, N., & Thaler, R. (2003). A survey of behavioral finance. *Handbook of the Economics of Finance, 1*, 1053-1128.

Barros, E., Popplewell, C., & Muhammad, T. (2021). Behavioral Finance -Impact of artificial intelligence and social media analytics on investor and trader. . . *ResearchGate*. https://www.researchgate.net/publication/355159676_Behavioral_Finance_-Impact_of_Artificial_Intelligence_and_Social_Media_Analytics_on_Investor_and_Trader_Behavior

Ben-Israel, D., Jacobs, W. B., Casha, S., Lang, S., Ryu, W. H. A., de Lotbiniere-Bassett, M., & Cadotte, D. W. (2020). The impact of machine learning on patient care: A systematic review. *Artificial Intelligence in Medicine, 103*, 101785. DOI: 10.1016/j.artmed.2019.101785 PMID: 32143792

Bhatia, A., Chandani, A., & Chhateja, J. (2020). Robo advisory and its potential in addressing the behavioral biases of investors—A qualitative study in Indian context. *Journal of Behavioral and Experimental Finance, 25*, 100281. DOI: 10.1016/j.jbef.2020.100281

Bhatnagar, A. (2016). How robo technology is changing wealth management. *Journal of Financial Planning, 29*(5), 22–25.

Bisht, D., Singh, R., Gehlot, A., Akram, S. V., Singh, A., Montero, E. C., Priyadarshi, N., & Twala, B. (2022). Imperative role of integrating digitalization in the firms finance: A technological perspective. *Electronics (Basel), 11*(19), 3252. DOI: 10.3390/electronics11193252

Bredt, S. (2019). Artificial Intelligence (AI) in the financial sector—Potential and public strategies. *Frontiers in Artificial Intelligence, 2*, 16. DOI: 10.3389/frai.2019.00016 PMID: 33733105

Brodie, J., Daubechies, I., De Mol, C., Giannone, D., & Loris, I. (2009). Sparse and stable Markowitz portfolios. *Proceedings of the National Academy of Sciences of the United States of America, 106*(30), 12267–12272. DOI: 10.1073/pnas.0904287106 PMID: 19617537

Cao, L., Yang, Q., & Yu, P. S. (2021). Data science and AI in FinTech: An overview. *International Journal of Data Science and Analytics, 12*(2), 81–99. DOI: 10.1007/s41060-021-00278-w

Carter, S. M., Rogers, W., Win, K. T., Frazer, H., Richards, B., & Houssami, N. (2020). The ethical, legal and social implications of using artificial intelligence systems in breast cancer care. *The Breast : Official Journal of the European Society of Mastology, 49*, 25–32. DOI: 10.1016/j.breast.2019.10.001 PMID: 31677530

Chen, C. Y. H., Guo, L., & Renault, T. (2019). What Makes Cryptocurrencies Special? Investor Sentiment and Return Predictability. *Investor Sentiment and Return Predictability (June 3, 2019).*

Chen, J. (2021). What is High-Frequency Trading (HFT)? How it works and example. *Investopedia.* https://www.investopedia.com/terms/h/high-frequency-trading.asp

Dandapani, K. (2017). Electronic finance–recent developments. *Managerial Finance, 43*(5), 614–626. DOI: 10.1108/MF-02-2017-0028

Daniel, K., Hirshleifer, D., & Subrahmanyam, A. (1998). Investor psychology and security market under-and overreactions. *the Journal of Finance, 53*(6), 1839-1885.

De Prado, M. L. (2018). *Advances in financial machine learning*. John Wiley & Sons.

Desouza, K. C., Dawson, G. S., & Chenok, D. (2020). Designing, developing, and deploying artificial intelligence systems: Lessons from and for the public sector. *Business Horizons*, *63*(2), 205–213. DOI: 10.1016/j.bushor.2019.11.004

Dunis, C., Middleton, P. W., Karathanasopolous, A., & Theofilatos, K. (2016). *Artificial intelligence in financial markets*. Palgrave Macmillan. DOI: 10.1057/978-1-137-48880-0

Duz Tan, S., & Tas, O. (2021). Social media sentiment in international stock returns and trading activity. *Journal of Behavioral Finance*, *22*(2), 221–234. DOI: 10.1080/15427560.2020.1772261

Dwivedi, Y. K., Hughes, L., Ismagilova, E., Aarts, G., Coombs, C., Crick, T., Duan, Y., Dwivedi, R., Edwards, J., Eirug, A., Galanos, V., Ilavarasan, P. V., Janssen, M., Jones, P., Kar, A. K., Kizgin, H., Kronemann, B., Lal, B., Lucini, B., & Williams, M. D. (2021). Artificial Intelligence (AI): Multidisciplinary perspectives on emerging challenges, opportunities, and agenda for research, practice and policy. *International Journal of Information Management*, *57*, 101994. DOI: 10.1016/j.ijinfomgt.2019.08.002

Ferri, R. (2014). Now anyone can be a robo-adviser. *Journal of Financial Planning*, *27*(12), 28.

Ghoddusi, H., Creamer, G. G., & Rafizadeh, N. (2019). Machine learning in energy economics and finance: A review. *Energy Economics*, *81*, 709–727. DOI: 10.1016/j.eneco.2019.05.006

Gill, K. S. (2021). Ethical dilemmas: Ned Ludd and the ethical machine. *AI & Society*, *36*(3), 669–676. DOI: 10.1007/s00146-021-01260-7 PMID: 34421227

Güler, D. (2023). The impact of investor sentiment on Bitcoin returns and conditional volatilities during the era of covid-19. *Journal of Behavioral Finance*, *24*(3), 276–289. DOI: 10.1080/15427560.2021.1975285

Hasso, T., Müller, D., Pelster, M., & Warkulat, S. (2022). Who participated in the GameStop frenzy? Evidence from brokerage accounts. *Finance Research Letters*, *45*, 102140. DOI: 10.1016/j.frl.2021.102140

He, W., Yan, G., & Da Xu, L. (2014). Developing vehicular data cloud services in the IoT environment. *IEEE Transactions on Industrial Informatics*, *10*(2), 1587–1595. DOI: 10.1109/TII.2014.2299233

Hill, J. (2018). *Fintech and the remaking of financial institutions*. Academic Press.

Hilpisch, Y. (2020). *Artificial Intelligence in Finance*. O'Reilly Media.

Hougan, M. (2015). Robo-Advisers: What it means to you. *Journal of Financial Planning*, *28*(2), 26.

Huang, W., Nakamori, Y., & Wang, S. Y. (2005). Forecasting stock market movement direction with support vector machine. *Computers & Operations Research*, *32*(10), 2513–2522. DOI: 10.1016/j.cor.2004.03.016

Kamila, M. K., & Jasrotia, S. S. (2023). Ethical issues in the development of artificial intelligence: recognizing the risks. *International Journal of Ethics and Systems*.

Khanboubi, F., Boulmakoul, A., & Tabaa, M. (2019). Impact of digital trends using IoT on banking processes. *Procedia Computer Science*, *151*, 77–84. DOI: 10.1016/j.procs.2019.04.014

Königstorfer, F., & Thalmann, S. (2020a). Applications of Artificial Intelligence in commercial banks–A research agenda for behavioral finance. *Journal of Behavioral and Experimental Finance*, *27*, 100352. DOI: 10.1016/j.jbef.2020.100352

Königstorfer, F., & Thalmann, S. (2020b). Applications of Artificial Intelligence in commercial banks–A research agenda for behavioral finance. *Journal of Behavioral and Experimental Finance*, *27*, 100352. DOI: 10.1016/j.jbef.2020.100352

Kooli, C. (2023a). Chatbots in education and research: A critical examination of ethical implications and solutions. *Sustainability (Basel)*, *15*(7), 5614. DOI: 10.3390/su15075614

Kooli, C. (2023b). Artificial intelligence dissociative identity disorder (AIDIS): The dark side of ChatGPT. *QScience Connect*, *2023*(2), 2. DOI: 10.5339/connect.2023.2

Lei, X., Mohamad, U. H., Sarlan, A., Shutaywi, M., Daradkeh, Y. I., & Mohammed, H. O. (2022). Development of an intelligent information system for financial analysis depend on supervised machine learning algorithms. *Information Processing & Management*, *59*(5), 103036. DOI: 10.1016/j.ipm.2022.103036

Lo, A. W. (2017). Big Data and the Industrial Organization of Financial Markets. *Annual Review of Financial Economics*, *9*(1), 1–26.

Majchrzak, A., Markus, M. L., & Wareham, J. (2016). Designing for digital transformation. *Management Information Systems Quarterly*, *40*(2), 267–278. DOI: 10.25300/MISQ/2016/40:2.03

Margiono, A. (2021). Digital transformation: Setting the pace. *The Journal of Business Strategy*, *42*(5), 315–322. DOI: 10.1108/JBS-11-2019-0215

Mitchell, T. (2023, May 22). *What We Know About Gen Z So Far | Pew Research Center*. Pew Research Center's Social & Demographic Trends Project. https://www.pewresearch.org/social-trends/2020/05/14/on-the-cusp-of-adulthood-and-facing-an-uncertain-future-what-we-know-about-gen-z-so-far-2/

Munoko, I., Brown-Liburd, H. L., & Vasarhelyi, M. (2020). The ethical implications of using artificial intelligence in auditing. *Journal of Business Ethics*, *167*(2), 209–234. DOI: 10.1007/s10551-019-04407-1

Nezami, M., Tuli, K. R., & Dutta, S. (2022). Shareholder wealth implications of software firms' transition to cloud computing: A marketing perspective. *Journal of the Academy of Marketing Science*, *50*(3), 538–562. DOI: 10.1007/s11747-021-00818-7 PMID: 35079189

O'hara, M. (2015). High frequency market microstructure. *Journal of Financial Economics*, *116*(2), 257–270. DOI: 10.1016/j.jfineco.2015.01.003

Phoon, K., & Koh, F. (2017). Robo-advisors and wealth management. *Journal of Alternative Investments*, *20*(3), 79–94. DOI: 10.3905/jai.2018.20.3.079

Pretz, K. (2013). The Next Evolution of the Internet. *[cited 2013 May 20]; available from*http://theinstitute.ieee.org/technology-focus/technology-topic/the-next-evolution-of-the-internet

Qi, Y., & Xiao, J. (2018). Fintech: AI powers financial services to improve people's lives. *Communications of the ACM*, *61*(11), 65–69. DOI: 10.1145/3239550

Safdar, N. M., Banja, J. D., & Meltzer, C. C. (2020). Ethical considerations in artificial intelligence. *European Journal of Radiology*, *122*, 108768. DOI: 10.1016/j.ejrad.2019.108768 PMID: 31786504

Samuel, J. (2017). Information token driven machine learning for electronic markets: Performance effects in behavioral financial big data analytics. *JISTEM-Journal of Information Systems and Technology Management, 14*, 371-383.

Shiller, R. J. (2015). Irrational exuberance. In *Irrational exuberance*. Princeton university press.

Tang, C. P., Huang, T. C. K., & Wang, S. T. (2018). The impact of Internet of things implementation on firm performance. *Telematics and Informatics*, *35*(7), 2038–2053. DOI: 10.1016/j.tele.2018.07.007

Tapscott, D. (2010). Grown up digital. How the net generation is changing your world. *International Journal of Market Research*, *52*(1), 139–140. DOI: 10.2501/S1470785310201119

Tetlock, P. C. (2007). Giving content to investor sentiment: The role of media in the stock market. *The Journal of Finance, 62*(3), 1139–1168. DOI: 10.1111/j.1540-6261.2007.01232.x

Tetlock, P. C. (2011). All the news that's fit to reprint: Do investors react to stale information? *Review of Financial Studies, 24*(5), 1481–1512. DOI: 10.1093/rfs/hhq141

Tetlock, P. C., Saar-Tsechansky, M., & Macskassy, S. (2008). More than words: Quantifying language to measure firms' fundamentals. *The Journal of Finance, 63*(3), 1437–1467. DOI: 10.1111/j.1540-6261.2008.01362.x

Tokic, D. (2018). BlackRock Robo-advisor 4.0: When artificial intelligence replaces human discretion. *Strategic Change, 27*(4), 285–290. DOI: 10.1002/jsc.2201

Uhl, M. W., & Rohner, P. (2018). Robo-advisors versus traditional investment advisors: An unequal game. *The Journal of Wealth Management, 21*(1), 44–50. DOI: 10.3905/jwm.2018.21.1.044

Vial, G. (2019). Understanding digital transformation: A review and a research agenda. *The Journal of Strategic Information Systems, 28*(2), 118–144. DOI: 10.1016/j.jsis.2019.01.003

Yilmaz, N. K., & Hazar, H. B. (2019). The rise of internet of things (IoT) and its applications in finance and accounting. *PressAcademia Procedia, 10*(1), 32–35. DOI: 10.17261/Pressacademia.2019.1139

ENDNOTES

1 https://www.accaglobal.com/gb/en/student/exam-support-resources/fundamentals-exams-study-resources/f9/technical-articles/behavioural-finance.html

2 https://www.investopedia.com/terms/b/behavioralfinance.asp

3 https://nexusintegra.io/industrial-digital-transformation-what-is-benefits/

4 https://www.investopedia.com/terms/c/cloud-computing.asp

5 https://www.investopedia.com/terms/b/blockchain.asp

Chapter 7
Navigating Sustainability in Digital Financial Services:
Transforming the Future

Choi-Meng Leong
Swinburne University of Technology Sarawak Campus, Sarawak, Malaysia

ABSTRACT

The emergence of digital financial services offered by corporates has triggered the relation to sustainability. This chapter review the interconnection between Sustainable Development Goals (SDGs), Environmental, Social, and Governance (ESG) principles and digital financial services. A systematic review of 20 articles from Scopus database derives four themes for the development of digital financial services by integrating sustainable development from the perspectives of current trends and future. The findings reveal the importance of the convergence between digital finance and sustainable/green finance to unveil the potential benefits for the sustainable practices. The chapter provide useful insights for scholars and practitioners regarding the development of digital financial services from the sustainability point of view.

INTRODUCTION

Sustainable Development Goals (SDGs) and Environmental, Social, and Governance (ESG) principles have gained eminence in recent years across various sectors, together with digital financial services. When an industrialized era transits to a sustainable future, two dominant frameworks emerge that have grasped the

DOI: 10.4018/979-8-3693-7160-2.ch007

attention of individuals, businesses and governments are ESG principles and SDGs (Işık et al., 2024). The United Nations' SDGs consist 17 objectives that are used to advance sustainable development while one of the elements affecting the realization of SDGs is ESG (Işık et al., 2024).

Research has been conducted to explore the relation between financial technology (fintech) and sustainability objectives (Arner et al., 2020; Carè et al., 2023) while some studies explore the relationship between fintech and regulatory or ethical standards (Aitken et al., 2020; Anagnostopoulos, 2018; Brownsword, 2019). The comprehensive framework of SDGs enables alignment in goal design as well as method measurement, in which the development of the framework enables different stakeholders to readily understand and act upon (Mio et al., 2020). Corporates possess the ability in innovating, scaling, investing and employing tend to move forward to 17 SDG goals (Tulder, 2018). However, it is still yet totally or successfully promoting the adoption of sustainability policies such as corporate social responsibility (CSR) and ESG in private sector (Van Tulder et al., 2021). For fintech, progressive approach has been used to unveil its full potential in supporting SDGs via the infrastructure development that promote digital financial transformation (Arner et al., 2020).

The fundamental framework that pilot the sustainable development of corporates is ESG principles, in which the principles are integrated to management and decision-making processes (Escrig-Olmedo et al., 2019). The governance dimension serves as a key for sustainable integration as well as a pre-requisite for designing sustainability-oriented strategies (Annesi et al., 2024). On the other hand, when technology progress combines with sustainable finance, the capital is directed to generate positive impacts on environment and society (Galeone et al., 2024). In the same vein, Singh (2022) also has uncovered the combination of green finance and digital finance into green digital finance in enhancing green initiatives via financial system such as fintech. One of the main challenges is the lack of participation of private sector, which international organizations have worked to integrate private sector initiatives as well as investment into mainstream climate finance (Singh, 2022).

In view of the challenges, this review examines current trends and future perspectives of SDGs, ESG principles, and digital financial services nexus. The aims of this review are: (1) to identify the way digital financial services are integrated to SDGs and ESG, and (2) to identify the current trends in the adoption of SDG-aligned practices and ESG frameworks within digital financial services, and how do these initiatives contribute to long-term value creation in the financial sector for sustainable future development.

LITERATURE REVIEW

Current Landscape of SDG Integration in Digital Financial Services

The integration of SDGs within digital financial services signifies a proliferating trend that associates financial innovation with global sustainability objectives. In the era of digital finance, companies are progressively distinguishing their roles in advancing these goals through innovative solutions. With the improved quality of services offered, Fintech contributes to a more transparent, more safeguarded and less costly financial system as well as promotes a diversified and attractive financial landscape (Moro-Visconti et al., 2020). As financial resources are channelled towards sustainable investments, this enables fintech contributes to the achievements of SDGs' 2023 Agenda (Dwivedi et al., 2021). Fintech promotes private savings mobilization towards green initiatives via institutional investors (i.e. insurance, pension funds, banks and investment companies) by repossessing non-financial data and information that is useful to integrate ESG principles in investment analysis and decision-making (Wang et al., 2020). Green fintech has emerged as technology-oriented innovation to support related SDGs (Puschmann et al., 2020). Green fintech also offers solutions to policymakers in terms of alleviating climate change risks, specifically in developing countries (Carè et al., 2023).

ESG Dimensions: Pillars of Responsible Digital Financial Services

ESG dimensions are fundamental principles that guide responsible business practices in the digital financial services sector. Last decade has witnessed the adoption of a new method for sustainable development by all business organizations (includes financial institutions) - the three dimensions of ESG - that are not limited to ethical issues but are priority contributors to economic aspect (Campanella et al., 2023). The best revolutionary technology in financial services such as artificial intelligence (AI) and machine learning tools are used to retrieve data that is useful for ESG ratings determination while promote renewable energy-oriented projects financing as well as environmental, social and ecology benefits generation (Zhou et al., 2020). ESG and technological enhancement are crucial for governance in terms of the reconsideration of business logic such as organizational models' evolution; processes revision from digital aspect; new skills and working logic advancement that call for ESG-oriented governance system to maximize stakeholders' involvement (Galeone et al., 2024). Corporate governance involves internal and external mechanisms that are designed to reinforce efforts of a company in attaining its objectives as well as utilized to establish and handle the relation with all stakeholders (Ahmed & Anifowose, 2024). Corporates with high ESG are less susceptible to litigation risk as a result of the effort to reduce environmental damage (Chen et al., 2023). Therefore, ESG dimensions are often used to operationalize and assess corporate social performance of a corporate (Schommer et al., 2019).

Future Perspective: Harnessing SDGs and ESG for Sustainable Innovation

Looking forward, the convergence of SDGs and ESG criteria is dignified to drive transformative innovation and sustainable growth within digital financial services. The continuous evolvement of technology prompts fintech companies to explore new ways to integrate sustainability into their products and services. The paradigm shift in finance landscape integrates the deliberation for ESG connection, increased fintech and increased demand for sustainable investments alternatives that have given birth to green finance (Dadabada, 2024). This leads to the integration of ESG principles and fintech in fostering green finance practices for enhanced transparency, responsible investment practices as well as positive societal outcomes (Dadabada, 2024). The role of private sector is crucial for the scaling up of SDG implementation by integrating ESG dimensions to business strategies (Mohieldin et al., 2023). Therefore, shaping the compliance could start with introducing the strategic-oriented and sustainability-oriented compliance programme within the corporate to promote the awareness of sustainability issues (Reis, 2022).

METHODS

Identification

The initial step for the systematic literature review is the selection of keywords. The relevant terms for digital financial services were determined based on the study of Hasan et al. (2022). On the other hand, the sustainable future influential frameworks are Environmental, Social, and Governance (ESG) and Sustainable Development Goals (SDGs) (Işık et al., 2024) and therefore ESG and SDG were included in the search terms. The creation of search strings enables all relevant terms be identified via Scopus database (see Table 1). There were 135 publications that were retrieved using Scopus database.

Screening

The screening step encompasses the evaluation of the consistency between the collection of relevant research items and the research questions. The selection of research items related to sustainability and digital financial services was based on content-related criteria. There were 82 papers excluded during the first stage of screening while 53 papers were examined founded on numerous exclusion and inclusion criteria that was detailed to this study (see Table 2). Literature was the main criterion applied and was fundamentally the research papers that serve as the key source of practical recommendations. As a result, meta-synthesis, meta-analyses, reviews, books, book chapters as well as conference proceedings were not included in the recent study. In addition, the publications selected was limited to English language for this review and only focused on the years ranged from 2020 to 2024.

Eligibility

A total of 53 papers were included in eligibility assessment. A careful examination based on the titles and core content for a compilation of 53 papers was carried out to ensure their consistency with the inclusion criteria as well as research objectives. As a result, 30 papers were excluded due to out of field, title and abstract not significantly related on the objective of the study, and full text access based on empirical evidence was not available. Therefore, a sum of 23 papers were remained for the following review.

Data Abstraction and Analysis

During this stage, the topics and subtopics were identified. This leads to the development of the themes. Figure 1 exhibits the processes of the careful selection of a total of 23 papers for analysis. The evaluation of the studies relate to sustainability and digital financial services was performed, which include the investigation of the method used as well as the research results.

Table 1. The search strings

Scopus	TITLE-ABS-KEY (SDG OR ESG) AND (fintech OR "Digital Finance" OR insurtech OR "mobile payment" OR "online payment" OR "Digital financial services" OR "Internet finance" OR "Mobile technology" OR "Mobile banking" OR "digital banking" OR "online banking" OR "internet banking" OR "financial technology" OR "insurance technology" OR "digital payment") AND (LIMIT-TO (PUBYEAR, 2020) OR LIMIT-TO (PUBYEAR, 2021) OR LIMIT-TO (PUBYEAR, 2022) OR LIMIT-TO (PUBYEAR, 2023) OR LIMIT-TO (PUBYEAR, 2024)) AND (LIMIT-TO (SUBJAREA, "BUSI") OR LIMIT-TO (SUBJAREA, "ECO")) AND (LIMIT-TO (DOCTYPE, "ar")) AND (LIMIT-TO (PUBSTAGE, "final")) AND (LIMIT-TO (SRCTYPE, "j")) AND (LIMIT-TO (LANGUAGE, "English")) Date of Access: 9 July 2024

Source: Author's Creation

Table 2. The selection criterion in searching

Criterion	**Inclusion**	**Exclusion**
Language	English	Non-English
Time line	2020 – 2024	< 2020
Literature type	Journal (Article)	Conference, Book Chapter, Review
Publication Stage	Final	In Press
Subject	Business, management and accounting; and Economics, Econometrics and Finance	Besides Business, management and accounting; and Economics, Econometrics and Finance

Figure 1. Flow diagram of the proposed searching study (Moher et al., 2010).

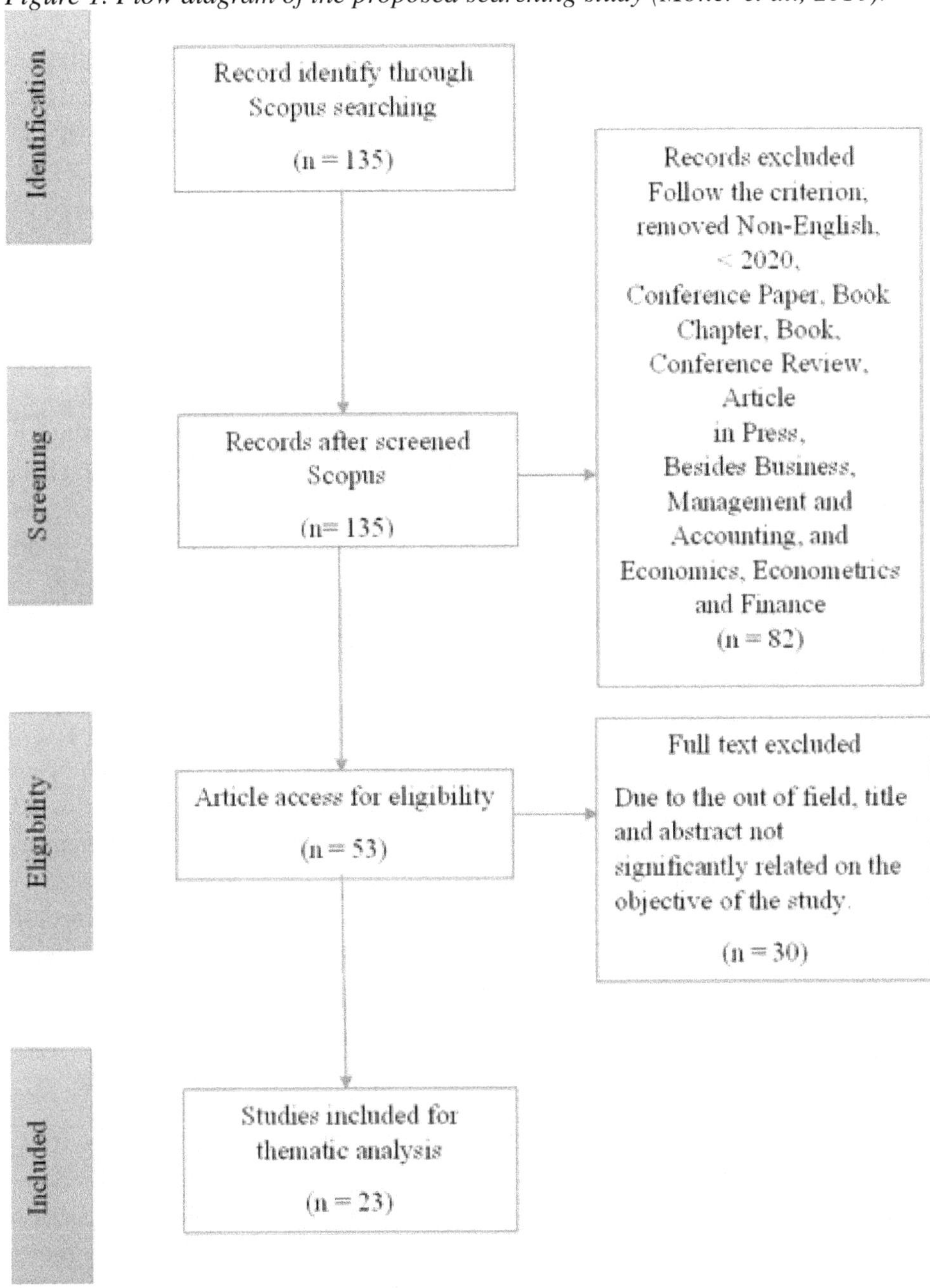

FINDINGS AND DISCUSSIONS

The systematic review has uncovered five themes based on the previous literature, comprises "Enhancing Corporate ESG Practices and Performance via Fintech's Role", "Interdisciplinary Investigation of Digital Financial Services, Fintech and Sustainable Development", "Contribution of Fintech to Financial Inclusion and Sustainable Development" and "Fintech Innovations, ESG Disclosure, IT Governance".

Enhancing Corporate ESG Practices and Performance via Fintech's Role

Innovations in fintech significantly shapes corporate strategies towards enhanced ESG practices, specifically in emerging markets. Development in fintech has enhanced corporate ESG activities; improved corporate ESG practices such as easing the financial constraints; increased attention of stakeholders that contributes to the strategic participation of firms in ESG behaviours (Ding et al., 2024); and accelerated digital transformation (Sang et al., 2024). Key mechanisms such as reducing the cost of equity and increasing issuance of equity and short-term loan in financial markets enable firms to adopt ESG practices effectively (Ding et al., 2024). Fintech also enhances transparency and accessibility of information relate to ESG via reduced financial constraints and information asymmetry (Liu & Li, 2024) and therefore promote greater stakeholder engagement and accountability.

Leveraging technologies via fintech promotes solutions formation that enables the participation of investors and companies in ESG-related areas, which has enhanced the ESG performance among banks (Dicuonzo et al., 2024). Financial technologies also encourage the embracing and amalgamation of ESG practices in financial sector (El Khoury et al., 2023). Therefore, it is critical to uncover the impact of financial technologies on financial sector such as in enhancing the sustainability.

Future Perspective

As fintech development leads to enhanced corporate ESG services, there is an accelerated role of government in promoting fintech growth for sustainable development. It is critical to consider the tax payment and incentives to encourage corporates for the innovation. Besides, the techniques for developing fintech index in a more comprehensive manner such as from demand and supply of financial services will be useful for the projection of its impact on real economy (Ding et al., 2024). On the other hand, the associate risk should be taken into consideration by the corporates in formulating the strategies to handle crisis. As the growth of artificial intelligence

(AI) could be speeding, the risk assessment associate with the integration of AI in financial services will be significant.

Interdisciplinary Investigation of Digital Financial Services, Fintech and Sustainable Development

ESG has played significant role in digital finance that contributes to the sustainable development. Digital finance contributes to the reduction in financial constraints among corporates that promote the ESG activities' engagement. The financial constraints reduction can be achieved by reducing asymmetric information between banks and firms that leads to the financing costs reduction via digital channels; availability of alternative financing sources that boost ESG activities to catch the attention of stakeholders; and improving sales cash inflow that enhances ESG activities participation (Mu et al., 2023). With the presence of the impact of corporate ESG performance, digital finance put forwards green innovation via research and development investment, and tackles financing constraints of firms through provision of alternative funding sources (Chen et al., 2024). In the same vein, Yang and Hui (2024) discover that digital finance enhances green innovation via financing constraints and financial costs reduction, in which ESG also possesses moderating effect. Ren et al. (2023) also uncover that digital finance improves corporate ESG performance via both green innovation and external supervision. Digital finance also improves corporate ESG performance and enhances investment in ESG activities (Mu et al., 2023). Interestingly, digital financial inclusion is used to proxy digital finance (Ren et al., 2023), which reflects the interrelationship between digital finance and financial inclusion. However, the support from government and financial institutions in the digital finance advancement is essential for enhancing efficiency in energy, protection in environment and performance in sustainability, in which the sustainable growth in digital finance is rely on the construction of infrastructure and depth of use (Zhang, 2023). Zhang (2023) also further highlight the role of digital finance in solving asymmetric information in ESG performance as well as promoting efficiency via facilitating digital finance resources by government regulators. Nevertheless, the emerging of "Green Fintech" aims to bridge the gap of the implementation of Fintech that requires engaging in technical and legal impediments to achieve the undertakes or prospective of sustainable finance (Macchiavello & Siri, 2022).

Regional fintech development also possesses impact on green innovation of corporate and Li et al. (2023) argue that higher degree of external attention such as media and analysts impose more impactful regional fintech in promoting corporate green innovation. Fintech companies contributes to SDG achievements directly and indirectly in various perspectives such as sustainability education and impact tracking advancement (Carè et al., 2023). However, the understanding of business model for fintech companies is in early stage (Laidroo et al., 2021) and therefore the needs to develop a new business model that considers social or environmental impact via transfer of created values to communities is essential (Carè et al., 2023).

Future Perspective

Sustainable digital financial services are the area worth for the exploration that could tie players, strategies and outcomes together in the integration of "digital" element and "sustainable" element in financial services such as the emerging concept of "Green Fintech". The green financing and SDG financing leads to innovative financing models (Devidze, 2022). For instance, green lending and green investments that are inexpensive, easy, transparent and inclusive are developed by fintech and innovative start-ups (Devidze, 2022). The business model in a corporate that could support the "Green Fintech" or sustainable/green finance would be crucial.

Contribution of Fintech to Financial Inclusion and Sustainable Development

Fintech platforms provide avenue to mobilize resources in the funding of sustainable development and therefore contribute significantly to SDGs. The funding or 'fintech dividend' is stemmed from accelerated savings and investments via the use of fintech platforms; resource diversions from conventional financial intermediaries; and reduced transactions costs (Michael & Latkovska, 2021). Regulatory frameworks and institutional reforms are critical to enable the direct contributions of fintech such as tax payment to support government spending in SDG; SDG-related ventures as well as conventional funding for public-private partnerships in banks, governments or international organizations (Michael & Latkovska, 2021). The extensive potential of fintech in supporting sustainability could be unravelled via the alliances of conventional businesses, governments and international organizations by creating innovative solutions that can resolve challenges in environment and social perspectives (Dicuonzo et al., 2024). A study by Showkat et al. (2024) found that the embracing of digital financial services leads to improvement in financial independence of women, which supports digital financial services promotes financial inclusion. Fintech companies promote financial inclusion and enhance social and environment impacts via provision of instruments and tools in achieving SDGs, for instance, technologies are used to reach to the communities (Carè et al., 2023). Fintech drives financial inclusion, in which companies could gain competitive advantage via initiatives such as subsidies and tax reductions to promote sustainable behaviours (Merello et al., 2023).

Future Perspective

Fintech's ability to stimulate financial inclusion and SDG-related initiatives highlights its transformative potential in global sustainability efforts. The achievement of SDGs relies on the collaboration between regulators and government on digital financial inclusion such as the creation of Digital ID, in which digital infrastructure would be the fundamental for long-run development (Zetzsche et al., 2019). Regulatory challenges and policy interventions are two of the areas needed to leverage fintech effectively for achieving SDGs, accentuating inclusive growth and equitable access to financial services. The greatest potential could be achieved for the countries who possess high penetration rates of smart phones and disorganized conventional financial systems (Zetzsche et al., 2019).

Fintech Innovations, ESG Disclosure, IT Governance

Fintech innovations are reshaping sustainability practices, which is crucial for sustainable finance. Conventionally, Fintech and sustainable finance are treated self-sufficiently, but their convergence offers new opportunities. Digital Finance/Fintech Action Plan has been trea(Almaqtari, 2024)ted independently with Sustainable Finance Strategy under the European Union (EU) policy agenda, in which the recent COVID-19 pandemic emphasizes the urgency for countries reconsider for integration of technology and sustainability (Macchiavello & Siri, 2022). Specifically, Fintech possesses the potential to tackle the challenges in present sustainable finance frameworks, such as access to retail financing, ESG disclosure and others (Macchiavello & Siri, 2022).

ESG disclosure for compliance is another area of concern due to the fast pace evolution in regulations. Government regulation is still the ground for humanization of fintech but could be enhanced to improve institutional support (Kazachenok et al., 2023). The current Fintech models possess a data infrastructure framework that is sustainable and able to caters the ESG data challenges such as concerns regarding data governance (Duran & Tierney, 2023). Information Technology (IT) governance is also crucial in shaping strategic planning of business. For instance, sustainability performance of banks is determined by sustainable activities, fintech evolution and advancement of technologies that are counted on strategic planning with IT governance (Almaqtari, 2024). Effective IT governance that combines with emphasis on ESG factors lead to improved sustainability performance (Almaqtari, 2024). The latest fintech development, such as the emergence of Initial Coin Offerings, also called for the link to ESG (Bitetto & Cerchiello, 2023).

Future Perspective

The impact of the support of governments in terms of the establishment of fintech projects, refinement of market laws and regulations, creation of optimal environment for business and financial services, improving asymmetric in information as well as implementation of green development strategies (Li et al., 2023) would be crucial for the sustainable development in financial services. Authorities also possess the role in proposing solutions that could enhance the scale and reliability of ESG disclosures with the participations from corporates, which could lead to the support for informed decision-making as well as regulatory compliance in financial markets. The governance framework such as IT governance, is essential for sustainability, in which the framework should align with the ESG objectives. IT governance is one of the priorities for policymakers and corporates to promote sustainable practices, foster economic resilience as well as create long-term value. Balancing technology advancement with ethical considerations in achieving sustainable growth is essential for corporates by leveraging IT governance strategically such as in their business models. Regulatory alignment and policy interventions are crucial to maximize fintech's impact on achieving SDGs. There is a need for robust governance frameworks to harness fintech's full potential in endorsing global sustainability.

CONCLUSION

Digital finance is an area that have grown tremendously with the advancement of technology. The integration of digital finance with sustainable finance or green finance would further discover the potential benefits in the sector of digital financial services. In corporate level, Tulder (2018) proposes seven guiding principles for strategic planning by integrating SDGs, which include: (i) depart from societal needs and ambitions as defined by the SDGs; (ii) make a gap analysis; (iii) access present materiality; (iv) define present and potential spill-over effects; (v) assess your stakeholder portfolio; (vi) define a future agenda; and (vii) connected leadership challenge.

Following the successor countries, Arner et al. (2020) and Zetzsche et al. (2019) recommended four pillars for the development of digital financial infrastructure which contributes to the digital financial transformation. The four pillars include: availability of identification such as Digital ID and eKYC as well as account opening simplification (Pillar 1); foster electronic payment systems, infrastructure, and an accommodating regulatory and policy framework that enhances the digital transfer of funds from conventional financial intermediaries as well as emerging market participants (Pillar 2); availability of initiatives to open account as well as electronic government services delivery, offering crucial tools for accessing services and saving (Pillar 3); and advancement of digital financial market infrastructure as well as systems that boost value-added financial services at the same time refining access, usage, and stability (Pillar 4). Strengthening the guiding principles at corporate level and the four pillars at country level will further promote sustainable digital financial services.

Regulatory framework in guiding this development will be crucial to facilitate the growth of digital platforms such as green bonds and robo-advisors while ethical dilemmas are another aspect that corporates ought to address on their journey to integrating fintech with sustainable finance (Dadabada, 2024). Moving forward, it is imperative for all stakeholders to collaboratively enhance the integration of ESG principles, fintech, and green/sustainable finance. The subsequent phase will involve evaluating the impact of this integration within the digital financial services sector.

REFERENCES

Ahmed, A., & Anifowose, M. (2024). Corruption, corporate governance, and sustainable development goals in Africa. *Corporate Governance (Bradford), 24*(1), 119–138. Advance online publication. DOI: 10.1108/CG-07-2022-0311

Aitken, M., Toreini, E., Carmichael, P., Coopamootoo, K., Elliott, K., & van Moorsel, A. (2020). Establishing a social licence for Financial Technology: Reflections on the role of the private sector in pursuing ethical data practices. *Big Data & Society, 7*(1). Advance online publication. DOI: 10.1177/2053951720908892

Almaqtari, F. A. (2024). The moderating role of IT governance on the relationship between FinTech and sustainability performance. *Journal of Open Innovation, 10*(2), 100267. https://doi.org/https://doi.org/10.1016/j.joitmc.2024.100267. DOI: 10.1016/j.joitmc.2024.100267

Anagnostopoulos, I. (2018). Fintech and regtech: Impact on regulators and banks. *Journal of Economics and Business, 100*, 7–25. Advance online publication. DOI: 10.1016/j.jeconbus.2018.07.003

Annesi, N., Battaglia, M., Ceglia, I., & Mercuri, F. (2024). Navigating paradoxes: building a sustainable strategy for an integrated ESG corporate governance. *Management Decision, ahead-of-print*(ahead-of-print). DOI: 10.1108/MD-10-2023-2006

Arner, D. W., Buckley, R. P., Zetzsche, D. A., & Veidt, R. (2020). Sustainability, FinTech and Financial Inclusion. *European Business Organization Law Review, 21*(1), 7–35. Advance online publication. DOI: 10.1007/s40804-020-00183-y

Bitetto, A., & Cerchiello, P. (2023). Initial coin offerings and ESG: Allies or enemies? *Finance Research Letters, 57*, 104227. Advance online publication. DOI: 10.1016/j.frl.2023.104227

Brownsword, R. (2019). Regulatory Fitness: Fintech, Funny Money, and Smart Contracts. *European Business Organization Law Review, 20*(1), 5–27. Advance online publication. DOI: 10.1007/s40804-019-00134-2

Campanella, F., Serino, L., Battisti, E., Giakoumelou, A., & Karasamani, I. (2023). FinTech in the financial system: Towards a capital-intensive and high competence human capital reality? *Journal of Business Research, 155*, 113376. Advance online publication. DOI: 10.1016/j.jbusres.2022.113376

Carè, R., Boitan, I. A., & Fatima, R. (2023). How do FinTech companies contribute to the achievement of SDGs? Insights from case studies. *Research in International Business and Finance, 66*, 102072. https://doi.org/https://doi.org/10.1016/j.ribaf.2023.102072. DOI: 10.1016/j.ribaf.2023.102072

Chen, S., Song, Y., & Gao, P. (2023). Environmental, social, and governance (ESG) performance and financial outcomes: Analyzing the impact of ESG on financial performance. *Journal of Environmental Management, 345*, 118829. Advance online publication. DOI: 10.1016/j.jenvman.2023.118829 PMID: 37688968

Chen, W., Arn, G., Song, H., & Xie, Y. (2024). The influences of digital finance on green technological innovation in China's manufacturing sector: The threshold effects of ESG performance. *Journal of Cleaner Production, 467*, 142953. https://doi.org/https://doi.org/10.1016/j.jclepro.2024.142953. DOI: 10.1016/j.jclepro.2024.142953

Dadabada, P. K. (2024). Analyzing the Impact of ESG Integration and FinTech Innovations on Green Finance: A Comparative Case Studies Approach. *Journal of the Knowledge Economy*. Advance online publication. DOI: 10.1007/s13132-024-02197-0

Devidze, N. (2022). Current State of Green Digital Financing and the Associated Challenges. In *Economics*. Law, and Institutions in Asia Pacific., DOI: 10.1007/978-981-19-2662-4_2

Dicuonzo, G., Palmaccio, M., & Shini, M. (2024). ESG, governance variables and Fintech: An empirical analysis. *Research in International Business and Finance, 69*, 102205. https://doi.org/https://doi.org/10.1016/j.ribaf.2023.102205. DOI: 10.1016/j.ribaf.2023.102205

Ding, J., Li, L., & Zhao, J. (2024). How does fintech prompt corporations toward ESG sustainable development? Evidence from China. *Energy Economics, 131*, 107387. Advance online publication. DOI: 10.1016/j.eneco.2024.107387

Duran, R. E., & Tierney, P. (2023). Fintech Data Infrastructure for ESG Disclosure Compliance. *Journal of Risk and Financial Management, 16*(8), 378. Advance online publication. DOI: 10.3390/jrfm16080378

Dwivedi, P., Alabdooli, J. I., & Dwivedi, R. (2021). Role of FinTech Adoption for Competitiveness and Performance of the Bank: A Study of Banking Industry in UAE. *International Journal of Global Business and Competitiveness, 16*(2), 130–138. Advance online publication. DOI: 10.1007/s42943-021-00033-9

El Khoury, R., Nasrallah, N., Hussainey, K., & Assaf, R. (2023). Spillover analysis across FinTech, ESG, and renewable energy indices before and during the Russia–Ukraine war: International evidence. *Journal of International Financial Management & Accounting*, *34*(2), 279–317. Advance online publication. DOI: 10.1111/jifm.12179

Escrig-Olmedo, E., Fernández-Izquierdo, M., Ferrero-Ferrero, I., Rivera-Lirio, J. M., & Muñoz-Torres, M. J. (2019). Rating the raters: Evaluating how ESG rating agencies integrate sustainability principles. *Sustainability (Basel)*, *11*(3), 915. Advance online publication. DOI: 10.3390/su11030915

Galeone, G., Ranaldo, S., & Fusco, A. (2024). ESG and FinTech: Are they connected? *Research in International Business and Finance*, *69*, 102225. Advance online publication. DOI: 10.1016/j.ribaf.2024.102225

Hasan, M. M., Yajuan, L., & Khan, S. (2022). Promoting China's Inclusive Finance Through Digital Financial Services. *Global Business Review*, *23*(4), 984–1006. Advance online publication. DOI: 10.1177/0972150919895348

Işık, C., Ongan, S., Islam, H., Pinzon, S., & Jabeen, G. (2024). Navigating sustainability: Unveiling the interconnected dynamics of ESG factors and SDGs in BRICS-11. *Sustainable Development*, *n/a*(n/a). https://doi.org/https://doi.org/10.1002/sd.2977

Kazachenok, O. P., Stankevich, G. V., Chubaeva, N. N., & Tyurina, Y. G. (2023). Economic and legal approaches to the humanization of FinTech in the economy of artificial intelligence through the integration of blockchain into ESG Finance. *Humanities & Social Sciences Communications*, *10*(1), 167. Advance online publication. DOI: 10.1057/s41599-023-01652-8

Laidroo, L., Koroleva, E., Kliber, A., Rupeika-Apoga, R., & Grigaliuniene, Z. (2021). Business models of FinTechs – Difference in similarity? *Electronic Commerce Research and Applications*, *46*, 101034. https://doi.org/https://doi.org/10.1016/j.elerap.2021.101034. DOI: 10.1016/j.elerap.2021.101034

Li, B., Du, J., Yao, T., & Wang, Q. (2023). FinTech and corporate green innovation: An external attention perspective. *Finance Research Letters*, *58*, 104661. https://doi.org/https://doi.org/10.1016/j.frl.2023.104661. DOI: 10.1016/j.frl.2023.104661

Liu, Z., & Li, X. (2024). The impact of bank fintech on ESG greenwashing. *Finance Research Letters*, *62*, 105199. Advance online publication. DOI: 10.1016/j.frl.2024.105199

Macchiavello, E., & Siri, M. (2022). Sustainable Finance and Fintech: Can Technology Contribute to Achieving Environmental Goals? A Preliminary Assessment of "Green Fintech" and "Sustainable Digital Finance.". *European Company and Financial Law Review*, *19*(1), 128–174. Advance online publication. DOI: 10.1515/ecfr-2022-0005

Merello, P., Barbera, A., & De la Poza, E. (2023). Analysing the determinant factors of the sustainability profile of Fintech and Insurtech companies. *Journal of Cleaner Production*, *421*, 138437. Advance online publication. DOI: 10.1016/j.jclepro.2023.138437

Michael, B., & Latkovska, T. (2021). The FinTech Dividend: How Much Money Is FinTech Likely to Mobilize for Sustainable Development? *Global Policy*, *12*(5), 677–688. Advance online publication. DOI: 10.1111/1758-5899.12994

Mio, C., Panfilo, S., & Blundo, B. (2020). Sustainable development goals and the strategic role of business: A systematic literature review. *Business Strategy and the Environment*, *29*(8), 3220–3245. Advance online publication. DOI: 10.1002/bse.2568

Moher, D., Liberati, A., Tetzlaff, J., & Altman, D. G. (2010). Preferred reporting items for systematic reviews and meta-analyses: The PRISMA statement. *International Journal of Surgery*, *8*(5), 336–341. https://doi.org/https://doi.org/10.1016/j.ijsu.2010.02.007. DOI: 10.1016/j.ijsu.2010.02.007 PMID: 20171303

Mohieldin, M., Wahba, S., Gonzalez-Perez, M. A., & Shehata, M. (2023). How Businesses Can Accelerate and Scale-Up SDG Implementation by Incorporating ESG into Their Strategies. In *Business, Government and the SDGs*. DOI: 10.1007/978-3-031-11196-9_3

Moro-Visconti, R., Rambaud, S. C., & Pascual, J. L. (2020). Sustainability in FinTechs: An explanation through business model scalability and market valuation. *Sustainability (Basel)*, *12*(24), 10316. Advance online publication. DOI: 10.3390/su122410316

Mu, W., Liu, K., Tao, Y., & Ye, Y. (2023). Digital finance and corporate ESG. *Finance Research Letters*, *51*, 103426. https://doi.org/https://doi.org/10.1016/j.frl.2022.103426. DOI: 10.1016/j.frl.2022.103426

Puschmann, T., Hoffmann, C. H., & Khmarskyi, V. (2020). How green fintech can alleviate the impact of climate change—The case of Switzerland. *Sustainability (Basel)*, *12*(24), 10691. Advance online publication. DOI: 10.3390/su122410691

Reis, L. (2022). How Can Compliance Steer Companies to Deliver on ESG Goals? In *The Palgrave Handbook of ESG and Corporate Governance*. DOI: 10.1007/978-3-030-99468-6_16

Ren, X., Zeng, G., & Zhao, Y. (2023). Digital finance and corporate ESG performance: Empirical evidence from listed companies in China. *Pacific-Basin Finance Journal*, *79*, 102019. https://doi.org/https://doi.org/10.1016/j.pacfin.2023.102019. DOI: 10.1016/j.pacfin.2023.102019

Sang, Y., Xie, M., Bai, X., & Guo, F. (2024). Does natural resource dependence influence the impact of financial technologies on corporate ESG and digital governance in China's listed enterprises? *Resources Policy*, *91*, 104948. https://doi.org/https://doi.org/10.1016/j.resourpol.2024.104948. DOI: 10.1016/j.resourpol.2024.104948

Schommer, M., Richter, A., & Karna, A. (2019). Does the Diversification–Firm Performance Relationship Change Over Time? A Meta-Analytical Review. *Journal of Management Studies*, *56*(1), 270–298. Advance online publication. DOI: 10.1111/joms.12393

Showkat, M., Nagina, R., Nori, U., Baba, M. A., & Shah, M. A. (2024). Empowering women in the digital age: Can digital financial services fulfil the promise of financial autonomy and gender equality in the attainment of Sustainable Development Goal 5? *Cogent Economics & Finance*, *12*(1), 2342459. DOI: 10.1080/23322039.2024.2342459

Singh, V. K. (2022). Regulatory and Legal Framework for Promoting Green Digital Finance. In *Economics*. Law, and Institutions in Asia Pacific., DOI: 10.1007/978-981-19-2662-4_1

van Tulder, R. (2018). Business & The Sustainable Development Goals: A Framework for Effective Corporate Involvement. In *Rotterdam School of Management*. Erasmus University.

Van Tulder, R., Rodrigues, S. B., Mirza, H., & Sexsmith, K. (2021). The UN's Sustainable Development Goals: Can multinational enterprises lead the Decade of Action? In *Journal of International Business Policy* (Vol. 4, Issue 1). DOI: 10.1057/s42214-020-00095-1

Wang, R., Mirza, N., Vasbieva, D. G., Abbas, Q., & Xiong, D. (2020). The nexus of carbon emissions, financial development, renewable energy consumption, and technological innovation: What should be the priorities in light of COP 21 Agreements? *Journal of Environmental Management*, *271*, 111027. Advance online publication. DOI: 10.1016/j.jenvman.2020.111027 PMID: 32778307

Yang, J., & Hui, N. (2024). How digital finance affects the sustainability of corporate green innovation. *Finance Research Letters*, *63*, 105314. https://doi.org/https://doi.org/10.1016/j.frl.2024.105314. DOI: 10.1016/j.frl.2024.105314

Zetzsche, D. A., Buckley, R. P., & Arner, D. W. (2019). FinTech for Financial Inclusion: Driving Sustainable Growth. *Journal of Finance, first edit*(February).

Zhang, D. (2023). Can digital finance empowerment reduce extreme ESG hypocrisy resistance to improve green innovation? *Energy Economics*, *125*, 106756. Advance online publication. DOI: 10.1016/j.eneco.2023.106756

Zhou, X., Tang, X., & Zhang, R. (2020). Impact of green finance on economic development and environmental quality: A study based on provincial panel data from China. *Environmental Science and Pollution Research International*, *27*(16), 19915–19932. Advance online publication. DOI: 10.1007/s11356-020-08383-2 PMID: 32232752

Chapter 8
Artificial Intelligence and the Future of Financial Decision-Making

Amna Naeem
Iqra University, Pakistan

ABSTRACT

Abstract: Artificial intelligence (AI) has transformed and modernized the process of financial decision making in the future; it also offers several opportunities and advancement for the users to make informed and effective decisions. Thus, the objective of this conceptual paper is to analyze the usage and application of AI in the finance sectors, specifically the role of AI in the future of financial decision-making. Finding of the conceptual paper has highlighted several significant usage and applications of Artificial intelligence in the financial decision making. These applications can be divided into six fundamental areas with reference to future of financial decision making: data analysis and insight, risk assessment, automation and efficiency, trading and investment strategies, personalized financial services, and fraud detection and security.

1. INTRODUCTION

Artificial intelligence is the system's capacity to comprehend and interpret external data, to learn and use the same data to accomplish tasks, goals, objectives via easy and flexible adaptation (Kaplan & Haenlein, 2019). Artificial Intelligence (AI) has become an increasingly important topic in recent years, as it has the potential to revolutionize many areas of life. The effectiveness of AI is highly dependent on its functionality, and its application in diverse fields presents both opportunities and

DOI: 10.4018/979-8-3693-7160-2.ch008

challenges (Chen et al, 2022). Artificial intelligence is a fundamental component in modern society; as it performs an essential role. Multiple factors determine the effectiveness of AI such as its accuracy, speed, and adaptability. The ability of AI to correctly identify and classify data is referred to as accuracy. Speed refers to an AI's capacity for quick data processing while adaptability refers to an AI's capacity for long-term learning and improvement. Additionally, processing large and vast data quickly and accurately is one of the predominant advantages of Artificial Intelligence.

Accordingly, the increased computing power has significantly improved the quality and quantity of big data; thus, significant advances have been made in various research areas, including machine learning, neural networks, and speech recognition in recent years (Brynjolfsson & McAfee, 2017). AI technology has advanced quickly and is now used extensively in all spheres of society. Artificial intelligence technology is rapidly transforming and widely used in all spheres of life. Recently, AI has penetrated in different industrial sectors including health care, manufacturing, transportation, economics and finance, etc. In addition, AI is also augmenting in the field of economics and finance, and intensifying its significance in the field. Artificial Intelligence (AI) has revolutionized and transformed the future of financial decision-making, while simultaneously offering numerous opportunities and advancements. Artificial Intelligences' impact in the Finance domain can be observed in various areas.

According to Brynjolfsson and McAfee (2017), AI and machine learning (ML) are identified as the most crucial technologies with wide-ranging applications in the present era. As a significant driver in the fourth industrial revolution, AI is predicted to exert a profound influence on economies and societies, globally. PricewaterhouseCoopers' study (2018) suggests that the adoption of AI technology holds the potential to contribute to a remarkable increase in global GDP by up to USD $15.7 trillion, equivalent to 14% by the year 2030. Particularly, the financial services industry has been an early adopter, with almost 30% of companies successfully incorporating one or more AI technologies into their core operations at a substantial scale in 2020. For instance, Banks have implemented AI-powered applications like digital payments, chat bots, and biometric fraud detection systems to enhance their customer service. Banks also utilized AI to collect and analyze borrowers' data to obtain useful insights and make better-informed decisions (Huang & You, 2022).

AI-powered risk control systems analyze vast amounts of data, identify trends and patterns, and evaluate potential threats and risks; thus, improving the overall risk management capabilities of financial institutions by incorporating advanced algorithms (Li et al., 2021). Transaction data analysis, enhanced chatbots, identity verification during client registration, fraud detection, bond trading pricing, monetization of money laundering, price differentiation in auto insurance, automated analysis of legal articles, risk control, portfolio management, client relationship control, and trade and investment transaction execution are some examples of contemporary applications of artificial intelligence in finance (Xiao and Ke, 2021). Additionally, AI is predicted to be able to extract hidden data insights more quickly by focusing on the decision making patterns, as validated by Brock and Von Wangenheim (2019), AI is a network "to support decision-making and knowledge management, and to automate customer interfaces" (p.115).

Artificial intelligence (AI) and Machine learning (ML) are augmented by the consistent growth in storage and computational power; hence, firms are investing in AI and ML to manage contemporary Financial Technology also known as "Fin-Tech" (Xiao and Ke, 2021). Machine learning is significantly contributing towards the multiple aspects of Finance i.e. research and development, identification of gaps, developing understanding and targeting unrealistic expectations; previously, all these tasks were usually performed by a team that would require additional cost and lack accuracy. Irrespective of these common tasks. According to Kitsios and Kamariotou (2021), Artificial intelligence (AI) and Machine learning (ML) provides financial monitoring, automation of repetitive tasks, formulation of investment plans, identification of transactional frauds, algorithm trading, etc. Correspondingly, AI also effectively analyzes the decision making process of structure and unstructured data accurately and precisely.

The rapid development of intelligent technology has resulted in the production of enormous amounts of data, which has the potential to greatly improve decision-making in the financial markets (Huang & You, 2022). The complicated procedures required in gathering, processing, and analyzing numerous information resources are just one of the new challenges that this technological advancement has posed for financial activities (Kumar et al., 2023). Additionally, the financial market functions in a volatile environment where unforeseen occurrences like the COVID-19 epidemic and government interventions further exacerbate the challenges of asset pricing and management (Mushafiq, 2021).

However, owing to the substantial advancement in the field of artificial intelligence (AI), it has witnessed rapid development in the features in recent years and has significantly catered these challenges by offering promising solutions for the financial sector (Malali & Gopalakrishnan, 2020). Nevertheless, AI is becoming more widely acknowledged as a viable tool to overcome the aforementioned challenges due to its capacity to efficiently mine patterns from large-scale information (Krollner et al., 2010). Correspondingly, financial institutions can improve their decision-making processes, risk assessment and management, asset pricing, and portfolio management methods by utilizing AI technologies (Kumar et al., 2021).

1.1 Purpose and Objective of the Paper

Moreover, limited literature has accentuated the role of AI in the decision making process; as this sector is comparatively new from other sectors like healthcare, manufacturing, transportation, and others. Therefore, this conceptual review is an attempt to analyze the contribution of Artificial intelligence in the field of Finance. In this article, we will explore the usage and application of AI in the finance sectors, specifically with the emphasis on the future of decision-making. This conceptual review will also highlight the intelligent tools available, and the challenges that must be addressed to fully realize the potential of AI. Therefore, the objective of the paper is to examine the role of Artificial intelligence in the future of financial decision making. Additionally, the study will also evaluate the influence and consequence of Artificial intelligence on the financial decision making in the near future.

2. LITERATURE REVIEW

2.1 Theoretical Background

Multiple theories assist the decision making process of AI and Financial decision-making process; these theories are commonly for the hypothesis proposed owing to the different covered dimensions. Initially, intelligence-design-choice theory proposed by Simon (1947) provides a more realistic view of the world. This framework includes the process of making decisions in between different and alternative elements and actions. This theory also accentuated multiple psychological factors that impact the human decision making ability i.e. stress, motivation, etc. Poromel (1997) further added three processes in the framework that direct the end results of any process; the process includes initial diagnosis and identification, choice and preference, and followed by the individual course of actions. Accordingly, these schools of thought provide pathways for the two developments that connect AI with the decision-making process.

During the initial stage, expert systems were considered a form of artificial intelligence (AI) designed to capture knowledge (Liao, 2005). These systems were focused on decision-making (Gupta, 2000) and aimed to replicate the decision-making abilities of experienced human experts. Accordingly, three stages of technology were introduced; rule-based systems, case-based reasoning systems, and machine learning systems (Cao e al., 2021). These systems were strong in terms of analyzing and reasoning which led to accurate decision making. Newell (1982) replaced these expert systems by the term knowledge-based systems, as it was considered a "black-box" system with varied functions. Furthermore, another argument related to the AI-decision making process included the competent and incompetent method. Dreyfus and Dreyfus (2005) elaborated that human decision making processes include a quick and intuitive approach while Artificial intelligence formulated the decision by slowed and reasoned; thus, making AI as the most effective and competent decision maker.

Therefore, multiple theories have been further proposed to determine the effectiveness, accuracy, acceptance, consequence, and limitations of Artificial intelligence; these theoretical frameworks include Theory of Planned Behavior (Ajzen, 1985), Technology Acceptance Model (Davis, 1989), Innovation Diffusion Theory (Rogers, 1958), Theory of Acceptance & Use of Technology (Venkatesh et al., 2003), and Extended UTAUT-2 (Venkatesh et al., 2016), Threat Avoidance Theory (Liang & Xue, 2010). Although these theories have generalized multiple aspects of Artificial intelligence; nevertheless, minimal resistance and ignorance is observed in all the fields of finance with the increased development in Artificial intelligence.

Accordingly, Artificial Neural Network models (ANN) is inspired by the functioning of the Human Brain; it also contains elements for establishing links which create advanced algorithms. With reference to financial decisions, ANN models analyze the complex financial data set and formulate predictions. Irrespective of identifying, recognizing, and classifying Financial data, these networks include feedback to analyze risk and further modify the decisions and approaches. ANNs contain three artificial nodes organized into layers; Input, hidden, and output layers (Leke and Marwala, 2019). Input layers receive financial data i.e. market variables, economic indicators. Hidden layers process the series of data to examine connection and transformations. While the output layer produces the predictions and classification of the examined indicators and variables. It can be utilized for various functions including forecasting stock market, credit-risk assessment, portfolio optimization, and fraud detection.

Neuroplasticity Theory refers to the brain ability to adapt, formulate, and function with respect to different conditions, situations, learning, and environmental influences. Thus, neuroplasticity theory suggests that machine learning algorithms are designed to learn and adapt from financial data and experiences. Analogous with the human brain that continuously improves decisions based on neural connection and experiences; as a result, AI algorithms can be programmed to continuously learn and modify systems contingent on the new financial information. Owing to Neuroplasticity, systems develop and modify financial skills, knowledge, and decision-making indicators. Adaptability allows systems to adjust their financial strategies based on new information or changing circumstances. Moreover, it can control and manage risk preferences and aversions to losses.

2.2 A Brief Overview of AI in the Financial Decision Making

Reviewed literature has accentuated various dimensions with respect to Artificial intelligence and Finance. Additionally, several studies have accentuated the escalating role of AI in economics and finance together with the substantial influence of Artificial Intelligence on decision-making. However, no study has emphasized the association between Artificial Intelligence and the Future of Financial Decision-Making. Therefore, this conceptual review is an essential attempt to eliminate the existing gap in the pertinent literature. Artificial intelligence and Financial decision making are two major domains that are crucial yet dissimilar from one another. Accordingly, McCarthy introduced the term Artificial intelligence (AI) in 1956, referring to it as intelligent machines. It accentuated and studied the design of intelligent agents that were vigilant for noticing the environment and taking actions accordingly. While decision making refers to the challenges and opportunities an individual encounter by examining available options and making vigilant decisions related to the organizations or firms (Amoako et al., 2021). Decision making process includes a few prerequisite steps that includes identification of challenges, data collection, forming options, and judging course of action (Amoaka et al., 2021). Similarly, Hellriegel et al. (2005) affirmed that ambiguity and doubt while making decisions can be conveniently solved by authentic information in order to make well informed and realistic decisions.

Financial decision making is considered as the most substantial process. Accordingly, Davidsson and Klofsten (2003) ascertain financial decision making as a means to ensure that profitable, effective, and best decisions are executed. The findings affirm better comprehension and understanding provide the ground for creating and exploiting better business opportunities. Multiple areas that also required effective decision making are identification of business, creating opportunities, refining market standards, acquiring resources, generating ideas, addressing technical challenges, etc (Astebro and Tag, 2017). In addition, Reuber and Fisherman (1997) established that these areas require complex and critical reasoning to formulate any decision; as these factors have long term consequences on the business performance and achievement. Therefore, entrepreneurs should enhance their decision making process to emphasize value for society and incorporate sustainability concerns that considerably affect the consumers and business; these processes also ensure inclusion of Artificial intelligence in the finance industry.

Similarly, Syam and Sharma (2018) suggest that decisions programmed by machines require Artificial intelligence. Few studies have documented the evolution and challenges in the era of big data (Duan et al., 2019) while others have studied the trends and future of AI in the field of business and finance (Ruiz-Real et al., 2021). In addition, Kitsios and Kamariotou (2021) conducted a systematic review by analyzing artificial intelligence and corporate strategy. The findings developed a model addressing the previous challenges encountered due to the adoption of AI and the corporate sector. Theory addresses digital transformation of AI in the finance sector and accentuated four crucial aspects: inclusion of AI and ML in organization, connectivity between AI tools with corporate strategy, knowledge management and decision-making process, and innovation and significance.

Correspondingly, the decision making process became more digitized with the modernization of intelligent technology. Cao et al. (2021) analyzed managers' understanding and attitude towards the role of artificial intelligence for organizational decision making. The outcomes validate the AI acceptance avoidance model (IAAAM) model justifies the positive and negative attitudes of managers towards the role of AI in decision making. Another conceptual review investigates the correlation among the ability of AI to make better entrepreneurial decisions (Amoako et al., 2021). Findings indicate AI better facilitates the decision making process. Moreover, findings validate that the contribution of employees and stakeholders mediates the association between AI and Decision making. Similarly, Albaek et al. (2022) examine the different ways AI assists in financial decision making.

Huang and You (2022) evaluate the applications of AI, AI algorithms for unstructured data, and the role of AI to explore structure and unstructured data for the financial decision making process. Moreover, study also ascertains the partnership of AI and humans to assist the financial decision making in several areas like investments and lending. Chen et al. (2022) investigate the adoption of Artificial intelligence in business-marketing; outcomes suggest seven key areas of business marketing that are proficiently targeted by AI which includes efficient and accurate improvement, effective decision making, enhanced customer relationship, increased sales, decreased risk, and cost reductions, respectively.

Furthermore, another study analyzed the Multi-Criterion Decision-Making (MCDM) approach in finance by utilizing artificial intelligence (Cerneviciene & Kabašinskas, 2021). This study underlines the dire need of explainability in the practical application of AI in different areas of business and finance in order to enhance interpretability and accuracy to make more effective decisions. Accordingly, decision making is a complex task that requires an integrated approach to manage different functions i.e. programming, complex statistical modeling, risk management, advance algorithm, and project planning. Nevertheless, MCDM makes these programs more manageable by dividing it into three categories; identification of problems, stipulating recommendations, and technical support. Therefore, this conceptual review is an attempt to address the explainability gap related to the efficiency of Artificial intelligence with reference to future financial decision-making.

3. METHODOLOGY

This section includes the selection and exclusion criteria of the conceptual papers. All the subject area, key words, and document type are listed below. The selection of database includes 52 articles based on the subject areas and relevant keywords of the current conceptual paper.

Figure 1. Conceptual review

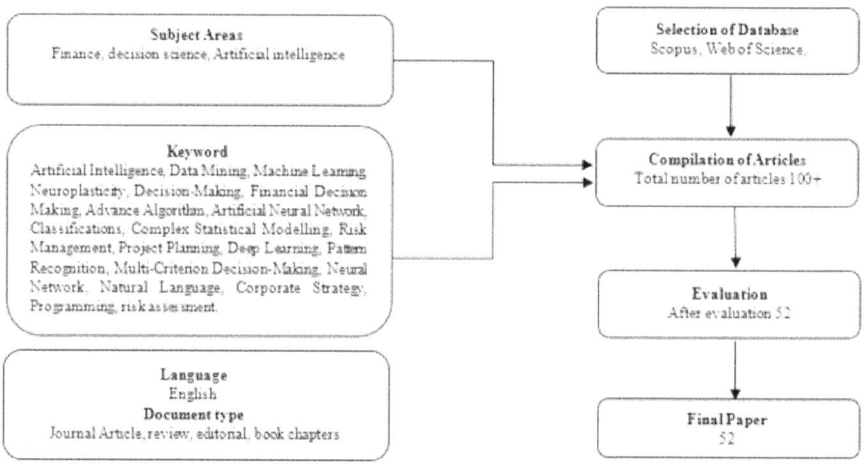

4. DISCUSSION

Artificial intelligence performs a substantial role in the finance industry; especially in the decision making sector. Nevertheless, the increasing demand of AI has caused a dire need for AI to handle advanced functions of decision making in various domains. Accordingly, AI algorithms, machine learning, and advanced technologies can be integrated to augment and assist efficiency, accuracy, and automation in the different areas of financial decision-making. Therefore, Artificial intelligence will perform a crucial role in the future of decision making with reference to data analysis and insights, risk assessment, automation and efficiency, trading and investment, personalized financial services, fraud detection and security, compliance and regulatory adherence, collaboration of AI-decisions and Human decisions.

4.1 Data Analysis and Insights

AI can interpret and analyze vast dataset; thus, in future AI will be able to examine structure and unstructured data more efficiently for various sources including text, images, videos, audios etc. AI algorithms excel at Pattern recognition and anomaly detection in large datasets. Thus, AI can reveal correlations and trends via machine learning that would otherwise be impossible to detect for humans (Brynjolfsson & McAfee, 2017). Pattern recognition will be crucial for fraud detection, predictive maintenance, and quality control. Secondly, AI will be able to efficiently predict and forecast by statistically examining historical data and identifying patterns to determine future outcomes (Kar & Kushwaha, 2021). Owing to feedback processing, AI can generate accurate predictions and forecasts for finance, sales, marketing, and supply chain management.

The third element of data analysis is Natural Language Processing (NLP) that assist AI to interpret and extract the data from human language, such as customer reviews, survey responses, recommendations, social media posts, news, and articles (García-Méndez et al., 2022; Fisher et al., 2016). Hence, AI text analysis provides insights regarding customer's opinion, responses, market trends by evaluating modeling, sentiment analysis, and summarization (Zaremba & Demire, 2023). Moreover, it provides automated data visualization to represent the meaningful datasets by identifying complex patterns, trends, development, etc. Lastly, AI will also enhance cognitive insights and will direct the human decision making process. Thus, AI will significantly assist decision makers to explore and evaluate complex patterns, alternative options, various circumstances, and simulate outcomes for more informed and data driven decisions.

4.2 Risk Assessment

AI can investigate large financial data sets that include transaction records, and economic indicators. It can better identify various types of risk such as market risk, credit risk, operational risk, and liquidity risk. In addition, AI detects fraudulent activities by thoroughly examining fraud detection and proposing possible prevention techniques. Anomaly detection algorithms assist in identifying suspicious patterns or trends that may cause apprehensive transactions, unauthorized access, or account hacking (Bao et al., 2022). AI will help financial institutions to mitigate the risk and minimize the loss via monetization of potential risk and fraudulent activities. Secondly, AI will augment credit scoring and underwriting. Previously, traditional scoring methods included a limited set of factors, such as credit history and income while we will be able to incorporate a broad range of data points and alternative data sources with the help of AI-credit scoring (Dhaigude & Lawande,

2022). Accordingly, analysis of social media activity, utility bill payments, online behavior, and credit enable financiers to make informed decisions related to the credit and manage default risk (Golden, 2016).

In addition, Stress testing and situation analysis is another feature of risk management that simulates different scenarios and conducts stress testing with the help of AI in order to inspect the resilience of financial portfolios or institutions. Moreover, Algorithms can evaluate adverse market conditions, risk factors, economic downturns, that will help decision-makers to comprehend potential vulnerable factors (Modgil et al., 2021). Moreover, AI will further assist in Regulatory compliance and risk management to ensure compliance with regulatory requirements. AI systems will ascertain potential compliance issues and implement measures to regulate standards. AI-powered risk management solutions will also help to identify and mitigate risks associated with non-compliance; hence, enabling better governance and risk control.

4.3 Automation and Efficiency

Artificial Intelligence can also process robotic process automation. Organizations may optimize workflows and minimize manual labor by using AI-powered bots to automate routine, rule-based tasks (McKinsey & Company, 2017). Robotic Process Automation (RPA) can perform data entry, data extraction, report production, and other mundane processes by simulating human interactions with software systems, freeing up workers to concentrate on more strategic and complicated duties. Secondly, AI offers intelligent document processing to automate the extraction, classification, and analysis of information from unstructured documents such as invoices, contracts, and forms (Yarlagadda, 2018). Techniques like Optical Character Recognition (OCR) and Natural Language Processing (NLP) help in validating information, automated processes, data extraction, improved efficiency, etc. Moreover, AI has introduced multiple Intelligent Chatbots and Virtual Assistants that can perform automated tasks with or without human intervention (Battina, 2018); For example, including self-driving vehicles, smart factories, and autonomous robots. Additionally, ML and NLP can provide personalized responses, automated tasks, etc. similarly, AI algorithms can process optimization and allocate resources by data analysis, identification, feedback, and improvements. Machine learning algorithms will assist in reducing cost, allocating resources, improving operation flow, etc.

4.4 Trading and Investment

Advanced machine learning algorithms can substantially contribute towards trading and investment strategies (Trippi & Turban, 1992). These AI driven trading systems will contribute to the monetization of swift trading and capitalized market opportunities. Artificial intelligence (AI) performs a transformative role in trading and investment across financial markets (Waisi, 2020). Therefore, AI will efficiently analyze data, trading volumes, patterns and correlation with the help of data analysis and pattern recognition that will be difficult for human traders to detect. Secondly, AI systems will effectively contribute towards predictive analysis and forecasting the movements, trends, and asset prices to assist traders to make informed decisions. Additionally, AI will excel in algorithm trading that will determine predefined rules and parameters for rapid execution of trades and ensuring increased opportunities. AI-driven trading techniques will also respond quickly to shifting market conditions, minimizing the influence of human emotions on trading choices (D'Hondt, 2020).

Similarly, sentiment analysis will allow traders to acquire information related to different commodities, stocks, resources, currencies and others to adjust their strategies accordingly. Moreover, Artificial Intelligence will allow trading execution and order routing via thoroughly analyzing market liquidity, order book depth, and transaction costs. Routing systems will also help in navigation of packages, tracking the order depth, splitting or combining large or small orders; all these practices will contribute to the stable market conditions and better prices. Therefore, advanced contributions of AI have significantly transformed the dynamic and decision making of trading and investment strategies via data analysis, predictive analytics, algorithmic trading, sentiment analysis, portfolio optimization (Waisi, 2020). Irrespective of the remarkable contribution of AI in the trade and investment strategies, human expertise and brain is necessary to comprehend the insights and judgements generated by AI.

4.5 Personalized Financial Services

Personalization in financial services includes transformation of customer's interactions with firms via data and analytics to anticipate needs and build deeper relationships with the customers. Artificial intelligence will also excel in the Personalization and recommendation systems; it will provide more personalized recommendations by investigating behavior, patterns, trends, preferences, and structure and unstructured data. AI can enhance individual experience by examining individual profiles to provide relevant services and products (Manser Payne, 2021). Initially, AI will provide Data-driven personalization services for all customers. AI-data analytics will process data related to transactional history, investing behavior, risk management, expenditure and consumption, etc. These practices will enable AI to generate customer profiles to offer individuals with customized recommendations (Hentzen, 2022). Accordingly, machine learning will suggest personalized financial products and services to customers by comprehending customer preference, risk tolerance, and financial objectives.

AI-driven robo-advisors will examine financial data and risk profile by offering automated investment management services (Shanmuganathan, 2020); AI will create customized investment portfolios consistent with customer's goals to offer wealth management and investment advice. These services will be cost-effective, diversified, and tailored investment solutions to a broader range of customers. Moreover, AI will help individuals to create personalized budgets, set financial goals, and track progress by integrating data from financial accounts and transactions; these tools will provide actual insights into spending patterns that will help users to make informed decisions regarding their financial objectives (Mogaji, 2020). Furthermore, the feedback feature of AI and its systems continuously learn from customer interactions and feedback, improving their ability to deliver more accurate and relevant personalized financial services over time. Therefore, AI will enable personalized financial services for financial institutions to provide customers with specialized and effective solutions. AI will further revolutionize financial services by incorporating data-driven insights with automated procedures in order to increase client satisfaction, engagement, and with better personal financial management.

4.6 Fraud Detection and Security

Artificial intelligence also offers fraud detection and security services to the customers and users to assist the process of financial decision making. Irrespective of providing multiple financial services and decision making in the core areas, AI provides fraud detection services and security for the users (Bao et al., 2022). Firstly, AI constantly monitors vast financial data and track record, behaviors, patterns. Moreover, AI can identify potential threat fraudulent activities in case of Anomaly detection. In future, these services will enable users to either prompt further investigation or allow AI to make informed decisions. Therefore, AI will be more competent in future and make more informed and technically sound decisions. For instance, real-time monitoring of financial transactions and activities will be made possible by AI. AI systems will immediately detect and react to suspect behaviors by evaluating data, reducing potential impact of fraud, prohibiting fraudulent activities, and stopping unauthorized transactions.

Additionally, AI will further develop fraud prevention models to provide sound services and analyze fraud data more competently (Hasan & Rizvi, 2022). These fraud detection models will enable AI to direct customers or users to analyze the data, patterns and activities to prevent loss and make their decisions based on AI. Moreover, behavioral biometrics will be easily examined by AI: as it will analyze user behavior, such as typing patterns, mouse movements, and navigation habits, to create unique behavioral biometric profiles. These behavioral profiles will provide a gateway to biometric authentication systems that will verify customers credential via facial, voice, and fingerprint recognition.

Therefore, AI and its different components will evolve further and incorporate more stimulating and advanced algorithms in the domain of financial decision making. These algorithms will help users to make decisions by offering relevant recommendations, suggestions, and analysis.

5. CONCLUSION

Globally, the role of AI is essential in determining The purpose of this conceptual paper is to evaluate the role of AI in the future of financial decision making. Findings of the review conclude that the role of artificial intelligence in financial decision-making is undeniably substantial and transformative. The increasing demand for AI-driven solutions has led to advancements in data analysis, risk assessment, automation, trading, personalized financial services, fraud detection, and security. AI's ability to process vast amounts of data, recognize patterns, and make predictions has empowered decision-makers with data-driven insights and more informed choices. AI-driven algorithms have revolutionized trading strategies, portfolio optimization, and risk management, leading to improved efficiency and accuracy in financial operations. AI-Personalized financial services offer tailored recommendations and solutions to customers, enhancing their overall experience. However, it is essential to acknowledge that while AI brings numerous benefits, it also raises critical ethical and regulatory considerations. Hence, striking a balance between AI-driven decisions and human oversight remains crucial to ensure responsible and sustainable implementation in the finance industry. Therefore, continuous and consistent revolutionization of AI will be imperative to address these challenges proactively to maximize the positive impact of AI on financial decision-making while minimizing potential risks.

REFERENCES

Agarwal, A., Singhal, C., & Thomas, R. (2021). *AI-powered Decision Making for the Bank of the Future. McKinsey Global Banking & Securities.* March. https://www.mckinsey.com/industries/financial-services/our-insights/ai-powered-decision-making-for-the-bank-of-the-future

Ajzen, I. (1985). From intentions to actions: A theory of planned behavior. In Kuhl, J., & Beckman, J. (Eds.), *Action-control: From cognition to behavior* (pp. 11–39). Springer. DOI: 10.1007/978-3-642-69746-3_2

Bag, S., Gupta, S., Kumar, A., & Sivarajah, U. (2021). An integrated artificial intelligence framework for knowledge creation and B2B marketing rational decision making for improving firm performance. *Industrial Marketing Management, 92*, 178–189. DOI: 10.1016/j.indmarman.2020.12.001

Bao, Y., Hilary, G., & Ke, B. (2022). Artificial intelligence and fraud detection. *Innovative Technology at the Interface of Finance and Operations, 1*, 223–247. DOI: 10.1007/978-3-030-75729-8_8

Battina, D. S. (2018). The future of artificial intelligence at work: A review on effects of decision automation and augmentation on workers targeted by algorithms and third-party observers. *International Journal of Innovations in Engineering Research and Technology, 5*(7).

Brock, J. K. U., & Von Wangenheim, F. (2019). Demystifying AI: What digital transformation leaders can teach you about realistic artificial intelligence. *California Management Review, 61*(4), 110–134. DOI: 10.1177/1536504219865226

Brynjolfsson, E., & McAfee, A. (2017). The business of artificial intelligence. *Harvard Business Review*, •••, 1–20.

Chen, L., Jiang, M., Jia, F., & Liu, G. (2022). Artificial intelligence adoption in business-to-business marketing: Toward a conceptual framework. *Journal of Business and Industrial Marketing, 37*(5), 1025–1044. DOI: 10.1108/JBIM-09-2020-0448

D'Hondt, C., De Winne, R., Ghysels, E., & Raymond, S. (2020). Artificial Intelligence Alter Egos: Who might benefit from robo-investing? *Journal of Empirical Finance, 59*, 278–299. DOI: 10.1016/j.jempfin.2020.10.002

Davis, F. D. (1989). Perceived usefulness, perceived ease of use, and user acceptance of information technology. *Management Information Systems Quarterly, 13*(3), 319–340. DOI: 10.2307/249008

Dhaigude, R., & Lawande, N. (2022). Impact of Artificial Intelligence on Credit Scores in Lending Process. In *2022 Interdisciplinary Research in Technology and Management (IRTM)* (pp. 1-5). IEEE. DOI: 10.1109/IRTM54583.2022.9791511

Dreyfus, H. L., & Dreyfus, S. E. (2005). Peripheral vision: Expertise in real world contexts. *Organization Studies, 26*(5), 779–792. DOI: 10.1177/0170840605053102

Fisher, I. E., Garnsey, M. R., & Hughes, M. E. (2016). Natural language processing in accounting, auditing and finance: A synthesis of the literature with a roadmap for future research. *Intelligent Systems in Accounting, Finance & Management, 23*(3), 157–214. DOI: 10.1002/isaf.1386

García-Méndez, S., de Arriba-Pérez, F., Barros-Vila, A., & González-Castaño, F. J. (2022). Detection of temporality at discourse level on financial news by combining Natural Language Processing and Machine Learning. *Expert Systems with Applications, 197*, 116648. DOI: 10.1016/j.eswa.2022.116648

Golden, L. L., Brockett, P. L., Ai, J., & Kellison, B. (2016). Empirical evidence on the use of credit scoring for predicting insurance losses with psycho-social and biochemical explanations. *North American Actuarial Journal : NAAJ, 20*(3), 233–251. DOI: 10.1080/10920277.2016.1209118

Goodell, J. W., Kumar, S., Lim, W. M., & Pattnaik, D. (2021). Artificial intelligence and machine learning in finance: Identifying foundations, themes, and research clusters from bibliometric analysis. *Journal of Behavioral and Experimental Finance, 32*, 100577. DOI: 10.1016/j.jbef.2021.100577

Gupta, M. (2000). Implications of expert systems for the operations of financial institutions. *Technovation, 20*(9), 509–516. DOI: 10.1016/S0166-4972(99)00165-0

Hasan, I., & Rizvi, S. A. M. (2022). AI-driven fraud detection and mitigation in e-commerce transactions. [Springer Singapore.]. *Proceedings of Data Analytics and Management: ICDAM, 2021*(1), 403–414. DOI: 10.1007/978-981-16-6289-8_34

Hentzen, J. K., Hoffmann, A., Dolan, R., & Pala, E. (2022). Artificial intelligence in customer-facing financial services: A systematic literature review and agenda for future research. *International Journal of Bank Marketing, 40*(6), 1299–1336. DOI: 10.1108/IJBM-09-2021-0417

Hilal, W., Gadsden, S. A., & Yawney, J. (2022). Financial fraud: A review of anomaly detection techniques and recent advances. *Expert Systems with Applications, 193*, 116429. DOI: 10.1016/j.eswa.2021.116429

Huang, A., & You, H. (2022). Artificial Intelligence in Financial Decision Making. *Handbook of Financial Decision Making, Forthcoming.*

Kaplan, A., & Haenlein, M. (2019). Siri, Siri, in my hand: Who's the fairest in the land? On the interpretations, illustrations, and implications of artificial intelligence. *Business Horizons*, *62*(1), 15–25. DOI: 10.1016/j.bushor.2018.08.004

Kar, A. K., & Kushwaha, A. K. (2021). Facilitators and barriers of artificial intelligence adoption in business–insights from opinions using big data analytics. *Information Systems Frontiers*, •••, 1–24.

Kitsios, F., & Kamariotou, M. (2021). Artificial intelligence and business strategy towards digital transformation: A research agenda. *Sustainability (Basel)*, *13*(4), 2025. DOI: 10.3390/su13042025

Krollner, B., Vanstone, B. J., & Finnie, G. R. (2010, April). Financial time series forecasting with machine learning techniques: a survey. In *ESANN*.

Kumar, A., Sharma, S., & Mahdavi, M. (2021). Machine learning (ML) technologies for digital credit scoring in rural finance: A literature review. *Risks*, *9*(11), 192. DOI: 10.3390/risks9110192

Kumar, D., Singh, R. K., Mishra, R., & Vlachos, I. (2023). Big data analytics in supply chain decarbonisation: A systematic literature review and future research directions. *International Journal of Production Research*, •••, 1–21.

Kushwaha, A. K., Kumar, P., & Kar, A. K. (2021). What impacts customer experience for B2B enterprises on using AI-enabled chatbots? Insights from Big data analytics. *Industrial Marketing Management*, *98*, 207–221. DOI: 10.1016/j.indmarman.2021.08.011

Leke, C. A., & Marwala, T. (2019). *Deep learning and missing data in engineering systems*. Springer International Publishing. DOI: 10.1007/978-3-030-01180-2

Liang, H., & Xue, Y. L. (2010). Understanding security behaviors in personal computer usage: A threat avoidance perspective. *Journal of the Association for Information Systems*, *11*(7), 1. DOI: 10.17705/1jais.00232

Liao, S. H. (2005). Technology management methodologies and applications: A literature review from 1995 to 2003. *Technovation*, *25*(4), 381–393. DOI: 10.1016/j.technovation.2003.08.002

Malali, A. B., & Gopalakrishnan, S. (2020). Application of artificial intelligence and its powered technologies in the indian banking and financial industry: An overview. *IOSR Journal Of Humanities And Social Science*, *25*(4), 55–60.

Manser Payne, E. H., Dahl, A. J., & Peltier, J. (2021). Digital servitization value co-creation framework for AI services: A research agenda for digital transformation in financial service ecosystems. *Journal of Research in Interactive Marketing, 15*(2), 200–222. DOI: 10.1108/JRIM-12-2020-0252

Modgil, S., Gupta, S., Stekelorum, R., & Laguir, I. (2021). AI technologies and their impact on supply chain resilience during COVID-19. *International Journal of Physical Distribution & Logistics Management, 52*(2), 130–149. DOI: 10.1108/IJPDLM-12-2020-0434

Mogaji, E., Soetan, T. O., & Kieu, T. A. (2020). The implications of artificial intelligence on the digital marketing of financial services to vulnerable customers. *Australasian Marketing Journal*, j-ausmj.

Mushafiq, M. (2021). Industry-level analysis of COVID-19's impact in emerging markets–evidence from Pakistan. *International Journal of Emerging Markets*, (ahead-of-print).

Mushafiq M, Sindhu M, Sohail M (2021) Financial performance under influence of credit risk in nonfinancial firms: evidence from Pakistan. J Econ Admin Sci 1026–4116

Newell, A. (1982). The knowledge level. *Artificial Intelligence, 18*(1), 87–127. DOI: 10.1016/0004-3702(82)90012-1

Njegovanović, A. (2018). Digital financial decision with a view of neuroplasticity/neurofinancy/neural networks.

Pomerol, J. C. (1997). Artificial intelligence and human decision making. *European Journal of Operational Research, 99*(116), 3–25. DOI: 10.1016/S0377-2217(96)00378-5

Ren, J. (2021). Research on financial investment decision based on artificial intelligence algorithm. *IEEE Sensors Journal, 21*(22), 25190–25197. DOI: 10.1109/JSEN.2021.3104038

Rodgers, W., Murray, J. M., Stefanidis, A., Degbey, W. Y., & Tarba, S. Y. (2023). An artificial intelligence algorithmic approach to ethical decision-making in human resource management processes. *Human Resource Management Review, 33*(1), 100925. DOI: 10.1016/j.hrmr.2022.100925

Rogers, E. M. (1995). *Diffusion of innovations* (4th ed.). New York Free Press.

Ruiz-Real, J. L., Uribe-Toril, J., Torres, J. A., & De Pablo, J. (2021). Artificial intelligence in business and economics research: Trends and future. *Journal of Business Economics and Management, 22*(1), 98–117. DOI: 10.3846/jbem.2020.13641

Shanmuganathan, M. (2020). Behavioural finance in an era of artificial intelligence: Longitudinal case study of robo-advisors in investment decisions. *Journal of Behavioral and Experimental Finance, 27*, 100297. DOI: 10.1016/j.jbef.2020.100297

Simon, H. A. (1947), Administrative Behavior, The Macmillan Company, New York, NY (2nd ed. published in 1957).

Trippi, R. R., & Turban, E. (Eds.). (1992). *Neural networks in finance and investing: Using artificial intelligence to improve real world performance*. McGraw-Hill, Inc.

Venkatesh, V., Morris, M. G., Davis, G. B., & Davis, F. D. (2003). User acceptance of information technology: Toward a unified view. *Management Information Systems Quarterly, 27*(3), 425–478. DOI: 10.2307/30036540

Venkatesh, V., Thong, J. Y., & Xu, X. (2016). Unified theory of acceptance and use of technology: A synthesis and the road ahead. *Journal of the Association for Information Systems, 17*(5), 328–376. DOI: 10.17705/1jais.00428

Waisi, M. (2020). Advantages and disadvantages of aI-based trading and investing versus traditional methods.

Xiao, F., & Ke, J. (2021). Pricing, management and decision-making of financial markets with artificial intelligence: Introduction to the issue. *Financial Innovation, 7*(1), 1–3. DOI: 10.1186/s40854-021-00302-9 PMID: 35024295

Yarlagadda, R. T. (2018). The RPA and AI automation. *International Journal of Creative Research Thoughts (IJCRT), ISSN*, 2320-2882.

Zaremba, A., & Demir, E. (2023). ChatGPT: Unlocking the future of NLP in finance. *Available atSSRN* 4323643.

Chapter 9
The Future of Personal Finance:
Artificial Intelligence, Machine Learning, and Big Data

Komal Akram Akram Khan
Iqra University, Pakistan

ABSTRACT

The rise of Artificial Intelligence, Machine Learning, and Big Data has resulted in a revolutionary shift in personal finance. The technologies leading this revolution have the potential to redefine financial strategies, bringing about a new era of accurate decision-making and well-informed decisions. Amid an ever-expanding landscape of data generation and consumption, individuals increasingly seek innovative methods to efficiently manage their finances. These technologies have emerged as powerful tools, providing exceptional capabilities for data forecasting, analysis, and decision-making. The primary emphasis of the paper is to comprehend how these technologies are set to revolutionize personal finance by allowing individuals to make more informed financial decisions, optimize investments, and diminish risks. It adds to the academic literature by synthesizing existing knowledge and provides individuals with helpful recommendations on finances using these technologies. Financial institutions can learn how to enhance customer experiences, streamline operations, and improve security.

DOI: 10.4018/979-8-3693-7160-2.ch009

1. INTRODUCTION

Personal finance involves managing an individual's or a household's financial resources to achieve specific financial objectives and maintain financial stability. This includes various aspects such as budgeting, saving, investing, and making wise financial decisions, covering all facets of an individual's financial life, including earning and spending money, as well as planning for retirement and managing debt (Garman & Forgue, 2014). However, personal finance demands critical skills and knowledge to handle financial resources responsibly. Traditionally, consumers lack ample knowledge about financial concepts and resources necessary to make decisions that are best for their financial well-being (Hwang & Park, 2023). In recent research, Xiao and Porto (2022) asserted that consumer financial choices have an impact on a person's or family's current financial well-being and capacity to save for long-term objectives like home ownership, pursuing higher education, or funding retirement (Xiao & Porto, 2022). Additionally, as seen by the economic crisis series, consumer actions significantly impact the nation's overall economic health (Hira, 2009). Therefore, personal finance is the area where ample financial literacy and innovative methods are required to ensure well-being.

Before the growth of the internet and digital technology, personal finance management mainly depended on manual processes and physical interactions. People used to record financial transactions by hand, conducted paper-based transactions, and managed finances through direct, face-to-face dealings with banks and financial institutions (Zhu et al., 2016). For example, before the advent of digital tools and apps, individuals tracked their earnings, expenses, and account balances using physical ledgers, checkbooks, and paper statements. Moreover, access to financial news, interest rates, and stock prices was limited to specific platforms, leaving investors with less real-time information (Wen et al., 2023). Investment options, tax management, transactions, statements, and banking affairs also required labor-intensive manual processes that demanded in-person efforts.

However, in an era of constant technological advancements, personal finance is experiencing a fundamental shift (Prete, 2022). Today, the future of personal finance is closely linked to Artificial Intelligence (AI), Machine Learning, and Big Data. AI assists automated decision-making and personalized financial insights by simulating human cognitive functions. On the other hand, machine learning boosts predictive analytics by identifying complex patterns and continuously improving financial forecasting models. Simultaneously, big data permits the processing and analysis of vast and diverse financial datasets that ultimately elevates risk assessment, fraud detection, and customer-centric financial strategies. Financial management has been transformed by integrating these technologies as they have enhanced efficiency, accessibility, and accuracy, thereby reshaping the landscape of modern finance.

As AI, Machine Learning, and Big Data continue to evolve, their integration into personal finance holds the promise of revolutionizing how individuals manage, invest, and secure their financial resources (Singh et al., 2022). Financial planning become less laborious and time-consuming compared to traditional practices. According to Ugwuanyi et al. (2022), traditionally, personal finances included much manual work and were prone to human error. In addition to this, the understanding that one may get through financial planning was limited. In contrast, Nguyen et al. (2023) stressed that the convergence of these cutting-edge technologies has ushered in an era where financial decision-making is becoming more accurate, personalized, and adaptive. One of the main reasons for the emergence of personal finance is the potential of AI and machine learning algorithms to process vast amounts of financial data with unprecedented speed and accuracy (Mer & Virdi, 2025). The authors further claimed that these technologies are proficient in analyzing market behavior, assessing potential risks, and providing investment recommendations. Thus, these practices enable individuals to make informed financial decisions, promptly respond to evolving circumstances, and take advantage of potential opportunities. AI systems have the remarkable ability to adapt and enhance their performance frequently (Krichen & Abdalzaher, 2024). These technologies go beyond just investment and asset management; they are on the cusp of transforming everyday financial decisions for individuals. Whether it's optimizing household budgets, managing debt more effectively, or offering personalized financial guidance, these technologies are poised to become essential tools for individuals striving to reach their sustainable financial goals (Kumar et al., 2022).

1.1 Research Purposes

The primary purpose of this discussion-based conceptual paper is to shed light on how the dynamic trio of AI, Machine Learning, and Big Data transforms the landscape of personal finance. Furthermore, it aims to provide valuable practical insights and considerations for individuals, financial institutions, and policymakers for making well-informed decisions and developing effective strategies in the current era of AI, Machine Learning, and Big Data. Another motivation of the paper is to promote forward-thinking and adaptability among stakeholders. The goal is to enable them to harness the full potential of these technologies for better financial well-being while dealing with potential challenges and ethical concerns in an open and reflective manner.

1.2 Research Gap and Research Contributions

In recent years, artificial intelligence, machine learning, and big data have gained significant attention in the realm of financial systems. It has revolutionized decision-making processes in financial technology, corporate finance, and banking. The current literature extensively explored several aspects of these technologies such as their role in financial inclusion (Ozili, 2021), application of reinforcement learning and deep learning algorithms in big data-based decision-making in financial industries (Singh et al., 2022), and their influence on sustainable finance (Kumar et al., 2022a). Additionally, Mishra et al. (2024) explored the role of machine learning and artificial intelligence in banking and finance. Likewise, Mer and Virdi (2025) recently studied the exclusive impact of AI on personal and corporate finance. Nguyen et al. (2023) conducted a multidimensional descriptive investigation to elucidate how big data, machine learning, and artificial intelligence have been integrated into the financial technology sector over time.

Above mentioned studies offer valuable insights into the broader financial system but they primarily emphasize institutional and corporate finance, disregarding the role of AI, machine learning, and big data for personal financial management. The potential of these technologies to improve personal finance through automated financial planning, predictive analytics, and AI-driven decision support remains underexplored context. The literature lacks descriptive study that solely explains how these technologies can transform personal finance and how an individual gets benefits from these emerging technologies. Therefore, a comprehensive discussion on this topic is crucial to equip individuals, financial institutions, and policymakers with the knowledge needed to navigate the opportunities and challenges of AI, machine learning, and big data in personal finance effectively. In a nutshell, this chapter aims to fill the literary gap by investigating how artificial intelligence, machine learning, and big data can transform personal finance. It is designed to offer practical insights for individuals, financial institutions, and policymakers so that they can make well-informed decisions and develop financing strategies accordingly.

This conceptual paper has the potential to significantly contribute to the literature, society, and various stakeholders in the following ways. To begin with, it contributes to the academic literature by providing a comprehensive investigation regarding the emerging role of artificial intelligence, machine learning, and big data in shaping the future of personal finance. This comprehensive perspective will be valuable for academics and researchers, serving as a fundamental reference for future research in this field. Secondly, in an era where personal finance is increasingly driven by technology, this paper provides practical insights and recommendations for individuals. Readers will better understand how AI and machine learning can be leveraged to manage their finances more efficiently, make informed investment decisions, and enhance their financial security. Thirdly, financial institutions can benefit from the paper's insights into the potential applications of AI, machine learning, and big data. It highlights how these technologies can improve customer experiences, streamline operations, and enhance security. Financial institutions can adapt their services and strategies by understanding the evolving landscape to remain competitive and better serve their clients.

2. LITERATURE REVIEW

2.1 Scholarly Analysis

Reviewed literature has accentuated various dimensions concerning artificial intelligence and personal finance. Several studies have validated the intensifying role of AI in the finance and economic industry. AI has found significant utility in delivering diverse financial services, leveraging its application in this domain to exploit the emerging potential in recent times (Fernandez, 2019). In reality, the concurrent progressions have enabled the creation of multiple pragmatic implementations catering to different requirements within the financial services sector. These encompass the automation of assorted functions and the amplification of analytical capabilities. These yields escalated efficiency, heightened quality, enriched customer contentment, and diminished operational expenditures (Grigoroudis et al., 2013). According to Donepudi (2017), digitized banking services via AI can host a larger audience and achieve higher customer satisfaction.

Huang et al. (2019) established that AI will manage the future of the economy by performing all analytical and critical tasks. Similarly, Panos and Wilson (2020) highlighted the revolutionary performance of financial technology in the transformation of the service industry. For instance, Financial planning, financial well-being, and economic inequality have all been impacted by FinTech advancements, including mobile payments, robo-advising, app-based investing platforms, and online banking options (Frame et al., 2019). FinTech also improves an individual's financial capabilities. According to Aoun (2017), improved finance and technology literacy enable individuals to utilize AI more productively. Mogaji et al. (2021) examined AI's implication for financial services of vulnerable customers; outcomes elaborate key implications for developers and managers to introduce a holistic system to optimize customer experience and enhance engagement with financial services providers. The study also emphasizes the importance of human connection.

However, the field continually embraces and adjusts to emerging technological prospects (Gimpel et al., 2018; Zheng et al., 2019) encompassed under the term FinTech, denoting financial technology. Prior studies primarily explored the integration of AI within Finance (Cao, 2020; Zheng et al., 2019). Cao (2022) examined the obstacles encountered by financial enterprises and delivered a comprehensive panorama of remedies utilizing both traditional and contemporary AI methods in the realm of Finance and economics. Another study also evaluates AI and machine learning to determine the foundation, underlying themes, and functions concerning finance (Goodell et al., 2021).

Correspondingly, Königstorfer and Thalmann (2020) analyzed the applications of Artificial Intelligence in commercial banks and established digitization and improvements in data analytics are substantial for various industries. The results highlight several benefits of AI in commercial banks, such as reduced financial losses, faster payment processing, automated compliance, and improved customer service. Mogaji and Nguyen (2022) evaluate managers' understanding of challenges and problems encountered during incorporating AI into different financial services. Findings reveal managers encounter problems with AI adoption but are aware of the crucial role of AI in financial services, especially marketing. Another study by Sohangir et al. (2018) validated the substantial role of data analytics, deep learning, and machine learning in financial sentiment analysis.

Simultaneously, Ma and Luv (2019) utilized three typical test functions to analyze the accuracy of financial credit risk prediction in Internet financials via machine learning. Results exhibit the high prediction ability of machine learning regarding financial credit risk prediction. Dixon et al. (2020) evaluate different dimensions, contributions, and performance of machine learning in finance. Results highlight that machine learning contributes to computational analysis, risk assessment and management, algorithmic trading, fraud detection, customer service and personalization, portfolio management, sentiment analysis, and regulatory compliance. In addition, Kumar et al. (2022) validated that machine learning and deep learning algorithms can tackle traditional problems like customer analytics, financial services, forecasting, risk detection, recommendations, network-based solutions, etc. Moreover, application of machine learning assists in effortlessly acquiring, analyzing, and organizing vast data (Sawwalakhe et al., 2023)

Another study analyzed the present, past, and future of sustainable finance (Kumar et al., 2022). The systematic review highlights the high performance and intellectual structure of sustainable finance via big data analytics and machine learning. Additionally, Weber et al. (2023) provide a systematic review related to the application of artificial intelligence in finance; the review contains extensive studies related to the field of finance, information systems, and computer science. Kshetri (2016) highlighted the role of big data in expanding financial services in China. Findings reveal an adverse effect on financial institutions and commercial banks due to lack of information, trustworthiness, and ineffective services. Cockcroft and Russell (2018) investigated the opportunities and benefits of Big Data in the accounting and financing sectors. Outcomes revealed trust and reputation in customer service were significantly researched areas with reference to Big Data. In addition, Hasan et al. (2020) explore the landscape and impact of Big Data on Finance. Results established that AI, machine learning, and Big data encourage the finance industry to proceed toward digitization. Finally, Big data has modernized and transformed the finance industry while substantially structuring future research and applications in finance. However, no study has incorporated the future of personal finance with respect to AI, Machine Learning, And Big Data.

Accordingly, the future of personal finance is undeniably intertwined with AI, Machine Learning, and Big Data. The ongoing refinement of these technologies will likely result in even more accurate predictions, enhanced automation, and smarter financial management. While challenges persist, the potential for improving financial literacy, optimizing investments, and securing individual financial futures is vast. Individuals can navigate the evolving landscape of personal finance with greater confidence and empowerment by embracing these technologies thoughtfully and responsibly. Therefore, there is an urgent need to analyze various dimensions of Artificial Intelligence, Machine Learning, and Big Data to develop a comprehensive understanding of multiple aspects of personal financing. These advanced technologies reshape how individuals manage, optimize, and plan their financial lives. Thus, personal finance can provide unprecedented benefits and possibilities through the utilization of AI, Machine Learning, and Big Data analytics.

3. DISCUSSION

AI, machine learning, and big data are expected to have a big impact on personal finance in the future. Numerous advantages of these technologies enable better decision-making, better financial management, and more individualized financial services. As the scope of personal finance lies in the integration of technology with financial services, various applications can be endorsed in multiple fields.

For instance, making educated investment decisions and maximizing savings strategies requires using technology like AI and machine learning, which can more accurately foresee future market circumstances and financial trends (Bharadiya, 2023). Big Data analytics has the potential to examine news stories, financial reports, and social media to analyze market sentiment and give investors information on possible market movements (Lee, 2017). Financial institutes can utilize AI-enabled retirement planning. AI-enabled retirement planning solutions can employ machine learning to estimate a person's future financial requirements, which will help them better retirement plans. Moreover, Robo-Advisors are yet another powerful machine learning tool. Financial agencies are expected to use them to automate the creation and management of investment portfolios suited to a person's financial objectives, level of risk tolerance, and time horizon (Fisch et al., 2017). Similarly, specific functions relating to tax management in virtual applications can also be beneficial. Personalized features of AI can analyze a person's financial condition and offer tax-saving tips, such as recommending tax-advantaged investments or suggesting deductions and credits. This can become a game changer for individuals and firms for real-time suggestions and evaluations of tax strategies.

In general, companies in the personal finance industry use AI, machine learning, and big data to improve client experiences, improve financial products, manage risk, and run more smoothly. These technologies are essential in the modern financial landscape because they allow businesses to respond to shifting market dynamics and client expectations.

3.1 The Roles and Advantages of AI, Machine Learning, and Big Data in the Future of Personal Finance

Firstly, AI is poised to revolutionize personal finance by providing intelligent, automated solutions for financial management, planning, and decision-making (Shanmuganathan, 2020). Another research revealed that AI-driven financial tools can promptly evaluate vast amounts of data, enabling them to make real-time recommendations and predictions based on individual financial situations and goals (Hentzen et al., 2022). AI has the following advantages: (i) according to Mer and Virdi (2025), AI can offer highly personalized financial advice, considering an individual's income, expenses, savings goals, and risk tolerance. This personalization helps users make informed decisions tailored to their unique circumstances. (ii) A scholar highlighted that AI-powered chatbots and virtual financial advisors can efficiently manage routine financial tasks like bill payments, budget tracking, and investment management, releasing individuals from time-consuming tasks (Mori, 2021). (iii) Abu Jamie et al. (2024) revealed that AI algorithms continuously monitor financial markets. Thus, the third advantage is that it can identify investment opportunities and potential risks, enabling users to adjust their portfolios accordingly. (iv) AI reduces the risk of financial fraud (Hasan & Rizvi, 2022) by detecting unusual transactions or patterns. It implies that AI has the potential to enhance security significantly.

Furthermore, within the realm of personal finance, the utilization of machine learning can be observed across many facets, encompassing but not limited to investment strategies, credit risk evaluation, and identifying fraudulent activities (Bhatore et al., 2020; Balcıoğlu, 2024). The advantages of machine learning are various: (i) It assists in analyzing historical financial data to predict future market trends, helping investors make more informed decisions. (ii) It provides more accurate and fair credit scores by considering a wider range of data points, potentially expanding access to credit for individuals with limited credit histories (Kozodoi et al., 2022). (iii) Further, the scholars stated that machine learning can optimize investment portfolios by continuously adjusting asset allocations based on market conditions and individual goals, aiming for better returns and risk management (Al Janabi, 2024). (iv) It identifies patterns in spending behavior and provides recommendations for budgeting and saving, helping individuals meet their financial goals (Alam et al., 2022).

Thirdly, Big Data, characterized by collecting and analyzing vast and varied datasets, is integral to AI and Machine Learning applications in personal finance. According to Singh et al. (2022), it provides the raw material for these technologies to generate insights and make informed recommendations. Big data has numerous benefits concerning personal finance. For instance, (i) Financial institutions can analyze a client's financial history, risk tolerance, investment goals, and even their social and economic context through Big Data. This data includes vast activities of finance, from income and expenses to past investment decisions (Edu, 2022). (ii) Big Data continuously feeds information into AI and Machine Learning algorithms, allowing for real-time adjustments to investment portfolios. If a client's financial situation changes or market conditions shift, the portfolio can be adapted accordingly. (iii) Personal finance apps can leverage Big Data to provide tailored savings and budgeting recommendations. They can analyze spending patterns, income sources, and financial goals to suggest strategies for achieving them (Agarwal & Ann, 2024; Talasila, 2024). (iv) Further, it can assess and mitigate financial risks for individuals. For instance, it can identify potential vulnerabilities in a person's financial portfolio and suggest diversification strategies to reduce risk exposure. (v) Most importantly, it evaluates transaction data on a massive scale to identify unusual patterns indicative of fraudulent activity, thereby strengthening security.

3.2 Challenges and Solutions

The future of personal finance, driven by AI, Machine Learning, and Big Data, offers immense promise and innovation. However, it also presents various complex challenges that demand careful consideration. One of the foremost concerns is data privacy and security. The proliferation of AI-driven financial tools has increased the collection and processing of vast amounts of personal and financial data, giving rise to legitimate concerns about protecting this sensitive information (Al-Okaily et al., 2022). Further, Kajol et al. (2022) stated that to mitigate these concerns, it is imperative to establish robust data protection regulations and enforce strict cybersecurity measures to ensure the confidentiality and integrity of individuals' financial data.

According to Akter et al. (2022), algorithm bias and fairness represent another substantial challenge. The scholars further mentioned that AI and machine learning algorithms can inadvertently perpetuate biases present in historical data, resulting in unequal or discriminatory financial outcomes. To tackle this issue, continuous monitoring and auditing of algorithms, transparent decision-making processes, and ethical AI development practices are imperative to rectify biases and promote fairness.

Moreover, there is a significant challenge in the form of a lack of understanding and trust among the general public regarding utilizing AI and Big Data in personal finance. A substantial segment of individuals may not have a comprehensive grasp of how these technologies function, which can lead to mistrust or hesitancy in adopting them (Zarifis & Cheng, 2022). The solution to this challenge lies in investment by financial institutions and policymakers in educational initiatives and enhanced transparency to enhance public comprehension and trust in these tools (Goyal & Kumar, 2021).

Navigating evolving regulatory landscapes is also a prominent challenge. Financial institutions must continually adapt to comply with new regulations related to AI and Big Data (Himeur et al., (2023). To address this challenge effectively, it is essential to foster close collaboration between regulators, financial institutions, and technology companies to develop and maintain regulatory frameworks that balance innovation and consumer protection.

Another challenge is striking the right balance between human expertise and AI-driven financial tools (Sheth et al., 2022). In addition, as per the scholarly work of Zhai et al. (2023), overreliance on automation may lead to the neglect of human judgment, which remains crucial in critical financial decisions. Encouraging the use of AI as a tool to enhance rather than replace human decision-making, with human oversight and intervention retained, is essential.

Digital inclusion is a critical challenge, as not all individuals have equal access to technology and digital financial services (Jamil, 2021), potentially excluding them from the benefits of AI-driven finance. In a study, Li and Li (2022) suggested that policymakers and financial institutions must collaborate to improve digital infrastructure and promote financial inclusion to ensure that everyone can access and benefit from these technologies.

Finally, ethical considerations are also major challenges personal finance faces concerning AI, machine learning, and big data. Using these technologies in personal finance raises ethical questions concerning consent, data ownership, and responsible technology use (Rabbani et al., 2022). According to Nguyen et al. (2023), establishing clear ethical guidelines and promoting responsible practices is essential to prioritize the well-being of individuals in the financial ecosystem. Furthermore, addressing these multifaceted challenges is vital for harnessing the full potential of AI, machine learning, and Big Data in personal finance while upholding responsible and ethical use to benefit individuals and society.

4. CONCLUDING STATEMENT AND IMPLICATIONS

In conclusion, addressing the issues is essential for realizing the full potential of AI, Machine Learning, and Big Data in personal finance, notwithstanding the importance of their promises. This paper includes suggestions for individuals, financial institutions, and policymakers based on literary evidence and discussion.

First of all, for individuals, this paper suggests that individuals or customers must invest time in understanding how AI, machine learning, and big data are changing personal finance. Getting familiar with the tools and services available to manage finances is necessary. For instance, Mint, You Need a Budget (YNAB), Mobile Banking Apps, and Online Banking Services are emerging tools and services that can assist customers. Secondly, it is highly recommended to consider using robo-advisors and AI-driven financial apps to help with investment decisions and portfolio management. These tools can offer cost-effective and data-driven solutions. Thirdly, exercising caution is crucial when it comes to safeguarding personal financial data. Hence, all users should know financial institutions' privacy policies and applications and adopt necessary measures to safeguard sensitive financial information.

The paper includes the following implications for financial institutions. Based on the discussion, investing in cutting-edge technologies, i.e., AI, machine learning, and big data, is suggested to improve consumer experience, expedite operations, and provide unique financial products and services. In addition, we recommend that financial institutions safeguard transparency in AI-driven financial decisions and algorithms, as customers are highly concerned regarding privacy due to online fraudulent activities. Furthermore, financial institutions should conduct systematic strict audits on algorithms to explore and address discriminatory factors that will eventually support principles of fairness. Another major concern is the lack of awareness among customers that hinders the use of tech-based products and services for personal financing. Therefore, it is recommended that financial institutions provide educational resources and arrange awareness campaigns that can facilitate customers' understanding of AI, machine learning, and big data. For instance, financial institutions can arrange workshops, webinars, and financial literary events to spread awareness. Also, educational resources such as informative videos, research reports, and newsletter subscriptions on social networking sites and official websites can play a major role in spreading knowledge among consumers. Most importantly, online courses and financial simulations are also necessary to spread awareness. Furthermore, it is the responsibility of financial institutions to ensure that these technologies are supported by user-friendly interfaces and reliable customer support. Prioritizing data security and taking robust measures to safeguard customers' data from cyberattacks and breaches is critical. Furthermore, financial organizations should adhere to data protection rules to gain customers' confidence. Finally, AI-driven solutions are suggested to be developed, allowing clients to customize financial portfolios and plans based on new preferences.

This study offers the following implications for policymakers. First, we recommend policymakers to support research and development; hence, they must arrange sufficient funds to foster personal finance management and security. Moreover, it is suggested to enforce regulations addressing privacy and ethical concerns regarding AI, machine learning, and big data in personal finance. Also, collaboration with experts and industry stakeholders is recommended to develop ethical standards and guidelines for AI, machine learning, and big data usage in finance. Also, they must clarify data ownership rights and responsibilities between individuals, institutions, and technology providers. Most importantly, policymakers must predict future developments in personal finance driven by AI, machine learning, and big data, such as more advanced financial chatbots, AI-driven financial education, and improved risk assessment.

REFERENCES

Abu Jamie, N. H., Abu-Jamie, T. N., & Al-Absy, M. S. M. (2024). Advances in AI and Their Effects on Finance and Economic Analysis. The AI Revolution. *Driving Business Innovation and Research, 1*, 507–523.

Agarwal, S., & Ann, T. C. (2024). Personal Finance Applications of Fintech. In The Emerald Handbook of Fintech: Reshaping Finance (pp. 235-248). Emerald Publishing Limited.

Ahmed, S., Alshater, M. M., El Ammari, A., & Hammami, H. (2022). Artificial intelligence and machine learning in finance: A bibliometric review. *Research in International Business and Finance, 61*, 101646.

Akter, S., Dwivedi, Y. K., Sajib, S., Biswas, K., Bandara, R. J., & Michael, K. (2022). Algorithmic bias in machine learning-based marketing models. *Journal of Business Research, 144*, 201–216.

Bhatore, S., Mohan, L., & Reddy, Y. R. (2020). Machine learning techniques for credit risk evaluation: A systematic literature review. *Journal of Banking and Financial Technology, 4*(1), 111–138.

Balcıoğlu, Y. S. (2024). Revolutionizing Risk Management AI and ML Innovations in Financial Stability and Fraud Detection. In Navigating the Future of Finance in the Age of AI (pp. 109-138). IGI Global.

Aoun, J. E. (2017). *Robot-proof: higher education in the age of artificial intelligence*. MIT press.

Aslam, F., Hunjra, A. I., Ftiti, Z., Louhichi, W., & Shams, T. (2022). Insurance fraud detection: Evidence from artificial intelligence and machine learning. *Research in International Business and Finance, 62*, 101744.

Bharadiya, J. P. (2023). Machine Learning and AI in Business Intelligence: Trends and Opportunities. [IJC]. *International Journal of Computer, 48*(1), 123–134.

Kozodoi, N., Jacob, J., & Lessmann, S. (2022). Fairness in credit scoring: Assessment, implementation and profit implications. *European Journal of Operational Research, 297*(3), 1083–1094.

Talasila, S. D. (2024). AI-Driven Personal Finance Management: Revolutionizing Budgeting and Financial Planning. *International Research Journal of Engineering and Technology, 11*(7), 397–400.

Al Janabi, M. A. (2024). Insights into Liquidity Dynamics: Optimizing Asset Allocation and Portfolio Risk Management with Machine Learning Algorithms. In Liquidity Dynamics and Risk Modeling (pp. 257-303). Palgrave Macmillan, Cham.

Cao, L. (2020). AI in finance: A review. Available at *SSRN* 3647625.

Cockcroft, S., & Russell, M. (2018). Big data opportunities for accounting and finance practice and research. *Australian Accounting Review*, *28*(3), 323–333.

Dixon, M. F., Halperin, I., & Bilokon, P. (2020). *Machine learning in finance* (Vol. 1170). Springer International Publishing.

Donepudi, P. K. (2017). Machine Learning and Artificial Intelligence in Banking. *Engineering International*, *5*(2), 83–86.

Fang, B., & Zhang, P. (2016). Big data in finance. Big data concepts, theories, and applications, 391-412.

Fisch, J. E., Laboure, M., Turner, J. A., & Center, P. P. (2017). The economics of complex decision making: The emergence of the robo adviser. Recuperado de: http://www. geog. ox. ac. uk/events/170911/Robo-vs-Human-Advisers-Aug-28. pdf.

Frost, J., Gambacorta, L., Huang, Y., Shin, H. S., & Zbinden, P. (2019). BigTech and the changing structure of financial intermediation. *Economic Policy*, *34*(100), 761–799.

Garman, E. T., & Forgue, R. (2014). *Personal finance*. Cengage Learning.

Gimpel, H., Rau, D., & Röglinger, M. (2018). Understanding FinTech start-ups–a taxonomy of consumer-oriented service offerings. *Electronic Markets*, *28*, 245–264.

Goldstein, I., Spatt, C. S., & Ye, M. (2021). Big data in finance. *Review of Financial Studies*, *34*(7), 3213–3225.

Goodell, J. W., Kumar, S., Lim, W. M., & Pattnaik, D. (2021). Artificial intelligence and machine learning in finance: Identifying foundations, themes, and research clusters from bibliometric analysis. *Journal of Behavioral and Experimental Finance*, *32*, 100577.

Goyal, K., & Kumar, S. (2021). Financial literacy: A systematic review and bibliometric analysis. *International Journal of Consumer Studies*, *45*(1), 80–105.

Grigoroudis, E., Tsitsiridi, E., & Zopounidis, C. (2013). Linking customer satisfaction, employee appraisal, and business performance: An evaluation methodology in the banking sector. *Annals of Operations Research*, *205*, 5–27.

Hasan, I., & Rizvi, S. A. M. (2022). AI-driven fraud detection and mitigation in e-commerce transactions. In Proceedings of Data Analytics and Management: ICDAM 2021, Volume 1 (pp. 403-414). Springer Singapore.

Hasan, M. M., Popp, J., & Oláh, J. (2020). Current landscape and influence of big data on finance. *Journal of Big Data*, *7*(1), 1–17.

Wu, M., Subramaniam, G., Li, Z., & Gao, X. (2025). Using AI Technology to Enhance Data-Driven Decision-Making in the Financial Sector. Artificial Intelligence-Enabled Businesses: How to Develop Strategies for Innovation, 187-207.

Himeur, Y., Elnour, M., Fadli, F., Meskin, N., Petri, I., Rezgui, Y., & Amira, A. (2023). AI-big data analytics for building automation and management systems: A survey, actual challenges and future perspectives. *Artificial Intelligence Review*, *56*(6), 4929–5021.

Hira, T. K. (2009). *Personal finance: Past, present and future*. Networks Financial Institute Policy Brief.

Huang, M. H., Rust, R., & Maksimovic, V. (2019). The feeling economy: Managing in the next generation of artificial intelligence (AI). *California Management Review*, *61*(4), 43–65.

Hwang, H., & Park, H. I. (2023). The relationships of financial literacy with both financial behavior and financial well-being: Meta-analyses based on the selective literature review. *The Journal of Consumer Affairs*, *57*(1), 222–244.

Jamil, S. (2021). From digital divide to digital inclusion: Challenges for wide-ranging digitalization in Pakistan. *Telecommunications Policy*, *45*(8), 102206.

Kajol, K., Singh, R., & Paul, J. (2022). Adoption of digital financial transactions: A review of literature and future research agenda. *Technological Forecasting and Social Change*, *184*, 121991.

Königstorfer, F., & Thalmann, S. (2020). Applications of Artificial Intelligence in commercial banks–A research agenda for behavioral finance. *Journal of Behavioral and Experimental Finance*, *27*, 100352.

Krichen, M., & Abdalzaher, M. S. (2024). Performance enhancement of artificial intelligence: A survey. *Journal of Network and Computer Applications*, •••, 104034.

Kshetri, N. (2016). Big data's role in expanding access to financial services in China. *International Journal of Information Management*, *36*(3), 297–308.

Kumar, S., Sharma, D., Rao, S., Lim, W. M., & Mangla, S. K. (2022a). Past, present, and future of sustainable finance: Insights from big data analytics through machine learning of scholarly research. *Annals of Operations Research*, •••, 1–44.

Kumar, S., Akoglu, L., Chawla, N., Nagrecha, S., Naware, V. M., Faruquie, T., & McCormick, H. (2022b). KDD Workshop on Machine Learning in Finance. In Proceedings of the 28th ACM SIGKDD Conference on Knowledge Discovery and Data Mining (pp. 4882-4883).

Lee, I. (2017). Big data: Dimensions, evolution, impacts, and challenges. *Business Horizons*, *60*(3), 293–303.

Ma, X., & Lv, S. (2019). Financial credit risk prediction in internet finance driven by machine learning. *Neural Computing & Applications*, *31*, 8359–8367.

Mer, A., & Virdi, A. S. (2025). The Influence of Artificial Intelligence on Personal and Corporate Finance: A Comprehensive Literature Review with Prospects for Future Research. Financial Landscape Transformation: Technological Disruptions, 253-268.

Mishra, A. K., & Tyagi, A. K. Richa, & Patra, S. R. (2024). Introduction to Machine Learning and Artificial Intelligence in Banking and Finance. In Applications of Block Chain technology and Artificial Intelligence: Lead-ins in Banking, Finance, and Capital Market (pp. 239-290). Cham: Springer International Publishing.

Mogaji, E., & Nguyen, N. P. (2022). Managers' understanding of artificial intelligence in relation to marketing financial services: Insights from a cross-country study. *International Journal of Bank Marketing*, *40*(6), 1272–1298.

Mogaji, E., Soetan, T. O., & Kieu, T. A. (2021). The implications of artificial intelligence on the digital marketing of financial services to vulnerable customers. *Australasian Marketing Journal*, *29*(3), 235–242. DOI: 10.1016/j.ausmj.2020.05.003

Mori, M. (2021). AI-powered virtual assistants in the realms of banking and financial services. In *Virtual Assistant*. IntechOpen.

Nguyen, D. K., Sermpinis, G., & Stasinakis, C. (2023). Big data, artificial intelligence and machine learning: A transformative symbiosis in favour of financial technology. *European Financial Management*, *29*(2), 517–548.

Ozili, P. K. (2021). Big data and artificial intelligence for financial inclusion: benefits and issues. In *Artificial intelligence, fintech, and financial inclusion* (pp. 1–10). CRC Press.

Panos, G. A., & Wilson, J. O. (2020). Financial literacy and responsible finance in the FinTech era: Capabilities and challenges. *European Journal of Finance, 26*(4-5), 297–301.

Prete, A. L. (2022). Digital and financial literacy as determinants of digital payments and personal finance. *Economics Letters, 213*, 110378.

Sawwalakhe, R., Arora, S., & Singh, T. P. (2023). Opportunities and Challenges for Artificial Intelligence and Machine Learning Applications in the Finance Sector. Advanced Machine Learning Algorithms for Complex Financial Applications, 1-17.

Shanmuganathan, M. (2020). Behavioural finance in an era of artificial intelligence: Longitudinal case study of robo-advisors in investment decisions. *Journal of Behavioral and Experimental Finance, 27*, 100297.

Shawat, R., Wassef, A., & Badawy, H. (2023). Artificial Intelligence in Financial Services: Advantages and Disadvantages. In Artificial Intelligence for Capital Markets (pp. 28-40). Chapman and Hall/CRC.

Sheth, J. N., Jain, V., Roy, G., & Chakraborty, A. (2022). AI-driven banking services: The next frontier for a personalised experience in the emerging market. *International Journal of Bank Marketing, 40*(6), 1248–1271.

Singh, V., Chen, S. S., Singhania, M., Nanavati, B., & Gupta, A. (2022). How are reinforcement learning and deep learning algorithms used for big data based decision making in financial

(•••). industries–A review and research agenda. *International Journal of Information Management Data Insights, 2*(2), 100094.

Sohangir, S., Wang, D., Pomeranets, A., & Khoshgoftaar, T. M. (2018). Big Data: Deep Learning for financial sentiment analysis. *Journal of Big Data, 5*(1), 1–25.

Weber, P., Carl, K. V., & Hinz, O. (2023). Applications of Explainable Artificial Intelligence in Finance—a systematic review of Finance, Information Systems, and Computer Science literature. Management Review Quarterly, 1-41.

Wen, S., Li, J., Huang, C., & Zhu, X. (2023). Extreme risk spillovers among traditional financial and FinTech institutions: A complex network perspective. *The Quarterly Review of Economics and Finance, 88*, 190–202.

Wilson, J. O. S., & Molyneux, P. (Eds.). (2019). *The Oxford Handbook of Banking*. Oxford University Press.

Xiao, J. J., & Porto, N. (2022). Financial capability and wellbeing of vulnerable consumers. *The Journal of Consumer Affairs, 56*(2), 1004–1018.

Zarifis, A., & Cheng, X. (2022). A model of trust in Fintech and trust in Insurtech: How Artificial Intelligence and the context influence it. *Journal of Behavioral and Experimental Finance*, *36*, 100739.

Zheng, X. L., Zhu, M. Y., Li, Q. B., Chen, C. C., & Tan, Y. C. (2019). FinBrain: When finance meets AI 2.0. *Frontiers of Information Technology & Electronic Engineering*, *20*(7), 914–924.

Zhu, X., Song, B., Ni, Y., Ren, Y., Li, R., Zhu, X., ... & Li, R. (2016). Digital finance—from traditional finance to digital and internet finance. Business Trends in the Digital Era: Evolution of Theories and Applications, 161-190.

Chapter 10
Revolutionizing Financial Services With AI and Blockchain Pioneering Innovations for a Digital Future

Ganesan Alias Kanagaraj M.
https://orcid.org/0000-0001-6714-463X
Saveetha Engineering College, India

Ramar Veluchamy
Saveetha Engineering College, India

V. Vimalnath
Saveetha Engineering College, India

K. K. Karthick
https://orcid.org/0000-0002-9379-6794
Saveetha Engineering College, India

ABSTRACT

The integration of Artificial Intelligence (AI) and Blockchain technology is transforming the financial services sector, ushering in a new era of digital innovation. This chapter explores how these pioneering technologies are redefining traditional financial systems, enhancing security, efficiency, and transparency. AI's capabilities in predictive analytics and decision-making, combined with Blockchain's decentralized and immutable ledger, present unprecedented opportunities for financial institutions

DOI: 10.4018/979-8-3693-7160-2.ch010

to optimize operations and create novel business models. We delve into practical applications such as smart contracts, fraud detection, and personalized financial services, showcasing real-world case studies and future trends. This comprehensive analysis provides insights into the challenges and potential of AI and Blockchain, highlighting the strategic imperatives for stakeholders aiming to thrive in a rapidly evolving digital landscape.

1: INTRODUCTION TO AI AND BLOCKCHAIN IN FINANCIAL SERVICES

Overview of AI and Blockchain Technologies

Artificial Intelligence (AI) and Blockchain are revolutionizing the financial services industry by introducing groundbreaking changes. AI involves the simulation of human cognitive processes by computer systems, enabling them to execute tasks that typically require human intellect. These tasks include visual perception, speech recognition, decision-making, and language translation. AI contributes to enhanced efficiency and improved decision-making in financial services through the use of predictive analytics, automated customer interactions, fraud detection, and tailored financial advice (Belanche et al., 2019).

Conversely, Blockchain is a decentralized digital ledger designed to securely record transactions across a distributed network of computers, making it impossible to alter records retrospectively. This technology ensures transparency, security, and efficiency in financial operations, including cross-border payments, trade finance, and identity verification (Sun et al., 2021). By integrating blockchain, financial institutions can significantly reduce transaction costs and boost the reliability of financial transactions by removing the need for intermediaries.

Historical Context and Evolution

The inception of AI dates back to the mid-20th century, with significant advancements in machine learning, natural language processing, and robotics occurring over the past few decades. Early implementations in financial services focused on algorithmic trading and credit scoring. However, the proliferation of big data and advances in computational power have exponentially increased AI's capabilities and applications in the financial sector.

Blockchain technology was conceptualized with the introduction of Bitcoin by Satoshi Nakamoto in 2008. Since then, its use has expanded beyond cryptocurrencies to include smart contracts, supply chain management, and secure data sharing.

The financial industry quickly recognized blockchain's potential for enhancing transparency and reducing costs associated with traditional financial processes (Kim & Park, 2020).

Importance in Modern Financial Services

The importance of AI and blockchain in modern financial services cannot be overstated. AI-driven tools such as robo-advisors and chatbots are revolutionizing customer interaction, providing personalized and efficient services. Robo-advisors use AI algorithms to offer financial advice and portfolio management with minimal human intervention, making financial planning more accessible and affordable (Gürsoy et al., 2019).

Blockchain technology enhances security and transparency in financial transactions. Its immutable ledger system is invaluable in reducing fraud, ensuring data integrity, and facilitating secure cross-border transactions. Financial institutions are leveraging blockchain to streamline processes such as trade finance, know-your-customer (KYC) procedures, and asset management (Kombe et al., 2019).

Objectives and Scope of the Book Chapter

The objective of this book chapter is to provide a comprehensive introduction to the revolutionary impact of AI and blockchain technologies on financial services. It aims to:

- Explain the fundamental concepts of AI and blockchain technologies.
- Trace the historical evolution and significant milestones of these technologies.
- Highlight their critical importance and applications in modern financial services.
- Discuss the challenges and opportunities presented by the adoption of AI and blockchain in the financial sector.

The scope of this chapter will encompass a detailed exploration of these technologies, supported by case studies and real-world applications. It will also provide insights into future trends and potential developments in the integration of AI and blockchain in financial services.

AI and blockchain are at the forefront of the digital transformation in financial services, offering unprecedented efficiency, security, and accessibility. This chapter sets the stage for understanding how these technologies are not only changing the landscape of financial services but also paving the way for a more inclusive and transparent financial system.

2: FUNDAMENTALS OF AI AND BLOCKCHAIN

Core Concepts of Artificial Intelligence

Machine Learning, Deep Learning, and Neural Networks

Machine Learning (ML): Machine Learning is a specialized area within AI that employs algorithms and statistical models to enable systems to enhance their performance on specific tasks using data, without explicit programming. It encompasses various methodologies, including supervised learning, unsupervised learning, and reinforcement learning (Gulshan et al., 2016).

Deep Learning (DL): Deep Learning, a sophisticated subset of ML, utilizes neural networks with multiple layers (deep neural networks) to process and analyze different types of data. It is particularly effective in handling large-scale datasets and complex tasks, such as image and speech recognition. Deep learning models can learn complex patterns and representations from raw data, leading to significant advancements in areas like computer vision and natural language processing (Paul et al., 2017).

Neural Networks: Neural Networks are computational frameworks inspired by the architecture of the human brain. They consist of interconnected layers of nodes (neurons) that process data through a series of layers. Each connection between neurons has an associated weight that is adjusted during training to reduce errors. Deep neural networks, which include multiple hidden layers between input and output layers, are capable of modeling complex functions (Hung et al., 2017).

Core Concepts of Blockchain Technology

Distributed Ledgers, Smart Contracts, and Cryptocurrencies

Distributed Ledgers: A distributed ledger is a consensually shared and synchronized database that spans multiple locations, institutions, or geographic regions. This system allows transactions to have public witnesses, making it more resistant to cyberattacks. The most prevalent form of distributed ledger is blockchain, which organizes data into sequential blocks, enhancing security and transparency (Baumann, 2020).

Smart Contracts: Smart contracts are automated agreements where the terms are directly encoded into software. These contracts automatically execute and enforce the terms once predefined conditions are met. Operating on blockchain

platforms like Ethereum, smart contracts facilitate, verify, and enforce contractual obligations without the need for intermediaries (Shrestha et al., 2021).
Cryptocurrencies: Cryptocurrencies are digital or virtual currencies secured by cryptographic methods. They function on decentralized networks powered by blockchain technology. Bitcoin, the pioneering and most well-known cryptocurrency, introduced the blockchain concept. Cryptocurrencies enable secure, peer-to-peer transactions without relying on a central authority and are integral to decentralized finance (DeFi), which uses blockchain to replicate traditional financial systems (Arias-Oliva et al., 2019).

Synergies Between AI and Blockchain

The integration of AI and blockchain technologies offers synergistic benefits that enhance the capabilities and applications of both technologies.

Enhanced Security and Transparency:

Blockchain provides a secure and immutable ledger for storing AI models' data and decisions, ensuring transparency and auditability. This integration can enhance the security of AI systems, making them less vulnerable to tampering and ensuring that the decisions made by AI algorithms can be traced and verified (Ghorashi et al., 2023).

Decentralized AI:

AI models can be deployed in a decentralized manner using blockchain technology, reducing the dependency on centralized data centers. This approach can lead to more robust and resilient AI systems that are less prone to single points of failure (Sun et al., 2021).

Data Sharing and Collaboration:

Blockchain enables secure and transparent data sharing among various AI systems and stakeholders. This feature is particularly important in fields where data privacy and security are critical, such as healthcare and finance. By using blockchain, the authenticity and integrity of data shared across different AI models are maintained, ensuring that it has not been altered (Khan et al., 2021).

Smart Contracts for Autonomous AI:

Smart contracts can automate transactions and operations between AI systems, enabling the creation of autonomous organizations and applications that operate without human intervention. For instance, smart contracts can govern the interactions between different AI agents in a supply chain, ensuring that transactions are executed automatically when certain conditions are met (Harshvardhan & Teoh, 2022).

3: AI APPLICATIONS IN FINANCIAL SERVICES

AI in Risk Management and Fraud Detection

Artificial Intelligence (AI) has significantly enhanced the capabilities of financial institutions in managing risks and detecting fraud. By leveraging machine learning algorithms and data analytics, AI can identify patterns and anomalies that may indicate fraudulent activities or potential risks.

Risk Management: AI-driven risk management systems analyze large datasets to identify potential risks in real-time. These systems use predictive analytics to forecast market trends and assess the impact of various risk factors on financial portfolios. For instance, AI can predict credit risks by evaluating the creditworthiness of borrowers based on their financial history and other relevant data (Larkin et al., 2021).

Fraud Detection: AI systems enhance fraud detection by analyzing transaction patterns and flagging unusual activities. Machine learning models can identify subtle patterns that may be missed by traditional rule-based systems. For example, AI algorithms can detect anomalies in transaction data that suggest fraudulent behavior, such as unusual spending patterns or multiple transactions in a short period (Firdaus et al., 2022). Moreover, AI can also incorporate behavioral analytics to assess the likelihood of fraud based on user behavior, thus reducing false positives and enhancing detection accuracy (Boztepe & Usul, 2019).

AI in Customer Service and Personalization

AI has transformed customer service in the financial sector by delivering personalized and efficient customer interactions. Leveraging natural language processing (NLP) and machine learning, AI systems can comprehend and address customer inquiries, anticipate customer needs, and provide tailored financial advice.

Chatbots and Virtual Assistants: AI-powered chatbots and virtual assistants are increasingly being used by banks and financial institutions to handle customer inquiries. These AI systems can provide instant responses to common questions, guide customers through complex processes, and even execute transactions. This reduces the workload on human agents and enhances customer satisfaction by providing 24/7 service (Belanche et al., 2019).

Personalized Financial Advice: AI systems analyze customer data to offer personalized financial advice and product recommendations. By examining spending patterns, investment preferences, and financial goals, AI can suggest tailored financial products and strategies. This personalization helps customers make informed decisions and improves their overall financial well-being (Gürsoy et al., 2019).

AI in Investment and Portfolio Management

AI technologies are transforming investment and portfolio management by providing data-driven insights and automating complex trading strategies. AI algorithms can process vast amounts of financial data, identify market trends, and optimize investment portfolios.

Algorithmic Trading: AI-powered algorithmic trading systems execute trades at high speeds and frequencies based on pre-defined criteria. These systems can analyze market conditions, historical data, and predictive models to make trading decisions, thereby reducing human error and increasing trading efficiency (Damiani et al., 2023).

Portfolio Optimization: AI-driven portfolio management tools employ machine learning algorithms to assess investment data and optimize asset allocation. These tools take into account factors like risk tolerance, investment duration, and market conditions to suggest optimal investment strategies. Additionally, AI can continuously monitor and adjust portfolios to enhance returns and mitigate risks (Torrente et al., 2022).

AI in Regulatory Compliance and Reporting

Regulatory compliance is a crucial component of financial services, and AI significantly contributes to ensuring adherence to regulatory standards. AI systems can streamline compliance processes, lower operational costs, and improve the accuracy of regulatory reporting.

Automated Compliance Monitoring: AI technologies can automate the surveillance of transactions and other financial activities to ensure regulatory compliance. By continuously analyzing data, AI systems can identify instances of non-compliance and trigger alerts for further investigation. This automation reduces the manual effort required for compliance monitoring and enhances detection accuracy (Fitriyah, 2020).

Regulatory Reporting: AI systems can automate the creation of regulatory reports by extracting pertinent data from financial transactions and other records. This automation ensures timely and precise reporting, mitigating the risk of penalties due to non-compliance. AI can also help interpret complex regulatory requirements and adjust reporting processes accordingly (Hernandez, 2011).

By integrating AI across various aspects of financial services, institutions can boost efficiency, enhance customer experience, and ensure effective risk management and regulatory compliance. The transformative potential of AI continues to drive innovation within the financial sector, leading to a more secure and customer-centric future.

4: BLOCKCHAIN APPLICATIONS IN FINANCIAL SERVICES

Blockchain in Payments and Transactions

Blockchain technology has transformed the payments and transactions landscape by providing unmatched transparency, security, and efficiency. Traditional payment systems typically involve numerous intermediaries, resulting in delays, elevated costs, and increased fraud risk. Blockchain resolves these challenges by using a decentralized ledger that records transactions in an immutable way, fostering trust without the necessity of intermediaries.

Enhanced Transparency and Security

Blockchain's immutable ledger offers a transparent record of all transactions, which can be audited in real-time by any network participant. This transparency mitigates the risk of fraud and enhances security, as each transaction is cryptographically secured and linked to the previous one. This linkage makes it nearly impossible to alter any part of the ledger without being detected.

Reduction in Transaction Costs and Time

By eliminating intermediaries, blockchain significantly reduces transaction fees. Cross-border payments, which traditionally take several days and incur high costs, can be completed within minutes at a fraction of the cost. This efficiency is particularly beneficial for remittances and international trade, where speed and cost savings are crucial.

Case Studies

One prominent example is Ripple, a blockchain-based payment protocol that facilitates instant, low-cost international payments. Ripple's native cryptocurrency, XRP, acts as a bridge currency, further streamlining the process and reducing liquidity costs. Major financial institutions like Santander and American Express have adopted Ripple for cross-border transactions, demonstrating blockchain's potential to transform the payments industry.

Blockchain in Trade Finance and Supply Chain Management

Trade finance and supply chain management are areas where blockchain can address significant inefficiencies and risks. Traditional trade finance involves extensive paperwork, which can lead to delays, errors, and fraud. Blockchain offers a digital, secure, and transparent alternative that enhances efficiency and trust among all parties involved.

Streamlining Documentation and Reducing Fraud

Blockchain enables the digitization of trade documents, such as letters of credit and bills of lading, making them accessible in real-time to all authorized participants. This digitization reduces the risk of errors and fraud, as each document is timestamped and securely recorded on the blockchain. Smart contracts, self-executing contracts with the terms of the agreement directly written into code, further streamline the process by automating transactions once predefined conditions are met.

Enhancing Traceability and Transparency

In supply chain management, blockchain provides end-to-end visibility of goods as they move from manufacturers to consumers. Each step of the supply chain is recorded on the blockchain, enabling participants to track the provenance and status of products in real-time. This traceability enhances transparency and trust, helping to ensure the authenticity of goods and adherence to ethical standards.

Case Studies

IBM's Food Trust is a notable example of blockchain in supply chain management. By collaborating with major food producers and retailers, IBM's blockchain platform enhances food safety by providing traceability from farm to table. This initiative has significantly reduced the time required to trace foodborne illness outbreaks, demonstrating blockchain's potential to improve supply chain efficiency and safety.

Blockchain in Identity Verification and KYC

Ensuring identity verification and implementing Know Your Customer (KYC) processes are essential in the financial services sector. Traditionally, these processes are cumbersome and susceptible to security breaches. Blockchain technology presents a robust and streamlined alternative for managing identities. It empowers individuals to control their personal data securely while maintaining compliance with regulatory standards.

Secure and Self-Sovereign Identity

Blockchain technology facilitates the establishment of self-sovereign identities, allowing individuals to store their personal data on a secure, decentralized network. This enables them to share only necessary information with institutions, safeguarding their full identity. This method significantly enhances privacy and security, thereby minimizing the risks associated with identity theft and data breaches.

Streamlining KYC Processes

KYC processes involve verifying the identity of clients to prevent fraud and money laundering. Traditionally, this involves repetitive and time-consuming paperwork for each financial institution. Blockchain allows for a shared, immutable KYC record that can be accessed by multiple institutions with the customer's consent. This reduces redundancy, lowers costs, and accelerates onboarding processes.

Case Studies

Civic is a blockchain-based identity verification platform that enables individuals to manage their digital identities securely. Civic's platform allows users to verify their identity once and then reuse this verification with multiple service providers, streamlining the KYC process. Financial institutions using Civic have reported significant reductions in onboarding times and costs, showcasing the benefits of blockchain in identity verification.

Blockchain in Asset Tokenization and Management

Asset tokenization involves converting real-world assets into digital tokens on a blockchain, making them easier to trade, manage, and fractionalize. This process has the potential to democratize access to investment opportunities and enhance the liquidity of traditionally illiquid assets.

Increasing Accessibility and Liquidity

Tokenization enables the division of assets like real estate, art, and commodities into smaller, tradable units. This approach facilitates fractional ownership, allowing a wider range of investors to enter markets that were previously inaccessible due to high entry costs. Additionally, tokenized assets can be traded on blockchain-based platforms, offering enhanced liquidity and the convenience of 24/7 trading.

Enhancing Transparency and Efficiency

Blockchain ensures that all transactions involving tokenized assets are recorded on an immutable ledger, providing transparency and reducing the risk of fraud. Smart contracts can automate the execution of complex transactions, such as the distribution of dividends or the management of rental income, enhancing operational efficiency.

Case Studies

Real estate is a sector where asset tokenization has shown significant promise. Platforms like RealT and Brickblock use blockchain to tokenize real estate properties, allowing investors to purchase fractional ownership and receive rental income.

These platforms provide a transparent and efficient way to invest in real estate, demonstrating how blockchain can transform asset management.

Blockchain technology is revolutionizing financial services by enhancing transparency, security, and efficiency across various applications. From payments and transactions to trade finance, identity verification, and asset management, blockchain offers innovative solutions that address longstanding challenges in the industry. As adoption continues to grow, blockchain has the potential to reshape the financial landscape, making it more inclusive, efficient, and secure.

AI-Enhanced Blockchain Protocols

The integration of Artificial Intelligence (AI) with blockchain technology is poised to revolutionize the financial sector by combining the strengths of both technologies. AI's ability to analyze vast amounts of data and make predictive decisions complements blockchain's secure, transparent, and decentralized nature. Together, they can create more efficient, secure, and intelligent financial systems.

Optimizing Blockchain Operations

AI can enhance blockchain protocols by optimizing various aspects of blockchain operations. For example, AI algorithms can be used to manage blockchain scalability and efficiency. Machine learning models can predict network congestion and optimize the timing and size of transactions, thereby reducing latency and transaction costs.

Intelligent Smart Contracts

Smart contracts are self-executing contracts with the terms of the agreement directly written into code. AI can make smart contracts more intelligent by enabling them to learn from historical data and adapt to new conditions. For instance, an AI-enhanced smart contract in financial trading could adjust its parameters based on market trends and past performance, ensuring better decision-making and reducing risks.

Enhanced Security and Fraud Detection

AI's capabilities in pattern recognition and anomaly detection can significantly enhance the security of blockchain networks. AI algorithms can continuously monitor transaction patterns and flag suspicious activities in real-time, preventing fraud and ensuring the integrity of the blockchain. This proactive approach to security is crucial in the financial industry, where the cost of breaches can be substantial.

Case Study: AI for Blockchain Scalability

A practical example of AI-enhanced blockchain protocols is the use of AI in optimizing consensus mechanisms. Traditional consensus algorithms like Proof of Work (PoW) are energy-intensive and slow. AI can be employed to develop more efficient consensus algorithms that reduce energy consumption and increase transaction throughput. For instance, combining AI with Proof of Stake (PoS) mechanisms can help in selecting validators more effectively, balancing the load, and ensuring quicker consensus.

Blockchain-Based AI Models

Blockchain technology can provide a robust and transparent infrastructure for developing and deploying AI models. The decentralized nature of blockchain ensures that AI models are not controlled by a single entity, promoting fairness and accountability.

Decentralized AI Training

One of the key challenges in AI development is the need for vast amounts of data, which are often controlled by a few large entities. Blockchain can facilitate decentralized AI training by enabling data sharing among multiple parties without compromising privacy. Each party can contribute data to train AI models, and blockchain ensures that the data contributions are securely recorded and that the contributors are fairly compensated.

Trustworthy AI Models

Blockchain can enhance the trustworthiness of AI models by providing an immutable record of the data and processes used in model training and deployment. This transparency is essential for ensuring the integrity and accountability of AI models, especially in financial applications where trust is paramount. Stakeholders can verify that the models have been trained on unbiased data and that the decision-making processes are transparent and explainable.

Secure Model Deployment and Updates

Deploying AI models on a blockchain ensures that the models are secure from tampering. Any updates or changes to the models can be recorded on the blockchain, providing a clear audit trail. This is particularly important in financial services, where AI models must be regularly updated to adapt to changing market conditions and regulatory requirements.

Case Study: Federated Learning on Blockchain

Federated learning is a decentralized approach to training AI models where data remains on local devices, and only the model updates are shared. Integrating blockchain with federated learning can enhance the security and transparency of the process. For example, in the financial industry, multiple banks could collaboratively train an AI model for credit scoring without sharing sensitive customer data. Blockchain would ensure that each bank's contributions are securely recorded and that the final model is fair and unbiased.

Case Studies of Integrated AI and Blockchain Solutions

The integration of AI and blockchain has already led to innovative solutions in the financial sector, demonstrating the potential of these technologies to transform the industry.

Case Study 1: AI-driven Investment Platforms

AI-driven investment platforms leverage blockchain to enhance transparency and security. These platforms use AI algorithms to analyze market data and make investment recommendations. By recording all transactions and investment decisions on a blockchain, these platforms ensure that the process is transparent and that investors can trust the recommendations. For instance, a platform might use AI to identify profitable trading opportunities and execute trades automatically, with all actions being recorded on the blockchain for auditability.

Case Study 2: Decentralized Insurance with AI

In the insurance industry, blockchain and AI can be combined to create decentralized insurance platforms. These platforms use AI to assess risk and determine premiums, while blockchain ensures that the process is transparent and that claims are handled fairly and efficiently. For example, a decentralized insurance platform might use AI to analyze data from IoT devices to assess the risk of insuring a particular asset. Claims can be processed automatically using smart contracts, with the entire process being transparent and tamper-proof.

Case Study 3: Fraud Detection and Compliance

Financial institutions are increasingly using AI and blockchain to enhance fraud detection and compliance. AI algorithms can analyze transaction patterns to identify potential fraud, while blockchain provides a secure and transparent record of all transactions. For instance, a bank might use AI to monitor customer transactions for unusual activity and use blockchain to ensure that all transactions are securely recorded and easily auditable. This integration not only enhances security but also simplifies regulatory compliance by providing a clear and immutable audit trail.

The integration of AI and blockchain holds immense potential for financial innovation, offering solutions that are more secure, transparent, and efficient. AI-enhanced blockchain protocols optimize operations and security, while blockchain-based AI models ensure trust and accountability. Case studies of integrated solutions demonstrate the practical benefits and transformative potential of combining these technologies. As financial institutions continue to explore and adopt these innovations, the landscape of financial services is set to become more intelligent, secure, and inclusive.

6: REGULATORY AND ETHICAL CONSIDERATIONS

Regulatory Landscape for AI and Blockchain

As AI and blockchain technologies advance and penetrate different sectors, including finance, the regulatory environment is becoming more intricate. Governments and regulatory authorities globally are working to develop frameworks that foster innovation while safeguarding public interest.

AI Regulations

AI regulations focus on ensuring transparency, accountability, and fairness. Many countries are developing comprehensive AI strategies that include regulatory guidelines. For instance, the European Union's General Data Protection Regulation (GDPR) has specific provisions on automated decision-making and profiling, requiring transparency in AI algorithms and giving individuals the right to know when AI is being used.

The proposed EU Artificial Intelligence Act aims to classify AI applications by risk levels and establish strict requirements for high-risk AI systems, including financial applications. This regulation emphasizes the need for robust data governance, human oversight, and risk management.

Blockchain Regulations

Blockchain regulations focus on ensuring financial stability, preventing fraud, and protecting consumers. Regulatory agencies, such as the U.S. Securities and Exchange Commission (SEC) and the UK's Financial Conduct Authority (FCA), have issued guidelines for Initial Coin Offerings (ICOs) and the classification of digital assets. Globally, there is a movement towards developing legal frameworks that acknowledge blockchain transactions and smart contracts. Countries like Switzerland and Singapore are at the forefront, implementing blockchain-friendly regulations that offer legal certainty while ensuring adherence to anti-money laundering (AML) and counter-terrorism financing (CTF) laws.

Harmonization of Regulations

A key challenge is the harmonization of regulations across jurisdictions to facilitate international cooperation and innovation. Initiatives such as the Financial Action Task Force (FATF) guidelines on virtual assets aim to create a cohesive regulatory environment, but differences in national regulations still pose challenges for global blockchain and AI adoption.

Ethical Implications and Challenges

The integration of AI and blockchain raises several ethical concerns that need to be addressed to ensure responsible use of these technologies.

Bias and Fairness

AI systems can perpetuate and amplify biases present in the training data. Ensuring fairness in AI requires rigorous testing for biases and implementing corrective measures. Blockchain can aid in providing transparency in the AI decision-making process, but ethical frameworks are necessary to guide the design and deployment of these systems.

Accountability and Responsibility

Determining accountability in AI and blockchain applications can be challenging. Smart contracts, for example, execute automatically without human intervention, raising questions about responsibility in cases of unintended consequences or errors. Establishing clear legal and ethical guidelines is crucial to address these issues.

Impact on Employment

AI and blockchain can automate many tasks, leading to significant shifts in employment patterns. While these technologies can create new job opportunities, they can also displace certain roles. Ethical considerations must include strategies for workforce transition, reskilling, and ensuring equitable access to new job opportunities.

Data Privacy and Security Issues

Data privacy and security are paramount in AI and blockchain applications, especially given the sensitive nature of financial data.

Privacy in AI

AI systems often require large datasets, which can include personal information. Ensuring compliance with data protection laws like GDPR is essential. Techniques such as differential privacy and federated learning are being developed to enhance privacy in AI without compromising utility.

Privacy in Blockchain

Blockchain's inherent transparency can conflict with privacy requirements. Solutions such as zero-knowledge proofs and privacy-focused blockchains (e.g., Zcash, Monero) are being explored to address this issue. These technologies allow for transactions to be verified without revealing the underlying data, thus maintaining privacy.

Security Concerns

Both AI and blockchain face substantial security risks. AI systems are prone to adversarial attacks, where malicious inputs can mislead the AI, resulting in incorrect decisions. Blockchain networks, despite their inherent security, are not completely immune to threats such as 51% attacks, where a majority control of the network's mining power by a single entity can compromise the system. To protect data and maintain trust in AI and blockchain systems, it is essential to implement robust security measures, including encryption, secure coding practices, and regular security audits.

International Standards and Compliance

International standards are crucial for ensuring consistency and interoperability in AI and blockchain applications.

Standardization Efforts

Organizations such as the International Organization for Standardization (ISO) and the Institute of Electrical and Electronics Engineers (IEEE) are actively working on establishing standards for AI and blockchain technologies. ISO/IEC JTC 1/SC 42 focuses on AI standardization, covering aspects such as AI system lifecycle and trustworthiness. Similarly, ISO/TC 307 addresses blockchain standards, including interoperability, privacy, and security.

Compliance Challenges

Compliance with international standards requires alignment with local regulations, which can vary significantly. Financial institutions and technology providers must navigate these complexities to ensure that their AI and blockchain solutions meet both local and international requirements.

Role of Global Cooperation

Global cooperation among regulators, standard-setting bodies, and industry stakeholders is essential to create a cohesive framework that supports innovation while ensuring safety and compliance. Initiatives such as the G20's efforts to develop a global framework for digital assets are steps in the right direction.

7: CHALLENGES AND RISKS IN AI AND BLOCKCHAIN ADOPTION

Technical Challenges

The adoption of AI and blockchain in financial services faces several technical hurdles that need to be addressed for these technologies to reach their full potential.

Scalability

Improving scalability remains a critical hurdle for blockchain networks. As transaction volumes grow, so do the demands on processing time and computational resources. Innovations like sharding, off-chain transactions, and layer 2 protocols are actively being refined to address these challenges and bolster scalability.

AI systems, particularly those involving deep learning, require substantial computational resources. Efficient resource management and the development of more powerful hardware are crucial to support the growing demands of AI.

Interoperability

Seamless interoperability between diverse blockchain networks and between AI systems and other technologies is crucial for integrated functionality. The establishment of standardized protocols and APIs plays a pivotal role in facilitating this interoperability, allowing disparate systems to communicate and collaborate seamlessly.

Data Quality and Integration

AI systems rely on high-quality data for training and decision-making. Ensuring the accuracy, completeness, and timeliness of data is a significant challenge. Blockchain can help in providing a transparent and immutable record of data, but integrating data from diverse sources remains complex.

Operational Risks

Operational risks are inherent in the deployment and management of AI and blockchain systems.

System Reliability

Ensuring the reliability and uptime of AI and blockchain systems is crucial for financial applications. Any downtime or failure can lead to significant financial losses and damage to reputation. Robust testing, monitoring, and maintenance practices are essential to mitigate these risks.

Human Factors

Human error can have a substantial impact on the effectiveness of AI and blockchain systems. Training and education are critical to ensure that users and developers understand how to operate and manage these technologies correctly.

Regulatory Compliance

Meeting regulatory requirements is an ongoing operational challenge. Financial institutions must continuously monitor regulatory changes and ensure that their AI and blockchain systems comply with evolving standards and laws.

Cybersecurity Threats

Cybersecurity threats are a major concern for AI and blockchain applications, given the sensitive nature of financial data and transactions.

Threat of Attacks

Blockchain networks can be targeted by attacks such as 51% attacks, Sybil attacks, and smart contract vulnerabilities. AI systems can be susceptible to adversarial attacks and data poisoning, where malicious actors manipulate the data to deceive the AI.

Data Breaches

Data breaches can have severe consequences, including financial losses, legal repercussions, and damage to reputation. Ensuring robust encryption, access controls, and continuous monitoring is essential to protect data from unauthorized access.

Security Best Practices

Implementing best practices such as multi-factor authentication, regular security audits, and incident response plans can enhance the security of AI and blockchain systems. Collaboration with cybersecurity experts and staying updated with the latest security trends are also crucial.

Market and Adoption Barriers

Despite the potential benefits, several barriers hinder the widespread adoption of AI and blockchain in financial services.

Cost of Implementation

The cost of implementing AI and blockchain technologies can be prohibitive for many organizations. This includes the costs of infrastructure, development, and compliance. Financial institutions need to carefully assess the return on investment and develop cost-effective strategies for adoption.

Lack of Expertise

There is a shortage of skilled professionals who are proficient in AI and blockchain technologies. This skills gap can slow down adoption and lead to implementation challenges. Investing in education and training programs is essential to build a knowledgeable workforce.

Resistance to Change

Resistance to change is a common barrier to the adoption of new technologies. Employees and stakeholders may be reluctant to embrace AI and blockchain due to fears of job displacement or skepticism about the benefits. Effective change management and clear communication about the advantages and implications of these technologies are crucial to overcome resistance.

Regulatory Uncertainty

Regulatory uncertainty can deter investment and innovation in AI and blockchain. Clear and consistent regulatory frameworks are needed to provide the confidence required for widespread adoption. Engaging with regulators and participating in the development of regulatory policies can help shape a favorable environment for these technologies.

Conclusion

The integration of AI and blockchain in financial services introduces a spectrum of challenges and risks, encompassing technical complexities, operational hurdles, cybersecurity vulnerabilities, and market entry barriers. Addressing these multifaceted challenges demands a holistic strategy integrating robust technical solutions, rigorous risk management practices, and collaborative efforts among industry participants. By surmounting these obstacles collectively, the financial sector can unlock the transformative capabilities of AI and blockchain, fostering innovation and operational efficiency.

8: CASE STUDIES OF AI AND BLOCKCHAIN INNOVATIONS IN FINANCIAL SERVICES

Successful Implementations and Best Practices

The integration of AI and blockchain in financial services has led to several successful implementations, showcasing the transformative potential of these technologies. By examining these cases, we can identify best practices and draw valuable insights.

AI-Driven Fraud Detection in Banking

A leading international bank implemented an AI-driven fraud detection system integrated with blockchain technology. The AI system uses machine learning algorithms to analyze transaction patterns and identify unusual activities indicative of fraud. The blockchain component ensures that all transactions are recorded immutably, providing a transparent and tamper-proof audit trail.

Best Practices:

1. **Data Integration:** Ensuring seamless integration of diverse data sources to enhance the AI model's accuracy.
2. **Continuous Learning:** Implementing continuous learning algorithms to adapt to new fraud patterns.
3. **Regulatory Compliance:** Aligning the system with regulatory requirements to ensure data privacy and security.

Blockchain for Insurance Claims Processing

A major insurance company adopted a blockchain-based system for processing claims. The system utilizes smart contracts to automate claims verification and settlement. AI algorithms assess the validity of claims based on predefined criteria, and once verified, the smart contract executes the payment automatically.

Best Practices:

1. **Smart Contract Design:** Designing robust smart contracts that accurately reflect policy terms and conditions.
2. **Transparency and Trust:** Enhancing customer trust through transparent and immutable claim records.
3. **Efficiency and Speed:** Reducing processing time and administrative overhead by automating claim settlements.

Fintech Solutions for Cross-Border Payments

A fintech startup developed a blockchain-based platform for cross-border payments, leveraging AI to optimize currency exchange rates and transaction fees. The platform uses AI to predict market movements and recommend the best times to execute transactions, while blockchain ensures secure and quick settlement.

Best Practices:

1. **User-Centric Design:** Focusing on user experience to simplify cross-border transactions.
2. **AI Optimization:** Utilizing AI to continuously optimize exchange rates and minimize fees.
3. **Scalability:** Ensuring the platform can handle increasing transaction volumes efficiently.

Case Studies from Banking, Insurance, and Fintech Sectors

Banking: JPMorgan Chase's AI and Blockchain Initiatives

JPMorgan Chase has been at the forefront of integrating AI and blockchain technologies. The bank's AI initiatives include predictive analytics for customer service and credit risk assessment. Additionally, its blockchain-based platform, Quorum, facilitates secure and efficient interbank transactions.

Insights:

1. **Integration Strategy:** Successful integration of AI and blockchain requires a well-defined strategy that aligns with the bank's overall goals.
2. **Innovation Culture:** Fostering a culture of innovation and continuous improvement is crucial for staying ahead in technology adoption.

Insurance: AXA's Fizzy Platform

AXA, a global insurance leader, launched Fizzy, a blockchain-based flight delay insurance platform. Using smart contracts, Fizzy automatically compensates policyholders for flight delays without the need for claims submission. AI algorithms assess risk and pricing based on historical flight data.

Insights:

1. **Customer Experience:** Simplifying processes and enhancing customer experience through automation and transparency.

2. **Data Utilization:** Leveraging historical data and AI for accurate risk assessment and pricing.

Fintech: Revolut's AI and Blockchain Applications

Revolut, a leading fintech company, has integrated AI and blockchain to offer innovative financial services. AI powers personalized financial advice and fraud detection, while blockchain is used for secure and transparent cryptocurrency transactions.

Insights:

- **Personalization:** Using AI to deliver personalized financial services that meet individual customer needs.
- **Security:** Ensuring robust security measures for cryptocurrency transactions through blockchain technology.

Lessons Learned and Insights Gained

1. **Collaboration is Key:** Successful implementations often involve collaboration between technology providers, financial institutions, and regulatory bodies.
2. **Focus on Customer Needs:** Innovations should address real customer needs and pain points to drive adoption.
3. **Regulatory Alignment:** Ensuring that AI and blockchain solutions comply with existing regulations is crucial for gaining trust and avoiding legal issues.
4. **Scalability and Flexibility:** It is imperative that solutions are designed with scalability and flexibility at their core, enabling adaptation to dynamic market conditions and evolving technological advancements.

9: FUTURE TRENDS AND EMERGING TECHNOLOGIES

Next-Generation AI Technologies

The future of AI in financial services will be shaped by several emerging technologies and trends.

Explainable AI (XAI)

As AI becomes more integrated into decision-making processes, the need for transparency and explainability grows. Explainable AI aims to make AI models more understandable to humans, providing insights into how decisions are made.

AI-Driven Personalization

Next-generation AI will enable even more personalized financial services, leveraging deep learning and natural language processing to understand individual customer needs and preferences.

Autonomous AI Agents

Autonomous AI agents capable of executing complex tasks without human intervention will revolutionize areas such as trading, investment management, and customer service.

Advancements in Blockchain Technology

Blockchain technology continues to evolve, with several advancements poised to enhance its application in financial services.

Interoperability Solutions

Progress in interoperability will empower diverse blockchain networks to communicate and transact seamlessly, thereby promoting wider adoption and integration across various platforms.

Scalable Consensus Mechanisms

New consensus mechanisms, such as Proof of Stake (PoS) and sharding, aim to improve blockchain scalability, making it more viable for high-volume financial applications.

Privacy-Enhancing Technologies

Technologies like zero-knowledge proofs and confidential transactions will enhance privacy on blockchain networks, addressing concerns around data confidentiality.

Impact of Quantum Computing on AI and Blockchain

Quantum computing has the potential to significantly impact both AI and blockchain technologies.

Quantum AI

Quantum computing can accelerate AI computations, enabling the processing of larger datasets and more complex models at unprecedented speeds. This will lead to breakthroughs in AI capabilities and applications.

Quantum-Resistant Blockchain

The emergence of quantum computing poses a significant threat to the current cryptographic algorithms utilized in blockchain technology. Therefore, it is imperative to develop quantum-resistant cryptographic techniques to safeguard the long-term security and integrity of blockchain networks.

Predictions for the Future of Financial Services

Enhanced Decision-Making

AI and blockchain will enhance decision-making in financial services by providing real-time insights, predictive analytics, and automated processes. This will lead to more informed and timely decisions, benefiting both institutions and customers.

Greater Financial Inclusion

The convergence of AI and blockchain technology is poised to enhance financial inclusion by offering accessible and cost-effective financial services to underserved populations. Decentralized finance (DeFi) platforms will be pivotal in driving this transformative change.

Evolution of Regulatory Frameworks

Regulatory frameworks must evolve alongside technological advancements. Proactive collaboration among regulators, industry stakeholders, and technology experts will be crucial to establish a balanced and supportive regulatory environment.

Integration of Emerging Technologies

Financial services will increasingly integrate emerging technologies such as the Internet of Things (IoT) and 5G, enhancing connectivity, data collection, and real-time processing capabilities.

Sustainable Finance

AI and blockchain will contribute to sustainable finance initiatives by providing transparency and accountability in environmental, social, and governance (ESG) metrics. These technologies will help institutions track and report their sustainability efforts more effectively.

The future of financial services will be shaped by the continuous advancements in AI and blockchain technologies. By addressing current challenges and leveraging emerging trends, financial institutions can unlock new opportunities for innovation, efficiency, and inclusivity. The integration of these technologies will drive the industry towards a more transparent, secure, and customer-centric future.

10: CONCLUSION AND THE ROAD AHEAD

Summary of Key Insights

In this exploration of AI and blockchain innovations in financial services, we have delved into the transformative potential, challenges, and future trends of these cutting-edge technologies. Here are the key insights from our discussion:

1. **Integration of AI and Blockchain**: The fusion of AI and blockchain technologies offers significant advantages, including enhanced security, transparency, and efficiency. AI's ability to analyze large datasets complements blockchain's immutable ledger, creating a robust foundation for various financial applications.
2. **Regulatory and Ethical Considerations**: Navigating the regulatory landscape is crucial for the successful implementation of AI and blockchain. Compliance with existing laws, coupled with ethical considerations such as fairness, accountability, and privacy, are essential to gain public trust and ensure sustainable innovation.
3. **Challenges and Risks**: The adoption of AI and blockchain in financial services comes with technical, operational, and cybersecurity challenges. Addressing scalability, interoperability, and security vulnerabilities is vital for the widespread adoption of these technologies.

4. **Case Studies and Best Practices**: Real-world implementations in banking, insurance, and fintech sectors demonstrate the practical benefits and best practices of AI and blockchain integration. These cases highlight the importance of customer-centric design, robust security measures, and continuous innovation.
5. **Future Trends and Emerging Technologies**: The future of financial services will be shaped by advancements in AI, blockchain, and other emerging technologies such as quantum computing. These innovations will drive greater financial inclusion, enhanced decision-making, and sustainable finance practices.

Strategic Recommendations for Financial Institutions

To leverage the full potential of AI and blockchain, financial institutions should consider the following strategic recommendations:

1. **Invest in Research and Development**: Continuous investment in R&D is essential to stay ahead of technological advancements. Collaborate with academic institutions, technology firms, and industry consortia to drive innovation and develop cutting-edge solutions.
2. **Adopt a Customer-Centric Approach**: Focus on designing products and services that meet the evolving needs of customers. Use AI to provide personalized financial advice and blockchain to ensure transparency and security in transactions.
3. **Enhance Data Governance**: Implement robust data governance frameworks to ensure the accuracy, integrity, and privacy of data. Leverage blockchain's immutable ledger for secure data management and AI for real-time data analysis.
4. **Foster a Culture of Innovation**: Encourage a culture of experimentation and innovation within the organization. Provide training and development opportunities to build a knowledgeable workforce proficient in AI and blockchain technologies.
5. **Engage with Regulators**: Proactively engage with regulatory bodies to stay informed about evolving regulations and contribute to the development of regulatory frameworks. Ensure compliance with local and international standards to avoid legal and reputational risks.
6. **Implement Robust Security Measures**: Prioritize cybersecurity by adopting best practices such as multi-factor authentication, regular security audits, and incident response plans. Address potential vulnerabilities in AI and blockchain systems to safeguard against cyber threats.

The Role of Innovation in Shaping the Future of Finance

Innovation is the driving force behind the transformation of the financial sector. As AI and blockchain technologies continue to evolve, their integration will lead to more intelligent, secure, and efficient financial systems. Here are some ways innovation will shape the future of finance:

1. **Enhanced Financial Inclusion**: AI and blockchain can democratize access to financial services by providing affordable and accessible solutions to underserved populations. Decentralized finance (DeFi) platforms will play a crucial role in this transformation.
2. **Improved Risk Management**: AI's predictive capabilities combined with blockchain's transparency will enable better risk assessment and management. Financial institutions can make data-driven decisions to mitigate risks and enhance regulatory compliance.
3. **Streamlined Operations**: Automation of routine processes through AI and smart contracts will reduce operational costs and improve efficiency. This will allow financial institutions to focus on strategic initiatives and innovation.
4. **Sustainable Finance**: Innovations in AI and blockchain will contribute to sustainable finance practices by providing transparency and accountability in environmental, social, and governance (ESG) metrics. These technologies will help track and report sustainability efforts more effectively.
5. **New Business Models**: The convergence of AI and blockchain will lead to the emergence of new business models and revenue streams. Financial institutions can explore opportunities in areas such as tokenized assets, digital identity verification, and AI-driven investment platforms.

Final Thoughts

The journey of integrating AI and blockchain into financial services is just beginning. While there are challenges and risks, the potential benefits far outweigh the obstacles. Financial institutions that embrace these technologies and adopt a forward-thinking approach will be well-positioned to lead in the future of finance.

Innovation, collaboration, and a commitment to ethical practices will be the key drivers of success. By leveraging AI and blockchain, financial institutions can create more inclusive, transparent, and efficient financial systems that benefit individuals, businesses, and society as a whole.

As we look to the future, it is clear that AI and blockchain will play a pivotal role in shaping the financial landscape. The road ahead is filled with opportunities for those who are willing to innovate, adapt, and embrace the transformative power of these technologies.

REFERENCES

Antonopoulos, A. M., & Wood, G. (2018). *Mastering Ethereum: Building smart contracts and dApps*. O'Reilly Media.

Bahga, A., & Madisetti, V. (2014). *Blockchain Applications: A Hands-On Approach*. VPT.

Belanche, D., Casaló, L. V., & Flavián, C. (2019). Artificial Intelligence in FinTech: Understanding robo-advisors adoption among customers. *Industrial Management & Data Systems, 119*(7), 1411–1430. DOI: 10.1108/IMDS-08-2018-0368

Belanche, D., Casaló, L. V., & Flavián, C. (2019). Artificial Intelligence in FinTech: Understanding robo-advisors adoption among customers. *Industrial Management & Data Systems, 119*(7), 1411–1430. DOI: 10.1108/IMDS-08-2018-0368

Bostrom, N., & Yudkowsky, E. (2014). The Ethics of Artificial Intelligence. In Frankish, K., & Ramsey, W. M. (Eds.), *The Cambridge Handbook of Artificial Intelligence* (pp. 316–334). Cambridge University Press. DOI: 10.1017/CBO9781139046855.020

Boztepe, E., & Usul, H. (2019). *Using the Analysis of Logistic Regression Model in Auditing and Detection of Frauds*. Khazar Journal of Humanities and Social Sciences. DOI: 10.5782/2223-2621.2019.22.3.5

Chen, Y., & Bellavitis, C. (2020). Blockchain disruption and decentralized finance: The rise of decentralized business models. *Journal of Business Venturing Insights, 13*, e00151. DOI: 10.1016/j.jbvi.2019.e00151

Damiani, C., Kalliatakis, G., Sreenivas, M., Al-Attar, M., Rose, J., Pudney, C., Lane, E. F., Cuzick, J., Montana, G., & Brentnall, A. (2023). Evaluation of an AI Model to Assess Future Breast Cancer Risk. *Radiology, 307*(5), e222679. DOI: 10.1148/radiol.222679 PMID: 37310244

Firdaus, R., Xue, Y., Gang, L., & Sibt e Ali, M. (2022). Artificial Intelligence and Human Psychology in Online Transaction Fraud. *Frontiers in Psychology, 13*, 13. DOI: 10.3389/fpsyg.2022.947234 PMID: 36304851

Fitriyah, F. K. (2020). The Roles of Internal Auditor and Leadership Style in Fraud Prevention and Detection.

Gürsoy, D., Chi, O. H., Lu, L., & Nunkoo, R. (2019). Consumers acceptance of artificially intelligent (AI) device use in service delivery. *International Journal of Information Management, 49*, 157–169. DOI: 10.1016/j.ijinfomgt.2019.03.008

Gürsoy, D., Chi, O. H., Lu, L., & Nunkoo, R. (2019). Consumers' acceptance of artificially intelligent (AI) device use in service delivery. *International Journal of Information Management*, *49*, 157–169. DOI: 10.1016/j.ijinfomgt.2019.03.008

Hernandez, J. R. (2011). Good Value from Shared Values: A fraud and risk perspective.

Kim, S., & Park, H. (2020). An Exploratory Study on the Factors Determining Acceptance of Blockchain-Based Financial Platform by Gender. *Journal of Digital Convergence*, *18*(3), 139–147.

Kombe, C., Sam, A., Ally, M., & Finne, A. (2019). Blockchain Technology in Sub-Saharan Africa: Where does it fit in Healthcare Systems: A case of Tanzania. *Journal of Health Informatics in Developing Countries*, 13.

Larkin, C., Drummond Otten, C., & Arvai, J. (2021). Paging Dr. JARVIS! Will people accept advice from artificial intelligence for consequential risk management decisions? *Journal of Risk Research*, *25*(4), 407–422. DOI: 10.1080/13669877.2021.1958047

Mougayar, W. (2016). *The Business Blockchain: Promise, Practice, and the Application of the Next Internet Technology*. Wiley.

Sun, W., Dedahanov, A., Shin, H., & Li, W. (2021). Using extended complexity theory to test SMEs' adoption of Blockchain-based loan system. *PLoS One*, *16*(2), 16. DOI: 10.1371/journal.pone.0245964 PMID: 33544745

Tapscott, D., & Tapscott, A. (2016). *Blockchain Revolution: How the Technology Behind Bitcoin Is Changing Money, Business, and the World*. Penguin.

Torrente, M., Sousa, P., Hernández, R., Blanco, M., Calvo, V., Collazo, A., Guerreiro, G. R., Nuñez, B., Pimentão, J., Sánchez, J. C., Campos, M., Costabello, L., Novácek, V., Menasalvas, E., Vidal, M., & Provencio, M. (2022). An Artificial Intelligence-Based Tool for Data Analysis and Prognosis in Cancer Patients: Results from the Clarify Study. *Cancers (Basel)*, *14*(64041), 4041. DOI: 10.3390/cancers14164041 PMID: 36011034

Veuger, J. (2018). Trust in a viable real estate economy with disruption and blockchain. *Facilities*, *36*(1/2), 103–120. DOI: 10.1108/F-11-2017-0106

Zengler, T. J., & Zheng, Z. (2020). Application of AI in Financial Services: Opportunities, Challenges, and Regulatory Implications. *Journal of Financial Regulation and Compliance*, *28*(3), 285–303. DOI: 10.1108/JFRC-02-2020-0022

Chapter 11
Smart Contracts in AI-Driven Decentralized Finance:
Navigating Emerging Technologies and Market Dynamics

C. V. Suresh Babu
https://orcid.org/0000-0002-8474-2882
Hindustan Institute of Technology and Science, India

G. Gokul
https://orcid.org/0009-0003-5367-6901
Vel Tech Rangarajan Dr. Sagunthala R&D Institute of Science and Technology, India

ABSTRACT

This study aims to explore the integration of smart contracts within decentralized finance (DeFi) platforms, focusing on their security, functionality, and potential applications across various industries. Utilizing a comprehensive survey methodology, the research analyzes existing literature and case studies to identify the advantages and challenges associated with smart contracts. Key findings reveal that while smart contracts enhance efficiency and transparency, they also present significant security vulnerabilities that necessitate advanced mitigation strategies, including the use of artificial intelligence. The study concludes that addressing these challenges is crucial for the broader adoption of smart contracts, emphasizing the need for standardized frameworks and rigorous testing protocols. The implications of this research highlight the transformative potential of smart contracts in reshaping

DOI: 10.4018/979-8-3693-7160-2.ch011

traditional business models and regulatory landscapes.

1. INTRODUCTION

1.1 Background and Context

Nick Szabo introduced the idea of smart contracts for the first time. One of the most well-known platforms for smart contracts is Ethereum, which has a wide range of uses across various industries. At first, smart contracts were limited to use in financial applications, like ERC20 tokens. Because of different industrial requirements, smart contract platforms have been invented over time in a variety of ways. (Tharaka Hewa, et al. 2022)

Blockchain and Smart Contracts

With the help of distributed ledger technology, or Blockchain, transactions can be conducted safely and openly without the need for middlemen like governments or financial institutions. It is composed of a node network that collaborates to keep a shared transaction database up to date. A consensus process is used by the network to validate every transaction, and every node has a copy of the database (Suresh Babu, C. V. & Abhinaba Pal. 2023). This guarantees that all transactions are transparent and unchangeable, and that there is no way for the database to be tampered with. One important development in Blockchain technology is the idea of SCs. To automate complicated financial transactions without the need for middlemen, self-executing programs, or SCs, run on a Blockchain. When specific requirements are satisfied, they are automatically carried out and stored on the Blockchain. Applications for SCs include voting systems, financial derivatives, and supply chain management. Figure 1 depicts the general architecture of Blockchain.

Figure 1. General architecture of blockchain

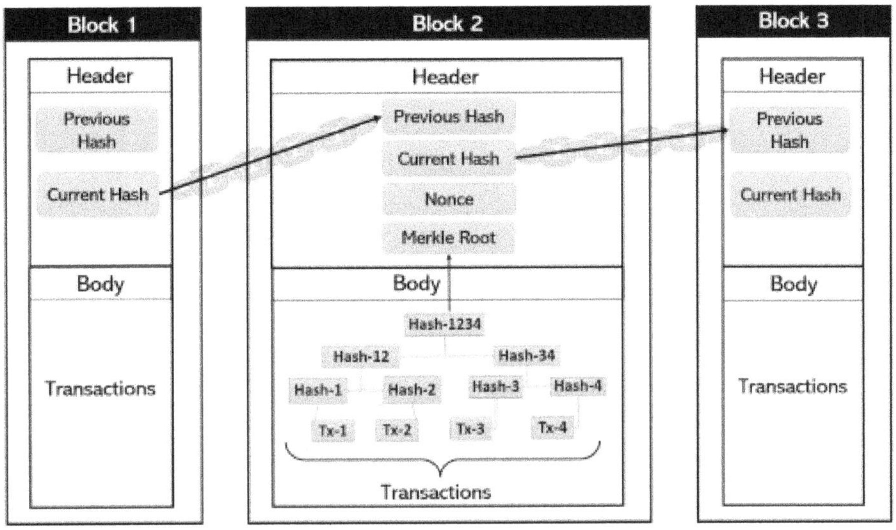

Application Domains

A number of markets could undergo substantial change if Blockchain and smart contract technologies are widely adopted. Blockchain technology, for example, can be used in the financial industry to create a more secure and dependable payment system. With SCs, the need for middlemen is eliminated and transaction fees are significantly reduced, completely changing the way business is done. Building decentralized lending and investing platforms with Blockchain technology can help increase the accessibility of financial services for individuals and businesses. (Moez Krichen 2023).

1.2 Relevance of Smart Contracts in DeFi

Smart contracts are autonomous programs that enforce and execute the terms of an agreement using software code and computational infrastructure. Initially proposed by Buterin et al., they were first applied in the financial industry, leveraging distributed ledger technology. Operating as decentralized programs on Blockchain networks, smart contracts are immutable and cryptographically verified to ensure program integrity and trustworthiness. They execute peer-to-peer, eliminating the need for centralized third-party intervention, and remain operational without dependency on centralized services. The key distinction of smart contracts lies in their ability to autonomously execute based on predefined conditions, rendering them intelligent compared to traditional paper-based agreements. (Tharaka Hewa, et al. 2020)

1.3 Objectives of the Chapter

To investigate the integration of AI technologies into DeFi platforms and smart contracts.
To identify and explain the advantages of combining AI with smart contracts in DeFi.
To analyze the risks and challenges involved in integrating AI and smart contracts into DeFi.
To examine the market dynamics and regulatory landscape impacting AI-driven DeFi platforms and smart contracts.
To present real-world examples and analyses of AI-powered smart contracts in DeFi.
To forecast future trends and potential developments at the intersection of AI, smart contracts, and DeFi.
To provide best practices and guidelines for successfully implementing AI-driven smart contracts in DeFi projects.

1.4 Architectural Framework

The structure of Blockchain networks is composed of the following layers: (Alfredo J. Perez and Sherali Zeadally 2022).

- **A P2P network:** Free communication between Blockchain nodes is ensured by the P2P network. The network of these Blockchain nodes is decentralized, with nodes dispersed throughout the world.
- **Global distributed ledger:** The storage protocol is implemented by the global distributed ledger in order to keep the ledger updated. Using public key cryptography, a distinct digital pseudonym (address) is generated for every user. A transaction facilitates communication between two addresses. Smart contracts, which carry out the transactions, are used to conduct data actions in the global ledger.
- **Applications:** Application Programming Interfaces (APIs) are implemented for different application scenarios by the Blockchain network's application layer. Digital document management platforms, telemetry systems, financial services, and copyright protection are a few examples of these applications.

Figure 2. Architectural framework

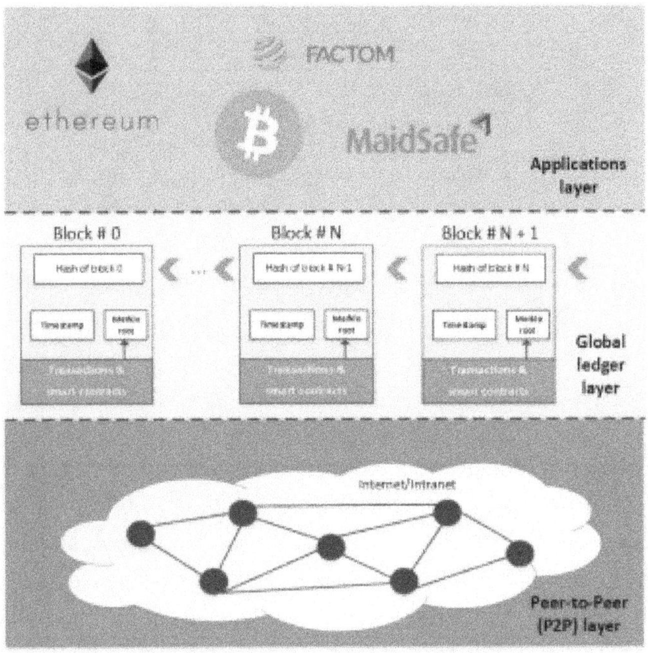

Ethereum Running Environment

Ethereum runs on blocks, Ethereum Virtual Machines (EVM), and smart-contact codes. Block mining basically identifies valid transactions and assembles the transformation of the corresponding state into a new block. The miner selects transactions, runs the smart contract's codes, modifies the state, computes the nonce (proof of work), and appends the recently mined block to the older Blockchain in order to accomplish this. The root of a modified Merkle Patricia tree (Modified MPT), which is a data structure used to store hashed Ethereum accounts, is hashed and kept in each block. To enhance comprehension of the smart contract, we elucidate the Ethereum block structure, as depicted in Figure 1.

Figure 3. Etherum block structure

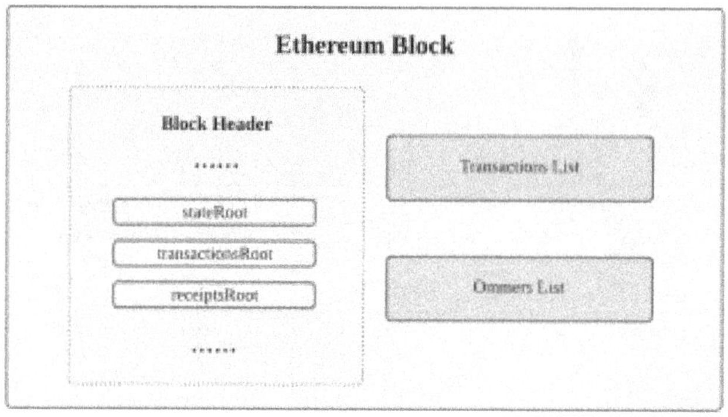

Block: Ethereum blocks consist of three components: a header, a transaction list, and an ommers list. Three Modified MPT root nodes—stateRoot, transactionRoot, and receiptsRoot—as well as additional block-specific data are contained in the header. The world state trie, transaction trie, and receipts trie Modified MPTs are those three. Every account, its status, and all transactions within those tries are kept in storage. Another Modified MPT exists, called the account storage content trie, whose root node is kept in the world state trie's account state. The actual transactions and ommers that the miner selects during the mining process are listed in the next two lists. Ommers are blocks whose parents are the same as the parents of the current block (Suresh Babu, C. V. & Sanjai Das 2023).

World state trie: A mapping between an account state and its address exists for each leaf node in this graph. Consequently, every account in this trial is linked to every other account, including the contract and external accounts. A single world state trie exists for each block.

Account storage contents trie: As we previously discussed, there are four fields in the account state. Field storage houses the trie root node of the account storage content. For this reason, this trie is included in the block as a component of the world state trie rather than being directly stored in the block header. This file holds all of the contract data.

Transaction trie: This table contains the hash of every transaction that is part of a block.

This transaction list and the block itself will remain unchanged after the block has been mined.

Receipts trie: Each receipt includes logs, the transaction status code, the accumulated gas used, and the results of the activity that was carried out. The serialization of this keys and information are kept together in the receipts trie. (Haozhe Zhou, et. al. 2022).

Figure 4. Block diagram

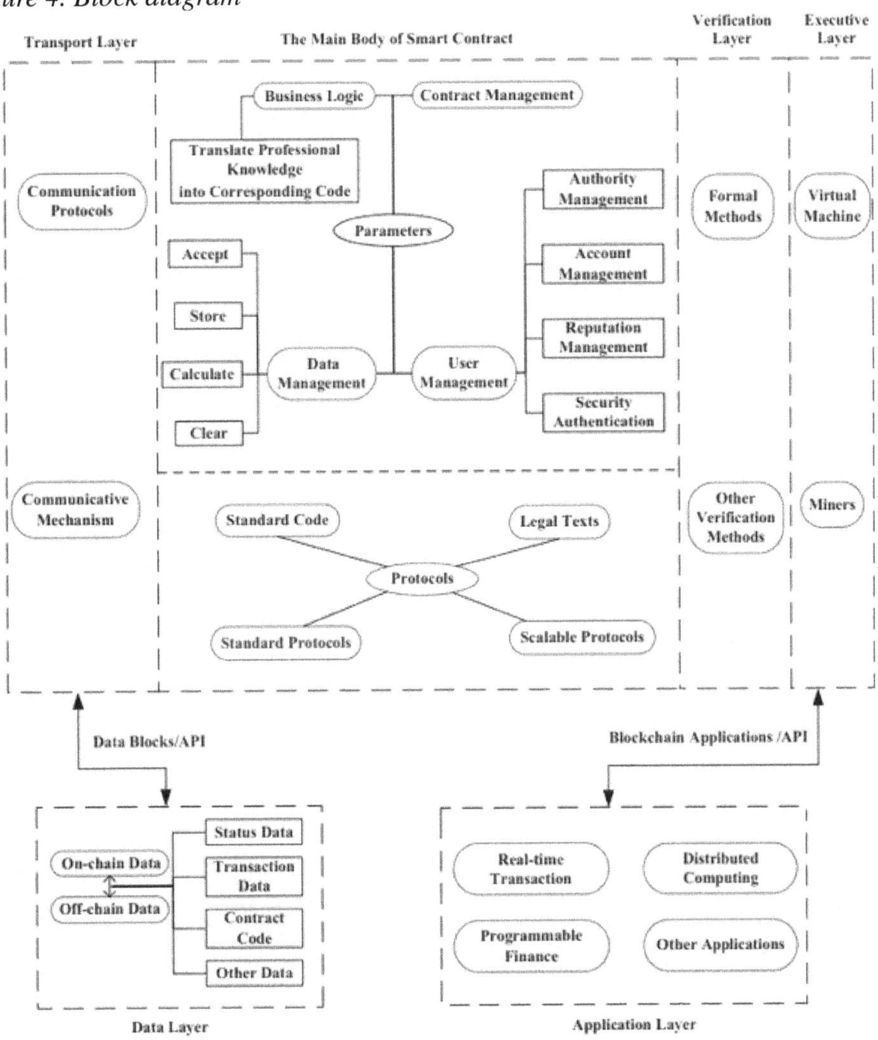

2. UNDERSTANDING SMART CONTRACTS

2.1 Definition and Key Features

Smart contracts, as defined by various experts, are self-executing programs stored and run on Blockchain to manage digital assets and agreements without needing third-party intervention. They are described as:

- "Computerized transaction protocols" that execute contract terms (Szabo, 1996).
- Programs for Blockchain applications like auctions, financial contracts, and permission management (Chen, Whitters, et al., 2022).
- Code deployed in or compiled from Blockchain environments (De Filippi, Primavera, et al., 2021).
- Digital agreements noted for automation and transparency but vulnerable to attacks due to complexity (Krichen, 2023).
- Self-executing programs ensuring peer agreements without third-party guarantees (Zhou, Fard, et al., 2022).

Smart contracts typically only perform basic functions, including:

- Issuing tokens for fundraising purposes, such as in token sales or Initial Coin Offerings (ICOs).
- Managing tokens as digital collectibles, as seen in examples like CryptoKitties.
- Facilitating decentralized marketplaces for trading digital tokens, like OpenSea.
- Enabling conditional or recurring payments based on predefined criteria.
- Operating joint savings accounts that restrict daily withdrawals.
- Implementing escrow systems to execute transactions upon specific conditions.
- Running simple lottery systems for collecting and redistributing funds to winners.
- Supporting transparent gambling systems such as prediction markets, like Augur.

However, combining multiple smart contracts can lead to more sophisticated applications. These include decentralized finance platforms such as lending protocols (e.g., MakerDAO) and liquidity pools (e.g., Uniswap, Aave). Smart contracts can also power social media platforms (e.g., Akasha, Karma, Peepeth) and decentralized governance systems for Blockchain assets, known as Decentralized Autonomous Organizations (e.g., TheDAO, MolochDAO, DxDAO) (De Filippi et. al. 2021)

2.2 Historical Development and Evolution

Figure 5. Evolution of smart contracts

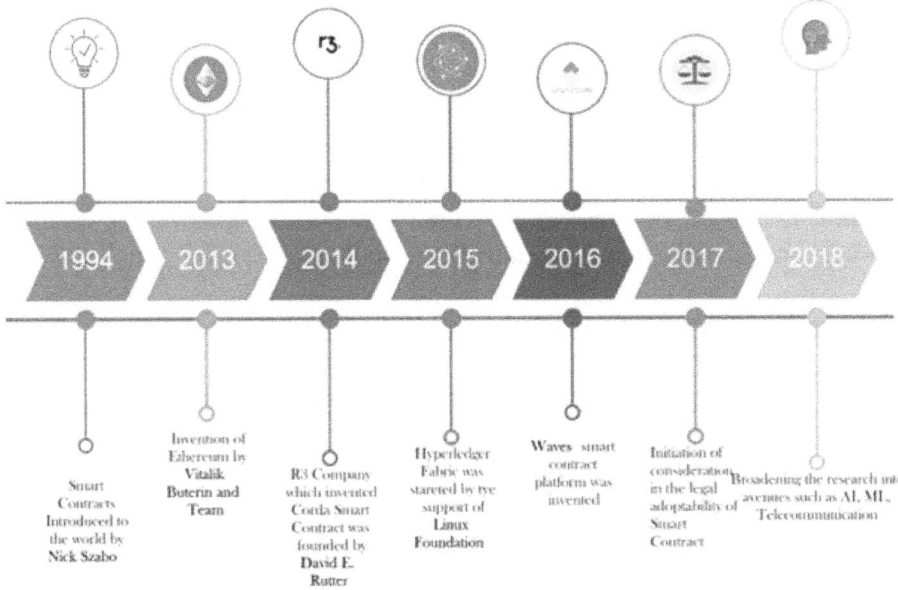

Figure 5 shows significant turning points in the development of Blockchain-based smart contracts across time. In 1994, Nick Szabo presented the notion of smart contracts to the public, marking the beginning of their existence. One of the biggest developments in smart contract history is the creation of Ethereum. Users are now able to roll out smart contract apps in public Blockchains thanks to the public Ethereum Blockchain (Tharaka Hewa, Mika et al. 2022). At first, the main purpose of Ethereum was currency exchange. In partnership with the Linux Foundation, the Hyperledger Fabric project was launched. Hyperledger Fabric's path has diverged from Ethereum's as the latter was meant to be a business Blockchain. A lot of platforms are being designed with enterprise requirements in mind.With the development of smart contracts across several platforms and a wide range of use cases, the research centered on the legalization of smart contracts. The place of smart contracts among the burgeoning computer science research subjects is a major area of concentration for the next study.

Nick Szabo (1996), an American computer scientist, coined the term "smart contract" in 1994. He defined it as a computerized protocol that executes contract terms. The goals of smart contracts include meeting common conditions (e.g., payment, confidentiality), minimizing exceptions, and reducing reliance on intermediaries. Economically, they aim to cut fraud, arbitration, and transaction costs. Szabo (1996) argued that contracts are crucial for trust in societies. By 1996, he noted that contracts are fundamental to free market economies. Since the 1990s, technology has evolved to automate contracts, with early examples like Chaum's DigitCash (1988) showcasing privacy-protecting payment systems. Szabo (1996) also emphasized that smart contracts should be verifiable, observable, and enforceable to be valuable. His predictions have proven accurate: smart contracts are now cutting costs and speeding up execution, as demonstrated by various examples.

Life Cycle of Smart Contracts

The four stages of a smart contract that the authors describe are creation, deployment, execution, and completion (Haozhe Zhou, et. al. 2022).

- **Creation**: Several high-level languages, including Solidity, Serpent, and Bamboo, can target an EVM during its creation phase. Solidity is the most often utilized one. It is Turing-complete and has features similar to JavaScript. The Solidity codes are compiled to opcodes, which are low-level instructions used by EVM, and encoded to bytecodes for storage purposes because EVM is unable to run the codes directly.
- **Deployment:** Based on the Ethereum protocol, there are two types of transactions: those that result in contract deployment and those that initiate message calls. A second piece of code that will be stored in the EVM running environment and executed at a later time is returned by the developer when they initiate a transaction containing bytecodes (which are kept in a field named init in the transaction structure).
- **Execution:** A smart contract that is in the execution stage is a program that is operating, much like a thread or process on a standalone computer. It will get data that will be sent to the contract as parameters as well as transactions (the first kind). The EVM then carries out each command one at a time until it is completed or the gas limit is reached. The moment a new block is mined, this process takes place. • Finalization. States are updated and recorded in Blockchains with transactions following execution. The smart contract's life cycle is now complete.

2.3 Types of Smart Contracts

In the Blockchain, there are three types of smart contracts. They are:

- Smart legal contracts
- Decentralized Autonomous Organizations (DAO)
- Application Logic Contracts (ALC)

Smart legal contract: It is lawful to get in touch with the most well-known smart contract. This includes all permissible clauses found in standard contracts, and incorporating standard legal regulations into a smart contract will meet both parties' needs by including the essential rules required by the agreement. The smart contract will adhere to the legal notes that will simultaneously fully satisfy the needs of the clients on both sides. As a result, users and agreement creators will be in balance.

Decentralized Autonomous Organizations: A decentralised autonomous organisation (DAO), also known as a decentralised autonomous corporation (DAC), is an association established by transparent rules encoded as a computer programme, subject to the constraints imposed by its members, and independent of any external influence. It is a localized component without a central authority. It's completely free and simple: smart contracts set the framework, carry out the decisions and proposals that have been agreed upon, and—surprisingly—the actual code is always available for public inspection.

Application Logic Contracts: ALC which ensure more widespread mechanization, more economical exchange, and versatility while enabling the devices to operate independently and safely. These agreements include code that is application-based and typically doesn't conflict with other Blockchain contracts. It utilizes cross-device communication, much like how Blockchain technology and the Internet of Things (IoT) combine. (Shobha tyagi, et al, 2022)

2.4 Role in Decentralized Finance (DeFi)

Cryptocurrencies and decentralized finance (DeFi) utilize Blockchain technology to facilitate peer-to-peer fund transfers without intermediaries. DeFi operates through the automated execution of smart contracts on Blockchain networks, enabling decentralized applications (DApps) to conduct financial functions on immutable, publicly visible ledgers. Smart contracts, often written in high-level languages like

Solidity, are self-executing programs triggered by predefined conditions that enforce agreements transparently on the Blockchain.

Figure 6. Blockchain in decentralized finance (DeFi)

Source: created in https://designer.microsoft.com/image-creator

Ethereum, the leading platform for smart contract implementation, supports a wide array of DeFi applications. As of June 2021, with a market capitalization of $317.3 billion, Ethereum hosts over 95% of DeFi projects. While Bitcoin also supports smart contracts, its script language is primarily focused on verifying signatures, limiting its functionality compared to Ethereum, which operates as a computation platform with the Ethereum Virtual Machine (EVM). The EVM serves as a secure execution environment where smart contracts reference the Blockchain ledger state (Haozhe Zhou et.al. 2022).

3. EMERGING TECHNOLOGIES ENHANCING SMART CONTRACTS

3.1 Artificial Intelligence (AI)

The study focuses on how to enhance SC security through artificial intelligence (AI). We present an overview of Blockchain technology and Smart Contracts (SCs), and we talk about potential attacks on SCs. Following a thorough examination of the ways in which AI can be leveraged to improve SC security, we go on to present the different categories of AI and their cybersecurity applications. Additionally, we highlight the unanswered problems and potential paths for this field's future study. Our study shows how AI can strengthen SC security and dependability while acting as an effective defense against attacks. In terms of AI for SC security, this paper establishes the foundation for upcoming investigations.

3.1.1 AI Integration with Smart Contracts

By examining the potential of artificial intelligence (AI) in this field, this work contributes to the field of SC security research. More specifically, it provides:

- An explanation of SCs and any possible vulnerabilities
- An explanation of Blockchain's role in SC security
- An outline of artificial intelligence, including its different subtypes and cybersecurity applications
- An analysis of the possible benefits of deploying AI for SC security, including its ability to recognize and neutralize threats
- A review of open issues and possible directions for future research in this area

3.1.2 Machine Learning and Predictive Analytics

People's interest in the potential applications of AI and machine learning to strengthen SC security is rising. These techniques may offer a more comprehensive and proactive approach to security by enabling the detection of anomalies and unusual activity that may indicate a security breach. These issues can be resolved to increase the trustworthiness of Blockchain technology and SCs (Moez Krichen 2023).

Artificial intelligence (AI) and machine learning, on the other hand, train computers on large datasets so they can identify patterns and render decisions. According to those figures. Since it wasn't specifically programmed, this approach is more flexible to new information and circumstances.

3.2 Blockchain Technology

Blockchain-based "smart contracts" (SCs) eliminate the need for middlemen like banks or lawyers by automating complex financial transactions. They guarantee that the database cannot be tampered with and that all transactions are transparent and unchangeable. They represent a significant breakthrough in Blockchain technology that has the potential to drastically alter how business is conducted.

The supply chain industry is another area where Blockchain technology shows promise. Blockchain technology makes it possible for businesses to monitor the entire product delivery process. It also makes financial transactions automated, removing the need for middlemen and enhancing speed and accuracy.

Blockchain technology is also applicable in the voting domain. Voter fraud can be completely eliminated and a fair and accurate count of all votes cast can be ensured with a Blockchain-based voting system. SCs can automate the process of tallying votes, resulting in a more precise and expedient process.

3.2.1 Blockchain Fundamentals

Network and security, finance and economy, cryptography, distributed networking, software engineering, and data structure are just a few of the domains that can be combined to evaluate Blockchain technology from version 1.0 to version 3.0 (Sangjukta Das, et al. 2023). In order to resolve the double spend issue, Satoshi Namakato published a Blockchain-based, cryptographically secure technique. When someone uses the same digital currency twice, it's known as double spending. This occurs when the attacker purchases multiple services. As a data structure consisting of a hashed chain of timestamps, Namakato defined Blockchain technology. There is a chain of hashes created by each timestamp, which includes the previous timestamp attached to it.

Below is a description of all three Blockchain versions:

1. **Version 1.0 (currency):** Security researcher Hall Finley first presented the concept of Blockchain version 1.0 in 2005, with the intention of generating money through the solution of mathematical puzzles. Following then, a large number of additional Blockchain-based cryptocurrencies were released to facilitate financial transactions.
2. **Blockchain Version 2.0 (smart contracts):** This version of the technology went beyond cryptocurrencies and included smart contracts, which are computer programs that run automatically whenever a certain condition is met. The Blockchain was able to handle more transactions on the public network in this version.

3. **Version 3.0 (D Apps):** Decentralized Applications (D Apps), which make use of decentralized communication and storage systems, are introduced by Blockchain version 3.0. Numerous decentralized applications, or D Apps, exist, including Tor, Popcorn, BitTorrent, Bit Message, and more. The most recent version, known as version 4.0 (Blockchain for the industry), presents business and industrial requirements-solving techniques enabled by Blockchain technology.

3.2.2 Smart Contract Platforms (e.g., Ethereum, Binance Smart Chain)

Another important topic covered in the paper is the Blockchain's design patterns. With the application on the Ethereum smart contracts platform, Marino et al. created a set of standards that allowed the smart contracts to modify or reverse a decision that had been made and communicated.

Different Blockchain platforms have different ways of implementing smart contracts in practice. Ethereum is the platform that introduced the concept of smart contracts in the real world among all of these others, and it is currently the most popular smart contract platform. (Kai Peng, Meijun Li, et al. 2021)

3.3 Quantum Computing

In contrast to other Blockchain implementations, its unique structural design makes it immune to the phenomenon of quantum computing. The main problem with tangle and not upholding any laws is deciding which of the two older transactions to approve. (Chandan Trivedi, et al. 2024)

3.3.1 Potential Impact on Smart Contracts

The supplier uses traditional factoring for post-shipment financing and bank financing for pre-shipment financing; first, we find that commitment frictions exist between the supplier and the bank under the baseline model. More precisely, the supplier cannot commit to the post-shipment factoring adoption decision, which changes the bank's risk exposure, until the bank decides on the interest rate during the pre-shipment loan request. The purchase order information (i.e., wholesale price and order quantity) would therefore be used by the bank to predict the supplier's factoring decision. Consequently, in order to persuade the bank to adopt post-shipment factoring and obtain a lower loan rate, the supplier may purposefully "overprice" in their wholesale price offering. Such overpricing severely damages the retailer's profit margin and causes a significant decrease in the order quantity. Using smart contracts allows the supplier to legitimately commit to factoring, which reduces overpricing brought on by commitment frictions and improves supply chain efficiency (Xiaoyu Wang and Fasheng Xu 2022).

Secondly, in the event that the retailer provides BDF as a substitute for pre-shipment financing, the smart contract may lower the profit margin for the supplier—and potentially the supply chain margin as well—provided that the cost of capital falls within a particular mode. Smart contracts dissuade retailers from offering Best and Final Price (BDF) because doing so requires them to trade off the capital cost of BDF against the wholesale cost resulting from the supplier's overpricing behavior in the absence of BDF. This is the main factor contributing to the negative impact. To be more precise, the retailer bears the reallocation of the production financing cost (capital cost) when BDF is implemented.

In the absence of interactions (and hence commitment frictions) with the bank, the supplier would be able to reciprocally maintain the relatively low optimal wholesale price, resulting in lower wholesale costs for the retailer. Additionally, the supplier's overpricing behavior is corrected and the commitment frictions are fully resolved upon adoption of smart contracts. Consequently, the benefit of BDF's lower wholesale costs is eliminated, discouraging the retailer from providing BDF and resulting in a precipitous drop in the supplier's profit because they can no longer offer interest-free financing.

Third, in cases where the supplier has access to both factoring and invoice trading as post-shipment financing, the supplier will always choose the latter due to its greater trading flexibility, which enables the supplier to keep accounts receivable on hand in the event of a liquidity shock, thereby avoiding needless post-shipment financing costs. Nevertheless, we discover that, surprisingly, the supplier may end up worse off with such a preferred option. Here is an explanation for the intuition. Invoice trading, in addition to the benefit of trading flexibility, by its very nature also renders commitment frictions ubiquitous and irreversible, whereas they may be mostly resolved. With factoring overpricing, Wang and Xu: Smart Contract in Trade Finance 5. The term "commitment trap" describes this phenomenon. In addition, the two elements that make up the value of invoice trading in comparison to factoring are:

(i) The premium difference plus trading flexibility together provide the explicit benefit.
(ii) The commitment trap brought about by invoice trading drives the implicit cost. The adoption dilemma of invoice trading can arise when there is a relatively high invoice trading premium because the implicit cost of commitment trap may outweigh the explicit benefit. Fortunately, by resolving the commitment frictions and the commitment trap, smart contracts (when combined with factoring) can add positive value in this situation.

3.3.2 Current Research and Future Prospects

Various research and development approaches are being used to integrate Blockchain technology with Internet of Things-based healthcare, with a focus on block size. On a Blockchain, transactions are just short statements of record-keeping that are stored in blocks. Encouraging all medical records to be stored on a Blockchain will result in a larger chain overall, requiring more data at every node. In this version, the difficulty lies in the fact that sensor devices used for smart healthcare have little processing power and storage, making it difficult to integrate them into a Blockchain. They frequently also oppose the installation of thin clients in order to allow users to connect to the Blockchain network (Chandan Trivedi, et al. 2024).

3.4 Other Relevant Technologies

3.4.1 Internet of Things (IoT)

In crowdsensing systems, large-scale sensor networks are deployed using consumer electronics like smartphones and Internet of Things gadgets. In this article, we list some of the most important privacy and security concerns that arise when developing crowdsensing systems using Blockchain and smart contracts (Alfredo J. Perez and Sherali Zeadally 2022).

In crowdsensing systems, large-scale sensor networks are deployed using consumer electronics like smartphones and Internet of Things gadgets. In this article, we list some of the most important privacy and security concerns that arise when developing crowdsensing systems using Blockchain and smart contracts.

3.4.2 Cryptographic Techniques

Modern cryptographic techniques, which have become indispensable in many industries, enable the protection of the security and integrity of Blockchain systems. These techniques have been successfully implemented in a variety of real-world scenarios by addressing particular issues and enhancing trust in decentralized networks. The following are some well-known instances of the application of cutting-edge cryptographic techniques in the Blockchain industry:

Enhanced Security in Supply Chain Management

In order to protect data and validate the flow of goods and information throughout the supply chain, supply chain management solutions based on Blockchain technology require sophisticated cryptographic techniques. With the use of multi-signature schemes, participants can verify transfers and transactions with the consent of multiple parties, reducing the possibility of fraud or tampering. In the supply chain, homomorphic encryption protects sensitive data like pricing or trade secrets, while zero-knowledge proofs offer privacy-preserving product authenticity and quality verification. These cryptographic techniques enhance supply chain operations' accountability, traceability, and transparency.

Authentication and Identity Management

Blockchain-based identity management systems streamline identity verification procedures while protecting personal data with cutting-edge cryptographic techniques. Zero-knowledge proofs allow people to confirm their identities without disclosing too much personal information. By distributing and strengthening private key management, threshold cryptography lowers the possibility of identity theft and unauthorized access. By offering enhanced privacy, data protection, and user control over personal information, this elevates digital identity systems to a new level (Karolina 2023).

Smart Contracts and Financial Transactions

Advanced cryptographic techniques play a crucial role in ensuring secure transactions and smart contract execution in cryptocurrency and Blockchain-based finance systems. While enabling transactions requiring the involvement of multiple parties, the use of multi-signature schemes helps increase the security surrounding cryptocurrency wallets. While homomorphic encryption safeguards private financial data kept on the Blockchain, zero-knowledge proofs allow for anonymous transactions and maintain regulatory compliance. Consequently, safe, open, and auditable financial transactions within decentralized networks are made possible by these cryptographic techniques.

4. MARKET DYNAMICS INFLUENCING SMART CONTRACTS

4.1 Technological Advancements

Enhancing Security

Smart contracts automate contractual obligations, replacing human agents with electronic counterparts. Traditional contract law emphasizes human autonomy in assuming obligations, such as through the autonomy principle or will theory. In smart contracting, machines utilize AI and machine learning to predict and fulfill promises, thereby reducing human involvement in contract formation. This shift prompts inquiries into the moral theory of contracting, as promises are pivotal in moral and legal interactions. Unlike traditional reliance on law, trust, and validation by a select group, smart contracts redefine how agreements are validated (Farshad Ghodoosi 2021).

For instance, when purchasing a used laptop on Amazon, the buyer relies on the platform and seller, believes in legal safeguards, checks reviews, and consults trusted acquaintances. Similar considerations are made by the seller.

This evolution challenges established norms, highlighting the transformative impact of smart contracts on contractual practices.

Advanced Auditing Tools

Ghaleb and Pattabiraman introduced SolidiFI, an automated tool designed to evaluate multiple static analysis tools used for smart contracts, including Oyente, Securify, Mythril, SmartCheck, Manticore, and Slither. SolidiFI injects seven distinct types of vulnerabilities into smart contracts and utilizes these security-analysis tools to identify them. This methodology aims to assess the effectiveness of these tools in detecting vulnerabilities such as timestamp dependency, unhandled exceptions, integer overflow/underflow, tx.origin usage, re-entrancy issues, unchecked send operations, and transaction order dependence.

While SolidiFI focuses on static analysis tools, it does not extend its evaluation to include dynamic analysis and formal verification tools. This study adopts a survey methodology similar to that of Praitheeshan et al., analyzing smart-contract security-analysis approaches across three categories: static, dynamic, and formal verification. It specifically examines newly proposed security-analysis tools and their contributions to enhancing smart-contract security (Zhou, H.; et.al 2022).

Role of AI in Identifying and Mitigating Security Threats

Recent advancements in mitigating smart contract threats highlight the adoption of AI-driven approaches utilizing machine learning (Suresh Babu, C. V., Sudhir Manoharan et a.l, 2024). These methodologies are particularly impactful for two primary reasons. Firstly, AI solutions leverage the robust capabilities inherent in modern smart contracts. Secondly, they have proven effective in bolstering security across diverse computing domains (N. Ivanov et.al 2023).

The inherent complexity of smart contracts poses challenges for traditional static and formal analytical methods. Contemporary smart contracts, often Turing-complete and implemented using languages like Solidity and Vyper, offer a wide array of coding possibilities. This diversity complicates the effectiveness of static methods, which typically rely on predefined patterns to identify vulnerabilities. In contrast, machine learning methods, while also pattern-based, benefit from recent advancements such as deep neural networks. These advancements enable them to explore vastly larger and more complex feature spaces compared to static approaches.

The use of AI and machine learning in security applications has been on the rise in recent years, notably in areas such as malware detection (N. Ivanov et.al 2023). Although the integration of machine learning methods for smart contract threat mitigation is still evolving, their inherent flexibility and adaptability hold promise for significantly enhancing smart contract security defenses in the foreseeable future.

Improving Scalability

In response to the scalability challenges faced by smart contracts, Layer 2 solutions have emerged as a pivotal strategy within Blockchain technology. While Layer 1 constitutes the fundamental architecture of the main Blockchain, Layer 2 functions as an overlay network built atop this foundational infrastructure. Layer 2 encompasses diverse protocols and solutions aimed at enhancing transaction speed and scalability across major cryptocurrency networks.

Layer 2 protocols establish a secondary framework where Blockchain transactions and operations can independently transpire outside the constraints of Layer 1, the primary Blockchain. This separation is designed to mitigate the inherent scaling limitations of the main-chain environment. Two prominent examples of Layer 2 solutions include the Bitcoin Lightning Network and Ethereum Plasma.

The Lightning Network, spearheaded in part by MIT Media Lab's Digital Currency Initiative, is a lightweight software solution tailored to scale public Blockchains and foster interoperability among cryptocurrencies. It achieves this by shifting small transactions to a secure "off-chain" setting, thereby reducing costs and processing times, and reserving direct Blockchain settlement for larger transactions.

In contrast, Ethereum Plasma consists of smart contracts that facilitate the creation of multiple Blockchains nested within a root Blockchain. The root Blockchain oversees the state of Plasma chains and intervenes only in instances of confirmed fraud. This architecture enables numerous Plasma Blockchains to coexist autonomously, each supporting its unique logic and smart contract capabilities, thereby enabling decentralized applications to operate efficiently at scale.

In summary, Layer 2 solutions alleviate a substantial portion of the workload traditionally borne by the main-chain, thereby enhancing scalability. While the main-chain remains pivotal for security and consensus, Layer 2 protocols offer enhanced throughput capable of supporting hundreds or even thousands of transactions per second. Consequently, Layer 2 solutions effectively address the scalability challenges inherent in Blockchain networks.

State Channels

State channels, first conceptualized by Coleman (Lydia d. Negka et. al. 2021), were initially implemented in practical applications like chess games around the same time. While state channels originated from the simpler concept of payment channels, which focused on facilitating off-chain payments to address Bitcoin's scalability issues, they have evolved into a more versatile solution. Platforms like Ethereum have adopted payment channel concepts, such as Raiden, and adapted them for broader Blockchain interactions.

Payment channels, despite their initial focus on payments, remain crucial for Blockchain scalability research. They serve as the foundation for state channels, enabling more complex interactions beyond simple payments. Innovations in payment channels often translate into advancements in state channels, as both share fundamental concepts and strategies.

State channels extend the capabilities of payment channels by allowing arbitrary state transitions and enabling off-chain execution of smart contracts without direct interaction with the Blockchain. This approach aims to reduce the number of on-chain transactions while maintaining security guarantees. State channels operate in two primary modes: optimistic, where participants assume honest behavior and exchange state updates off-chain, and pessimistic, where on-chain interactions resolve disputes arising from potential malicious actions.

However, state channels rely on the continuous operation (liveness) of the underlying Blockchain for security. Participants trust that any necessary transaction can be published on-chain to maintain security and resolve disputes. Blockchain systems act as trusted arbitrators, ensuring the integrity of state channel operations and ensuring fair outcomes.

Sidechains

In contrast to state channels, sidechains operate independently and in parallel to the main-chain. They offer scalability benefits by enabling secure asset transfers between the sidechain and main-chain. However, sidechains introduce trade-offs between scalability and security, as they may not share the same consensus protocol as the main-chain.

Role of Continuous Innovation and Global Collaboration

The future of AI-driven decentralized finance is being shaped by smart contracts, which integrate artificial intelligence (AI) to analyze data and identify patterns. In crowdsensing systems, data analysis outcomes may be disseminated to participants or external entities, depending on system design (Alfredo J. Perez and Sherali Zeadally 2022).

AI replicates human decision-making by learning from historical data and detecting patterns. In contrast, Blockchain operates as a decentralized ledger, employing consensus protocols among miners to record transactions securely.

While both AI and Blockchain have demonstrated success in various sectors, current applications often require more advanced solutions. Collaborating AI with Blockchain offers unique advantages that could significantly benefit industrial and academic sectors alike in development, implementation, and operation.

Cortex AI has pioneered a platform enabling developers to create AI-driven Blockchain applications through open participation, fostering innovation at the intersection of artificial intelligence and decentralized technologies.

4.2 Regulatory Landscape

4.2.1 Current Regulations and Compliance

Though smart contracts have benefits, there are a few obstacles to overcome when incorporating them into the legal system (Harshdeep Rapal 2024):

- **Legal Recognition:** A varied and dynamic legal environment is reflected in the differing legal statuses of smart contracts across jurisdictions. In the US, some states have passed legislation specifically recognizing and upholding smart contracts, including Tennessee and Arizona. The enforceability and legal standing of many other jurisdictions' laws, however, are seriously unclear since they haven't yet established clear frameworks. Due to the need to manage varying legal requirements and interpretations, this lack of consistency can present difficulties for companies that operate in multiple regions. That being said, in order to guarantee the widespread adoption and dependability of smart contracts, it is imperative that their legal status be recognized.
- **Enforceability**: Complying with current contract law principles, such as offer, acceptance, and consideration, is crucial to making sure smart contracts are enforceable in court. Smart contracts are self-executing and automated; they frequently do not have traditional written terms or signatures, which makes alignment difficult. The accuracy and lucidity of the code, which must

clearly express the goals and conditions of the parties involved, are also necessary for its legal enforceability. Local contract laws, which differ greatly amongst jurisdictions, must also be complied with by smart contracts. To ensure that smart contracts satisfy all legal requirements, businesses may need to seek legal expertise for the drafting and review process.

- **Jurisdictional Issues:** The decentralized nature of Blockchain makes it difficult to identify the relevant jurisdiction and legal framework for a smart contract, particularly when dealing with cross-border transactions. In contrast to traditional contracts, which are typically regulated by national laws, smart contracts function on an international network that crosses national borders. Conflicts of law may arise as a result, with several jurisdictions vying for control over the same contract. Clear language in the smart contract that specifies the selected jurisdiction and applicable law is necessary to resolve these conflicts. Enforcing these terms in practice can be challenging and may necessitate international legal cooperation, even with these provisions in place.
- **Regulatory Compliance:** To be reliable and legally sound, smart contracts need to abide by a number of laws, including those pertaining to know your customer (KYC) and anti-money laundering (AML). It can be difficult to incorporate these compliance measures into the code since it needs to be updated frequently to account for new rules and legislation. There are serious legal ramifications, including fines and penalties, for breaking these rules. Moreover, regulatory compliance entails making sure that the parties involved and the underlying Blockchain, as well as the smart contract itself, all comply with applicable laws and regulations. This intricacy highlights how crucial it is to keep up with regulatory changes and incorporate them into the designs of smart contracts.
- **Dispute Resolution:** Due to their automated and self-executing nature, smart contracts may not be appropriate for traditional dispute resolution processes like litigation or arbitration. Ensuring that parties have recourse in case of disagreements or issues requires the development of efficient dispute resolution procedures arising from smart contracts. One strategy is to incorporate decentralized arbitration systems that offer a Blockchain-based dispute resolution system. As an alternative, hybrid models that incorporate Blockchain technology with conventional legal procedures can also be successful. To improve the overall dependability and enforceability of the contract, these procedures must be precisely outlined in the smart contract to guarantee that all parties are aware of and consent to the dispute resolution procedures in place.

4.2.2 Future Regulatory Trends

Regulatory Sandboxes: Regulatory sandboxes offer a safe haven where entrepreneurs can test smart contracts while being watched over by regulatory bodies. With these sandboxes, businesses can test new technologies and business models without having to worry about facing penalties for noncompliance right away. Businesses can learn a great deal about the expectations and requirements of regulations by collaborating closely with regulators. This strategy guarantees that new solutions initially satisfy regulatory standards while also encouraging innovation. Regulatory sandboxes can also assist regulators in better understanding emerging technologies and creating more knowledgeable and efficient regulatory frameworks (Harshdeep Rapal 2024).

Standardization: To enable regulatory compliance, it is crucial to create standardized frameworks and templates for smart contracts. The complexity and legal ambiguities surrounding smart contracts are lessened by standardization, which offers a common language and set of rules that all parties can adhere to. Businesses can guarantee compliance with industry best practices and regulatory requirements for their smart contracts by using standardized templates. The assessment and verification of compliance by auditors and regulators is also made easier by this uniformity. Furthermore, by offering a dependable and predictable framework for a range of applications across diverse industries, standardized smart contracts can encourage wider adoption.

Interoperability: Improving communication between various Blockchain systems is essential to smart contract functionality and wider adoption. Smart contracts with interoperability function more smoothly across different Blockchain networks, increasing their usefulness and suitability for a wider range of situations. This feature is especially crucial for cross-border transactions because various Blockchain systems may be used in different jurisdictions. Interoperability lowers obstacles to cross-border trade and cooperation by allowing smart contracts to communicate and interact across platforms. It also improves legal recognition because contracts that are compatible with various systems have a higher chance of being recognized and upheld internationally.

AI Integration: By combining artificial intelligence (AI) and smart contracts, their potential and efficacy can be greatly increased. AI has the ability to automate compliance monitoring, guaranteeing in real time that smart contracts comply with regulatory requirements. Due to this integration, the contract terms can be dynamically modified in response to changing market conditions and regulatory frameworks. AI is also capable of conducting real-time risk assessments, spotting possible problems and taking action to mitigate them before they become serious ones. Artificial intelligence (AI) can make smart contracts more intelligent, adaptive, and able to handle complicated transactions with little need for human intervention. This will increase efficiency and lower compliance costs.

4.3 Consumer Expectations

4.3.1 Impact on Smart Contract Adoption

When it comes to applications, convenience, and enforcement costs, smart contracts are superior to traditional agreements. These agreements are universally applicable to all kinds of transactions in all domains (Dmytro.K 2020).

Whether you work as a business manager or an official in the public sector, adopting smart contracts will have a big impact on you in the long and short terms.

Now let's examine the key benefits of smart contracts:

Time-efficiency: It typically takes weeks to draft, approve, and implement a paper-based contract. The lengthy process is brought on by the need for numerous middlemen and an extensive feedback loop. Since Blockchain smart contracts don't need the involvement of a court to be enforced, using them doesn't require legal compliance or the need to contact attorneys.

Security: One of the safest methods to make sure no one else can alter the document is to use smart contracts, which employ data encryption. Smart contracts have a great deal of potential impact on political agreements and international relations because of their high level of security.

Precision: Compared to a paper contract, a smart contract is more adaptable and takes into consideration more information. An agreement like this can sort through a long list of complex requirements and select, from dozens of possibilities, the best one to carry out. Additionally, there are fewer chances of agreement deviations because there is no human error involved in the agreement's execution.

Money savings: Smart contracts eliminate the need for parties to engage in negotiations through middlemen. They take up no physical space, are simpler to store, and don't need to be printed.

Transparency: Both sides have the opportunity to review even the smallest details when developing a smart contract. This eliminates the possibility of miscommunication or missing out on crucial information. A smart contract inspires more confidence in both parties because of its resistance to tampering.

5. CASE STUDIES AND APPLICATIONS

5.1 Case Study 1: Implementing Smart Contracts for Transparency in Carbon Trading

Carbon trading markets are key tools for mitigating climate change by providing financial incentives to reduce greenhouse gas (GHG) emissions. However, traditional carbon trading systems face challenges related to data opacity, double-counting of credits, and lack of transparency in transactions (Kreibich & Hermwille, 2021). To address these issues, AI-driven smart contracts in decentralized finance (DeFi) provide a promising solution by enhancing transparency, accountability, and traceability in carbon markets. By automating transaction verification, tracking emissions data, and ensuring compliance, smart contracts can play a pivotal role in establishing a trustworthy carbon trading ecosystem.

1. Addressing Transparency and Traceability Issues

A major challenge in carbon trading lies in ensuring that carbon credits are not counted more than once across different markets or trading systems. Double-counting can undermine the integrity of carbon markets and reduce the overall effectiveness of carbon reduction goals (Bernstein et al., 2022). AI-driven smart contracts can mitigate this by implementing real-time tracking of carbon credits across decentralized ledgers. This tracking can provide a verifiable audit trail for each credit's lifecycle, from issuance to retirement, which is accessible to all market participants. The blockchain's immutable record ensures that each carbon credit is uniquely represented, preventing double-counting and increasing transparency (Zhao & Shi, 2021).

2. Automating Verification and Compliance

Ensuring that carbon credits accurately represent the GHG reductions they claim is crucial for maintaining credibility in carbon trading markets. Traditional verification processes are often time-consuming, costly, and vulnerable to manipulation (Broekhoff et al., 2019). By integrating AI algorithms, smart contracts can automate the verification of emissions reductions using data from Internet of Things (IoT) devices and remote sensing technologies, such as satellite imagery (Xie et al., 2023). These smart contracts can instantly cross-reference emissions data with predefined compliance criteria, ensuring that only verifiable reductions are tokenized as carbon credits. This automated process streamlines compliance checks and increases trustworthiness, as each carbon credit is backed by real-time, AI-verified data.

3. Enhancing Accountability Through Publicly Verifiable Data

Transparency in carbon markets is also enhanced by the ability of blockchain-based smart contracts to make transaction data publicly accessible. Each transaction involving a carbon credit—whether issuance, transfer, or retirement—is recorded on a decentralized ledger, which is open to scrutiny by regulators, investors, and the public. This transparency mitigates risks associated with greenwashing and builds investor confidence in carbon markets (Karp & Gaustad, 2022). For example, a case study in Switzerland demonstrated the use of blockchain-based smart contracts to record the lifecycle of carbon credits in a public ledger, allowing participants to verify the authenticity and environmental impact of each credit in real time (Meylan & Nastasi, 2020).

4. Case Example: Automated Carbon Credit Market on DeFi Platforms

A notable example of AI-driven smart contracts in carbon trading is the decentralized carbon credit trading platform, Toucan Protocol. Toucan leverages blockchain and AI-powered smart contracts to tokenize verified carbon credits, ensuring that credits on its platform represent legitimate, verifiable emissions reductions. Toucan Protocol's smart contracts automatically track credit ownership, enforce compliance with carbon standards, and provide real-time emissions data to participants, ensuring transparency and preventing double-counting. By doing so, it has established a transparent, efficient marketplace that aligns with the goals of sustainable finance (Toucan Protocol, 2022).

5.2 Case Study 2: AI-Powered Risk Assessment in Sustainable Investment

The integration of artificial intelligence (AI) within decentralized finance (DeFi) is revolutionizing the ability of financial systems to assess and manage investment risks, particularly in the context of sustainable investments aligned with environmental, social, and governance (ESG) criteria. Sustainable investment, characterized by its commitment to ethical and responsible financing, has unique risk considerations due to fluctuating regulatory standards, market perception, and the variability in environmental and social outcomes (Bennett & Lamming, 2022). AI-driven smart contracts, when applied to sustainable investments within DeFi ecosystems, enable automated and adaptive risk assessment that addresses these complexities. This section explores how AI-powered risk assessment frameworks within smart contracts are contributing to sustainable finance by minimizing investor risk, ensuring compliance, and enhancing transparency.

1. Leveraging Predictive Analytics for ESG Risk Assessment

Predictive analytics in AI can process large volumes of ESG-related data, such as historical performance of sustainable projects, environmental impact metrics, and market trends, to create robust risk profiles for investments. By incorporating predictive algorithms, AI-driven smart contracts in DeFi are able to continuously monitor and evaluate the risk levels associated with sustainable assets (Leong & Sung, 2023). For example, projects in renewable energy, such as solar and wind, carry unique operational risks due to weather dependencies and long-term financial return uncertainties. AI-powered smart contracts can evaluate these variables, forecast potential risks, and adjust investment terms in real-time to mitigate losses.

Furthermore, predictive AI algorithms embedded in smart contracts can factor in broader geopolitical and regulatory trends that impact sustainable projects, such as shifts in environmental legislation or subsidy policies (Grewal & Purnanandam, 2021). By doing so, smart contracts provide dynamic and responsive risk assessments that help investors make informed decisions while aligning their portfolios with sustainability goals.

2. Automating Compliance and Fraud Detection

Compliance with ESG standards is essential for sustainable investments but can be challenging due to the potential for fraud and greenwashing—where companies or projects falsely claim to be sustainable (Watson & White, 2022). AI-driven smart contracts can mitigate these risks by automatically verifying data sources, validating claims, and identifying discrepancies that may indicate fraudulent behavior. For instance, an AI-based compliance check can compare reported emissions data from a company with independently sourced environmental data from IoT sensors or satellite imagery to verify its authenticity. This feature is crucial for attracting more capital to sustainable projects by ensuring transparency and reducing the risk of investing in projects that do not meet ESG criteria.

Machine learning models within these smart contracts are trained to detect irregularities and patterns associated with non-compliance or fraud, which enables faster and more reliable identification of high-risk investments. The automated compliance capabilities of AI-driven smart contracts reduce operational overhead and minimize the risk associated with investing in unverified sustainable assets (Tang & Shi, 2024).

3. Case Example: AI in Carbon-Neutral Portfolio Management

A notable case study of AI-powered risk assessment in sustainable DeFi solutions can be seen in the management of carbon-neutral investment portfolios. Carbon-neutral portfolios focus on investments that offset carbon emissions by funding projects such as reforestation or renewable energy generation. By leveraging AI-driven smart contracts, DeFi platforms can evaluate the long-term sustainability and risk profiles of these projects through continuous monitoring and data analysis (Clark et al., 2021). For example, a decentralized platform might utilize AI algorithms to analyze trends in carbon credit prices, regulatory shifts, and environmental impact data to adjust the risk rating of different projects within the portfolio.

Through this approach, investors are empowered to participate in sustainable projects while minimizing exposure to volatile or high-risk assets. AI-driven smart contracts also provide real-time updates on portfolio compliance with carbon-neutral standards, enabling automated adjustments based on the latest environmental and market data. This ensures that the portfolio's sustainability objectives are maintained while managing potential financial risks.

5.3 Case Study 3: Decentralized Finance for Financing Renewable Energy

Cryptocurrencies and decentralized finance (DeFi) utilize Blockchain technology to facilitate peer-to-peer fund transfers without intermediaries. DeFi operates through the automated execution of smart contracts on Blockchain networks, enabling decentralized applications (DApps) to conduct financial functions on immutable, publicly visible ledgers. Smart contracts, often written in high-level languages like Solidity, are self-executing programs triggered by predefined conditions that enforce agreements transparently on the Blockchain.

ShafaqNaheedKhan et al. (2021) explore integration challenges between IoT devices and Blockchain, focusing on data integrity, synchronization, and security (ShafaqNaheedKhan et al., 2021). They discuss the need for improved protocols and authentication mechanisms.

This grouping of research gaps provides a structured overview of the current challenges and gaps in smart contract research, highlighting areas where further investigation and innovation are needed to advance the field within AI-driven decentralized finance and broader financial ecosystems.

5.4 Insights and Lessons from Existing AI-Driven DeFi Projects in Sustainability

The leading platform for smart contract implementation, supports a wide array of DeFi applications. As of June 2021, with a market capitalization of $317.3 billion, Ethereum hosts over 95% of DeFi projects. While Bitcoin also supports smart contracts, its script language is primarily focused on verifying signatures, limiting its functionality compared to Ethereum, which operates as a computation platform with the Ethereum Virtual Machine (EVM). The EVM serves as a secure execution environment where smart contracts reference the Blockchain ledger state (Haozhe Zhou et.al. 2022).

5.5 Lessons Learned and Best Practices

- Future smart contract-based financial systems should incorporate formal auditing procedures and adhere to PCI-DSS (Payment Card Industry Data Security Standards) and PA-DSS (Payment Application Data Security Standards) standards to facilitate widespread adoption (Tharaka Hewa 2020).
- Testing smart contract-based financial systems in closed-loop systems, such as unbanked villages, can reveal operational challenges in real-world scenarios, providing valuable insights into system resilience and usability.
- Addressing these challenges is crucial before deploying smart contract-based payment systems on a global scale, ensuring robustness and reliability across diverse environments.
- Future research in smart contracts is increasingly focused on enhancing the privacy of health information management systems, aiming to strengthen security measures and regulatory compliance in healthcare applications.

These best practices underscore the importance of rigorous testing, adherence to industry standards, and ongoing research to advance the reliability, security, and privacy of smart contract technologies.

5.6 Challenges and Failures

Smart contracts are a promising technology, but there are still a lot of issues that need to be resolved. We divide these significant obstacles into four categories based on the four stages of a smart contract's life cycle. In the interim, we also provide a summary of recent developments in addressing these problems (Zibin Zheng,Shaoan Xie, et al. 2019).

Creation Challenges: Creating contracts is a crucial step in putting smart contracts into practice. It is the responsibility of users to write their own contracts and implement them on different Blockchain systems. Smart contracts built on Blockchains are likewise non-modifiable once they are implemented, as Blockchains are by nature immutable. Developers must therefore carefully handle the following issues.

Readability: Solidity, Go, Kotlin, Java, and other programming languages are used to write the majority of smart contracts. Subsequently, the source codes will be assembled and run. Programs have different forms of codes as a result of different time periods. One of the biggest challenges still facing us is how to make programs readable in all forms.

6. TECHNICAL ASPECTS AND DESIGN OF SMART CONTRACTS

6.1. Smart Contract Design Principles

In order to address the problem of immutability, Marino and Juels proposed a set of guidelines for changing or revoked smart contracts. These norms are derived from contract law and reformulated for the smart contract environment. These standards are demonstrated to be realistic after being put to the test in Ethereum. That does, however, go somewhat against Ethereum's original design principles (Kai Peng, Meijun Li, et al. (2021).

6.2. Development Tools and Platforms

Solidity and Ethereum

For a specific Blockchain platform, programming languages define smart contracts. What kind of smart contracts can be written for a given Blockchain platform depends on the features of the programming language, specifically whether or not it is Turing complete. Popular programming languages like Python, C++, GO lang, and JavaScript are also common examples of programming languages for smart contracts in Blockchain platforms, such as Solidity (for Ethereum). (Alfredo J. Perez and Sherali Zeadally 2022).

Advanced Auditing Tools

Ghaleb and Pattabiraman introduced SolidiFI, an automated tool designed to evaluate multiple static analysis tools used for smart contracts, including Oyente, Securify, Mythril, SmartCheck, Manticore, and Slither. SolidiFI injects seven distinct types of vulnerabilities into smart contracts and utilizes these security-analysis tools to identify them. This methodology aims to assess the effectiveness of these tools in detecting vulnerabilities such as timestamp dependency, unhandled exceptions, integer overflow/underflow, tx.origin usage, re-entrancy issues, unchecked send operations, and transaction order dependence.

While SolidiFI focuses on static analysis tools, it does not extend its evaluation to include dynamic analysis and formal verification tools. This study adopts a survey methodology similar to that of Praitheeshan et al., analyzing smart-contract security-analysis approaches across three categories: static, dynamic, and formal verification. It specifically examines newly proposed security-analysis tools and their contributions to enhancing smart-contract security (Zhou, H.; et.al 2022).

7. ADDRESSING CHALLENGES IN SMART CONTRACTS

Emphasis on Addressing Challenges: QuarkChain employs a Blockchain interoperability framework that incorporates a reputation-based Proof-of-Authority consensus mechanism. This smart contract design is specifically tailored to address challenges within biopharmaceutical supply chain management. (Shafaq Naheed Khan, et al. (2021)

7.1 Security and Vulnerabilities

7.1.1 Common Security Issues

1. **Vulnerabilities and Attacks:** Exploiting vulnerabilities, bugs, and attacks in smart contracts has led to significant losses of cryptocurrencies, with some incidents resulting in millions of dollars in losses.
2. **IoT and Crowdsensing Systems:** Enhancing the security of smart contracts is critical for IoT and crowdsensing systems. Flawed smart contracts executed in cyber-physical systems could potentially reprogram devices via sensing tasks, leading to data theft or physical harm to users.

3. **Interconnected Devices and Services:** The challenge is compounded by the multitude of interconnected devices, software frameworks, and services. Many manufacturers and providers lack security by design in their devices and software/services, exacerbating the issue (Alfredo J. Perez et. al. 2022).

7.1.2 Mitigation Strategies

A recent noteworthy trend in mitigating smart contract threats involves AI-driven approaches utilizing machine learning (N. Ivanov et.al 2023).. These approaches are particularly impactful for two main reasons. Firstly, AI solutions enable the exploitation of the rich capabilities of modern smart contracts. Secondly, they have demonstrated success in enhancing security across various computing domains.

The expressive nature of smart contracts poses challenges for traditional static and formal analytical methods. Many contemporary smart contracts are Turing-complete, allowing complex algorithms to be implemented using languages like Solidity and Vyper (Suresh Babu, C. V., Sudhir Manoharan et a.l, 2024). However, this expressiveness also introduces a vast number of coding possibilities, making it difficult for static methods, which primarily rely on predefined patterns, to effectively address all potential vulnerabilities. While machine learning methods also rely on patterns, recent advancements in machine learning, such as deep neural networks, can explore significantly larger and more complex feature spaces compared to static approaches.

In recent years, there has been a noticeable rise in using AI and machine learning for security applications, such as malware detection. While the adoption of machine learning methods for smart contract threat mitigation is still evolving, their flexibility and adaptability are expected to increasingly contribute to enhancing smart contract security defenses in the future.

7.2 Scalability and Performance

1. **Ethereum Updates:** Ethereum initiated updates to its protocols and network architecture to securely handle thousands of transactions per second. This involved transitioning from Proof of Work (PoW) to Proof of Stake (PoS) and implementing shard chains to distribute network load across 64 parallel chains.
2. **Improvements and Future Needs:** These updates significantly reduced Ethereum's power consumption and improved scalability. However, the effectiveness of these changes in supporting secure crowdsensing systems on public Blockchains will require further observation in the coming years. Scaling crowdsensing systems based on public Blockchains will necessitate additional research and development. (Alfredo J. Perez et. al. 2022)

7.3 Legal and Compliance Issues

Enforcing Smart Contracts across Jurisdictions

Enforcing smart contracts globally presents challenges where legal frameworks may vary:

- Smart contracts may fall under legal contract definitions in some jurisdictions, while others require validation through traditional legal instruments.
- Despite their potential legal recognition in specific jurisdictions, independent Blockchains cannot entirely replace current contracts or serve as sole proof in court. However, they can enhance data sharing efficiency among businesses (Elizaveta Zinovyeva, et al. 2021).

Need for Standardized Legal Frameworks

1. Electronic agreements aim to replicate physical contracts visually and functionally.
2. Electronically signed documents hold equal legal validity as physically signed agreements in many jurisdictions, though not universally accepted.
3. Existing legal frameworks can directly or analogously apply to smart contracts (SCs), enabling Blockchain (BC) users to:
    - Be uniquely identified and associated with their signature.
    - Maintain control over signature creation.
    - Verify accompanying signed data on the Blockchain.
    - Easily demonstrate data integrity and withdraw consent.

These points underscore the parity between electronically signed agreements and the application of legal frameworks to smart contracts, leveraging Blockchain technology for enhanced security and verifiability (Vittorio Capocasale, et. al. 2022).

Interoperability:

1. A thorough analysis of interoperability solutions across various categories is conducted, and the results are tabulated to meaningfully depict the characteristics of these solutions. This analysis identifies several unresolved concerns and avenues for future research aimed at overcoming constraints and enhancing Blockchain interoperability performance (Sajjad Khan et. al. 2021).
2. Smart contracts play a crucial role in connecting Blockchains and enhancing interoperability. Their ability to enforce contractual terms in decentralized environments is the primary reason for their superior performance compared

to architecture-based interoperability solutions (Blockchain interoperability, decentralized apps, digital assets, smart contracts, chain code, cross-chain transactions, and sidechains).

8. FINDINGS AND SUGGESTIONS

8.1. Major Findings and Contributions of the Chapter

The chapter on smart contracts presents several significant findings and contributions that align with its objectives:

1. **Understanding Smart Contracts**: The chapter effectively elucidates the concept of smart contracts, detailing their functionality, benefits, and the underlying Blockchain technology that enables their operation. This foundational knowledge is crucial for stakeholders looking to implement or study smart contracts.
2. **Security and Vulnerability Analysis**: A thorough examination of the security challenges associated with smart contracts is provided, highlighting common vulnerabilities and potential attack vectors. This analysis contributes to the field by raising awareness of the risks involved and the need for robust security measures.
3. **Emerging Technologies**: The chapter discusses the integration of artificial intelligence (AI) and other emerging technologies with smart contracts, showcasing how these innovations can enhance security and functionality. This contribution opens avenues for future research and development in the intersection of these technologies.
4. **Regulatory Considerations**: The chapter emphasizes the importance of regulatory compliance and the need for standardized frameworks for smart contracts. This finding is critical for ensuring that smart contracts can be effectively integrated into existing legal systems and business practices.
5. **Interoperability Challenges**: The chapter identifies the need for interoperability among different Blockchain platforms, which is essential for the widespread adoption of smart contracts. This finding underscores the importance of developing solutions that facilitate communication between various Blockchain networks.

9. FUTURE RESEARCH DIRECTIONS

The study outlines several possible Future Research Directions concerning smart contracts, categorized into Emerging Trends, Innovations, and Recommendations for Future Research. Here's a detailed discussion on each category:

9.1 Emerging Trends in Smart Contracts

1. **New Use Cases and Applications**: As industries increasingly adopt Blockchain technology, there is a growing need to explore novel applications of smart contracts beyond traditional financial services. Research could focus on sectors such as healthcare, real estate, and supply chain management, identifying specific use cases that leverage the unique capabilities of smart contracts.
2. **Integration with Emerging Technologies**: The convergence of smart contracts with technologies like Artificial Intelligence (AI) and the Internet of Things (IoT) presents a rich area for exploration. Research could investigate how AI can enhance the decision-making processes within smart contracts or how IoT devices can trigger contract execution based on real-time data.
3. **Impact of Regulatory Changes**: As governments and regulatory bodies develop frameworks for Blockchain and smart contracts, it is crucial to study how these changes affect the design, implementation, and adoption of smart contracts. Research could focus on compliance challenges and the adaptability of smart contracts to evolving legal landscapes.

9.2 Innovations on the Horizon

1. **Advanced Cryptographic Techniques**: The security of smart contracts is paramount, and research into innovative cryptographic methods could enhance their resilience against attacks. This includes exploring zero-knowledge proofs and other advanced encryption techniques that can protect sensitive data while maintaining transparency.
2. **Interoperability Solutions**: As multiple Blockchain platforms emerge, the ability for smart contracts to operate across different networks is essential for broader adoption. Research could focus on developing protocols and standards that facilitate seamless interactions between disparate Blockchain systems, enhancing the functionality and utility of smart contracts.
3. **Decentralized Dispute Resolution Mechanisms**: Given the automated nature of smart contracts, traditional dispute resolution methods may not be suitable. Research could explore the design and implementation of decentralized arbitra-

tion systems that leverage Blockchain technology to resolve conflicts efficiently and fairly.

9.3 Suggestions and Recommendation

While the chapter covers a range of important topics, there may be specific objectives that were not fully addressed, including:

1. **Comprehensive Case Studies**: The chapter could benefit from more detailed case studies that illustrate successful implementations of smart contracts across various industries, providing practical examples of their application and impact.
2. **User Experience and Adoption Barriers**: An exploration of user experience issues and barriers to adoption for businesses and individuals could provide insights into the challenges faced in implementing smart contracts in real-world scenarios.
3. **Long-term Implications and Sustainability**: The chapter may not have sufficiently addressed the long-term implications of smart contracts on business models and economic systems, including considerations for sustainability and ethical concerns.
4. **Comparative Analysis with Traditional Contracts**: A comparative analysis that highlights the differences, advantages, and disadvantages of smart contracts versus traditional contracts could provide a clearer understanding of when and why to use smart contracts.
5. **Future Trends and Predictions**: While the chapter discusses emerging trends, it may not have provided specific predictions or scenarios for the future evolution of smart contracts and their potential impact on various sectors.

9.4 Recommendations for Future Research

1. **Interdisciplinary Research**: The complexity of smart contracts necessitates a multidisciplinary approach that combines insights from law, computer science, economics, and social sciences. Future research should encourage collaboration among experts from these fields to address the multifaceted challenges posed by smart contracts.
2. **Standardized Frameworks and Templates**: To facilitate regulatory compliance and enhance the reliability of smart contracts, there is a need for standardized frameworks and templates. Research should focus on developing best practices that can be adopted across industries, ensuring consistency and clarity in smart contract design.

3. **Rigorous Testing and Validation**: As smart contracts are immutable once deployed, ensuring their correctness and security before implementation is critical. Future research should emphasize the importance of rigorous testing methodologies, including formal verification and automated testing tools, to identify and mitigate vulnerabilities in smart contracts.

The future of smart contracts is promising, with numerous avenues for research that can drive innovation and address existing challenges. By focusing on these emerging trends, innovations, and recommendations, researchers and practitioners can contribute to the evolution of smart contracts, ensuring their successful integration into various sectors and enhancing their overall impact on society

10. CONCLUSION

10.1 Summary of Key Findings

This study has provided a comprehensive overview of smart contracts, highlighting their potential to revolutionize various sectors through automation, security, and transparency. Key findings indicate that smart contracts can significantly reduce transaction costs and time by eliminating intermediaries, while also enhancing trust among parties through immutable and verifiable agreements. The research has identified critical challenges, including security vulnerabilities, regulatory uncertainties, and the need for interoperability among different Blockchain platforms.

10.2. Implications for the Financial Services Industry

The implications of smart contracts for the financial services industry are profound. They offer the potential to streamline processes such as trade finance, insurance claims, and compliance reporting, thereby improving efficiency and reducing operational risks. Financial institutions can leverage smart contracts to automate complex transactions, enhance customer experiences, and ensure regulatory compliance. However, the industry must also address the associated risks, including cybersecurity threats and the need for robust governance frameworks to manage smart contract execution.

10.3. Final Thoughts and Recommendations

In conclusion, while smart contracts present exciting opportunities for innovation and efficiency, ongoing research and development are essential to overcome existing challenges. It is recommended that stakeholders, including developers, regulators, and industry leaders, collaborate to establish standardized practices and frameworks that promote security, interoperability, and compliance. Additionally, further exploration of emerging technologies and their integration with smart contracts will be crucial in unlocking their full potential. By fostering a proactive approach to research and development, the financial services industry can harness the transformative power of smart contracts to drive future growth and innovation

REFERENCES

Bennett, R., & Lamming, R. (2022). ESG risk and the role of AI in sustainable finance: A review. *Journal of Sustainable Finance & Investment, 12*(3), 207–220. DOI: 10.1080/20430795.2022.2050745

Bernstein, S., Jones, K., & Mitchell, D. (2022). Tackling double-counting in carbon markets: The role of blockchain and AI. *Environmental Research Letters, 17*(2), 025002. DOI: 10.1088/1748-9326/ac4f54

Broekhoff, D., Gillenwater, M., & Colbert-Sangree, T. (2019). Quality and integrity of carbon offset credits: Lessons from verification challenges. *Journal of Environmental Economics and Policy, 8*(4), 354–374. DOI: 10.1080/21606544.2019.1686611

Capocasale, V., & Perboli, G. (2022). Standardizing smart contracts. *IEEE Access : Practical Innovations, Open Solutions, 10*, 91203–91212. Advance online publication. DOI: 10.1109/ACCESS.2022.3202550

Chen, H., Whitters, G., Amiri, M. J., Wang, Y., & Loo, B. T.. (2022). Declarative smart contracts. In *Proceedings of the 30th ACM Joint European Software Engineering Conference and Symposium on the Foundations of Software Engineering (ESEC/FSE '22)*, November 14-18, 2022, Singapore, Singapore. ACM, New York, NY, USA, 13 pages. https://doi.org/DOI: 10.1145/3540250.3549121

Clark, . (2021). Smart Contracts Security Threats and Solutions. *International Journal of Information Technology and Web Engineering*. Advance online publication. DOI: 10.4018/IJITWE.304048

De Andrés, J., & Lorca, P. (2021). On the impact of smart contracts on auditing. *The International Journal of Digital Accounting Research, 21*, 155–181. DOI: 10.4192/1577-8517-v21_6

De Filippi, P., Wray, C., & Sileno, G. (2021). Smart contracts. *Internet Policy Review, 10*(2), 1–9. DOI: 10.14763/2021.2.1549

Dmytro, K. (2020). 5 benefits of using smart contracts & their problems. This manuscript is made available under the Blaize user license. https://blaize.tech/5-benefits-of

Ghodoosi, F. (2021). Contracting in the age of smart contracts. *Washington Law Review (Seattle, Wash.), 96*, 51.

Grewal, D., & Purnanandam, A. (2021). The impact of regulatory shifts on ESG risk management. *Journal of Financial Regulation, 8*(1), 43–57. DOI: 10.1093/jfr/fjab012

Hewa, T., Ylianttila, M., & Liyanage, M.. (2020). Survey on Blockchain based smart contracts: Applications, opportunities and challenges. *Journal of Network and Computer Applications*.

Ivanov, N., Li, C., Yan, Q., Sun, Z., Cao, Z., & Luo, X. (2023). Security threat mitigation for smart contracts: A comprehensive survey. *ACM Computing Surveys*, *55*(14s), 326. Advance online publication. DOI: 10.1145/3593293

Karolina. (2023). Advanced cryptographic techniques for secure Blockchain development. This manuscript is made available under the Nextrope user license. https://nextrope.com/

Karp, A., & Gaustad, G. (2022). Blockchain for sustainability: Enhancing accountability in carbon markets. *Sustainable Development*, *30*(3), 526–534. DOI: 10.1002/sd.2291

Khan, S. N., Loukil, F., Ghedira-Guegan, C., Benkhelifa, E., & Bani-Hani, A. (2021). Blockchain smart contracts: Applications, challenges, and future trends. *Peer-to-Peer Networking and Applications*, *14*(5), 2901–2925. DOI: 10.1007/s12083-021-01127-0 PMID: 33897937

Kreibich, N., & Hermwille, L. (2021). Transparency and credibility in the carbon markets: Blockchain applications and limitations. *Climate Policy*, *21*(7), 970–986. DOI: 10.1080/14693062.2021.1917685

Krichen, M. (2023). Strengthening the security of smart contracts through the power of artificial intelligence. *Computers*, *12*(107), 107. Advance online publication. DOI: 10.3390/computers12050107

Leong, P., & Sung, H. (2023). Predictive analytics and ESG risk management in decentralized finance. *Finance Research Letters*, *15*(2), 215–223. DOI: 10.1016/j.frl.2023.101298

Meylan, G., & Nastasi, P. (2020). Case study: Blockchain for carbon credits in Switzerland. *Energy Policy*, *146*, 111806. DOI: 10.1016/j.enpol.2020.111806

Negka, L. D., & Spathoulas, G. P. (2021). Blockchain state channels: A state of the art. *IEEE Access : Practical Innovations, Open Solutions*, *9*, 160277–160298. Advance online publication. DOI: 10.1109/ACCESS.2021.3131419

Peng, K., Li, M., Huang, H., Wang, C., Wan, S., & Choo, K. K. R. (2021). Security challenges and opportunities for smart contracts in internet of things: A survey. *IEEE Internet of Things Journal*, *8*(15), 12004–12020. https://www.ieee.org/publications/rights/index.html. DOI: 10.1109/JIOT.2021.3074544

Perez, A. J., & Zeadally, S. (2022). Secure and privacy-preserving crowdsensing using smart contracts: Issues and solutions. This manuscript is made available under the Elsevier user license. https://www.elsevier.com/open-access/userlicense/1.0/

Protocol, T. (2022). *Toucan's decentralized carbon market: Using blockchain to enhance transparency in carbon trading*. Retrieved from https://toucan.earth

Rapal, H. (2024). Smart contracts and regulatory compliance: Navigating the legal landscape. This manuscript is made available under the Legitt user license. https://legittai.com/

ShafaqNaheedKhan, FaizaLoukil, ChirineGhedira-Guegan, ElhadjBenkhelifa and AnoudBani-Hani et al. (2021). Blockchain smart contracts: Applications, challenges and future trends Special Issue on Blockchain for Peer-to-Peer Computing (2021) 14:2901–2925.https://doi.org/DOI: 10.1007/s12083-021-01127-0

Suresh Babu, C. V. & Abhinaba Pal. (2023). Securing Decentralized Finance Through Blockchain Technologies. In R. Thanigaivelan, S. Kaliappan, & C. Jegadheesan (Eds.), *Cyber-Physical Systems and Supporting Technologies for Industrial Automation* (pp. 351-372). IGI Global. https://doi.org/DOI: 10.4018/978-1-6684-9267-3.ch020

Suresh Babu, C. V. & Sanjai Das (2023). Impact of Blockchain Technology on the Stock Market. In K. Mehta, R. Sharma, & P. Yu (Eds.), *Revolutionizing Financial Services and Markets Through FinTech and Blockchain* (pp. 44-59). IGI Global. https://doi.org/DOI: 10.4018/978-1-6684-8624-5.ch004

SureshBabu. C. V., Sudhir Manoharan., L., G. K., & V., S. K. (2024). Application of Support Vector Machine Algorithm in Automated Lending Protocols for Decentralized Finance Platforms. In L. Vardari & I. Qabrati (Eds.), Decentralized Finance and Tokenization in FinTech (pp. 1-20). IGI Global. https://doi.org/DOI: 10.4018/979-8-3693-3346-4.ch001

Tang, X., & Shi, Z. (2024). Automation and fraud detection in sustainable finance: The role of AI and DeFi smart contracts. *Computational Economics*, *49*(2), 456–470. DOI: 10.1007/s10614-023-09987-5

Trivedi, C., Rao, U., Parmar, K., Bhattacharya, P., & Tanwar, S.. (2024). A transformative shift towards Blockchain-based IoT environments: Consensus, smart contracts, and future directions. https://doi.org/DOI: 10.22541/au.170663514.49171896/v1

Tyagi, S., Reddy, G. C., Chandu, V., & Koteswararao, N.. (2022). Study of smart contracts. https://doi.org/DOI: 10.2139/ssrn.4376852

Vigliotti, M. G. (2021). What do we mean by smart contracts? Open challenges in smart contracts. *Frontiers in Blockchain*, *3*, 553671. DOI: 10.3389/fbloc.2020.553671

Wang, X., & Xu, F. (2022). The value of smart contract in trade finance. https://doi.org/DOI: 10.1287/msom.2022.1126

Watson, K., & White, S. (2022). Greenwashing in sustainable finance: A challenge for ESG compliance. *Journal of Business Ethics*, *180*(1), 87–98. DOI: 10.1007/s10551-021-04928-7

Xie, H., Li, Q., & Zhang, Y. (2023). AI-powered verification of carbon credits: Leveraging IoT and blockchain technologies. *Environmental Science & Technology*, *57*(3), 1212–1223. DOI: 10.1021/acs.est.2c05565

Zhao, M., & Shi, L. (2021). Carbon market transparency through AI-driven blockchain solutions. *Journal of Cleaner Production*, *280*, 124618. DOI: 10.1016/j.jclepro.2020.124618

Zheng, Z., Xie, S., Dai, H. N., Chen, W., Chen, X., Weng, J., & Imran, M.. (2019). An overview on smart contracts: Challenges, advances and platforms. https://arxiv.org/abs/1912.10370

Zhou, H., Fard, A. M., & Makanju, A. (2022). The State of Ethereum Smart Contracts Security: Vulnerabilities, Countermeasures, and Tool Support. *Journal of Cybersecurity and Privacy.*, *2022*(2), 358–378. DOI: 10.3390/jcp2020019

Zhou, H., Milani Fard, A., & Makanju, A. (2022). The state of Ethereum smart contracts security: Vulnerabilities, countermeasures, and tool support. *Journal of Cybersecurity and Privacy*, *2*(2), 358–378. DOI: 10.3390/jcp2020019

Zinovyeva, E., Reule, R. C. G., & Hardle, W. K., et al. (2021). Understanding smart contracts: Hype or hope.

KEY TERMS AND DEFINITIONS

ERC20: Ethereum Request for Comment 20
SCs: Smart Contracts
P2P: Peer-to-peer
AI: Artificial Intelligence
DeFi: Decentralized Finance
APIs: Application Programming Interfaces
EVM: Ethereum Virtual Machines
MPT: Merkle Patricia Tree
ICOs: Initial Coin Offerings
DAO: Decentralized Autonomous Organization

ALC: Application Logic Contracts
DAC: Decentralized Autonomous Corporation
Dapps: Decentralized applications
BDF: Best and Final Price
IoT: Internet of Things
AML: Anti-money Laundering
KYC: Know your customer
PCI-DSS: Payment Card Industry Data Security Standards
PA-DSS: Payment Application Data Security Standards
PoW: Proof of Work
PoS: Proof of Stake
BC: Blockchain

Chapter 12
Robotic Process Automation (RPA): A Catalyst for Innovation in Financial Services

David P. Surenthran
https://orcid.org/0009-0001-7665-2406
St. Joseph's College of Engineering, India

R. Suguna
https://orcid.org/0009-0008-3892-9356
Jeppiaar College of Arts and Science, India

K. Balasubramanian
https://orcid.org/0000-0003-2141-4344
Jain University Kochi, India

D. Murugan
https://orcid.org/0009-0004-0225-5880
Hindustan College of Arts and Science, India

G. Magelesh
https://orcid.org/0009-0008-4683-5077
St. Joseph's College of Engineering, India

Joel Jebadurai Devapitchai
https://orcid.org/0000-0002-6947-8497
St. Joseph's College of Engineering, India

ABSTRACT

This chapter explores Robotic Process Automation (RPA) as a transformative force in the financial sector, examining its evolution, implementation strategies, and future trends. It highlights RPA's significant benefits, including cost reduction, improved accuracy, enhanced efficiency, and faster processing times. Diverse use cases demonstrate RPA's impact on data entry, financial reporting, compliance, planning, risk mitigation, and customer service. Real-world examples, such as DBS Bank's successful implementation, showcase RPA's transformative power. The chapter provides a comprehensive guide for effective RPA implementation, covering process selection, ROI analysis, tool selection, bot development, system

DOI: 10.4018/979-8-3693-7160-2.ch012

integration, security, compliance, and change management. It also presents case studies highlighting both the potential and challenges of RPA. Looking forward, the chapter identifies emerging trends that will shape RPA's future in finance, including, process mining, enhanced cybersecurity, integration with IoT and edge computing, and the rise of the digital workforce.

INTRODUCTION

The finance department encounters difficulties in manual labour, including inaccuracies and exhaustion resulting from the replication and migration of data across numerous systems. In order to tackle this issue, financial executives sought assistance from software robots powered by Robotic Process Automation (RPA). These robots exhibited exceptional ability, effortlessly managing invoices without experiencing weariness or making mistakes, and moving data between systems with great accuracy. The reports demonstrated precision and timeliness, enabling the finance team to perform data analysis and provide strategic input to enhance the organisation's financial health.

The adoption of RPA in the financial industry is motivated by the need to improve service offerings, decrease expenses, and sustain a competitive advantage. In the current fast-paced environment, clients place a high value on ease and efficient work completion. Personalisation is essential for achieving cost-effectiveness. RPA enables financial institutions to automate tasks as required, effectively meeting their needs and improving the financial health of their organisations. By integrating customised automation, RPA can assist financial institutions in preserving their competitive advantage and enhancing their client services.

JPMorgan Chase, a prominent worldwide financial institution, encountered the increasing difficulty of effectively handling extensive amounts of data and intricate procedures throughout its diverse range of operations. The bank's capacity to scale efficiently was limited by time-consuming manual operations such as loan processing, trade reconciliation, and compliance reporting, which were also prone to errors. In order to surmount these obstacles, JPMorgan Chase deliberately adopted RPA. The bank implemented a fleet of robots to automate various repetitive operations, so freeing workers from monotonous work and enabling them to concentrate on more valuable activities. For example, RPA bots were programmed to extract and verify data from loan applications, greatly speeding up the loan approval process and decreasing the chance of mistakes made by humans. Within the domain of compliance, RPA bots diligently oversee transactions to detect possible fraudulent activities, guaranteeing strict compliance with regulatory obligations with exceptional precision and swiftness. JPMorgan Chase's decision to implement RPA resulted in significant cost reductions, increased operational efficiency, greater risk management, and higher customer satisfaction. The bank established a precedent for the revolutionary capabilities of RPA in the financial sector by adopting this breakthrough technology. This has opened the door for a new age of growth and efficiency driven by automation. (jpmorgan.com)

METHODOLOGY

The methodology adopted for this chapter is based on secondary research, utilizing a comprehensive review and analysis of existing literature, industry reports, case studies, and surveys on the adoption and impact of RPA within the financial services sector. The research encompasses both academic publications and industry-specific sources to provide a well-rounded perspective on the topic. The research methodology involved a systematic approach to data collection and analysis. Relevant literature was identified through database searches and online repositories. The collected data was then critically evaluated and synthesized to identify key themes, trends, and patterns related to RPA adoption in finance. Additionally, the research draws on publicly available information from financial institutions regarding their RPA initiatives, including press releases, annual reports, and websites. This real-world data complements the academic and industry research, providing concrete examples of how RPA is being applied and the outcomes it is achieving. While this chapter relies on secondary research, it aims to provide a comprehensive and up-to-date overview of RPA in finance, supported by a diverse range of credible sources. The insights gleaned from this research will be used to inform the subsequent sections of this chapter, exploring the specific applications, benefits, challenges, and future outlook of RPA in the financial sector.

SIGNIFICANCE OF RPA IN THE FINANCE SECTOR

RPA, or Robotic Process Automation, Firstly, the term “robotic” might be deceptive. RPA is a software-driven system that does not utilise any real robots. Software robots are generally engineered to execute repetitive operations that are often executed within back-office environments. These operations include processing insurance claims, managing payroll, automating procurement processes, preparing bank reconciliation statements, accelerating the quote-to-cash cycle, and generating invoices, among other tasks. The potential consequences of this phenomenon might significantly impact a firm (Šperka R et.al., 2023)

Leslie Willcocks, a globally renowned expert in automation and technology management, provides the following statement. RPA refers to the use of software robots, sometimes referred to as "bots," within the financial sector to automate monotonous and rule-governed activities like as data entry, reconciliation, and report generation. Automated tools employ mimicking human actions to execute tasks across many systems and applications, hence enhancing productivity, precision, and cost-efficiency in financial operations (Rutschi et al., 2020). The significance of RPA in the finance sector is as follows:

Increased Productivity and Efficiency

RPA technologies surpass humans in terms of repetitive activities, operating at a quicker pace. This enables individuals in the financial sector to effectively manage strategic planning and decision-making processes (Yao et.al., 2024).

Error Elimination and Enhanced Precision

RPA greatly diminishes mistakes made during data entry, calculations, or any other activities, leading to the generation of more dependable reports. This is achieved by strictly following clear and specific directions (Christian Flechsig et.al., 2022).

Cost Reduction

RPA decreases the operational costs associated with human work. Minimising errors also serves to decrease the necessity for rework and any penalties resulting from noncompliance (Mohamed Saleh et.al., 2024).

Enhanced Compliance

Through strict adherence to established protocols and meticulous documentation of all activities, it enhances compliance and diminishes the probability of incurring penalties from regulatory bodies or experiencing negative publicity that may harm the organisation's reputation (Treacy et.al., 2023).

Scalability

Scalability refers to the ability of a system, network, or method to effectively handle or accommodate growing workloads while maintaining its functioning without any compromise (Mandvikar et.al., 2023).

Enhancing the Client Experience Indirectly

Enhanced customer experience may be achieved by implementing RPA, which leads to expedited processing times, fewer operational mistakes, and a more agile workforce that is relieved from monotonous activities (infosysbpm.com).

EVOLUTION OF RPA ADOPTION IN FINANCIAL INSTITUTIONS

The adoption of RPA in the financial sector has been a dynamic journey, characterized by distinct phases of exploration, growth, and maturity. Each phase represents a significant shift in how financial institutions perceive and utilize RPA, leading to transformative changes in operational efficiency, customer experience, and overall business strategy (Gunisity et.al., 2024).

Figure 1. Evolution of RPA

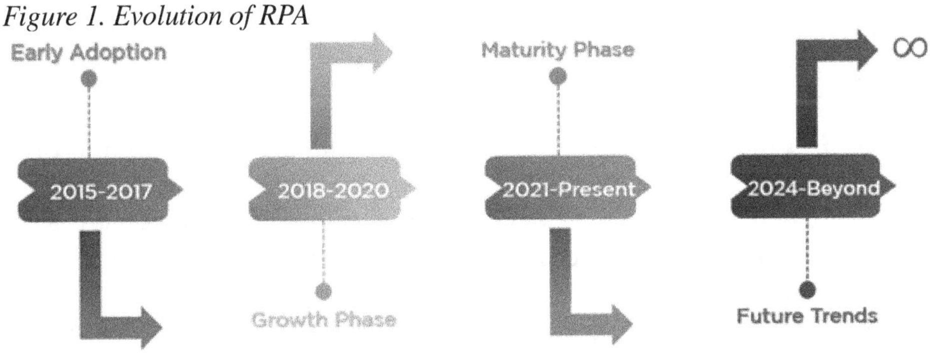

Phase 1: Early Adoption (2015-2017)

The initial phase of RPA adoption was marked by a sense of cautious optimism and a focus on testing the waters (pwc.de).

- **2015 - Initial Exploration and Regulatory Compliance:** Financial institutions began experimenting with RPA through pilot projects, primarily targeting low-risk, high-volume tasks like data entry, reconciliation, and report generation. A key driver for early adoption was the need for regulatory compliance. RPA's ability to execute tasks with precision and generate detailed audit trails made it an attractive solution for meeting stringent regulatory requirements.
- **2016 - First Implementations and Focus on Cost Savings:** The success of pilot projects led to the first full-scale implementations of RPA. Financial institutions began automating more complex processes like invoice processing, claims management, and KYC procedures. Cost reduction remained a primary motivator. RPA's ability to replace manual labor with software robots promised significant savings in operational costs.
- **2017 - Expansion of Use Cases and Regulatory Emphasis:** As confidence in RPA grew, financial institutions expanded its use to encompass a wider range of processes, including customer onboarding, loan origination, and fraud detection. Regulatory bodies continued to emphasize the importance of data accuracy and operational resilience, further reinforcing the value of RPA in maintaining compliance and mitigating risks.

Phase 2: Growth Phase (2018-2020)

This phase witnessed a rapid acceleration in RPA adoption as financial institutions recognized its potential to transform their operations (capco.com).

- **2018 - Integration with Core Systems and Enhanced Capabilities:** RPA was integrated with core banking systems, ERP platforms, and other critical applications, enabling seamless automation of end-to-end processes. RPA vendors introduced advanced capabilities, such as machine learning-based decision-making, natural language processing for unstructured data, and computer vision for image recognition, expanding the scope of automation.
- **2019 - Operational Efficiency and Scalability:** Financial institutions focused on achieving operational excellence by scaling RPA across the enterprise. Centers of Excellence (CoEs) were established to manage, govern, and standardize RPA initiatives. RPA became a key driver of cost reduction, efficiency gains, and improved accuracy in areas like trade processing, compliance reporting, and customer service.
- **2020 - Enterprise-wide Adoption and Customer Interaction:** RPA evolved into a strategic tool for digital transformation. It was no longer confined to back-office operations but was increasingly used to enhance customer-facing

processes. Chatbots and virtual assistants powered by RPA began to handle customer inquiries, provide personalized financial advice, and streamline customer onboarding.

Phase 3: Maturity Phase (2021-Present)

In this phase, RPA has reached a level of maturity where it is deeply embedded in the fabric of financial institutions (deloitte.com).

- **2021 - Strategic Implementation and Hyperautomation:** RPA adoption shifted from a tactical approach to a strategic imperative. Organizations developed comprehensive RPA roadmaps aligned with their business objectives. The concept of hyperautomation gained traction, integrating RPA with AI, machine learning, process mining, and other technologies to achieve end-to-end automation of complex business processes.
- **2022 - Innovation in Customer Experience and New Financial Products:** RPA played a pivotal role in driving innovation in customer experience. Financial institutions leveraged RPA to deliver personalized recommendations, proactive service alerts, and self-service options, improving customer satisfaction and loyalty. RPA streamlined the development and launch of new financial products and services, reducing time-to-market and enabling rapid innovation.
- **2023 - Integration with Advanced Technologies and Self-Healing Systems:** The integration of RPA with emerging technologies like blockchain, Internet of Things (IoT), and cloud computing created a new paradigm of intelligent automation. Self-healing RPA systems were developed to automatically identify and resolve issues, ensuring the continuous operation of automated processes.

Future Trends (2024 and Beyond)

As RPA continues to mature and permeate financial institutions, its future holds exciting possibilities. These are some key trends that are likely to shape the RPA landscape in the coming years (Doguc et. al., 2020 & automationedge.com).

- **Autonomous Processes:** RPA will evolve towards greater autonomy, enabling software robots to handle increasingly complex tasks and make decisions with minimal human intervention.
- **Ethical AI and RPA:** As AI becomes more integrated with RPA, ethical considerations will become paramount. Financial institutions will need to es-

tablish robust governance frameworks to ensure transparency, fairness, and accountability in automated decision-making.

- **Dynamic Compliance:** RPA will play a crucial role in maintaining compliance in a rapidly changing regulatory landscape. Intelligent automation solutions will enable real-time monitoring, risk assessment, and automated reporting to ensure adherence to regulatory requirements.
- **Continued Growth:** The adoption of RPA in the financial sector is expected to continue its upward trajectory. As the technology matures and its capabilities expand, financial institutions will find new and innovative ways to leverage RPA to achieve their strategic objectives.
- **Focus on Customer Experience:** RPA will be increasingly utilized to deliver exceptional customer experiences. Personalization, speed, and convenience will be key priorities, and RPA will be instrumental in achieving these goals.

ADVANTAGES AND POTENTIAL IMPACT OF RPA ON FINANCE OPERATIONS

RPA holds significant potential for enhancing financial processes. It has the capability to significantly minimise costs by automating repetitive activities and improving accuracy by reducing human errors. RPA enhances compliance and auditability by expediting procedures and reducing mistakes. This liberates employees from mundane tasks, allowing them to focus on more advanced analytics and decision-making. In the future, RPA has the potential to completely transform financial operations, leading to improved efficiency, data-driven analysis, and eventually enhancing total corporate performance.

Cost Reduction

According to research conducted by Oyeniyi et.al., 2024 and McKinsey & Company, the implementation of RPA has the potential to reduce expenses associated with diverse financial and accounting activities by a range of 20% to 40%. Financial institutions have the ability to automate repetitive rules-based processes through the use of RPA, resulting in a reduction of manual participation and a considerable decrease in labour expenses.

Improved Accuracy and Compliance

According to Cooper et.al., 2019 and Deloitte, the integration of RPA in financial processes has the potential to decrease errors by as much as 90%, leading to enhanced accuracy and compliance. RPA reduces human mistakes by automating repetitive tasks like as data input and reconciliation. It also ensures compliance with regulatory regulations, hence improving overall organisational compliance.

Enhanced Efficiency and Productivity

According to a recent study conducted by Patricio et.al., 2023 and Ernst & Young, the implementation of RPA has the potential to enhance process efficiency by around 80%, hence resulting in increased levels of production. Streamlining processes using RPA enhances the pace of tasks, allowing financial teams to focus on value-adding activities like analysis and strategic decision-making. This, in turn, boosts overall productivity.

Faster Processing and Reporting

According to research conducted by Fernandez et.al., 2023 and KPMG, the utilisation of robots has been found to result in a reduction in processing time for financial services activities by around 50% to 75%. Consequently, this leads to an acceleration of reporting cycles. Automating operations like as data extraction, validation, and report production with RPA expedites financial closing procedures. This automation also enables real-time access to reliable financial information, supporting rapid decision-making.

Scalability and Flexibility

According to a survey conducted by Roszkowska et.al., 2020 and PwC, more than 90% of CFOs who had used this technology saw scalability as a significant benefit resulting from its integration within their organisations. Scalability pertains to the capacity to adapt in accordance with transaction volumes or business requirements, whereas flexibility entails the ability to swiftly adapt to changes in market conditions, hence affording banks a wider range of choices during various economic eras.

Strategic Insights and Analytics

According to a survey done by Ivančić et.al., 2019 and UiPath, a significant majority of financial professionals, namely 91%, hold the belief that the implementation of (RPA) results in enhanced accessibility to strategic insights and analytics. According to the same survey, RPA allows financial professionals to save time by automating repetitive processes and data processing duties. This allows them to focus more on value-added activities such as analysis, leading to better choices and improved business outcomes.

USE CASES AND APPLICATIONS

RPA has various applications in the field of finance. It is particularly efficient in handling jobs that are repeated and dependent on rules. RPA excels in the domains of accounts payable and receivable, financial reporting, reconciliations, and regulatory compliance. Another notable illustration may be the process of loan origination or any other procedure that involves consumer interaction. Technology enhances their speed and reduces their susceptibility to errors. Consequently, this allows for a greater allocation of staff time towards strategic analysis and decision-making inside the department. As the development of RPA technology progresses, its potential benefits in reducing complexity will also be extended to numerous financial sector tasks that are now considered challenging to automate.

Figure 2. Applications of RPA

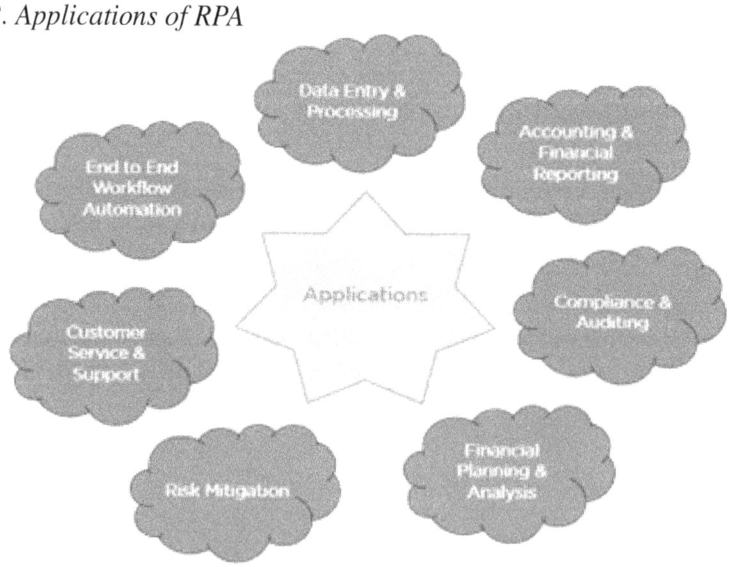

Data Entry and Processing Automation

The primary and extensive use of RPA in the field of finance is in the automation of manual data input and processing operations. For instance, the extraction of data from various financial records such as invoices, purchase orders, and bank statements can be efficiently performed by robotic process automation bots. These bots possess the capability to handle substantial volumes of information at a faster pace than humans, while maintaining unparalleled accuracy. This entails eliminating the tedious and error-prone elements linked to the manual input of numerical data into computer systems, which have a significant impact on several accounting departments. RPA has the potential to decrease processing time for data-intensive financial activities by as much as 80%. Furthermore, what distinguishes RPA from other software applications is its capacity to operate in conjunction with pre-existing systems and databases, hence minimising the need for human involvement in the transfer of information across various locations. The enhanced quality and reliability of such data directly influence subsequent activities such as financial reporting, analysis, and forecasting, resulting in more profound understanding of an organisation's operations and facilitating improved decision-making at different levels of management (Nilesh D Kulkarni et.al., 2023 & deloitte.com).

Streamlining Accounting and Financial Reporting

RPA revolutionises accounting and financial reporting operations by automating laborious and repetitive procedures. Bots provide the capability to efficiently do account reconciliations by effectively comparing transactions across several systems and detecting any inconsistencies. The financial closure process is expedited by the utilisation of RPA, which automates the creation of journal entries, consolidations, and the compilation of financial statements such as balance sheets and income statements. This automation guarantees the timely and correct delivery of crucial financial information. Ernst & Young's analysis indicates that RPA has the capacity to decrease the expenses associated with financial reporting procedures by 30-40%. Furthermore, in order to ensure audit readiness, each stage of an automated process is meticulously recorded, therefore establishing a visible audit trail that serves the aim of compliance (Arkadiusz Januszewskia et.al., 2021 & ey.com)

Enhancing Compliance and Auditing Processes

Compliance and auditing are crucial duties for financial organisations due to the highly regulated environment in which they operate. RPA is crucial in reducing risk and optimising these operations. Bots can be instructed to autonomously oversee transactions to ensure compliance with regulatory rules, identifying possible warning signs. The capacity of RPA to provide comprehensive audit trails, which meticulously record every stage of a procedure, greatly enhances the preparedness for audits and promotes openness. Furthermore, the implementation RPA in the collecting and processing of compliance reports serves to alleviate the administrative workload placed on compliance teams. RPA has the potential to decrease compliance expenses by as much as 50%. This enables specialists in the field of compliance to concentrate on strategic risk assessments and proactive steps in order to maintain the organisation's compliance (Thekkethil et.al., 2021).

Optimizing Financial Planning and Analysis

RPA has the potential to enhance the efficiency and accuracy of financial decision-making within finance teams through the integration and automation of key components of financial planning and analysis (FP&A). Robotic systems have the capability to effectively retrieve various types of information from enterprise resource planning systems, spreadsheets, or databases. Put simply, they achieve this by minimising the requirement for laborious human data processing. Consequently, analysts are capable of focusing their attention on tasks that contribute value. RPA facilitates the expeditious generation and evaluation of diverse financial models through the automation of processes such as scenario modelling, forecasting, budgeting, and others. According to the findings of the McKinsey & Company Report on Business Technology Office in 2016, it was observed that there were potential savings of up to 40% in labour hours worked. This implies that there is an increased availability of time for strategic insights, since RPA has the capability to save 40% of the time spent on Financial Planning and Analysis (FP&A) tasks. This results in enhanced decision-making capacity and a proactive approach to adapting to new business circumstances (Kulkarni et.al., 2023 & mckinsey.com).

Mitigating Risks Through Automation

RPA is an effective method for reducing operational risks in financial organisations. The implementation of RPA effectively mitigates the risk associated with human error by automating repetitive and manual operations. Bots demonstrate exceptional proficiency in activities such as data validation, cross-system inspections, and compliance monitoring. RPA has the capability to proactively detect inconsistencies, possible instances of fraud, or difficulties related to regulatory compliance. In addition, the meticulous recording of each step in the process by RPA establishes a thorough record of activities, so improving transparency and accountability, both of which are essential for effective risk management. According to a research published by the Institute for Robotic Process Automation & Artificial Intelligence (IRPAAI), the installation of RPA has the potential to result in a significant decrease of 25% to 50% in operational risk exposure (Villar et.al., 2021 & irpaai.com)

Improving Customer Service and Support

RPA in the banking industry extends beyond back-office activities and can even be applied to customer care and support functions. Everyday routine customer inquiries, such as balance checks, password resets, and transaction history requests, can be automated using chatbots and virtual assistants powered by RPA. These automated systems provide immediate and accurate answers, significantly reducing response time and increasing customer satisfaction. UiPath's poll revealed that 91% of financial professionals acknowledge the positive impact of RPA on their ability to gain strategic insights and data. This, in turn, indirectly enhances customer service by facilitating more informed and personalised interactions. Furthermore, the use of RPA helps streamline loan application processes, resulting in faster approval durations and an enhanced overall experience for clients. Concrete data on the precise impact of RPA on customer service in the finance industry is limited. However, there are numerous instances where institutions have successfully implemented this technology, resulting in faster and more efficient relationships with consumers that are customised to their individual needs rather than a generic approach (Khan et.al., 2023 & uipath.com).

Automating End-to-End Workflows for Efficiency

RPA is an exceptional technology that can efficiently handle the full financial workflow from start to finish. This type of comprehensive automation streamlines complex procedures like loan origination, account opening, and claims processing, hence minimising the need for manual involvement and reducing associated errors. According to a study conducted by Everest Group, the implementation of RPA can result in a reduction of 30%-50% in both processing time and cost for full cycle financial procedures. It enhances operational efficiency and boosts client satisfaction by expediting service delivery. Another advantage of RPA is its capacity to seamlessly interact with various systems and applications, facilitating the efficient transfer of information between departments. This integration eliminates obstacles and enhances process optimisation. (Sumathi, N et.al., 2022 & everestgrp.com)

IMPLEMENTATION STRATEGIES

To achieve success and fully exploit the benefits, a strategic strategy is crucial for implementing RPA in the finance sector. Despite its considerable potential, there are certain challenges associated with the implementation of this technology. Deloitte's analysis reveals that 78% of financial institutions have either adopted or intend to adopt RPA. However, a mere 3% have successfully expanded its use to numerous functions. Hence, it is crucial to devise a meticulously planned implementation strategy that effectively tackles potential hurdles and aligns with broader organisational objectives. The following paragraphs will analyse various essential tactics for applying RPA in financial institutions, which can unlock its complete potential and bring about substantial transformations in their operations (Grande et.al., 2024 & deloitte.com)

Identifying Suitable Processes for Automation

Deciding which tasks to automate is crucial for the successful implementation of RPA. An effective starting point is to identify tasks that are characterised by being rule-based, repetitive, and high-volume, as these tasks tend to consume significant amounts of time and resources. Typically, these operations mostly deal with structured data, with only a few exceptions. This makes them ideal candidates for automation. McKinsey research indicates that 42% of finance activities can be completely automated, while 19% can be mostly automated. However, not all procedures are suitable for RPA. It is essential to give priority to those initiatives that have the highest potential for return on investment and are in line with an organisation's strategic goals. When choosing them, it is important to examine variables like as process complexity, degrees of standardisation, data quality considerations, and scalability possibilities (Choi et.al., 2021 & mckinsey.com).

Assessing ROI and Cost-Benefit Analysis

In order to accomplish a successful implementation of RPA, it is essential to conduct an assessment of Return on Investment (ROI) and do a cost-benefit analysis. This involves quantifying the advantages of automation in financial terms, such as cost savings from reduced labour, improved efficiency, or less errors, compared to the expenses associated with purchasing RPA software packages, infrastructure, and setup. Based on research completed by Automation Anywhere in 2021, financial institutions can anticipate substantial returns on investment from this technology. In fact, certain organisations were able to recover their initial capital expenditure within a mere 6-9 months. However, it is important to also consider intangible advantages such as increased compliance levels, elevated customer care standards, and improved team morale, among other perks. Hence, during a comprehensive assessment, it is crucial to include elements such as the potential of these robots to provide long-term value by being scalable and adaptable to evolving corporate contexts (Santos et.al., 2019 & automationanywhere.com)

Selecting Appropriate RPA Tools and Technologies

In order to achieve a successful deployment, it is imperative to carefully select the appropriate tools and technology for RPA. Each of these software applications possesses distinct advantages and disadvantages, as well as numerous additional features within the realm of RPA technology. Gartner's Magic Quadrant for RPA research identifies UiPath, Automation Anywhere, and Blue Prism as leaders in the field. However, there are also numerous other providers that offer strong competition. When choosing an RPA tool, it is important to examine variables like as usability, scalability, security features, integration capabilities, and cost. Assessing the particular requirements of the organisation in relation to strategic goals will guarantee alignment, while also considering the reputation of vendors, customer service, and training resources. This will not only facilitate a smooth transition but also improve the adoption process (González Enríquez et.al., 2020 & gartner.com).

Designing, Developing, and Deploying RPA Bots

The design phase of a bot encompasses the establishment of the process flow, the definition of input and output parameters, and the identification of exception management. This is done to ensure compatibility and seamless integration with other systems. Development utilises a specific RPA tool, where the bot is constructed by employing drag-and-drop interfaces and occasionally implementing bespoke programming. According to a research analysis by UiPath, 88% of organisations who utilise RPA have observed a gain in productivity. Once the development is completed, rigorous testing should be conducted to ensure that the product functions as intended and fulfils all the predetermined criteria for success. Deployment encompasses various tasks, such as integrating the system into the production environment, determining the schedule for its execution, and monitoring its performance. Effective change management, coupled with well-executed communication strategies, is essential for ensuring seamless transitions and user buy-in during this period (Egger et.al., 2020 & uipath.com)

Integrating RPA With Existing Systems Securely

To effectively integrate RPA with existing systems, it is crucial to implement a robust approach that guarantees the protection of sensitive financial data and maintains uninterrupted operating processes. An area of worry regarding security is the manner in which bots engage with various apps and databases throughout the integration of RPA. Forrester's research revealed that security was the most significant difficulty in the implementation processes of 53% of organisations. It is crucial to incorporate secure authentication systems, together with encryption mechanisms for data in transit and at rest, and role-based access rules that restrict bot rights. These measures are necessary to minimise risks. Furthermore, it is essential to conduct regular security audits and vulnerability assessments on a frequent basis to identify any potential weaknesses within the integrated environment. The IT team must closely engage with the security team to ensure that industry standards compliance needs are met while integrating RAPs, following best practices (Pratik et.al., 2023 & forrester.com).

Addressing Regulatory Compliance and Data Privacy Concerns

The banking business is bound by rigorous regulatory frameworks, and any technology installation must adhere to these regulations. A poll conducted by Thomson Reuters reveals that 91% of global financial services firms perceive compliance with regulatory requirements as a significant obstacle. When implementing automation processes, it is crucial for RPA to adhere to data protection regulations and not disrupt regulatory compliance. To ensure the safety and protection of stored information, it is crucial to combine RPA with robust security systems such as encryption methods, access controls, and audit trails. These measures not only ensure the security of the data but also enable tracking its source in case it becomes unknown during transit. Furthermore, workflows must be developed to comply with specific regulations such as General Data Protection Regulation (GDPR) or California Consumer Privacy Act (CCPA), ensuring that the privacy rights of customers are consistently respected and maintained throughout the entire process. In order to maintain the security of their systems and avoid violating consumer protection laws, organisations must regularly perform risk assessments and compliance audits. Failure to do so may result in unauthorised access and the loss of public confidence, which can have negative consequences for all stakeholders involved (Jain et.al., 2024 & thomsonreuters.com).

Managing Organisational Change and Gaining Stakeholder Buy-In

In order to achieve success in implementing RPA in the banking sector, businesses must effectively manage and navigate through internal changes and also secure the support and agreement of all stakeholders involved. A poll done by Deloitte revealed that 52% of organisations encountered resistance while deploying RPA, indicating a reluctance to embrace change. Therefore, it is crucial to establish effective communication channels and implement comprehensive training programmes. Stakeholders should be informed about the various advantages of using RPA, emphasising its capacity to improve efficiency, minimise errors, and empower individuals to assume more valuable responsibilities. Furthermore, engaging key stakeholders in the selection and design stages of robotic process automation will foster a sense of accountability and inclusivity. Organisations may secure essential support for successful adoption by actively managing changes and showcasing the value proposition of RPA (Rodrigo et.al., 2023 & deloitte.com).

BEST PRACTICES AND CASE STUDIES

Implementing RPA successfully requires adhering to established best practices and learning from real-world case studies. While the potential benefits of RPA are substantial, a study by EY found that 30-50% of initial RPA projects fail to meet expectations due to various factors such as lack of clear objectives, inadequate change management, and unrealistic expectations. In this section, we will delve into best practices that can guide organisations towards successful RPA implementation, drawing insights from case studies that showcase the transformative power of this technology in the finance industry (Osman et.al., 2019).

DBS Bank: Transforming Operations with RPA

DBS Bank, in response to difficulties with manual procedures and operational inefficiencies, initiated a substantial installation of RPA. A specialised Centre of Excellence (CoE) was created to identify and streamline appropriate procedures, such as customer onboarding, loan processing, and trade finance operations. An important obstacle that needed to be overcome was the reluctance of employees to accept and adapt to change. This was successfully tackled by implementing a thorough change management programme. The outcomes were remarkable. DBS documented significant cost reductions, enhanced productivity, less errors, and expedited turnaround times. By shifting their attention to jobs that provide greater value, employees experienced higher work satisfaction and improved operational efficiency (fintechfutures.com).

AT&T's RPA Journey: Lessons in Change Management and Process Selection

Real-world RPA implementations have shown that effective planning and alignment with stakeholders are crucial. When AT&T made the decision to automate its financial operations, certain employees expressed reluctance due to concerns that computers might replace their jobs. However, the company successfully addressed this challenge by involving employees in the design and implementation phases of RPA, while also clearly communicating the advantages of automation for both the workforce and the organisation. As a result, there was a significant 44% decrease in manual labour for specific procedures. This occurrence exemplifies the necessity of transparent change management in the successful implementation of robotic process automation, as demonstrated by the crucial role of effective communication. Furthermore, it emphasises the importance of selecting the appropriate procedure in automation. While AT&T made significant strides in improving efficiency in several areas, they faced challenges when attempting to automate complicated processes that require human judgement and decision-making abilities. Consequently, it is necessary to thoroughly assess the appropriateness of a particular process before determining whether or not to automate it, in order to avoid wasting time on such endeavours (about.att.com).

Streamlining Operations at a Big Four Accounting Firm

A leading global professional services firm, widely recognized as one of the "Big Four" accounting firms, sought to enhance operational efficiency and reduce errors by automating repetitive tasks. With a vast network spanning 158 countries and over 236,000 employees, the firm partnered with Cognizant Softvision to develop and implement a tailored robotic process automation (RPA) solution. This initiative aimed to streamline workflows and improve quality and risk management, all without requiring a major overhaul of their existing IT infrastructure. Cognizant Softvision's team of experts, organized into "Virtual Pods" of remote, globally distributed specialists, collaborated closely with the firm to identify key processes for automation and implement the RPA solution. Despite the challenges posed by the COVID-19 pandemic, these virtual teams successfully delivered the project on time and within budget. The implemented RPA bots have already eliminated 6,000 hours of manual labor, a number projected to increase to 100,000 hours in the coming year. Additionally, the firm has realized annual savings of $8 million and experienced significant improvements in accuracy, quality, and risk management (cognizant.com).

Turbocharging Invoice Processing at Acme Manufacturing

Acme Manufacturing, a multinational corporation grappling with difficulties in managing its intricate and high-capacity invoice processing workflow, sought out Robotic Process Automation (RPA) as a remedy. The process of manually entering data from different invoice formats was both time-consuming and prone to errors, resulting in payment delays and operational inefficiencies. In order to tackle these problems, Acme Manufacturing adopted an RPA solution that includes advanced document parsing features. This solution facilitated the extraction of crucial invoice data by RPA bots, irrespective of the format. The extracted data was then cross-validated with internal systems and automatically inputted into the ERP system for approval. The incorporation of an exception handling mechanism guaranteed that there would be very little need for manual intervention, thereby making the process more efficient. Consequently, the company witnessed a substantial 80% decrease in the time it took to process invoices, accomplished an impressive 99.5% accuracy rate in data entry, and generated noteworthy cost savings. In addition, better insight into the invoice lifecycle and expedited payment timelines strengthened supplier relationships, hence enhancing overall operational efficiency and financial performance (tungstenautomation.com).

FUTURE TRENDS AND OUTLOOK

The potential of RPA to revolutionise the financial environment is becoming more apparent as it continues to develop and mature. The future of RPA in the banking industry goes beyond simply automating monotonous work. It involves rethinking and redesigning company processes, improving customer experiences, and fostering strategic growth. In the future, we anticipate that RPA will evolve to possess greater intelligence, adaptability, and integration with other developing technologies, leading to a new era of automation and improved productivity. The subsequent parts will explore the precise patterns and progressions that are poised to mould the future of RPA in finance, emphasising its capacity to transform the industry.

Low-Code/No-Code RPA Platforms

A big trend in the future of RPA is the democratisation of automation. Business users who don't know a lot about coding can still be involved in the automation process with low-code or no-code methods. The visual, user-friendly interfaces of these platforms let users create and set up automation workflows by dragging and dropping pre-built components. This not only speeds up the implementation of RPA but also encourages employees to find and automate jobs that make their work easier and more efficient, which leads to a culture of innovation within organisations. This trend shows a change from automation being led by IT to a more joint approach where business users are more involved in driving automation projects (Doguc et.al., 2020).

Increased Focus on Process Discover

To get the most out of RPA, you need to figure out which tasks to automate. More and more businesses are buying process mining and discovering tools to learn more about how their current workflows work. These tools analyse a huge amount of operational data to find slowdowns, waste, and jobs that are done over and over again that could be easily automated. Companies can make sure that their RPA projects have the biggest effect on increasing productivity, cutting costs, and making customers satisfied by prioritising automation efforts based on data-driven insights. Companies use RPA more strategically, focusing on improving whole business processes instead of just automating certain chores (El-Gharib et.al., 2022).

Enhanced Cybersecurity Measures

Strong cybersecurity steps are more important than ever as RPA becomes increasingly prevalent in finance. RPA bots deal with confidential financial data a lot, which means they could be attacked online. To protect RPA equipment and data, companies are spending money on high-tech security tools like encryption, access controls, and intrusion detection systems. Also, security-by-design ideas are getting more and more attention. This means that security is thought about at every stage of developing and deploying RPA. It is important it is to find a balance between the advantages of technology and the need to keep important financial data safe (Balamurugan A et.al., 2023).

Integration with IoT and Edge Computing

When RPA, the Internet of Things (IoT), and edge computing converge together, they make it possible for financial automation to go to new heights. Sensors, wearable technology, and financial terminals are just some of the IoT gadgets that collect huge amounts of real-time data. RPA can use this information to make automated choices and actions, which will make operations more responsive and efficient. For example, RPA bots can look at real-time market data and make trades automatically. They can also use data from IoT-enabled cars to handle insurance claims. Edge computing brings processing closer to the data source. This makes RPA even more useful by lowering latency and letting people make decisions more quickly in financial processes that need to be done quickly (Liao et.al., 2018).

The Rise of the Digital Workforce

In banking, the idea of a digital workforce is becoming more popular. People no longer see RPA bots as just tools for automating tasks; they see them as virtual coworkers who work with real employees to improve productivity and come up with new ideas. Companies are making their workplaces flexible so they can accommodate both human and digital workers, giving each group of workers jobs that match their skills. People can focus on making strategic decisions and handling complex problems while bots take care of repetitive tasks that are based on rules. This collaborative approach makes the workplace more productive and flexible. As more people work from home, the rise of the digital workforce is transforming the way work is done in finance redefining the roles and responsibilities of both humans and machines (Madakam et.al., 2019).

CONCLUSION

RPA is profoundly changing the financial industry by replacing human operations with automated processes, resulting in increased efficiency and fostering innovation. Originally centred on basic, recurring assignments. RPA has evolved in parallel with breakthroughs in Artificial Intelligence (AI), Machine Learning (ML), and Natural Language Processing (NLP) to address increasingly intricate procedures. This not only expedites procedures and reduces expenses, but also promotes a more flexible, customer-focused financial environment. As RPA merges with AI and ML, it will have a significant impact on decision-making, risk management, and customer service, leading to even more promising outcomes in the future. Nevertheless, it is imperative to prioritise appropriate deployment, which requires a strong emphasis on data protection, ethical use of AI, and the retraining of the workforce. Looking to the future, the financial industry is ready for a new era driven by intelligent automation based on RPA. Low-code/no-code platforms will facilitate the democratisation of automation, while strengthened security measures will preserve critical data. The combination of Internet of Things (IoT) and edge computing enables immediate decision-making and automated physical chores. The collaboration between humans and machines will progress alongside the digital workforce, leading to additional advancements and increased effectiveness. RPA has become essential for financial organisations as they navigate the digital world. In order to survive and succeed in the constantly changing financial world, it is crucial to adopt this technology, tackle its difficulties, and take use of its extensive possibilities. RPA is a fundamental element of the future of banking, facilitating the development of an efficient, secure, and customer-focused financial ecosystem (Ayinla et.al., 2024).

Strategic Roadmap for RPA Success in Finance

RPA may change finance, but a holistic approach is needed. Organisations should prioritise integrating RPA activities with business goals to ensure that automation is driven by strategy rather than technology. RPA is a dynamic tool that demands continual improvement. AI, machine learning, and process mining can unleash hyperautomation, allowing organisations to automate increasingly complex processes and achieve unparalleled efficiency. Upskilling and reskilling personnel ensures they can collaborate with digital workforces and adapt to changing jobs. RPA implementations require a strong governance framework to ensure openness, accountability, and ethical decision-making. Cybersecurity must be a major focus for RPA because it handles sensitive financial data. Creating an innovative culture and guaranteeing RPA adoption across the organisation requires open communication and collaboration between IT, finance, and other stakeholders. Starting with pilot projects and scaling up based on learnings and achievements reduces risks and maximises RPA advantages. Partners with the proper RPA provider can greatly impact automation projects, so vendor selection is vital. Change management solutions must also address staff concerns, give comprehensive training, and promote automation positivity. Financial institutions may transform RPA from a tactical tool to a strategic asset that improves operational excellence, client experiences, and long-term success in the ever-changing finance industry by following these tips (Fernandez et.al., 2023 & Ivančić et.al., 2019).

Table 1. Abbreviations

AI	**Artificial Intelligence**
CCPA	California Consumer Privacy Act
CoE	Centre of Excellence
ERP	Enterprise Resource Planning
FP&A	Financial Planning and Analysis
GDPR	General Data Protection Regulation
IoT	Internet of Things
IRPAAI	Institute for Robotic Process Automation & Artificial Intelligence
KYC	Know Your Customer
ML	Machine Learning
NLP	Natural Language Processing
ROI	Return on Investment
RPA	Robotic Process Automation

REFERENCES

AT&T. (2022). *AT&T.*https://about.att.com/

Automation Anywhere. (2021). *Automation Anywhere.* https://www.automationanywhere.com/

Automation Edge. (2024). *Automation Edge.* https://automationedge.com/

Ayinla, B., Atadoga, A., Ike, C., Ndubuisi, N., Asuzu, O. F., & Adeleye, R. (2024). The role of robotic process automation (RPA) in modern accounting: A review—Investigating how automation tools are transforming traditional accounting practices. *Engineering Science & Technology Journal, 5*(2), 427–447. DOI: 10.51594/estj.v5i2.804

Balamurugan, A., Vamsi, M., Bhattacharya, R., Mohammed, S., Kaushik, P., & Haralayya, D. (2023). Robotic process automation (RPA) in accounting and auditing of business and financial information. *Manager, 58*, 127–142.

Capco. (2019). *Capco.* https://www.capco.com/

Choi, D., R'bigui, H., & Cho, C. (2021). Robotic process automation implementation challenges. In *Proceedings of [Conference or Book Title]* (pp. [pages]). Springer. DOI: 10.1007/978-981-15-7990-5_29

Cognizant. (2024). *Cognizant.* https://www.cognizant.com/

Cooper, L., Holderness, D.Jr, Sorensen, T., & Wood, D. (2019). Robotic process automation in public accounting. *Accounting Horizons, 33*(4), 15–35. DOI: 10.2308/acch-52466

Deloitte. (2024). *Deloitte.* https://www2.deloitte.com

Doğuc, Ö. (2020). Robot process automation (RPA) and its future. In *Handbook of Research on Strategic Fit and Design in Business Ecosystems.* IGI Global., DOI: 10.4018/978-1-7998-1125-1.ch021

Egger, A., Ter, A., Kratsch, W., Leemans, S., Röeglinger, M., & Wynn, M. (2020). Bot log mining: Using logs from robotic process automation for process mining. In *Business Process Management: BPM 2020.* Springer.

El-Gharib, N., & Amyot, D. (2022). A review of data-driven robotic process automation exploiting process mining.

Everest Group. (2022). *Everest Group.* https://www.everestgrp.com/

Fernandez, D., Dastane, O., Omar Zaki, H., & Aman, A. (2023). Robotic process automation: Bibliometric reflection and future opportunities. *European Journal of Innovation Management, 27*(2), 692–712. DOI: 10.1108/EJIM-10-2022-0570

Fintech Futures. (2018). *Fintech Futures.* https://www.fintechfutures.com/

Flechsig, C., Anslinger, F., & Lasch, R. (2022). Robotic process automation in purchasing and supply management: A multiple case study on potentials, barriers, and implementation. *Journal of Purchasing and Supply Management, 28*(1), 100718. DOI: 10.1016/j.pursup.2021.100718

Forrester. (2021). *Forrester.* https://www.forrester.com/

Gartner. (2021). *Gartner.* https://www.gartner.com/

González Enríquez, J., Jimenez Ramirez, A., Domínguez Mayo, F. J., & Garcia-Garcia, J. A. (2020). Robotic process automation: A scientific and industrial systematic mapping study. *IEEE Access : Practical Innovations, Open Solutions, 8*, 214072–214095. DOI: 10.1109/ACCESS.2020.2974934

Grande, V., Campos, R., Facin, A., & Batistela, G. (2022). An analysis of the benefits, challenges and methods of process selection to adopt robotic process automation. *Revista Gestão da Produção. Operações e Sistemas, 17*(1), 89–108.

Gunisity, S. R. (2024). Evolution of automation to hyperautomation: Leveraging RPA, AI, ML, NLP for optimal operational efficiency. *International Journal of Computer Trends and Technology, 72*(5), 76–83. DOI: 10.14445/22312803/IJCTT-V72I3P111

Infosys, B. P. M. (2024). *Infosys BPM.* https://www.infosysbpm.com/

IRPAAI. (2024). *Institute for Robotic Process Automation & Artificial Intelligence.* https://irpaai.com/

Ivančić, L., Suša Vugec, D., & Vukšić, V. (2019). Robotic process automation: Systematic literature review. In *Organizational Transformation and Managing Innovation in the Fourth Industrial Revolution.* Springer., DOI: 10.1007/978-3-030-30429-4_19

Jadhav, P., & Dongare, R. (2023). Robotic process automation (RPA) in business processes: Benefits and challenges. *International Journal of Advanced Research in Science, Communication and Technology, 3*(1). ISSN 2581-9429.

Jain, V., Balakrishnan, A., Beeram, D., Najana, M., & Chintale, P. (2024). Leveraging artificial intelligence for enhancing regulatory compliance in the financial sector. *International Journal of Computer Trends and Technology, 72*(5), 124–140. DOI: 10.14445/22312803/IJCTT-V72I5P116

Januszewski, A., Kujawski, J., & Buchalska-Sugajska, N. (2021). Benefits of and obstacles to RPA implementation in accounting firms. *Procedia Computer Science*, *192*, 4672–4680. DOI: 10.1016/j.procs.2021.09.245

Khan, A., Khalid, W., Faisal, S., & Suliman Fadl Elseed, E. (2023). The future: Artificial intelligence's profound impact on accounting and society—Anticipating job market dynamics and evolving skill requirements for accountants. *Seybold Report*, *18*(11), 1596–1622.

KPMG. (2024). *KPMG*. https://assets.kpmg.com/

Kulkarni, N., & Bansal, S. (2023). Finance business process automation using RPA. *Journal of Economics & Management Research*, *4*(3), 1–5. DOI: 10.47363/JESMR/2022(4)220

Liao, Y., Rocha Loures, E., & Deschamps, F. (2018). Industrial internet of things: A systematic literature review and insights. *IEEE Internet of Things Journal*, *5*(6), 4515–4525. DOI: 10.1109/JIOT.2018.2834151

Madakam, S., Holmukhe, R., & Jaiswal, D. (2019). The future digital workforce: Robotic process automation (RPA). *Journal of Information Systems and Technology Management*, *16*(e201916005). Advance online publication. DOI: 10.4301/S1807-1775201916001

Mandvikar, S. (2023). Indexing robotic process automation products. *International Journal of Computer Trends and Technology*, *71*(4), 52–56. DOI: 10.14445/22312803/IJCTT-V71I8P108

McKinsey & Company. (2018–2023). *McKinsey & Company*. https://www.mckinsey.com/

Medium. (2024). *Medium*. https://medium.com/

Mohamed, S., & Frank, L. (2024). Improved efficiency and reduced costs: The role of robotic process automation (RPA) in automating price adjustments.

Moreira, S., Mamede, H. S., & Santos, A. (2023). Process automation using RPA – A literature review. *Procedia Computer Science*, *219*, 244–254. DOI: 10.1016/j.procs.2023.01.287

Morgan, J. P. (2020–2021). *J.P. Morgan*. https://www.jpmorgan.com/

Osman, C.-C. (2019). Robotic process automation: Lessons learned from case studies. *Informações Econômicas*, *23*(3), 66–71. DOI: 10.12948/issn14531305/23.4.2019.06

Oyeniyi, L., Ugochukwu, C., & Mhlongo, N.Lawrence Damilare OyeniyiChinonye Esther UgochukwuNoluthando Zamanjomane Mhlongo. (2024). Robotic process automation in routine accounting tasks: A review and efficiency analysis. *World Journal of Advanced Research and Reviews, 22*(2), 695–711. DOI: 10.30574/wjarr.2024.22.1.1156

Patrício, L., Costa, L., Varela, L., & Avila, P. (2023). Sustainable implementation of robotic process automation based on a multi-objective mathematical model. *Sustainability (Basel), 15*(18), 15045. DOI: 10.3390/su152015045

PwC Germany. (2019). *PwC*. https://www.pwc.de/

Ribeiro, J., Lima, R., Eckhardt, T., & Paiva, S. (2021). Robotic process automation and artificial intelligence in Industry 4.0: A literature review. *Procedia Computer Science, 181*, 51–58. DOI: 10.1016/j.procs.2021.01.104

Rodrigo, R. (2023). Impact of robotic process automation (RPA) implementation in banking sector of South Asian countries. DOI: 10.13140/RG.2.2.20867.27680

Roszkowska, P. (2020). Fintech in financial reporting and audit for fraud prevention and safeguarding equity investments. *Journal of Accounting & Organizational Change, Advance online publication.*

Rutschi, C., & Dibbern, J. (2020). Towards a framework of implementing software robots: Transforming human-executed routines into machines. *The Data Base for Advances in Information Systems, 51*(2), 104–128. DOI: 10.1145/3380799.3380808

Santos, F., Pereira, R., & Braga de Vasconcelos, J. (2019). Toward robotic process automation implementation: An end-to-end perspective. *Business Process Management Journal, 26*(2), 405–420. Advance online publication. DOI: 10.1108/BPMJ-12-2018-0380

Šperka, R., & Halaška, M. (2023). The performance assessment framework (PPAFR) for RPA implementation in a loan application process using process mining. *Information Systems and e-Business Management, 21*(2), 277–321. DOI: 10.1007/s10257-022-00602-2

Sumathi, N., & Jeyalakshmi, A. (2022). Implementing robotic process automation to improve operational efficiency in the health-care sector. *International Journal of Health Sciences, 6*(S1), 9666–9672. Advance online publication. DOI: 10.53730/ijhs.v6nS1.7256

Thekkethil, M., Shukla, V., Beena, F., & Chopra, A. (2021). Robotic process automation in banking and finance sector for loan processing and fraud detection. In *2021 6th International Conference on Recent Innovations in Technology and Engineering (ICRITO)* (pp. 1–6). IEEE. DOI: 10.1109/ICRITO51393.2021.9596076

Thomson Reuters. (2022). *Thomson Reuters*. Retrieved May 18, 2024, from https://www.thomsonreuters.com/

Treacy, S., Adyanthaya, A., Kearny, C., Anand, J., O'Sullivan, K., & Xu, Y. (2023). From hype to reality: Navigating the challenges of RPA implementation. In *Proceedings of the 18th European Conference on Innovation and Entrepreneurship* (pp. 875–882). DOI: 10.34190/ecie.18.2.1721

Tungsten Automation. (2023). *Tungsten Automation*. Retrieved May 21, 2024, from https://www.tungstenautomation.com/

UiPath. (2021, 2022, 2023). *UiPath*. Retrieved May 20, 2024, from https://www.uipath.com/

Vijai, C., Suriyalakshmi, S., & Elayaraja, M. (2020). The future of robotic process automation (RPA) in the banking sector for better customer experience. *Shanlax International Journal of Commerce*, *8*(3), 61–65. DOI: 10.34293/commerce.v8i2.1709

Villar, A., & Khan, N. (2021). Robotic process automation in banking industry: A case study on Deutsche Bank. *Journal of Banking and Financial Technology*, *5*(1). Advance online publication. DOI: 10.1007/s42786-021-00030-9

Yao, M. (2024). RPA technology enables highly automated development of corporate financial accounting processes. *Applied Mathematics and Nonlinear Sciences*, *9*(1), 1–13. DOI: 10.2478/amns-2024-0541

Chapter 13
Quantum Computing: Transforming the Landscape of Financial Markets

Maiyra Ahmed
Iqra University, Pakistan

ABSTRACT

Quantum-computers can assist to resolve and answer particular problems and issues which are not solvable by binary computers or classical hardware. Considering the prompt response offered by quantum-computers hence has the possibility to assist any sector, market or division which utilizes estimations, such as financial markets. Initially, the quantum-computer applications for financial markets included, machine-learning, optimization and simulation issues which have been discussed by most of the studies. Therefore, in this study we aim to analyze the use-cases like risk management, portfolio management and pricing of derivatives to provide insight about the usefulness of quantum-computers in financial markets. This indicates that financial markets can benefit from quantum-computers in the upcoming years.

BACKGROUND OF QUANTUM COMPUTER

The integration of physics in solving complex issues within financial services dates back several decades. For instance, the Black-Scholes-Merton framework employs the Brownian motion approach to price financial instruments like European call options (Ederington & Guan, 2000; Nestler, 2017). The advent of quantum computing brings innovative capabilities for financial calculations and problem-solving, particularly in navigating uncertainty and optimizing artificial processes. Early adopters of quantum computers stand to benefit from these advancements by uncovering "Dynamic Arbitrage Opportunities" overlooked by competitors.

DOI: 10.4018/979-8-3693-7160-2.ch013

Additionally, quantum computers enhance compliance, leverage behavioral data to improve customer service, and provide rapid responses to market volatility (Egger et al., 2020).

The primary advantage of quantum computers lies in their vast "Solution-space" compared to classical binary computers, despite their fragility (Hassija et al., 2020). Quantum computing's power exponentially increases with each additional qubit, far surpassing the capabilities of traditional computers that rely on multiplying transistors to tackle problems. This exponential power allows quantum computing to transform financial services operations, including client management, treasury and asset management, trading, and compliance and risk management.

Quantum computing's applications in financial services can be categorized into three main areas: (a) prediction and targeting, (b) trading optimization, and (c) risk profiling. Each category offers potential use cases, such as in insurance, banking, and financial markets (Pistoia et al., 2021). Quantum computers, supported by quantum mechanical phenomena, manage data through qubits, which are highly effective in handling probability distributions, data mapping, sample evaluation, and summarization. These capabilities lead to more precise calculations, reduced runtimes, and solutions to previously unsolvable problems (Marella & Parisa, 2020).

Modern financial service users demand personalized and rapidly adaptive services to meet their evolving needs (Jacobi & Brenner, 2018). Small and medium-sized financial institutions risk losing up to 25% of their customer base by offering non-customer-centric products. Developing an analytic framework that swiftly and accurately processes behavioral data to determine real-time customer needs is challenging. This limitation prevents financial institutions from providing prompt, personalized services and products, missing opportunities to grow their customer base and reach the 1.7 billion unbanked adults worldwide.[1]

Fraud detection is another significant challenge, with financial institutions losing an estimated 10 to 40 billion USD annually due to poor data management and fraud practices. Current fraud detection methods yield an 18% false-positive rate, causing institutions to be overly cautious. This inefficiency extends the credit scoring process to as long as 12 weeks. With 70% of banking transactions now conducted online, customers favor systems that are quick and efficient.[2] Financial institutions that delay communication with customers risk losing them to more responsive, customer-focused competitors.

Quantum computing offers groundbreaking potential for expanding customer bases and enhancing forecasting models (Renduchintala et al., 2022). Quantum computers excel in data modeling, identifying trends, classifying data, and making predictions, which are currently impractical due to the complexities of intricate data networks.

Financial markets face increased complexity, such as the XVA (valuation adjustment) framework, which now includes components like debit (DVA), capital (KVA), credit (CVA), margin (MVA), and funding (FVA).[3] Heightened transparency and rigorous validation processes impact risk management calculations, aligning credit exposure with credit limits on derivatives portfolios. Additionally, financing models and assets, such as ETFs and ESG financing, have evolved significantly.

In this complex trading landscape, finance managers struggle to incorporate real-world constraints, like market volatility and customer life events, into portfolio optimization. Traditional portfolio managers simulate numerous scenarios to ensure sensitivities align with projected returns. However, current computational limitations and transaction costs make balancing investment portfolios with market movements almost impossible.[4]

Quantum computing aids in navigating current trading complexities. Its combinatorial optimization capabilities help finance managers improve portfolio diversification, balance investments with market environments and investor goals, and streamline trading settlement processes for greater cost efficiency (Omarova, 2020).

Financial institutions are pressured to balance risk, enhance hedging strategies, and conduct broader distress assessments to meet regulatory requirements (Williams, 2010). Managing liquidity, pricing derivatives, and assessing risk involve complex computations, making it challenging to accurately handle risk costs in trading. The Monte Carlo simulation is widely used to evaluate volatility and risk in financial modeling, but it has limitations due to estimation errors (Portmann & Renner, 2022).

Quantum computing helps financial institutions address these challenges by offering superior solutions to balance risk, optimize hedging, and conduct comprehensive distress assessments while complying with regulatory standards.

LITERATURE REVIEW

Various financial activities, from optimization of portfolio to pricing of securities and derivatives, possess the capability needed to evaluate the extend of probable results. In this era, banking sector is applying models and algorithms which compute probabilities (Bouland et al., 2020). These are moderately efficient yet these are not perfect, as portrayed at the time of financial turmoil years ago, when allegedly few-possible crisis happened more rapidly than projected.

In world with huge-data, more robust computing machines are necessary to compute exact possibilities or probabilities. Considering the notion that various financial institutions are willing to adopt an advance generation processor which operate on quantum physics fundamentals to decode massive level of information at high-speed. The most prominent in the field named "Google" revealed that

Sycamore quantum-processor usually takes more than or equal to 180 seconds to complete the activity which can take years for super-computers to perform the same task. The trail efficiently exhibited potential of quantum-computers which presently is unimaginable.

Financial markets and institutions which can exploit quantum-computers are more-likely to emphasize on its considerable advantages. Specifically, they will be capable to efficiently examine huge data sets which are unstructured. Distinct understanding into these segments can assist financial markets as well as institutions to take best possible decision and enhance services provided to customers, for instance via relevant schemes or well-timed announcement of projects. There are evenly high-powered use scenarios in corporate finance, management of portfolios, capital markets and activities related to encryption. In a frequently commoditized atmosphere, it can be a track towards competitive-edge. Quantum-computers are specifically positive where algorithms are charged via data-steams, for example prices of equity in real-time which includes a higher degree of noise randomly.

The influence of pandemic has exhibited that exact and on-time evaluation of risk stays a crucial issue for financial markets and institutions. Although, earlier the happenings of 2020, the past years have witnessed economic and financial catastrophes which cause frequent deviation in how institutions and market stakeholders analyze, price and risk dissimilar asset categories. It drives the initiation of elevating difficulties and real-time risk framework energized via AI however still operational on fundamental computers.

According to Albareti et al. (2022), quantum-computers can answer particular queries which are not workable on basic hardware, increasing the power offered via quantum-computers hence has the possibility to transform any sector which utilizes calculation, comprising finance. Initially, applications of quantum-computer for financial sector includes simulation, machine learning and optimization of issues which have previously been offered and employed to uses scenarios like management of portfolio, pricing and management of risk. This analysis evaluated methodologies, platforms, algorithms and use scenarios of quantum-computers for numerous uses in finance within a structured manner. It is intended at employees employed in the financial sector and aids to earn understanding of the present transformation and abilities and insight the possibility of quantum-computers within the financial sector.

Another study, of Orús et al. (2019) explored the application of quantum-computers to solve financial issues along with the present techniques and future's overview. This study analyzed quantum-computer use in algorithms optimization and depicted its use for portfolio optimization, searching for opportunities for arbitrage and credit scoring. It is observed that quantum-computers amplitude computations can help in various presently use financial models and techniques due to its high-speed.

In the similar context, the study of Egger et al. (2020) discussed the capability and use of quantum-computers for financial queries. The study also focuses on algorithms, optimization, machine learning and simulation of quantum-computers. As per the analysis, quantum-computing advantages are more likely to bring revolution in the financial institutions which will enhance financial services for customer.

According to Mosteanu and Faccia (2021), the revolution of financial markets includes fintech technology which has become one of the leading application. The presently changing and shifting paradigm in many field of science, physics, database management and geometry considerably play a crucial role towards a massive change in the structure of finance sector, while being a major concern regarding cyber-threat. To explore the innovations strength, weakness, opportunities and threats, SWOT analysis was applied. The outcome verified that availability of information and the elevating connection of crosswise uses tends to be a first step towards transformation due to the change in economic paradigms. The developing computing ability and the growth of elevating sturdy forecasting software provide competitive edge, important dynamics, and computation of difficult problem. In this scenario, as evident earlier, there is a greater probability of market concentration in which, although limited firms or leader of innovations can afford to invest in these advancements, to gain competitive edge against their rival companies.

Subsequently, Gupta and Sharma (2023) observed the impact of quantum-computer on firms. The analysis provides understanding regarding this type of computer along with its benefits and also revealing the drawbacks or shortcomings of quantum-computers for firms. This comprises of enhanced functioning, elevated effectiveness and improved measures of privacy. As per the analysis it was concluded that quantum-computers have the capability to basically modify operations of the firm and offer novel opportunities for advancement. It further reveals that the businesses need to finance in evolving own quantum-computers ability and to determine the possible issues and risks related with this innovation.

QUANTUM COMPUTERS IN FINANCIAL MARKETS

Quantum computing is in its developmental phase, yet experiments have shown its high potential for the finance sector. According to the World Economic Forum in 2022, governments have invested approximately $25 billion in quantum computing research and development, and about $1 billion in venture capital deals were finalized in the recent financial year (Tawiah & Keefe, 2022). Despite being in its early stages, various mechanical complexities need to be resolved before quantum computing can be widely used for routine tasks.

However, quantum computing has already demonstrated significant potential for various fields, including finance. Its capability to solve complex mathematical problems much faster than classical computers makes it ideal for numerous applications. While finance is one of the early adopters, other industries like logistics, military, manufacturing, and pharmaceuticals are also testing quantum computing.

The unique characteristics of quantum computing can profoundly impact financial markets. Tasks such as financial forecasting and modeling could benefit greatly from quantum computing's enhanced precision and processing capabilities. Portfolio optimization, risk management, and asset pricing are some of the most frequently cited applications. Additionally, the implications for cryptography make it crucial for financial markets to monitor quantum computing advancements (Gill et al., 2022).

Collaboration is essential in quantum computing development due to the need for software and hardware innovation. Leading technology companies such as Amazon, IBM, Microsoft, and Google have initiated projects to experiment with quantum software, cloud solutions, and hardware (El-Seoud et al., 2017).

For instance, Microsoft Azure Quantum has partnered with Goldman Sachs to explore quantum computing for pricing. JPMorgan is experimenting with quantum solutions for risk management and optimization, while HSBC has teamed up with IBM to explore the technology's applications for pricing, risk reduction, and portfolio optimization (Owolabie et al., 2024).

Quantum computers operate on the principles of quantum mechanics, an extension of physics dealing with the behavior of matter and light at atomic and subatomic scales (Henkle et al., 2024). Unlike classical computers that process and store data in bits (binary values of 0 or 1), quantum computers use qubits, which can exist in multiple states simultaneously—a property known as superposition. This allows quantum computers to handle vastly more data than classical bits (Erwin & Engelbrecht, 2023).

Another key property of qubits is entanglement, where pairs of qubits are interconnected such that changing the state of one instantly affects the other, regardless of distance. This gives quantum computers additional processing power. While adding bits to a classical computer linearly increases its processing power, adding qubits to a quantum computer exponentially increases its processing capacity.[5]

However, working with qubits is challenging because they must be maintained in a delicate quantum state, which is highly sensitive to physical disturbances.[6] This requires sophisticated safeguards, such as ultra-cooled refrigerators, vacuum chambers, and insulation, to protect the qubits from environmental interference.

Furthermore, quantum computers require entirely new software, hardware, and algorithms to fully exploit their properties. While research has highlighted quantum computers' benefits in AI, cryptography, and machine learning, there is a need to develop new algorithms specifically designed for quantum computing, rather than adapting existing ones meant for classical computers.[7]

The potential impact of quantum computers on the banking sector is significant due to their ability to handle vast amounts of transactions and calculations quickly (Costa et al., 2022). Currently, some financial institutions are using quantum algorithms that leverage unique quantum properties like superposition and entanglement, though these capabilities are still being fully realized.

For example, Grover's algorithm can rapidly search large, unstructured databases of financial information, such as identifying specific transactions or trends. Shor's algorithm allows for the fast factoring of large numbers, which is crucial for encryption and could be used for portfolio optimization (Montanez-Barrera et al., 2024).

Asset pricing is another application where quantum computing can make a significant impact. Traditional methods for pricing financial assets, such as derivatives, rely on complex mathematical models like Monte Carlo simulations, which involve generating numerous potential outcomes to estimate value. Quantum Monte Carlo (QMC) methods can handle complex financial instruments, such as options with non-linear payoffs, more efficiently (Ajagekar & You, 2019).

A common question about quantum computers is whether they can predict the stock market. While quantum computers may outperform classical machines in certain financial modeling tasks, it is unlikely they will predict the stock market with high precision.[8] Moreover, like any new technology, quantum computing introduces new complexities and limitations that need to be addressed before its full potential in financial applications can be realized.

Financial institutions have high hopes for quantum computing's impact on risk management, which involves identifying, assessing, classifying, and mitigating risks. Each step involves complex modeling and simulations to predict risk outcomes, where accuracy and speed are critical. Quantum computing can enhance cybersecurity through more advanced encryption methods.

Data encryption is crucial in finance to protect sensitive information from unauthorized access. Quantum computers could break many current encryption methods but also offer the potential to develop new, more secure encryption techniques resistant to classical attacks. For example, quantum key distribution can create and distribute a secret key between parties, ensuring data privacy and integrity even if an unauthorized party intercepts the communication.[9]

Quantum computing's properties pose challenges and opportunities for blockchain technologies. While quantum computers could potentially break current encryption methods used in blockchain, researchers are working on quantum-proof encryption techniques for blockchain to withstand such attacks, like IBM's Crystals Kyber.[10] Additionally, quantum computing could improve blockchain performance and security, enhancing transaction efficiency.

Financial markets and trading could see a significant boost in efficiency through advanced algorithms capable of conducting multiple calculations simultaneously, revealing numerous possibilities and predictions for market behavior (Hofmann et al., 2022). Despite quantum computing's demonstrated capabilities in addressing various financial challenges, current machines' limited scale and the lack of a classical model for quantum algorithms pose challenges.

Possible Applications of Quantum Computing in Finance

Quantum computers can transform financial markets by solving complex problems faster and more accurately than classical computers. Applications in finance include:

Digital Communication Security: Quantum computers can disrupt cryptography, affecting electronic fund transfers and banking transactions. This could lead to new, more secure cryptographic methods.

Fraud Detection: Quantum computing can optimize fraud detection systems to use robust elements efficiently, enhancing fraud detection systems to use robust elements efficiently, enhancing their ability to detect and prevent fraudulent activities. For example, Mastercard has projected that its network has saved about $30 billion in fraud over the past two years, showcasing the potential impact of advanced technology in this area.

Optimization: Quantum computers excel at solving optimization problems. Various algorithms can be used to tackle specific optimization challenges, such as portfolio optimization or arbitrage opportunities. Quantum computers can assess multiple scenarios simultaneously, providing high-quality solutions and reducing computation time. For instance, algorithms like QAOA/VQE are used for quadratic unconstrained binary optimization (QUBO) problems (Gupta & Kekatos, 2023).

Monte Carlo Simulations: Monte Carlo simulations, used for risk analysis and options pricing, require extensive computational resources. Quantum algorithms like Quantum Amplitude Estimation (QAE) can perform these simulations more efficiently, offering faster and more accurate results (Bouchmal et al., 2023).

Quantum Machine Learning: Quantum machine learning can be applied to various financial tasks, such as principal component analysis and credit scoring. Quantum computers can handle large datasets more effectively, providing timely analysis and more accurate models.

Portfolio Management: Quantum computing can optimize portfolio management by quickly evaluating numerous potential combinations of assets. This allows for rapid updates and identification of optimal portfolios, even in complex scenarios. For example, quantum computers can help form trading strategies that consider various rates of return and risk levels. When quantum hardware matures, optimization algorithms could significantly enhance the evaluation of trading strategies and collateral management for loan portfolios.

Risk Management: Quantum computers can precisely handle different types of financial risk, including credit risk, market risk, and operational risk. By processing large datasets quickly, quantum computing can improve the accuracy of risk assessments and reduce the time needed for complex simulations like Monte Carlo simulations. This can help financial institutions hold lower capital buffers and enhance overall market stability.

CONCLUSION

This study examined the current state of quantum computing in financial markets and highlighted various use cases. The review of existing research demonstrated that quantum computers offer significant benefits in portfolio optimization, risk management, and other financial applications. Quantum computing can quickly identify optimal portfolio combinations, enhance derivative pricing accuracy, and improve risk management precision, ultimately reducing financial instability.

While financial firms are experimenting with quantum computing and its various applications, the technology's full potential has yet to be realized. Achieving this potential requires advancements in quantum computer hardware, such as increasing the number of qubits and minimizing current hardware errors. Additionally, quantum computers need to become cost-effective and economically viable for widespread adoption.

In conclusion, quantum computing holds the promise of revolutionizing the financial sector by providing faster and more accurate solutions to complex problems. As the technology matures, its impact on financial markets is expected to grow, leading to more efficient, secure, and innovative financial services.

REFERENCES

Ajagekar, A., & You, F. (2019). Quantum computing for energy systems optimization: Challenges and opportunities. *Energy*, *179*, 76–89. DOI: 10.1016/j.energy.2019.04.186

Bouchmal, O., Cimoli, B., Stabile, R., Vegas Olmos, J. J., & Tafur Monroy, I. (2023). From classical to quantum machine learning: Survey on routing optimization in 6G software defined networking. *Frontiers in Communications and Networks*, *4*, 1220227. DOI: 10.3389/frcmn.2023.1220227

Bouland, A., van Dam, W., Joorati, H., Kerenidis, I., & Prakash, A. (2020). Prospects and challenges of quantum finance. arXiv preprint arXiv:2011.06492.

Costa, P. C., An, D., Sanders, Y. R., Su, Y., Babbush, R., & Berry, D. W. (2022). Optimal scaling quantum linear-systems solver via discrete adiabatic theorem. *PFX Quantum : a Physical Review Journal*, *3*(4), 040303. DOI: 10.1103/PRXQuantum.3.040303

Ederington, L. H., & Guan, W. (2000). Why are those options smiling? *Univ. of Oklahoma Center for Financial Studies Working Paper*.

Egger, D. J., Gambella, C., Marecek, J., McFaddin, S., Mevissen, M., Raymond, R., Simonetto, A., Woerner, S., & Yndurain, E. (2020). Quantum computing for finance: State-of-the-art and future prospects. *IEEE Transactions on Quantum Engineering*, *1*, 1–24. DOI: 10.1109/TQE.2020.3030314

El-Seoud, S. A., El-Sofany, H. F., Abdelfattah, M., & Mohamed, R. (2017). Big Data and Cloud Computing: Trends and Challenges. *International Journal of Interactive Mobile Technologies*, *11*(2), 34. DOI: 10.3991/ijim.v11i2.6561

Erwin, K., & Engelbrecht, A. (2023). Meta-heuristics for portfolio optimization. *Soft Computing*, *27*(24), 19045–19073. DOI: 10.1007/s00500-023-08177-x

Gill, S. S., Kumar, A., Singh, H., Singh, M., Kaur, K., Usman, M., & Buyya, R. (2022). Quantum computing: A taxonomy, systematic review and future directions. *Software, Practice & Experience*, *52*(1), 66–114. DOI: 10.1002/spe.3039

Gupta, S., & Kekatos, V. (2023, June). A quantum approach for stochastic constrained binary optimization. In *ICASSP 2023-2023 IEEE International Conference on Acoustics, Speech and Signal Processing (ICASSP)* (pp. 1-5). IEEE. DOI: 10.1109/ICASSP49357.2023.10097179

Gupta, S., & Sharma, V. (2023, May). Effects of Quantum computing on Businesses. In 2023 4th International Conference on Intelligent Engineering and Management (ICIEM) (pp. 1-6). IEEE. DOI: 10.1109/ICIEM59379.2023.10166880

Hassija, V., Chamola, V., Saxena, V., Chanana, V., Parashari, P., Mumtaz, S., & Guizani, M. (2020). Present landscape of quantum computing. *IET Quantum Communication, 1*(2), 42–48. DOI: 10.1049/iet-qtc.2020.0027

Henkle, E., Igur, V., Karnik, S., & Velaga, S. (2024). Quantum Finance: Exploring Asset Management with QAOA.

Hofmann, J. S., Khalaf, E., Vishwanath, A., Berg, E., & Lee, J. Y. (2022). Fermionic Monte Carlo study of a realistic model of twisted bilayer graphene. *Physical Review X, 12*(1), 011061. DOI: 10.1103/PhysRevX.12.011061

Jacobi, R., & Brenner, E. (2018). How large corporations survive digitalization. *Digital marketplaces unleashed*, 83-97.

Loizou, P., & French, N. (2012). Risk and uncertainty in development: A critical evaluation of using the Monte Carlo simulation method as a decision tool in real estate development projects. *Journal of Property Investment & Finance, 30*(2), 198–210. DOI: 10.1108/14635781211206922

Marella, S. T., & Parisa, H. S. K. (2020). *Introduction to quantum computing*. Quantum Computing and Communications.

Montanez-Barrera, J. A., Willsch, D., Maldonado-Romo, A., & Michielsen, K. (2024). Unbalanced penalization: A new approach to encode inequality constraints of combinatorial problems for quantum optimization algorithms. *Quantum Science and Technology*, *9*(2), 025022. DOI: 10.1088/2058-9565/ad35e4

Nestler, G. (2017). *The Derivative Condition: A Present Inquiry into the History of Futures* (Doctoral dissertation, Goldsmiths, University of London).

Omarova, S. T. (2020). Dealing with disruption: Emerging approaches to fintech regulation. *Wash. UJL & Pol'y, 61*, 25.

Orús, R., Mugel, S., & Lizaso, E. (2019). Quantum computing for finance: Overview and prospects. *Reviews in Physics, 4*, 100028. DOI: 10.1016/j.revip.2019.100028

Owolabi, O. S., Uche, P. C., Adeniken, N. T., Tanoh, V., & Emi-Johnson, O. G. (2024). Quantum computing applications, challenges, and prospects in financial portfolio optimization. *World Journal of Advanced Research and Reviews, 22*(3), 014-022.

Pistoia, M., Ahmad, S. F., Ajagekar, A., Buts, A., Chakrabarti, S., Herman, D., . . . Yalovetzky, R. (2021, November). Quantum machine learning for finance ICCAD special session paper. In *2021 IEEE/ACM international conference on computer aided design (ICCAD)* (pp. 1-9). IEEE. DOI: 10.1109/ICCAD51958.2021.9643469

Portmann, C., & Renner, R. (2022). Security in quantum cryptography. *Reviews of Modern Physics*, *94*(2), 025008. DOI: 10.1103/RevModPhys.94.025008

Renduchintala, T., Alfauri, H., Yang, Z., Pietro, R. D., & Jain, R. (2022). A survey of blockchain applications in the fintech sector. *Journal of Open Innovation*, *8*(4), 185. DOI: 10.3390/joitmc8040185

Tawiah, B., & Keefe, M. O. C. (2022). Financing a corporate venture capital program. *Journal of Banking & Finance*, *135*, 106364. DOI: 10.1016/j.jbankfin.2021.106364

Williams, C. P. (2010). *Explorations in quantum computing*. Springer Science & Business Media.

ENDNOTES

1 https://www.worldbank.org/en/news/press-release/2018/04/19/financial-inclusion-on-the-rise-but-gaps-remain-global-findex-database-shows

2 https://www.javelinstrategy.com/press-release/identity-fraud-losses-totaled-43-billion-2022-affecting-40-million-us-adults

3 https://www.risk.net/technology/5732851/xva-management-challenges-and-solutions

4 https://www.cfainstitute.org/en/membership/professional-development/refresher-readings/asset-allocation-alternative-investments

5 https://medium.com/@kareldumon/the-computational-power-of-quantum-computers-an-intuitive-guide-9f788d1492b6

6 https://www.technologyreview.com/2024/01/04/1084783/quantum-computing-noise-google-ibm-microsoft/

7 https://quantumzeitgeist.com/why-quantum-computing-ai-technonology-era/

8 https://cointelegraph.com/explained/how-does-quantum-computing-impact-the-finance-industry

9 https://www.sciencedirect.com/topics/physics-and-astronomy/quantum-key-distribution

10 https://www.nist.gov/news-events/news/2022/07/nist-announces-first-four-quantum-resistant-cryptographic-algorithms

Chapter 14
Virtual Reality and Augmented Reality in Financial Services

Amna Masood
Iqra University, Pakistan

ABSTRACT

Virtual and augmented reality systems of modern technology have grasped much attention due to their extraordinary effect on traditional ways of operating business in diverse fields. One of the prone industries to these changes is financial service industry. Thus, this paper pens down the insights about virtual and augmented reality and its role in financial services. The article utilizes library research approach to analyze the information from existing scholarly articles and literature. The study describes the dimensions of virtual and augmented realities and their convincing benefits in financial industry. Some significant practices have been described explaining how AR and VR modernize traditional financial services i.e., analyzing risks, investment portfolios, virtual biddings, and other services. Hence, the research contributes to advancing comprehension of virtual and augmented reality in financial and banking industry. Various financial policymakers, technology providers, bankers, financial experts, and financial firms are the key beneficiaries of the present research paper.

1. INTRODUCTION

With evolving digital technological tools, a pool of demand exists to industrialize updated platforms that not only meet technological needs but also harness industrial productivity and efficiency. Learning about technological history, it can be assumed that new and updated computing platforms advance with every passing decade.

DOI: 10.4018/979-8-3693-7160-2.ch014

Hence, there is a dire need to propel and get ready for digital services for tomorrow. One of the future-oriented and by far most extraordinary technological platforms revolves around vision in order to construct riveting augmented experience (Yung & Khoo-Lattimore, 2019). As stated by Mark Zuckerberg, the CEO of Facebook in 2014 after acquiring the Virtual Reality company named: Oculus for USD 2 billion "When you put on their goggles, you enter a completely immersive computer-generated environment, like a game, or a movie scene or a place far away. Today, social networks are about sharing moments. And tomorrow, they'll be about sharing experiences", the world is now moving towards not just materialistic technological advancement but also experiential virtual technologies (Thomson Reuters, 2014). Hence, various technological firms i.e., Oculus, Sony, Samsung, Google, HTC, and Microsoft adopted their biggest projects of virtual and augmented reality into the mass market by the end of 2016.

Augmented Reality

Augmented reality is a hybrid system of real and virtual scenes viewed by users that are generated by digital gadgets which ultimately augments scenes to enhance users' experience and perception of the external world with additional information (Vallino, 2002; Guttentag, 2010; Jung et al., 2015). Recent developments in mobile computing have sparked the creation and growth of AR applications, which take advantage of mobile devices' geolocation capabilities to give users context-sensitive information about their immediate surroundings (Yovcheva et al., 2012). Medical, entertainment, military, engineering design, robotics and telerobotics, manufacturing, maintenance, and repair, as well as consumer designs, are just a few examples of uses for augmented reality (Maad et al., 2007). AR seamlessly incorporates digital information like 3D objects, text, or animations into the user's perspective of the real world using cameras, sensors, and display devices like smartphones or AR glasses. It provides a variety of applications in the gaming and entertainment, healthcare, industrial, and educational fields. Real-time information is provided, productivity is increased, and our perception of and interaction with the world around us is revolutionized by AR, which connects the virtual and actual worlds. Three essential conditions are satisfied by using augmented reality: integrating virtual and actual items, their alignment, and enabling dynamic interactions between them. This is done in a way that the technologies including wearable computing, global positioning systems, and wireless connectivity, location-based computing help provide immersive user experience. Augmented reality apps were initially introduced by the gaming and entertainment businesses, but they are now being used by a few other areas, including marketing, education, communications, healthcare, public safety, education, and tourism. It is feasible to combine the digital visual, aural, and tactile information superimposed on the screen with augmented reality software and hardware.

Virtual Reality

Generally, Virtual reality is referred to as the use of a 3D computer-generated world that the user can travel and interact with, producing a real-time simulation of one or more of the user's senses (Gutierrez et al., 2008; Guttentag, 2010). According to Cruz-Neira et al. (1992) and Williams and Hobson (1995), virtual reality can be categorized owing to its four key elements: (i) Visualization, which typically makes use of a head-mounted display and allows the user to gaze about; (ii) Suspension of disbelief and the physical depiction of objects; (iii) Interactivity, the degree to which the experience can be controlled, typically through the use of sensors and an input device like joysticks or keyboards etc. Moreover, Virtual Environments and Virtual Worlds are the two core words that are frequently used in the concept of virtual reality. According to Guttentag (2010), the experience of VR involves the user becoming fully involved in a virtual environment. On the contrary, according to Penfold (2009), virtual worlds are persistent virtual spaces that are always accessible and allow users to create, play, and interact in real time as avatars. Consistent to Penfold's phenomenon, Huang et al. (2016) suggest second Life, an online virtual environment where avatars can socialize, network, and design their own virtual settings, as one of the most popular platforms for virtual worlds. To account for the gravity of second life, it is expected that with over 1 million active users per month since its launch in 2003, Second Life accounted for 36 million residents. The virtual world economy also witnessed USD 3.2 billion in transactions over a ten-year period (Linden Lab, 2013).

Although augmented and virtual realities indicate similar properties; however, the concepts are quite varying when it comes to functionality. While augmented reality (AR) applications blend virtual reality with images of real-world items, virtual reality (VR) applications immerse the user in a three-dimensional experience that closely resembles the actual world. The degree of immersion is what makes a difference for the user. While with VR, the user is completely immersed in a virtual environment, with AR, the user still sees a big portion of the real world.

Along with various industries such as medical, education, entertainment, and tourism, financial sector is also exposed to the dynamic shifts of traditional services to digitization. For instance, Unquestionably, the shift towards entirely digital banks has been the most significant turning point and fundamental transformation in recent years. The banking sector as one of the prime financial service provider, is evolving as a result of environmental shocks, the development and advancement of digital technologies, the emergence of the digital age, and the offering of cutting-edge services. Therefore, key fields like artificial intelligence (AI), robotics, digitization, nanotechnology, the internet of things (IOT), augmented reality, and the main fields of digital learning like big data, cloud computing, smart phones technologies, and social media are also changing quickly (Komulainen et al., 2018; Sousa & Rocha, 2019). These developmental changes are enabling shift in needs of customer, economies, businesses and societies. According to Li (2018), as a new route for information, simplification, and the creation of new partnerships, digital technologies are also being utilized to create a new interface between vendors and buyers. The user experience will also improve, and new revenue streams will be created (Svahn et al., 2017). The old commercial structures of banks are under significant challenge from growing digital advances in financial services. Banking and financial services are the first to address problems because they are heavily digitized than other sectors worldwide (Komulainen et al., 2018). With regard to making digital technologies difficult for rivals to imitate, today's profitable finance companies need a distinctive value rule (Ross et al., 2017).

Diving deep into the universe of digitalization, another contemporary phenomenon cannot be put aside. In recent years, there has been great attention transcended upon the word “metaverse”. It is the concept of a replica of the real world which provides a virtual experience. Although the virtual universe has received a lot of attention, it is crucial to comprehend the environment in which it operates and the value that it generates. For example, the sale and purchase of various assets are now being carried out on multiple metaverse platforms. Nicholls and Le-Khac, (2021) recommend that the land prices associated with digital land have been increasing since Republic Real Estate introduced a fund for investors to buy virtual land. The fund intends to acquire virtual properties in different online metaverses and turn them into lodgings, shops, and other uses. This will result in customers placing a higher value on these features. Similarly, on a digital asset platform based on blockchain technology, it is anticipated that stocks and bonds will be hosted. The steady shift to online-only shopping and experiences, meaning that people buy completely virtual assets, is another significant aspect of the metaverse.

Provided the metaverse's increasing significance, the financial sector has been examining ways to add value virtually and how fintech companies may provide financial services in this new setting. Additionally, metaverse technology opens up novel business models and structures that could improve the use of cryptography as a substitute for traditional financial systems. The metaverse's underlying technologies mix augmented reality- AR with virtual reality- VR (Katterbauer et al., 2022). Hence, the interactivity of virtual universe realities can be implemented through games, but it could also be done through real estate, business transactions, and other related contexts (Karpoff, 2021). Financial data and transaction management will play a crucial role in the metaverse, enabling people and businesses to interact and operate throughout various universes, as indicated by Facebook's conversion into Meta. Digital assets, are available for purchase and can even be transferred across universes (Leukfeldt et al., 2017). Along with various advantages and competitive edge, challenges owing to virtual reality i.e., cybercrimes can also be attributed to in the virtual space of the metaverse. While it is renowned for fusing artificial intelligence, open source software, augmented reality, and 3D virtual reality, other important elements are also present in the metaverse are peer-to-peer payments and non-fungible tokens (Mohamed & Ali, 2018). This explains in detail a number of obstacles that may prevent the use of these equipment.

Some of the real life examples of AR and VR being implemented in financial institutes across the world can be taken into consideration. For instance, financial institutions like JP Morgan Chase have experimented with VR to demonstrate their investing strategies, giving clients the opportunity to engage in simulated market settings and make informed choices (Forbes, 2022)[1]. Recently, J.P. Morgan has enlisted itself as the first bank to open a branch in the metaverse. Likewise, J.P. Morgan Asset Management also launched "New Guide to the Markets Mobile-Based Augmented Reality (AR) Experience" with collaboration with Coffee Labs in 2021. Customers now have a new method to get interactive information on important economic themes affecting markets and investors thanks to the smartphone and tablet led platforms[2]. Additionally, insurance companies like AXA are investigating the use of augmented reality that allows underwriters to evaluate property risks, allowing underwriters to precisely overlay risk data onto actual structures, identify potential hazards, and determine insurance premiums. Similarly, other financial institutes such as ARK invest, UBS, HSBC and Barclays are implementing VR and AR collaborative applications to provide clients with digital information, investment options, track market trends and expose employees with immersive training programs. The above discussed examples show how international financial institutions have utilized virtual reality and augmented reality to boost training for workers, revolutionize many elements of their business, and improve consumer experiences.

In spite of these implementations and advantages, the literature is contemplated on the potential of technology that can transform businesses. However, there is a dire need to evaluate the dynamic avenues of information dissemination positioned by augmented reality and virtual reality. In addition, financial institutes that are the driving forces of an economic development are the foremost entities exposed to the challenges and opportunities of AR and VR. Therefore, it is pertinent to explore how financial institutes implement these technological advancements and what challenges are exposed when it comes to providing financial services.

2. LITERATURE REVIEW

Technological adoption in various institutes have been vastly discussed in prior literature; however, very limited scholarly work is penned down in terms of virtual and augmented reality and its implication in financial sector. This section broadly analyzes the theoretical roots of the virtual and augmented reality in the said context in order to better comprehend the theoretical justifications and foundations of the technology in financial services.

VR-AR and Financial Inclusion

One strand of literature pens down the role of virtualization and digitalization in endorsing financial inclusion and business/ economic development. Numerous financial services have been moved online, fostering the growth of alternative finance through the use of internet platforms for money raising and borrowing. As a result, financial inclusion steps in to upscale the potential of a country's innovation for the extensive volume of alternative finance (Bilan et al., 2019). Moreover, according to Shofawati (2019), digital finance has a conspicuous contribution in the overall growth of Small and Medium Enterprise and financial inclusion ultimately. Therefore, easy accessibility of digital finance can promote financial inclusion, facilitating easier access to financing for all businesses, especially SMEs, the majority of which are not bankable. Moreover, Rumiński et al. (2019) also presented a specific augmented reality system for the visualization of stock data. Based on the notion that AR can improve the working settings of equity managers and traders, the research examined how hand gestures can be used to engage with 3D financial data representations created artificially by computers to increase human cognitive skills. Therefore, the authors coupled the nVisor ST50 headset with the InteriaCube4 and Leap Motion gadgets to enable tracking of head orientation and hand-based AR environment control. This way, a user can generate virtual charts showing real-time stock data and financial TV broadcasts in his or her surroundings by using hand gestures.

VR-AR and Islamic Financial Literacy and Sharia Compliance

The in-depth analysis of the literature also reveals that augmented and virtual reality has also been an eye-catching phenomenon in the Islamic financial literacy and banking sector for enhanced financial services. To dig deep into the concept, various renowned research articles have shed light on the ways, virtual and augmented realities endorse enhanced and better financial services and financial literacy. For instance, Katterbauer et al (2022) accentuated the underlying cybercrime associated with financial services under the umbrella of the metaverse. The enormous theft of cryptocurrency from exchanges of false or questionable NFT and other financial goods that have lost a lot of value instantly are two recent examples of financial cybercrimes that have expanded dramatically in the metaverse. Despite the fact that cybercrimes have occurred on a large scale in the metaverse, few of these crimes have been brought to justice due to the lack of legislation and the virtual nature of these activities. Subsequently, to address this concerned matter, Katterbauer et al (2022) demonstrated that Islamic finance and Sharia compliance could provide the metaverse with significant potential by linking financial services and instruments to speculative-free real and virtual assets. Given the virtual and augmented reality, cryptocurrencies and NFTs are the by-products that open room for financial fraud and cybercrimes. Therefore, the study articulated that Islamic law forbids uncertainty and any dishonest behavior, which significantly reduces the likelihood that cybercriminals will be able to take advantage of such situations for their own gain. This necessarily lowers the likelihood of fraud because there must be a connection to either a physical object or a virtual asset with little opportunity for speculation. Extending the literature to teaching of sharia financial literacy system, Candra Sari et al. (2022) analyzed elementary students' financial socialization using augmented reality (AR) technology in the hopes of enhancing their understanding of sharia finance. The authors reported that the treatment group's sharia financial knowledge increased more than that of the control group after they were exposed to sharia financial socialization through AR media making AR technology to be a game changer in the advancement of shariah financial literacy.

VR-AR and Banking Sector

Given the importance of digital platforms, virtual reality is one of the cutting-edge approaches that has been adopted over time in the banking services industry. As a result, Kołodziej (2017) aimed to prove the effective implementation of VR for banking activities while generating a competitive advantage. The study also suggests that VR and AR are the prime sources that reduce business cost, and improves communication channels between banking agents and customers. Additionally, VR systems are able to improve and advance internal processes such as recruitment, training, and auditing of financial firms. Later on, Boshkov (2019) assessed the ways virtual banking facilitates financial inclusion. The author suggests that banking systems are evolving from conventional strategies to smart virtual platforms like mobile applications to ensure effective digital payments and P2P services. This way, financial institutions make sure to use virtual and digital platforms as a medium to facilitate online business and economic development.

Dubey (2019) in his study conferred that progressive financial institutions have boosted their spending on internal banking systems, particularly those that use permanent ledgers due to the increasing role of Fintech technologies in shaping digital banking globally. He further stated that the latest technologies such as augmented reality, artificial intelligence, and block chain technology are the most critical aspects that induce vibrational influence on various industries including financial markets. According to the study, AR technologies are used to improve process efficiency, cut costs, and produce a wide range of beneficial effects for businesses.

In a similar strand, the digital transformation of the value chain has also been assessed in the banking sector by Naimi-Sadigh et al. (2021). The scholars articulate that digital technologies have been widely employed by firms to revolutionize their performance. Businesses now are in dire need of having strong organizational structures with appropriate strategies, stable governance systems, and digital competencies to transform the world with digital change. Concerning banking services, pioneering digital models such as big data, IoT, AI, cloud computing, fin-tech, VR, AR, and blockchain are some of the groundbreaking opportunities in order to serve valued financial services. Therefore, the authors explained the strategic ways to apply these digital models in Iranian Bank by using the Delphi method in their study. The scholars established a process of information technology project with three categories. It is concluded that infrastructure, development, and the level and nature of business are the significant determinants for effective utilization of technology in business operations. An earlier study of Maad et al. (2007) also accentuated the potential of augmented reality in financial trading. The study forecasted the higher value gained from AR while discussing the challenges of augmented realism in achieving higher electronic commerce and electronic financial trading. Therefore, augmented reality of rendering, usability, and system profitability are the key considerations for the successful initiation of financial services.

In spite of the rapid utilization of technological advancements in financial systems, there is a need to systematically review the ways financial institutes specifically the banking industry can be integrated with Industry 4.0. To account for this concern, Mehdiabadi et al. (2020) studied some of the prominent global banks that applied advanced technologies. The study reveals that Industry 4.0's Banking 4.0 is an integrated value creation system made up of six design tenets and fourteen technological trends. Among these 14 trends is augmented reality. The banks with the full potential to apply these trends have the tendency to grow and prosper in service value creation and chain. Hence, financial institutes opt for developed and mature technologies such as AI and VR to pass out traditional, time-consuming and old-fashioned tasks and to increase financial development swiftly (David and Kaulihowa 2018).

Subsequently, the adoption of metaverse, virtual, and augmented realities is a driving force to support the economy and excel in the financial sector. With the help of these, multiple opportunities can be grabbed in the field of customer communications, global-level transactions, digital assets, loan plans, and mortgages (Dubey et al., 2022; Seth et al., 2022). Because of this, several experts have made predictions about a time in the future when only platforms for virtual reality (VR) like Metaverse will be necessary for communication (Jovanović & Milosavljević, 2022). Mozumder et al. (2023) also corroborated that people's financial trustworthiness rose as a result of Metaverse's safe and dependable technologies. Extended reality, blockchain decentralization, AI applications, IoT systems, digital twins, and digital virtual identities are all used in the metaverse to manage its finances. It would be advantageous for banking and financial services in particular to be able to manage their accounts and perform transactions through a virtualized environment (Chen, 2024). According to Banaeian Far and Imani Rad (2020), one of the key benefits of AR, VR, and metaverse to deliver superior financial services include: Banks' monthly statements can easily be delivered through web portals or virtual reality platforms thanks to metaverse. Furthermore, Butt et al. (2024) also endorse the use of mobile augmented reality adoption in the financial sector particularly banking sector as the study revealed the significance of augmented reality brand experience in the realm of digital banking.

3. DISCUSSION

Role of VR and AR in Financial Services

Virtual and augmented realities allow users to discern visual data and information in a more immersive and engaging way. As a result, advanced technology incorporating AR and VR has transformed consumer patterns towards financial services. Banks and other financial service providers are currently working to develop tactics that will improve the participation of younger clients who are unwilling to do their banking business in physical locations. As a result, banks are currently thinking about using mobile technology to increase consumer engagement, especially those that are having trouble boosting engagement among clients of the new generation (Dubey, 2019). Increasing client choice and giving improved visibility of spending behaviors and trends are two of the main issues banks face today (Yagol et al., 2018). This is one area in particular where AR may significantly help clients make better decisions by exposing them to new ways of reading financial information and data.

Therefore, the aim of this paper lies in the comprehension of AR and VR technologies and their developments in financial services. This stance discusses how these advanced technologies can impact firms' ability for efficient financial services and the challenges posed along the way.

Additionally, it is plausible to pinpoint the drivers that push financial institutions to adopt convergent and advanced technologies for facilitating superior financial services. One of the prime causes is the augmented development of modern technologies with advanced business models altering present-day financial services. Some of the exponential technologies include cloud computing, artificial intelligence (AI), robotics, distributed ledger technologies (blockchain), biometrics, the Internet of Things (IoT), and virtual-augmented reality. The aforementioned technologies are effective at promoting challenges as they enable low-cost entry-level business models. Moreover, the shift in consumer choices is another driving force. Customers are now accustomed to digital environments and demand a positive digital experience as well as free, individualized services that are simple to use (Jünger & Mietzner, 2020). Lastly, newly enacted financial policies and regulations owing to the financial crisis, globalization, and modernization also contribute as the driving force to propel financial institutes in adopting the latest virtual technologies.

Application of VR and AR Technologies in Financial Services

Corresponding to driving forces, virtual and augmented realities (AR-VR) constantly transform the traditional financial service industry in multiple aspects. These dramatic shifts are being brought about by the promise of augmented reality and virtual reality to improve decision-making, expedite operations, and improve customer experiences (Martins et al., 2022). When compared to AR and VR technology, traditional financial services commonly depend on static information. financial organizations, for instance, can utilize VR to build virtual worlds where customers can explore investment ideas, model market conditions, and make wise judgments. Financial advisors are able to offer dynamic visualizations of investment portfolios and tailored recommendations by using augmented reality (AR), which can overlay real-time data onto physical locations (Schroeder et al., 2020).

Moreover, data analytics and visualization in financial services are being revolutionized by AR and VR technology. AR and VR make it possible to visually represent complex data in immersive and interactive ways as opposed to using conventional charts and graphs (Yagol et al., 2018). The ability to overlay data onto actual environments enables financial professionals to explore and comprehend big datasets more naturally. With correspondence of internal efficiency, employees can practice interactions with clients, risk evaluations, and compliance procedures through realistic VR simulations (Khandelwal & Upadhyay, 2021; Xie et al., 2021).

The improvement of employee abilities and knowledge retention results from the switch from conventional classroom-style teaching to hands-on virtual experiences. Hence, the financial industry pursues to gain a higher competitive edge by embracing these technologies.

Pertaining to the implementation of these technologies, trading in financial markets has previously employed virtual reality. However, there is a shift from the use of VR to AR in digital financial trading (Maad et al., 2007). According to the author, this shift results from a focus on realism and limited interaction constraints. The study proposes, a CYBERII augmented reality financial application that places the user—who is assuming the role of a financial dealer—into a virtual setting and makes use of the slider technique to create "active regions" that allow for full-body engagement. The dealer sets his or her bid/ask prices during interaction with the 3D environment in which he is inserted to draw in traders. Body involvement initiates the flow of buyers and sellers, illuminating the idea of the augmented reality interaction method created by CYBERII. The simulation adds perceptual information about the bid-ask spread variation and the flow of traders. These examples indicate the advanced use of AR and VR in promoting the modern digitized financial world. Subsequently, we can anticipate many more innovative use cases that fundamentally alter how financial institutions connect with their clients and run their operations as technology continues to advance while taking a competitive edge.

Furthermore, numerous recent real case studies or real life examples of the integration of AR and VR with financial services also prevail. For instance, by developing holographic workstations that depict complex financial data using augmented and virtual reality, Citi Bank has embraced AR and VR in the financial services industry. This tool enables traders to respond swiftly to shifts in the market. The workstation is a notable example of augmented reality in banking since it allows users to edit data in a three-dimensional space, offering a more dynamic and interesting method of analyzing financial data. Likewise, Bank of America has incorporated AR and VR into financial services by training its staff in virtual reality. VR-based training programs offered by the bank help employees improve their problem-solving and customer-interaction abilities by simulating customer service scenarios. Employees are more equipped to manage intricate financial issues effectively thanks to this augmented reality example in banking, which enhances the overall client experience.

Challenges and Promises

In spite of the propelling promises of the said technologies in the financial industry, various challenges prevail in the way of adopting augmented reality technologies. For instance, a heavy investment plan is required owing to software/ hardware and infrastructure complementing the implication of AR and VR. Financial institutions are required to set aside funds for the acquisition of AR/VR equipment as well as for the development of specialized apps and system integration. Smaller organizations or those with tighter budgets may find this initial expense to be a hurdle (Koohang et al., 2023). Secondly, the handling of sensitive client data by financial firms raises new privacy and data security concerns (Mazurek & Małagocka, 2019; Quach et al., 2022). Institutions must make sure that consumer data is shielded from unauthorized access or breaches and that interactions within AR/VR settings are safe. Compliance with data protection laws, such as the GDPR or CCPA, is essential and could call for extra precautions. Additionally, financial institutions can use cutting-edge encryption methods and reliable authentication processes for AR/VR apps to address data security concerns. Sensitive client information can be safeguarded by using biometric authentication and secure data transmission (Yang et al., 2021; Baig et al., 2023).

Another key challenge for financial firms to keep in mind is that bandwidth and connections become crucial concerns for VR applications that depend on real-time data. To provide clients with the latest information in immersive settings, smooth data transmission is necessary. A seamless AR/VR experience may be difficult to deliver in areas with poor internet infrastructure. In response to the prevailing challenge, financial institutions can investigate edge computing solutions, which perform data processing closer to the user, lowering latency and reliance upon high-speed internet connections, to address bandwidth difficulties. Even in areas with poor connectivity, this can dramatically improve the performance of real-time AR/VR applications.

Moreover, applications for AR and VR must provide simple, straightforward user interfaces. It can be difficult to create interfaces that are simple to use and comprehend, especially when working with complicated financial data and transactions (Su et al., 2020; Rumiński et al., 2019). Making sure that users with impairments can access content is also crucial, but it could take extra work. Accessibility elements in AR and VR systems design ensure that all users, even individuals with disabilities, may use these technologies. It makes AR and VR experiences more inclusive to offer alternatives for speech recognition technology, verbal commands, as well as other accessibility tools.

Furthermore, various serious security and regulatory issues with the use of augmented reality (AR) and virtual reality (VR) in financial services also prevail. These technologies raise concerns about cybersecurity, privacy, and compliance since they gather and handle enormous volumes of sensitive financial and biometric data. In order to ensure secure data encryption and fraud protection, financial institutions must comply with complicated rules including the CCPA, PSD2, and GDPR. Cyberthreats, such as deepfake fraud, identity theft, and phishing assaults, present significant concerns in online banking settings. Similarly, collaborations between financial institutions, technology companies, and regulators to create uniform standards for data protection, international transactions, and moral AI application can lead to regulatory clarity. Building trust in AR/VR financial apps will also be aided by initiatives for consumer education and transparency in data collecting.

Notwithstanding their potential, obstacles to acceptance for AR and VR include high implementation costs, problems integrating legacy systems, and customer distrust. Concerns around accessibility and security prevent AR/VR banking experiences from being widely adopted, and many users are not familiar with them. To improve customer experience and operational efficiency, financial institutions are investigating use cases such as immersive wealth management, virtual banking branches, AI-powered customer care, and risk assessment tools. Additionally, VR training simulations are being used to enhance fraud detection and staff onboarding. Even if there are still obstacles to overcome, AR and VR have the potential to revolutionize the financial services industry as long as organizations address security, regulatory, and usability issues.

Regardless of these difficulties, financial institutions are increasingly removing obstacles to the adoption of augmented reality and virtual reality by putting an emphasis on innovation, working with the suppliers of technology, and taking a customer-centric approach. The use of augmented reality and virtual reality in financial services is anticipated to become more efficient and profitable as technology develops and best practices become clear.

4. CONCLUSION

For over a decade, digital technologies have transformed the manual lifestyle in every sphere. The development in technologies also altered the traditional ways of doing finance and providing financial services. Digital finance has strengthened the banking systems, growth of business, and financial inclusion. Following this strand virtual and augmented realities made it possible to deliver future services in the present day. With the goal of complete integration with the virtual environment, the concept of VR enables the immersion to use the human senses. Subsequently, augmented reality (AR) allows for the self-portraiture of real and digital photographs with the use of specialized software and equipment. Based on the capabilities of AR and VR in the current modern world, this present research demonstrates the possibility of using virtual/ augmented reality-based financial services. AR and VR have the tendency to make the financial process fast, easier, and more effective in the fields of stocks, bonds, investment portfolios, digital currencies, and risk analysis. Along with the propelling benefits, these systems also indicate some grave challenges in terms of cybercrime, security risks, and financial theft. To account for these challenges, financial institutions are required to plan and integrate high-quality copyright and encryption systems.

Table 1. Abbreviations and key terms

AR	**Augmented Reality**
VR	Virtual Reality
AI	Artificial Intelligence
IoT	Internet of Things
NFT	Non Fungible Token

REFERENCES

Baig, A. F., Eskeland, S., & Yang, B. (2023). Privacy-preserving continuous authentication using behavioral biometrics. *International Journal of Information Security*, •••, 1–15.

Banaeian Far, S., & Imani Rad, A. (2023). What are the benefits and opportunities of launching a Metaverse for NEOM city? *Security and Privacy*, *6*(3), e282. DOI: 10.1002/spy2.282

Bilan, Y., Rubanov, P., Vasylieva, T. A., & Lyeonov, S. (2019). The influence of industry 4.0 on financial services: Determinants of alternative finance development. *Polish Journal of Management Studies*.

Boshkov, T. (2019). Virtual Banking and Financial Inclusion.

Butt, A. H., Ahmad, H., & Muzaffar, A. (2024). Augmented reality is the new digital banking–AR brand experience impact on brand loyalty. *International Journal of Bank Marketing*, *42*(2), 156–182. DOI: 10.1108/IJBM-11-2022-0522

Candra Sari, R., Rika Fatimah, P. L., Ilyana, S., & Dwi Hermawan, H. (2022). Augmented reality (AR)-based sharia financial literacy system (AR-SFLS): A new approach to virtual sharia financial socialization for young learners. *International Journal of Islamic and Middle Eastern Finance and Management*, *15*(1), 48–65. DOI: 10.1108/IMEFM-11-2019-0484

Chen, X. (2024). Research on the Application of Machine Learning Technology in Enterprise Intelligent Finance. *International Journal of Computer Science and Information Technologies*, *3*(3), 199–205. DOI: 10.62051/ijcsit.v3n3.20

Cruz-Neira, C., Sandin, D. J., DeFanti, T. A., Kenyon, R. V., & Hart, J. C. (1992). The CAVE: Audio visual experience automatic virtual environment. *Communications of the ACM*, *35*(6), 64–73. DOI: 10.1145/129888.129892

David, L., & Kaulihowa, T. (2018). The impact of E-banking on commercial banks' performance in Namibia. *International Journal of Economics and Financial Research*, *4*(10), 313–321.

Dubey, V. (2019). FinTech innovations in digital banking. [IJERT]. *International Journal of Engineering Research & Technology (Ahmedabad)*, *8*(10), 597–601.

Dubey, V., Mokashi, A., Pradhan, R., Gupta, P., & Walimbe, R. (2022). Metaverse and Banking Industry–2023 The Year of Metaverse Adoption.

Gutierrez, M., Vexo, F., & Thalmann, D. (2008). *Stepping into virtual reality*. Springer Science & Business Media. DOI: 10.1007/978-1-84800-117-6

Guttentag, D. A. (2010). Virtual reality: Applications and implications for tourism. *Tourism Management*, *31*(5), 637–651. http://www.samsung.com/global/galaxy/gear-vr/ https://am.jpmorgan.com/us/en/asset-management/adv/about-us/media/press-releases/jp-morgan-asset-management-launches-new-guide-to-the-markets-mobile-based-augmented-reality-ar-experience/ https://vr.google.com/ https://www.forbes.com/sites/ronshevlin/2022/02/16/jpmorgan-opens-a-bank-branch-in-the-metaverse-but-its-not-for-what-you-think-its-for/?sh=689ac290158d. DOI: 10.1016/j.tourman.2009.07.003

Huang, Y. C., Backman, K. F., Backman, S. J., & Chang, L. L. (2016). Exploring the implications of virtual reality technology in tourism marketing: An integrated research framework. *International Journal of Tourism Research*, *18*(2), 116–128. DOI: 10.1002/jtr.2038

Jovanović, A., & Milosavljević, A. (2022). VoRtex Metaverse platform for gamified collaborative learning. *Electronics (Basel)*, *11*(3), 317. DOI: 10.3390/electronics11030317

Jung, T., Chung, N., & Leue, M. C. (2015). The determinants of recommendations to use augmented reality technologies: The case of a Korean theme park. *Tourism Management*, *49*, 75–86. DOI: 10.1016/j.tourman.2015.02.013

Jünger, M., & Mietzner, M. (2020). Banking goes digital: The adoption of FinTech services by German households. *Finance Research Letters*, *34*, 101260. DOI: 10.1016/j.frl.2019.08.008

Karpoff, J. M. (2021). The future of financial fraud. *Journal of Corporate Finance*, *66*, 101694. DOI: 10.1016/j.jcorpfin.2020.101694

Katterbauer, K., Hassan, S. Y. E. D., & Cleenewerck, L. (2022). Financial cybercrime in the Islamic finance metaverse. *Journal of Metaverse*, *2*(2), 56–61. DOI: 10.57019/jmv.1108783

Khandelwal, K., & Upadhyay, A. K. (2021). Virtual reality interventions in developing and managing human resources. *Human Resource Development International*, *24*(2), 219–233. DOI: 10.1080/13678868.2019.1569920

Kołodziej, M. (2017). Virtual reality as the indicator of the modern banking. *Financial Sciences*. Nauki o finansach, (2 (31)).

Komulainen, H., Saraniemi, S., Ulkuniemi, P., & Ylilehto, M. (2018). End-customer value restructuring the financial service supply chain. *Marketing Intelligence & Planning, 36*(6), 709–720. DOI: 10.1108/MIP-11-2017-0320

Koohang, A., Nord, J. H., Ooi, K. B., Tan, G. W. H., Al-Emran, M., Aw, E. C. X., Baabdullah, A. M., Buhalis, D., Cham, T.-H., Dennis, C., Dutot, V., Dwivedi, Y. K., Hughes, L., Mogaji, E., Pandey, N., Phau, I., Raman, R., Sharma, A., Sigala, M., & Wong, L. W. (2023). Shaping the metaverse into reality: A holistic multidisciplinary understanding of opportunities, challenges, and avenues for future investigation. *Journal of Computer Information Systems, 63*(3), 735–765. DOI: 10.1080/08874417.2023.2165197

Leukfeldt, E. R., Lavorgna, A., & Kleemans, E. R. (2017). Organised cybercrime or cybercrime that is organised? An assessment of the conceptualisation of financial cybercrime as organised crime. *European Journal on Criminal Policy and Research, 23*(3), 287–300. DOI: 10.1007/s10610-016-9332-z

Li, F. (2020). The digital transformation of business models in the creative industries: A holistic framework and emerging trends. *Technovation, 92*, 102012. DOI: 10.1016/j.technovation.2017.12.004

Linden Lab. (2013). Infographic–10 Years of Second Life.

Maad, S., Garbaya, S., & Bouakaz, S. (2007). From virtual to augmented reality in financial trading: A CYBERII application. *Journal of Enterprise Information Management, 21*(1), 71–80. DOI: 10.1108/17410390810842264

Martins, N. C., Marques, B., Alves, J., Araújo, T., Dias, P., & Santos, B. S. (2022). Augmented reality situated visualization in decision-making. *Multimedia Tools and Applications, 81*(11), 14749–14772. DOI: 10.1007/s11042-021-10971-4

Mazurek, G., & Małagocka, K. (2019). Perception of privacy and data protection in the context of the development of artificial intelligence. *Journal of Management Analytics, 6*(4), 344–364. DOI: 10.1080/23270012.2019.1671243

Mehdiabadi, A., Tabatabeinasab, M., Spulbar, C., Karbassi Yazdi, A., & Birau, R. (2020). Are we ready for the challenge of Banks 4.0? Designing a roadmap for banking systems in Industry 4.0. *International Journal of Financial Studies, 8*(2), 32. DOI: 10.3390/ijfs8020032

Mohamed, H., & Ali, H. (2018). Blockchain, Fintech, and Islamic Finance. In *Blockchain, Fintech, and Islamic Finance*. de Gruyter.

Mozumder, M. A. I., Theodore, A. T. P., Athar, A., & Kim, H. C. (2023, February). The metaverse applications for the finance industry, its challenges, and an approach for the metaverse finance industry. In *2023 25th International Conference on Advanced Communication Technology (ICACT)* (pp. 407-410). IEEE.

Naimi-Sadigh, A., Asgari, T., & Rabiei, M. (2021). Digital transformation in the value chain disruption of banking services. *Journal of the Knowledge Economy*, ●●●, 1–31.

Nicholls, J., Kuppa, A., & Le-Khac, N. A. (2021). Financial cybercrime: A comprehensive survey of deep learning approaches to tackle the evolving financial crime landscape. *IEEE Access : Practical Innovations, Open Solutions*, *9*, 163965–163986. DOI: 10.1109/ACCESS.2021.3134076

Penfold, P. (2009). Learning through the world of second life—A hospitality and tourism experience. *Journal of Teaching in Travel & Tourism*, *8*(2-3), 139–160. DOI: 10.1080/15313220802634224

Quach, S., Thaichon, P., Martin, K. D., Weaven, S., & Palmatier, R. W. (2022). Digital technologies: Tensions in privacy and data. *Journal of the Academy of Marketing Science*, *50*(6), 1299–1323. DOI: 10.1007/s11747-022-00845-y PMID: 35281634

Ross, J. W., Beath, C. M., & Sebastian, I. M. (2017). How to develop a great digital strategy. *MIT Sloan Management Review*, *58*(2), 7.

Rumiński, D., Maik, M., & Walczak, K. (2019). Visualizing Financial Stock Data within an Augmented Reality Trading Environment. *Acta Polytechnica Hungarica*, *16*(6), 223–239. DOI: 10.12700/APH.16.6.2019.6.14

Rumiński, D., Maik, M., & Walczak, K. (2019). Visualizing Financial Stock Data within an Augmented Reality Trading Environment. *Acta Polytechnica Hungarica*, *16*(6), 223–239. DOI: 10.12700/APH.16.6.2019.6.14

Schroeder, K., Ajdadilish, B., Henkel, A. P., & Calero Valdez, A. (2020, April). Evaluation of a financial portfolio visualization using computer displays and mixed reality devices with domain experts. In *Proceedings of the 2020 CHI Conference on Human Factors in Computing Systems* (pp. 1-9). DOI: 10.1145/3313831.3376556

Seth, D., Gupta, M., & Singh, B. J. (2022). A Study to Analyse the Impact of Using the Metaverse in the Banking Industry to Augment Performance in a Competitive Environment. In *Applying Metalytics to Measure Customer Experience in the Metaverse* (pp. 9–16). IGI Global. DOI: 10.4018/978-1-6684-6133-4.ch002

Shofawati, A. (2019). The role of digital finance to strengthen financial inclusion and the growth of SME in Indonesia. *KnE Social Sciences*, 389-407.

Sousa, M. J., & Rocha, Á. (2019). Digital learning: Developing skills for digital transformation of organizations. *Future Generation Computer Systems, 91*, 327–334. DOI: 10.1016/j.future.2018.08.048

Su, K. W., Chen, S. C., Lin, P. H., & Hsieh, C. I. (2020). Evaluating the user interface and experience of VR in the electronic commerce environment: A hybrid approach. *Virtual Reality (Waltham Cross), 24*(2), 241–254. DOI: 10.1007/s10055-019-00394-w

Svahn, F., Mathiassen, L., Lindgren, R., & Kane, G. C. (2017). Mastering the digital innovation challenge. *MIT Sloan Management Review, 58*(3), 14.

Thomson Reuters. (2014). Edited transcript: FB – Facebook M&A call to acquire oculus. In *Thomson Reuters Streetevents* (pp. 1–13). Thomson Reuters.

Vallino, J. (2002). *Introduction to augmented reality*. Rochester Institute of Technology.

Williams, P., & Hobson, J. P. (1995). Virtual reality and tourism: Fact or fantasy? *Tourism Management, 16*(6), 423–427. DOI: 10.1016/0261-5177(95)00050-X

Xie, B., Liu, H., Alghofaili, R., Zhang, Y., Jiang, Y., Lobo, F. D., Li, C., Li, W., Huang, H., Akdere, M., Mousas, C., & Yu, L. F. (2021). A review on virtual reality skill training applications. *Frontiers in Virtual Reality, 2*, 645153. DOI: 10.3389/frvir.2021.645153

Yagol, P., Ramos, F., Trilles, S., Torres-Sospedra, J., & Perales, F. J. (2018). New trends in using augmented reality apps for smart city contexts. *ISPRS International Journal of Geo-Information, 7*(12), 478. DOI: 10.3390/ijgi7120478

Yang, W., Wang, S., Sahri, N. M., Karie, N. M., Ahmed, M., & Valli, C. (2021). Biometrics for internet-of-things security: A review. *Sensors (Basel), 21*(18), 6163. DOI: 10.3390/s21186163 PMID: 34577370

Yovcheva, Z., Buhalis, D., & Gatzidis, C. (2012). Smartphone augmented reality applications for tourism. [ertr]. *Ereview of Tourism Research, 10*(2), 63–66.

Yung, R., & Khoo-Lattimore, C. (2019). New realities: A systematic literature review on virtual reality and augmented reality in tourism research. *Current Issues in Tourism, 22*(17), 2056–2081. DOI: 10.1080/13683500.2017.1417359

ENDNOTES

1. https://www.forbes.com/sites/ronshevlin/2022/02/16/jpmorgan-opens-a-bank-branch-in-the-metaverse-but-its-not-for-what-you-think-its-for/?sh=689ac290158d

2. https://am.jpmorgan.com/us/en/asset-management/adv/about-us/media/press-releases/jp-morgan-asset-management-launches-new-guide-to-the-markets-mobile-based-augmented-reality-ar-experience/

Compilation of References

Abu Jamie, N. H., Abu-Jamie, T. N., & Al-Absy, M. S. M. (2024). Advances in AI and Their Effects on Finance and Economic Analysis. The AI Revolution. *Driving Business Innovation and Research, 1*, 507–523.

Adams, K. M., Choe, J., Mostafanezhad, M., & Phi, G. T. (2021). (Post-) pandemic tourism resiliency: Southeast Asian lives and livelihoods in limbo. *Tourism Geographies, 23*(4), 915–936. DOI: 10.1080/14616688.2021.1916584

Agarwal, A., Singhal, C., & Thomas, R. (2021). *AI-powered Decision Making for the Bank of the Future. McKinsey Global Banking & Securities*. March. https://www.mckinsey.com/industries/financial-services/our-insights/ai-powered-decision-making-for-the-bank-of-the-future

Agarwal, S., & Ann, T. C. (2024). Personal Finance Applications of Fintech. In The Emerald Handbook of Fintech: Reshaping Finance (pp. 235-248). Emerald Publishing Limited.

Agarwal, R., Gao, G., DesRoches, C., & Jha, A. K. (2010). Research commentary—The digital transformation of healthcare: Current status and the road ahead. *Information Systems Research, 21*(4), 796–809. DOI: 10.1287/isre.1100.0327

Ahmad, A., Sohail, A., & Hussain, A. (2021). Emergence of financial technology in Islamic banking industry and its influence on bank performance in covid-19 scenario: A case of developing economy. *Gomal University Journal of Research, 37*(1), 97–109. DOI: 10.51380/gujr-37-01-09

Ahmed, A., & Anifowose, M. (2024). Corruption, corporate governance, and sustainable development goals in Africa. *Corporate Governance (Bradford), 24*(1), 119–138. Advance online publication. DOI: 10.1108/CG-07-2022-0311

Ahmed, M. A., Khattak, M. S., & Anwar, M. (2022). Personality traits and entrepreneurial intention: The mediating role of risk aversion. *Journal of Public Affairs, 22*(1), e2275. DOI: 10.1002/pa.2275

Ahmed, S., Alshater, M. M., El Ammari, A., & Hammami, H. (2022). Artificial intelligence and machine learning in finance: A bibliometric review. *Research in International Business and Finance*, *61*, 101646.

Aitken, M., Toreini, E., Carmichael, P., Coopamootoo, K., Elliott, K., & van Moorsel, A. (2020). Establishing a social licence for Financial Technology: Reflections on the role of the private sector in pursuing ethical data practices. *Big Data & Society*, *7*(1). Advance online publication. DOI: 10.1177/2053951720908892

Ajagekar, A., & You, F. (2019). Quantum computing for energy systems optimization: Challenges and opportunities. *Energy*, *179*, 76–89. DOI: 10.1016/j.energy.2019.04.186

Ajzen, I. (1980). *Understanding attitudes and predicting social behavior*. Prentice Hall.

Ajzen, I. (1985). From intentions to actions: A theory of planned behavior. In Kuhl, J., & Beckman, J. (Eds.), *Action-control: From cognition to behavior* (pp. 11–39). Springer. DOI: 10.1007/978-3-642-69746-3_2

Akter, S., Dwivedi, Y. K., Sajib, S., Biswas, K., Bandara, R. J., & Michael, K. (2022). Algorithmic bias in machine learning-based marketing models. *Journal of Business Research*, *144*, 201–216.

Al Janabi, M. A. (2024). Insights into Liquidity Dynamics: Optimizing Asset Allocation and Portfolio Risk Management with Machine Learning Algorithms. In Liquidity Dynamics and Risk Modeling (pp. 257-303). Palgrave Macmillan, Cham.

Aldboush, H. H., & Ferdous, M. (2023). Building trust in fintech: An analysis of ethical and privacy considerations in the intersection of big data, AI, and customer trust. *International Journal of Financial Studies*, *11*(3), 90. DOI: 10.3390/ijfs11030090

Ali, F., Khurram, M. U., & Jiang, Y. (2021). The five-factor asset pricing model tests and profitability and investment premiums: Evidence from Pakistan. *Emerging Markets Finance & Trade*, *57*(9), 2651–2673. DOI: 10.1080/1540496X.2019.1650738

Ali, H., Abdullah, R., & Zaini, M. Z. (2019). Fintech and its potential impact on Islamic banking and finance industry: A case study of Brunei Darussalam and Malaysia. [IJIEF]. *International Journal of Islamic Economics and Finance*, *2*(1), 73–108. DOI: 10.18196/ijief.2116

Aljifri, R. (2023). Investor psychology in the stock market: An empirical study of the impact of overconfidence on firm valuation. *Borsa Istanbul Review*, *23*(1), 93–112. DOI: 10.1016/j.bir.2022.09.010

Allam, Z., Sharifi, A., Bibri, S. E., Jones, D. S., & Krogstie, J. (2022). The metaverse as a virtual form of smart cities: Opportunities and challenges for environmental, economic, and social sustainability in urban futures. *Smart Cities*, *5*(3), 771–801. DOI: 10.3390/smartcities5030040

Almaqtari, F. A. (2024). The moderating role of IT governance on the relationship between FinTech and sustainability performance. *Journal of Open Innovation*, *10*(2), 100267. https://doi.org/https://doi.org/10.1016/j.joitmc.2024.100267. DOI: 10.1016/j.joitmc.2024.100267

Aloosh, A., & Ouzan, S. (2020). The psychology of cryptocurrency prices. *Finance Research Letters*, *33*, 101192. DOI: 10.1016/j.frl.2019.05.010

Alshater, M. M., Saba, I., Supriani, I., & Rabbani, M. R. (2022). Fintech in islamic finance literature: A review. *Heliyon*, *8*(9), 8. DOI: 10.1016/j.heliyon.2022.e10385 PMID: 36060472

Anagnostopoulos, I. (2018). Fintech and regtech: Impact on regulators and banks. *Journal of Economics and Business*, *100*, 7–25. Advance online publication. DOI: 10.1016/j.jeconbus.2018.07.003

Anifa, M., Ramakrishnan, S., Joghee, S., Kabiraj, S., & Bishnoi, M. M. (2022). Fintech Innovations in the Financial Service Industry. *Journal of Risk and Financial Management*, *15*(7), 287. Advance online publication. DOI: 10.3390/jrfm15070287

Annesi, N., Battaglia, M., Ceglia, I., & Mercuri, F. (2024). Navigating paradoxes: building a sustainable strategy for an integrated ESG corporate governance. *Management Decision, ahead-of-print*(ahead-of-print). DOI: 10.1108/MD-10-2023-2006

Antonopoulos, A. M., & Wood, G. (2018). *Mastering Ethereum: Building smart contracts and dApps*. O'Reilly Media.

Antony, A. (2020). Behavioral finance and portfolio management: Review of theory and literature. *Journal of Public Affairs*, *20*(2), e1996. DOI: 10.1002/pa.1996

Aoun, J. E. (2017). *Robot-proof: higher education in the age of artificial intelligence*. MIT press.

Arner, D. W., Buckley, R. P., Zetzsche, D. A., & Veidt, R. (2020). Sustainability, FinTech and Financial Inclusion. *European Business Organization Law Review*, *21*(1), 7–35. Advance online publication. DOI: 10.1007/s40804-020-00183-y

Arslanian, H., & Fischer, F. (2019). *The future of finance: The impact of FinTech, AI, and crypto on financial services*. Springer. DOI: 10.1007/978-3-030-14533-0

Asif, M., Khan, M. N., Tiwari, S., Wani, S. K., & Alam, F. (2023). The Impact of Fintech and Digital Financial Services on Financial Inclusion in India. *Journal of Risk and Financial Management, 16*(2), 122. Advance online publication. DOI: 10.3390/jrfm16020122

Aslam, F., Hunjra, A. I., Ftiti, Z., Louhichi, W., & Shams, T. (2022). Insurance fraud detection: Evidence from artificial intelligence and machine learning. *Research in International Business and Finance, 62*, 101744.

AT&T. (2022). *AT&T.*https://about.att.com/

Automation Anywhere. (2021). *Automation Anywhere.* https://www.automationanywhere.com/

Automation Edge. (2024). *Automation Edge.* https://automationedge.com/

Ayinla, B., Atadoga, A., Ike, C., Ndubuisi, N., Asuzu, O. F., & Adeleye, R. (2024). The role of robotic process automation (RPA) in modern accounting: A review—Investigating how automation tools are transforming traditional accounting practices. *Engineering Science & Technology Journal, 5*(2), 427–447. DOI: 10.51594/estj.v5i2.804

Ayoola, T. (2013). The effect of cashless policy of government on corruption in Nigeria. *International Review of Management and Business Research, 2*(3), 682–690.

Aziz, B., & Khan, A. (2016). Behavioral factors influencing individual investor's investment decision and performance, Evidence from Pakistan Stock Exchange. *International journal of research in finance and marketing, 6*(7), 74-86.

Babajide, A. A., & Adetiloye, K. A. (2012). Investorsâ€™ Behavioural Biases and the Security Market: An Empirical Study of the Nigerian Security Market. *Accounting and Finance Research, 1*(1), 219–219. DOI: 10.5430/afr.v1n1p219

Baba, M. A., Haq, Z. U., Dawood, M., & Aashish, K. (2023). FinTech Adoption of Financial Services Industry: Exploring the Impact of Creative and Innovative Leadership. *Journal of Risk and Financial Management, 16*(10), 453. Advance online publication. DOI: 10.3390/jrfm16100453

Baber, H. (2020). FinTech, crowdfunding and customer retention in Islamic banks. *Vision (Basel), 24*(3), 260–268. DOI: 10.1177/0972262919869765

Badakhshan, E., & Ball, P. (2023). Applying digital twins for inventory and cash management in supply chains under physical and financial disruptions. *International Journal of Production Research, 61*(15), 5094–5116. DOI: 10.1080/00207543.2022.2093682

Bag, S., Gupta, S., Kumar, A., & Sivarajah, U. (2021). An integrated artificial intelligence framework for knowledge creation and B2B marketing rational decision making for improving firm performance. *Industrial Marketing Management, 92*, 178–189. DOI: 10.1016/j.indmarman.2020.12.001

Bahga, A., & Madisetti, V. (2014). *Blockchain Applications: A Hands-On Approach*. VPT.

Bahrammirzaee, A. (2010). A comparative survey of artificial intelligence applications in finance: Artificial neural networks, expert system and hybrid intelligent systems. *Neural Computing & Applications, 19*(8), 1165–1195. DOI: 10.1007/s00521-010-0362-z

Baig, A. F., Eskeland, S., & Yang, B. (2023). Privacy-preserving continuous authentication using behavioral biometrics. *International Journal of Information Security*, •••, 1–15.

Bakar, S., & Yi, A. N. C. (2016). The impact of psychological factors on investors' decision making in Malaysian stock market: A case of Klang Valley and Pahang. *Procedia Economics and Finance, 35*, 319–328. DOI: 10.1016/S2212-5671(16)00040-X

Baker, H. K., & Ricciardi, V. (2014). How biases affect investor behavior. *The European Financial Review*, •••, 7–10.

Baker, M., Bradley, B., & Wurgler, J. (2011). Benchmarks as limits to arbitrage: Understanding the low-volatility anomaly. *Financial Analysts Journal, 67*(1), 40–54. DOI: 10.2469/faj.v67.n1.4

Balamurugan, A., Vamsi, M., Bhattacharya, R., Mohammed, S., Kaushik, P., & Haralayya, D. (2023). Robotic process automation (RPA) in accounting and auditing of business and financial information. *Manager, 58*, 127–142.

Balcıoğlu, Y. S. (2024). Revolutionizing Risk Management AI and ML Innovations in Financial Stability and Fraud Detection. In Navigating the Future of Finance in the Age of AI (pp. 109-138). IGI Global.

Banaeian Far, S., & Imani Rad, A. (2023). What are the benefits and opportunities of launching a Metaverse for NEOM city? *Security and Privacy, 6*(3), e282. DOI: 10.1002/spy2.282

Bao, Y., Hilary, G., & Ke, B. (2022). Artificial intelligence and fraud detection. *Innovative Technology at the Interface of Finance and Operations, 1*, 223–247. DOI: 10.1007/978-3-030-75729-8_8

Barber, B. M., & Odean, T. (2001). Boys will be boys: Gender, overconfidence, and common stock investment. *The Quarterly Journal of Economics, 116*(1), 261–292. DOI: 10.1162/003355301556400

Barberis, N., & Thaler, R. (2003). A survey of behavioral finance. *Handbook of the Economics of Finance, 1*, 1053-1128.

Barberis, N., & Thaler, R. H. (2002). A Survey of Behavioral Finance. SSRN Electronesearch, 15 (1), 55-72. DOI: 10.2139/ssrn.327880

Barberis, N., & Huang, M. (2001). Mental Accounting, Loss Aversion, and Individual Stock Returns. *The Journal of Finance*, *56*(4), 1247–1292. DOI: 10.1111/0022-1082.00367

Barberis, N., Thaler, R., Constantinides, G. M., Harris, M., & Stulz, R. (2003). *Handbook of the Economics of Finance. A Survey of Behavioral Finance (1052-1090)*. Elsevier Science BV.

Barros, E., Popplewell, C., & Muhammad, T. (2021). Behavioral Finance -Impact of artificial intelligence and social media analytics on investor and trader... *ResearchGate*. https://www.researchgate.net/publication/355159676_Behavioral_Finance_-Impact_of_Artificial_Intelligence_and_Social_Media_Analytics_on_Investor_and_Trader_Behavior

Bashir, T., Azam, N., Butt, A. A., Javed, A., & Tanvir, A. (2013). Are behavioral biases influenced by demographic characteristics & personality traits? Evidence from Pakistan. *European Scientific Journal*, *9*(29).

Battina, D. S. (2018). The future of artificial intelligence at work: A review on effects of decision automation and augmentation on workers targeted by algorithms and third-party observers. *International Journal of Innovations in Engineering Research and Technology*, *5*(7).

Belanche, D., Casaló, L. V., & Flavián, C. (2019). Artificial Intelligence in FinTech: Understanding robo-advisors adoption among customers. *Industrial Management & Data Systems*, *119*(7), 1411–1430. DOI: 10.1108/IMDS-08-2018-0368

Ben-Israel, D., Jacobs, W. B., Casha, S., Lang, S., Ryu, W. H. A., de Lotbiniere-Bassett, M., & Cadotte, D. W. (2020). The impact of machine learning on patient care: A systematic review. *Artificial Intelligence in Medicine*, *103*, 101785. DOI: 10.1016/j.artmed.2019.101785 PMID: 32143792

Bennett, R., & Lamming, R. (2022). ESG risk and the role of AI in sustainable finance: A review. *Journal of Sustainable Finance & Investment*, *12*(3), 207–220. DOI: 10.1080/20430795.2022.2050745

Bernstein, S., Jones, K., & Mitchell, D. (2022). Tackling double-counting in carbon markets: The role of blockchain and AI. *Environmental Research Letters, 17*(2), 025002. DOI: 10.1088/1748-9326/ac4f54

Bharadiya, J. P. (2023). Machine Learning and AI in Business Intelligence: Trends and Opportunities. [IJC]. *International Journal of Computer, 48*(1), 123–134.

Bhatia, A., Chandani, A., & Chhateja, J. (2020). Robo advisory and its potential in addressing the behavioral biases of investors—A qualitative study in Indian context. *Journal of Behavioral and Experimental Finance, 25*, 100281. DOI: 10.1016/j.jbef.2020.100281

Bhatnagar, A. (2016). How robo technology is changing wealth management. *Journal of Financial Planning, 29*(5), 22–25.

Bhatore, S., Mohan, L., & Reddy, Y. R. (2020). Machine learning techniques for credit risk evaluation: A systematic literature review. *Journal of Banking and Financial Technology, 4*(1), 111–138.

Bilan, Y., Rubanov, P., Vasylieva, T. A., & Lyeonov, S. (2019). The influence of industry 4.0 on financial services: Determinants of alternative finance development. *Polish Journal of Management Studies.*

Bisht, D., Singh, R., Gehlot, A., Akram, S. V., Singh, A., Montero, E. C., Priyadarshi, N., & Twala, B. (2022). Imperative role of integrating digitalization in the firms finance: A technological perspective. *Electronics (Basel), 11*(19), 3252. DOI: 10.3390/electronics11193252

Bitetto, A., & Cerchiello, P. (2023). Initial coin offerings and ESG: Allies or enemies? *Finance Research Letters, 57*, 104227. Advance online publication. DOI: 10.1016/j.frl.2023.104227

Błach, J., & Klimontowicz, M. (2021). The Determinants of PayTech's Success in the Mobile Payment Market – The Case of BLIK. *Journal of Risk and Financial Management, 14*(9), 422. Advance online publication. DOI: 10.3390/jrfm14090422

Blankespoor, E., deHaan, E., & Marinovic, I. (2020). Disclosure processing costs, investors' information choice, and equity market outcomes: A review. *Journal of Accounting and Economics, 70*(2-3), 101344. DOI: 10.1016/j.jacceco.2020.101344

Boda, J. R., & Sunitha, G. (2018). Investor's psychology in investment decision making: A behavioral finance approach. *International Journal of Pure and Applied Mathematics, 119*(7), 1253–1261.

Boshkov, T. (2019). Virtual Banking and Financial Inclusion.

Bostrom, N., & Yudkowsky, E. (2014). The Ethics of Artificial Intelligence. In Frankish, K., & Ramsey, W. M. (Eds.), *The Cambridge Handbook of Artificial Intelligence* (pp. 316–334). Cambridge University Press. DOI: 10.1017/CBO9781139046855.020

Bouchmal, O., Cimoli, B., Stabile, R., Vegas Olmos, J. J., & Tafur Monroy, I. (2023). From classical to quantum machine learning: Survey on routing optimization in 6G software defined networking. *Frontiers in Communications and Networks*, *4*, 1220227. DOI: 10.3389/frcmn.2023.1220227

Bouland, A., van Dam, W., Joorati, H., Kerenidis, I., & Prakash, A. (2020). Prospects and challenges of quantum finance. arXiv preprint arXiv:2011.06492.

Boztepe, E., & Usul, H. (2019). *Using the Analysis of Logistic Regression Model in Auditing and Detection of Frauds*. Khazar Journal of Humanities and Social Sciences. DOI: 10.5782/2223-2621.2019.22.3.5

Bredt, S. (2019). Artificial Intelligence (AI) in the financial sector—Potential and public strategies. *Frontiers in Artificial Intelligence*, *2*, 16. DOI: 10.3389/frai.2019.00016 PMID: 33733105

Brock, J. K. U., & Von Wangenheim, F. (2019). Demystifying AI: What digital transformation leaders can teach you about realistic artificial intelligence. *California Management Review*, *61*(4), 110–134. DOI: 10.1177/1536504219865226

Brodie, J., Daubechies, I., De Mol, C., Giannone, D., & Loris, I. (2009). Sparse and stable Markowitz portfolios. *Proceedings of the National Academy of Sciences of the United States of America*, *106*(30), 12267–12272. DOI: 10.1073/pnas.0904287106 PMID: 19617537

Broekhoff, D., Gillenwater, M., & Colbert-Sangree, T. (2019). Quality and integrity of carbon offset credits: Lessons from verification challenges. *Journal of Environmental Economics and Policy*, *8*(4), 354–374. DOI: 10.1080/21606544.2019.1686611

Brownsword, R. (2019). Regulatory Fitness: Fintech, Funny Money, and Smart Contracts. *European Business Organization Law Review*, *20*(1), 5–27. Advance online publication. DOI: 10.1007/s40804-019-00134-2

Brynjolfsson, E., & McAfee, A. (2017). The business of artificial intelligence. *Harvard Business Review*, •••, 1–20.

Butt, A. H., Ahmad, H., & Muzaffar, A. (2024). Augmented reality is the new digital banking–AR brand experience impact on brand loyalty. *International Journal of Bank Marketing*, *42*(2), 156–182. DOI: 10.1108/IJBM-11-2022-0522

Campanella, F., Serino, L., Battisti, E., Giakoumelou, A., & Karasamani, I. (2023). FinTech in the financial system: Towards a capital-intensive and high competence human capital reality? *Journal of Business Research, 155*, 113376. Advance online publication. DOI: 10.1016/j.jbusres.2022.113376

Candra Sari, R., Rika Fatimah, P. L., Ilyana, S., & Dwi Hermawan, H. (2022). Augmented reality (AR)-based sharia financial literacy system (AR-SFLS): A new approach to virtual sharia financial socialization for young learners. *International Journal of Islamic and Middle Eastern Finance and Management, 15*(1), 48–65. DOI: 10.1108/IMEFM-11-2019-0484

Cao, L. (2020). AI in finance: A review. Available at *SSRN* 3647625.

Cao, L., Yang, Q., & Yu, P. S. (2021). Data science and AI in FinTech: An overview. *International Journal of Data Science and Analytics, 12*(2), 81–99. DOI: 10.1007/s41060-021-00278-w

Caparrelli, F., D'Arcangelis, A. M., & Cassuto, A. (2004). Herding in the Italian stock market: A case of behavioral finance. *Journal of Behavioral Finance, 5*(4), 222–230. DOI: 10.1207/s15427579jpfm0504_5

Capco. (2019). *Capco*. https://www.capco.com/

Capocasale, V., & Perboli, G. (2022). Standardizing smart contracts. *IEEE Access : Practical Innovations, Open Solutions, 10*, 91203–91212. Advance online publication. DOI: 10.1109/ACCESS.2022.3202550

Carè, R., Boitan, I. A., & Fatima, R. (2023). How do FinTech companies contribute to the achievement of SDGs? Insights from case studies. *Research in International Business and Finance, 66*, 102072. https://doi.org/https://doi.org/10.1016/j.ribaf.2023.102072. DOI: 10.1016/j.ribaf.2023.102072

Carter, S. M., Rogers, W., Win, K. T., Frazer, H., Richards, B., & Houssami, N. (2020). The ethical, legal and social implications of using artificial intelligence systems in breast cancer care. *The Breast : Official Journal of the European Society of Mastology, 49*, 25–32. DOI: 10.1016/j.breast.2019.10.001 PMID: 31677530

Chauhan, M., Shingari, I., & Shingari, I. (2017). Future of e-wallets: A perspective from under graduates. *International Journal of Advanced Research in Computer Science and Software Engineering, 7*(8), 146. DOI: 10.23956/ijarcsse.v7i8.42

Chaurasia, S. S., Verma, S., & Singh, V. (2019). *Exploring the intention to use M-payment in India. Transforming Government: People*. Process and Policy., DOI: 10.1108/TG-09-2018-0060

Chawla, D., & Joshi, H. (2020). Role of Mediator in Examining the Influence of Antecedents of Mobile Wallet Adoption on Attitude and Intention. *Global Business Review, 24*(4), 609–625. DOI: 10.1177/0972150920924506

Chawla, D., & Joshi, H. (2021). *Degree of Awareness and the Antecedents of the Digital Media Platform: The Case of Mobile Wallets.* FIIB Business Review., DOI: 10.1177/23197145211023413

Chen, C. Y. H., Guo, L., & Renault, T. (2019). What Makes Cryptocurrencies Special? Investor Sentiment and Return Predictability. *Investor Sentiment and Return Predictability (June 3, 2019).*

Chen, J. (2021). What is High-Frequency Trading (HFT)? How it works and example. *Investopedia.* https://www.investopedia.com/terms/h/high-frequency-trading.asp

Chen, G., Kim, K. A., Nofsinger, J. R., & Rui, O. M. (2007). Trading performance, disposition effect, overconfidence, representativeness bias, and experience of emerging market investors. *Journal of Behavioral Decision Making, 20*(4), 425–451. DOI: 10.1002/bdm.561

Chen, H., Whitters, G., Amiri, M. J., Wang, Y., & Loo, B. T.. (2022). Declarative smart contracts. In *Proceedings of the 30th ACM Joint European Software Engineering Conference and Symposium on the Foundations of Software Engineering (ESEC/FSE '22),* November 14-18, 2022, Singapore, Singapore. ACM, New York, NY, USA, 13 pages. https://doi.org/DOI: 10.1145/3540250.3549121

Chen, L., Jiang, M., Jia, F., & Liu, G. (2022). Artificial intelligence adoption in business-to-business marketing: Toward a conceptual framework. *Journal of Business and Industrial Marketing, 37*(5), 1025–1044. DOI: 10.1108/JBIM-09-2020-0448

Chen, S., Song, Y., & Gao, P. (2023). Environmental, social, and governance (ESG) performance and financial outcomes: Analyzing the impact of ESG on financial performance. *Journal of Environmental Management, 345,* 118829. Advance online publication. DOI: 10.1016/j.jenvman.2023.118829 PMID: 37688968

Chen, W., Arn, G., Song, H., & Xie, Y. (2024). The influences of digital finance on green technological innovation in China's manufacturing sector: The threshold effects of ESG performance. *Journal of Cleaner Production, 467,* 142953. https://doi.org/https://doi.org/10.1016/j.jclepro.2024.142953. DOI: 10.1016/j.jclepro.2024.142953

Chen, X. (2024). Research on the Application of Machine Learning Technology in Enterprise Intelligent Finance. *International Journal of Computer Science and Information Technologies, 3*(3), 199–205. DOI: 10.62051/ijcsit.v3n3.20

Chen, Y., & Bellavitis, C. (2020). Blockchain disruption and decentralized finance: The rise of decentralized business models. *Journal of Business Venturing Insights*, *13*, e00151. DOI: 10.1016/j.jbvi.2019.e00151

Chia, W. T., Koh, K. F., Ng, W. K., & Yap, Z. H. (2023). *The linkage between behavioral factors and investment intention among youth in Malaysia* (Doctoral dissertation, UTAR).

Choi, D., R'bigui, H., & Cho, C. (2021). Robotic process automation implementation challenges. In *Proceedings of [Conference or Book Title]* (pp. [pages]). Springer. DOI: 10.1007/978-981-15-7990-5_29

Chowdhury, E. K., Khan, I. I., & Dhar, B. K. (2022). Catastrophic impact of Covid-19 on the global stock markets and economic activities. *Business and Society Review*, *127*(2), 437–460. DOI: 10.1111/basr.12219

Cisar, O.(2003). Strategies for using information technologies for curbing public-sector corruption: The case of the Czech Republic (CR). Budapest: Open society institute

Clark, . (2021). Smart Contracts Security Threats and Solutions. *International Journal of Information Technology and Web Engineering*. Advance online publication. DOI: 10.4018/IJITWE.304048

Cockcroft, S., & Russell, M. (2018). Big data opportunities for accounting and finance practice and research. *Australian Accounting Review*, *28*(3), 323–333.

Cognizant. (2024). *Cognizant*. https://www.cognizant.com/

Cooper, L., Holderness, D.Jr, Sorensen, T., & Wood, D. (2019). Robotic process automation in public accounting. *Accounting Horizons*, *33*(4), 15–35. DOI: 10.2308/acch-52466

Costa, P. C., An, D., Sanders, Y. R., Su, Y., Babbush, R., & Berry, D. W. (2022). Optimal scaling quantum linear-systems solver via discrete adiabatic theorem. *PFX Quantum : a Physical Review Journal*, *3*(4), 040303. DOI: 10.1103/PRXQuantum.3.040303

Creswell, J. W., & Creswell, J. D. (2017). *Research design: Qualitative, quantitative, and mixed methods approaches*. Sage publications.

Croushore, D. (2007). Money and banking: a policy-oriented approach.

Cruz-Neira, C., Sandin, D. J., DeFanti, T. A., Kenyon, R. V., & Hart, J. C. (1992). The CAVE: Audio visual experience automatic virtual environment. *Communications of the ACM*, *35*(6), 64–73. DOI: 10.1145/129888.129892

D'Hondt, C., De Winne, R., Ghysels, E., & Raymond, S. (2020). Artificial Intelligence Alter Egos: Who might benefit from robo-investing? *Journal of Empirical Finance, 59*, 278–299. DOI: 10.1016/j.jempfin.2020.10.002

Dadabada, P. K. (2024). Analyzing the Impact of ESG Integration and FinTech Innovations on Green Finance: A Comparative Case Studies Approach. *Journal of the Knowledge Economy*. Advance online publication. DOI: 10.1007/s13132-024-02197-0

Damiani, C., Kalliatakis, G., Sreenivas, M., Al-Attar, M., Rose, J., Pudney, C., Lane, E. F., Cuzick, J., Montana, G., & Brentnall, A. (2023). Evaluation of an AI Model to Assess Future Breast Cancer Risk. *Radiology, 307*(5), e222679. DOI: 10.1148/radiol.222679 PMID: 37310244

Dandapani, K. (2017). Electronic finance–recent developments. *Managerial Finance, 43*(5), 614–626. DOI: 10.1108/MF-02-2017-0028

Daniel, K., Hirshleifer, D., & Subrahmanyam, A. (1998). Investor psychology and security market under-and overreactions. *the Journal of Finance, 53*(6), 1839-1885.

David, L., & Kaulihowa, T. (2018). The impact of E-banking on commercial banks' performance in Namibia. *International Journal of Economics and Financial Research, 4*(10), 313–321.

Davis, F. D. (1989). Perceived usefulness, perceived ease of use, and user acceptance of information technology. *Management Information Systems Quarterly, 13*(3), 319–340. DOI: 10.2307/249008

Dawood, H. M., Liew, C. Y., & Lau, T. (2021). Mobile perceived trust mediation on the intention and adoption of FinTech innovations using mobile technology: A systematic literature review. F1000Research, 10. https://doi.org/DOI: 10.12688/f1000research.74656.2

De Andrés, J., & Lorca, P. (2021). On the impact of smart contracts on auditing. *The International Journal of Digital Accounting Research, 21*, 155–181. DOI: 10.4192/1577-8517-v21_6

De Bondt, W. F., & Thaler, R. H. (1995). Financial decision-making in markets and firms: A behavioral perspective. *Handbooks in Operations Research and Management Science, 9*, 385–410. DOI: 10.1016/S0927-0507(05)80057-X

De Filippi, P., Wray, C., & Sileno, G. (2021). Smart contracts. *Internet Policy Review, 10*(2), 1–9. DOI: 10.14763/2021.2.1549

De Prado, M. L. (2018). *Advances in financial machine learning*. John Wiley & Sons.

Deloitte. (2024). *Deloitte*. https://www2.deloitte.com

Desouza, K. C., Dawson, G. S., & Chenok, D. (2020). Designing, developing, and deploying artificial intelligence systems: Lessons from and for the public sector. *Business Horizons*, *63*(2), 205–213. DOI: 10.1016/j.bushor.2019.11.004

Devidze, N. (2022). Current State of Green Digital Financing and the Associated Challenges. In *Economics*. Law, and Institutions in Asia Pacific., DOI: 10.1007/978-981-19-2662-4_2

Dhaigude, R., & Lawande, N. (2022). Impact of Artificial Intelligence on Credit Scores in Lending Process. In *2022 Interdisciplinary Research in Technology and Management (IRTM)* (pp. 1-5). IEEE. DOI: 10.1109/IRTM54583.2022.9791511

Dicuonzo, G., Palmaccio, M., & Shini, M. (2024). ESG, governance variables and Fintech: An empirical analysis. *Research in International Business and Finance*, *69*, 102205. https://doi.org/https://doi.org/10.1016/j.ribaf.2023.102205. DOI: 10.1016/j.ribaf.2023.102205

Ding, J., Li, L., & Zhao, J. (2024). How does fintech prompt corporations toward ESG sustainable development? Evidence from China. *Energy Economics*, *131*, 107387. Advance online publication. DOI: 10.1016/j.eneco.2024.107387

Dixon, M. F., Halperin, I., & Bilokon, P. (2020). *Machine learning in finance* (Vol. 1170). Springer International Publishing.

Dmytro, K. (2020). 5 benefits of using smart contracts & their problems. This manuscript is made available under the Blaize user license. https://blaize.tech/5-benefits-of

Doğuc, Ö. (2020). Robot process automation (RPA) and its future. In *Handbook of Research on Strategic Fit and Design in Business Ecosystems*. IGI Global., DOI: 10.4018/978-1-7998-1125-1.ch021

Donepudi, P. K. (2017). Machine Learning and Artificial Intelligence in Banking. *Engineering International*, *5*(2), 83–86.

Dreyfus, H. L., & Dreyfus, S. E. (2005). Peripheral vision: Expertise in real world contexts. *Organization Studies*, *26*(5), 779–792. DOI: 10.1177/0170840605053102

Dubey, V., Mokashi, A., Pradhan, R., Gupta, P., & Walimbe, R. (2022). Metaverse and Banking Industry–2023 The Year of Metaverse Adoption.

Dubey, V. (2019). FinTech innovations in digital banking. [IJERT]. *International Journal of Engineering Research & Technology (Ahmedabad)*, *8*(10), 597–601.

Dunis, C., Middleton, P. W., Karathanasopolous, A., & Theofilatos, K. (2016). *Artificial intelligence in financial markets*. Palgrave Macmillan. DOI: 10.1057/978-1-137-48880-0

Duran, R. E., & Tierney, P. (2023). Fintech Data Infrastructure for ESG Disclosure Compliance. *Journal of Risk and Financial Management*, *16*(8), 378. Advance online publication. DOI: 10.3390/jrfm16080378

Duz Tan, S., & Tas, O. (2021). Social media sentiment in international stock returns and trading activity. *Journal of Behavioral Finance*, *22*(2), 221–234. DOI: 10.1080/15427560.2020.1772261

Dwivedi, P., Alabdooli, J. I., & Dwivedi, R. (2021). Role of FinTech Adoption for Competitiveness and Performance of the Bank: A Study of Banking Industry in UAE. *International Journal of Global Business and Competitiveness*, *16*(2), 130–138. Advance online publication. DOI: 10.1007/s42943-021-00033-9

Dwivedi, Y. K., Hughes, L., Ismagilova, E., Aarts, G., Coombs, C., Crick, T., Duan, Y., Dwivedi, R., Edwards, J., Eirug, A., Galanos, V., Ilavarasan, P. V., Janssen, M., Jones, P., Kar, A. K., Kizgin, H., Kronemann, B., Lal, B., Lucini, B., & Williams, M. D. (2021). Artificial Intelligence (AI): Multidisciplinary perspectives on emerging challenges, opportunities, and agenda for research, practice and policy. *International Journal of Information Management*, *57*, 101994. DOI: 10.1016/j.ijinfomgt.2019.08.002

Ederington, L. H., & Guan, W. (2000). Why are those options smiling? *Univ. of Oklahoma Center for Financial Studies Working Paper*.

Egger, A., Ter, A., Kratsch, W., Leemans, S., Röeglinger, M., & Wynn, M. (2020). Bot log mining: Using logs from robotic process automation for process mining. In *Business Process Management: BPM 2020*. Springer.

Egger, D. J., Gambella, C., Marecek, J., McFaddin, S., Mevissen, M., Raymond, R., Simonetto, A., Woerner, S., & Yndurain, E. (2020). Quantum computing for finance: State-of-the-art and future prospects. *IEEE Transactions on Quantum Engineering*, *1*, 1–24. DOI: 10.1109/TQE.2020.3030314

El Khoury, R., Nasrallah, N., Hussainey, K., & Assaf, R. (2023). Spillover analysis across FinTech, ESG, and renewable energy indices before and during the Russia–Ukraine war: International evidence. *Journal of International Financial Management & Accounting*, *34*(2), 279–317. Advance online publication. DOI: 10.1111/jifm.12179

El-Gharib, N., & Amyot, D. (2022). A review of data-driven robotic process automation exploiting process mining.

El-Seoud, S. A., El-Sofany, H. F., Abdelfattah, M., & Mohamed, R. (2017). Big Data and Cloud Computing: Trends and Challenges. *International Journal of Interactive Mobile Technologies*, *11*(2), 34. DOI: 10.3991/ijim.v11i2.6561

Erwin, K., & Engelbrecht, A. (2023). Meta-heuristics for portfolio optimization. *Soft Computing*, *27*(24), 19045–19073. DOI: 10.1007/s00500-023-08177-x

Esawe, A. T. (2022). Understanding mobile e-wallet consumers' intentions and user behavior. *Spanish Journal of Marketing - ESIC*, *26*(3), 363–384. Advance online publication. DOI: 10.1108/SJME-05-2022-0105

Escrig-Olmedo, E., Fernández-Izquierdo, M., Ferrero-Ferrero, I., Rivera-Lirio, J. M., & Muñoz-Torres, M. J. (2019). Rating the raters: Evaluating how ESG rating agencies integrate sustainability principles. *Sustainability (Basel)*, *11*(3), 915. Advance online publication. DOI: 10.3390/su11030915

Everest Group. (2022). *Everest Group*. https://www.everestgrp.com/

Fama, E. F. (1960). Efficient market hypothesis. *Diss. Ph.D. Thesis, Ph. D. dissertation*.

Fang, B., & Zhang, P. (2016). Big data in finance. Big data concepts, theories, and applications, 391-412.

Fernandez, D., Dastane, O., Omar Zaki, H., & Aman, A. (2023). Robotic process automation: Bibliometric reflection and future opportunities. *European Journal of Innovation Management*, *27*(2), 692–712. DOI: 10.1108/EJIM-10-2022-0570

Fernandez, V. (2006). The impact of major global events on volatility shifts: Evidence from the Asian crisis and 9/11. *Economic Systems*, *30*(1), 79–97. DOI: 10.1016/j.ecosys.2005.09.004

Ferri, R. (2014). Now anyone can be a robo-adviser. *Journal of Financial Planning*, *27*(12), 28.

Filbeck, G., Hatfield, P., & Horvath, P. (2005). Risk aversion and personality type. *Journal of Behavioral Finance*, *6*(4), 170–180. DOI: 10.1207/s15427579jpfm0604_1

Fintech Futures. (2018). *Fintech Futures*. https://www.fintechfutures.com/

Firdaus, R., Xue, Y., Gang, L., & Sibt e Ali, M. (2022). Artificial Intelligence and Human Psychology in Online Transaction Fraud. *Frontiers in Psychology*, *13*, 13. DOI: 10.3389/fpsyg.2022.947234 PMID: 36304851

Fisch, J. E., Laboure, M., Turner, J. A., & Center, P. P. (2017). The economics of complex decision making: The emergence of the robo adviser. Recuperado de: http://www. geog. ox. ac. uk/events/170911/Robo-vs-Human-Advisers-Aug-28. pdf.

Fishbein, M., & Ajzen, I. (1977). *Belief, attitude, intention, and behavior: An introduction to theory and research.* Addison-Wesley.

Fisher, I. E., Garnsey, M. R., & Hughes, M. E. (2016). Natural language processing in accounting, auditing and finance: A synthesis of the literature with a roadmap for future research. *Intelligent Systems in Accounting, Finance & Management*, *23*(3), 157–214. DOI: 10.1002/isaf.1386

Fitriyah, F. K. (2020). The Roles of Internal Auditor and Leadership Style in Fraud Prevention and Detection.

Flechsig, C., Anslinger, F., & Lasch, R. (2022). Robotic process automation in purchasing and supply management: A multiple case study on potentials, barriers, and implementation. *Journal of Purchasing and Supply Management*, *28*(1), 100718. DOI: 10.1016/j.pursup.2021.100718

Forrester. (2021). *Forrester*. https://www.forrester.com/

Frost, J., Gambacorta, L., Huang, Y., Shin, H. S., & Zbinden, P. (2019). BigTech and the changing structure of financial intermediation. *Economic Policy*, *34*(100), 761–799.

Gai, K., Qiu, M., Sun, X., & Zhao, H. (2017). Security and privacy issues: A survey on FinTech. In *Smart Computing and Communication: First International Conference, SmartCom 2016, Shenzhen, China, December 17-19, 2016* [Springer International Publishing]. *Proceedings*, *1*, 236–247.

Galeone, G., Ranaldo, S., & Fusco, A. (2024). ESG and FinTech: Are they connected? *Research in International Business and Finance*, *69*, 102225. Advance online publication. DOI: 10.1016/j.ribaf.2024.102225

Ganie, I. R., Wani, T. A., & Yadav, M. P. (2022). Impact of COVID-19 outbreak on the stock market: An evidence from select economies. *Business Perspectives and Research*, •••, 22785337211073635. DOI: 10.1177/22785337211073635

García-Méndez, S., de Arriba-Pérez, F., Barros-Vila, A., & González-Castaño, F. J. (2022). Detection of temporality at discourse level on financial news by combining Natural Language Processing and Machine Learning. *Expert Systems with Applications*, *197*, 116648. DOI: 10.1016/j.eswa.2022.116648

Garman, E. T., & Forgue, R. (2014). *Personal finance.* Cengage Learning.

Gartner. (2021). *Gartner*. https://www.gartner.com/

Ghoddusi, H., Creamer, G. G., & Rafizadeh, N. (2019). Machine learning in energy economics and finance: A review. *Energy Economics, 81*, 709–727. DOI: 10.1016/j.eneco.2019.05.006

Ghodoosi, F. (2021). Contracting in the age of smart contracts. *Washington Law Review (Seattle, Wash.), 96*, 51.

Gill, K. S. (2021). Ethical dilemmas: Ned Ludd and the ethical machine. *AI & Society, 36*(3), 669–676. DOI: 10.1007/s00146-021-01260-7 PMID: 34421227

Gill, S. S., Kumar, A., Singh, H., Singh, M., Kaur, K., Usman, M., & Buyya, R. (2022). Quantum computing: A taxonomy, systematic review and future directions. *Software, Practice & Experience, 52*(1), 66–114. DOI: 10.1002/spe.3039

Gimpel, H., Rau, D., & Röglinger, M. (2018). Understanding FinTech start-ups–a taxonomy of consumer-oriented service offerings. *Electronic Markets, 28*, 245–264.

Golden, L. L., Brockett, P. L., Ai, J., & Kellison, B. (2016). Empirical evidence on the use of credit scoring for predicting insurance losses with psycho-social and biochemical explanations. *North American Actuarial Journal : NAAJ, 20*(3), 233–251. DOI: 10.1080/10920277.2016.1209118

Goldstein, I., Spatt, C. S., & Ye, M. (2021). Big data in finance. *Review of Financial Studies, 34*(7), 3213–3225.

González Enríquez, J., Jimenez Ramirez, A., Domínguez Mayo, F. J., & Garcia-Garcia, J. A. (2020). Robotic process automation: A scientific and industrial systematic mapping study. *IEEE Access : Practical Innovations, Open Solutions, 8*, 214072–214095. DOI: 10.1109/ACCESS.2020.2974934

Goodell, J. W., Kumar, S., Lim, W. M., & Pattnaik, D. (2021). Artificial intelligence and machine learning in finance: Identifying foundations, themes, and research clusters from bibliometric analysis. *Journal of Behavioral and Experimental Finance, 32*, 100577. DOI: 10.1016/j.jbef.2021.100577

Goodfellow, C., Bohl, M. T., & Gebka, B. (2009). Together we invest? Individual and institutional investors' trading behaviour in Poland. *International Review of Financial Analysis, 18*(4), 212–221. DOI: 10.1016/j.irfa.2009.03.002

Goyal, K., & Kumar, S. (2021). Financial literacy: A systematic review and bibliometric analysis. *International Journal of Consumer Studies, 45*(1), 80–105.

Grande, V., Campos, R., Facin, A., & Batistela, G. (2022). An analysis of the benefits, challenges and methods of process selection to adopt robotic process automation. *Revista Gestão da Produção. Operações e Sistemas, 17*(1), 89–108.

Grewal, D., & Purnanandam, A. (2021). The impact of regulatory shifts on ESG risk management. *Journal of Financial Regulation, 8*(1), 43–57. DOI: 10.1093/jfr/fjab012

Grigoroudis, E., Tsitsiridi, E., & Zopounidis, C. (2013). Linking customer satisfaction, employee appraisal, and business performance: An evaluation methodology in the banking sector. *Annals of Operations Research, 205*, 5–27.

Güler, D. (2023). The impact of investor sentiment on Bitcoin returns and conditional volatilities during the era of covid-19. *Journal of Behavioral Finance, 24*(3), 276–289. DOI: 10.1080/15427560.2021.1975285

Gunisity, S. R. (2024). Evolution of automation to hyperautomation: Leveraging RPA, AI, ML, NLP for optimal operational efficiency. *International Journal of Computer Trends and Technology, 72*(5), 76–83. DOI: 10.14445/22312803/IJCTT-V72I3P111

Guo, M., Kuai, Y., & Liu, X. (2020). Stock market response to environmental policies: Evidence from heavily polluting firms in China. *Economic Modelling, 86*, 306–316. DOI: 10.1016/j.econmod.2019.09.028

Gupta, S., & Kekatos, V. (2023, June). A quantum approach for stochastic constrained binary optimization. In *ICASSP 2023-2023 IEEE International Conference on Acoustics, Speech and Signal Processing (ICASSP)* (pp. 1-5). IEEE. DOI: 10.1109/ICASSP49357.2023.10097179

Gupta, S., & Sharma, V. (2023, May). Effects of Quantum computing on Businesses. In 2023 4th International Conference on Intelligent Engineering and Management (ICIEM) (pp. 1-6). IEEE. DOI: 10.1109/ICIEM59379.2023.10166880

Gupta, M. (2000). Implications of expert systems for the operations of financial institutions. *Technovation, 20*(9), 509–516. DOI: 10.1016/S0166-4972(99)00165-0

Gupta, N. (2023). Volatility Response to "Black Swan Event" of COVID-19 in Asian Stock Market: An Empirical Study Using EGARCH Model. *International Journal of Engineering and Management Research*, •••, 13.

Gürsoy, D., Chi, O. H., Lu, L., & Nunkoo, R. (2019). Consumers acceptance of artificially intelligent (AI) device use in service delivery. *International Journal of Information Management, 49*, 157–169. DOI: 10.1016/j.ijinfomgt.2019.03.008

Gutierrez, M., Vexo, F., & Thalmann, D. (2008). *Stepping into virtual reality*. Springer Science & Business Media. DOI: 10.1007/978-1-84800-117-6

Guttentag, D. A. (2010). Virtual reality: Applications and implications for tourism. *Tourism Management, 31*(5), 637–651. http://www.samsung.com/global/galaxy/gear-vr/ https://am.jpmorgan.com/us/en/asset-management/adv/about-us/media/press-releases/jp-morgan-asset-management-launches-new-guide-to-the-markets-mobile-based-augmented-reality-ar-experience/ https://vr.google.com/ https://www.forbes.com/sites/ronshevlin/2022/02/16/jpmorgan-opens-a-bank-branch-in-the-metaverse-but-its-not-for-what-you-think-its-for/?sh=689ac290158d. DOI: 10.1016/j.tourman.2009.07.003

Han, H., Hsu, L. T. J., & Lee, J. S. (2009). Empirical investigation of the roles of attitudes toward green behaviors, overall image, gender, and age in hotel customers' eco-friendly decision-making process. *International Journal of Hospitality Management, 28*(4), 519–528. DOI: 10.1016/j.ijhm.2009.02.004

Hasan, I., & Rizvi, S. A. M. (2022). AI-driven fraud detection and mitigation in e-commerce transactions. In Proceedings of Data Analytics and Management: ICDAM 2021, Volume 1 (pp. 403-414). Springer Singapore.

Hasan, A., Sikarwar, P., Mishra, A., Raghuwanshi, S., Singhal, A., Joshi, A., Singh, P. R., & Dixit, A. (2024). Determinants of Behavioral Intention to Use Digital Payment among Indian Youngsters. *Journal of Risk and Financial Management, 17*(2), 87. Advance online publication. DOI: 10.3390/jrfm17020087

Hasan, I., & Rizvi, S. A. M. (2022). AI-driven fraud detection and mitigation in e-commerce transactions. [Springer Singapore.]. *Proceedings of Data Analytics and Management: ICDAM, 2021*(1), 403–414. DOI: 10.1007/978-981-16-6289-8_34

Hasan, M. M., Popp, J., & Oláh, J. (2020). Current landscape and influence of big data on finance. *Journal of Big Data, 7*(1), 1–17.

Hasan, M. M., Yajuan, L., & Khan, S. (2022). Promoting China's Inclusive Finance Through Digital Financial Services. *Global Business Review, 23*(4), 984–1006. Advance online publication. DOI: 10.1177/0972150919895348

Hasan, R., Hassan, M. K., & Aliyu, S. (2020). Fintech and Islamic finance: Literature review and research agenda. [IJIEF]. *International Journal of Islamic Economics and Finance, 3*(1), 75–94. DOI: 10.18196/ijief.2122

Hassija, V., Chamola, V., Saxena, V., Chanana, V., Parashari, P., Mumtaz, S., & Guizani, M. (2020). Present landscape of quantum computing. *IET Quantum Communication, 1*(2), 42–48. DOI: 10.1049/iet-qtc.2020.0027

Hasso, T., Müller, D., Pelster, M., & Warkulat, S. (2022). Who participated in the GameStop frenzy? Evidence from brokerage accounts. *Finance Research Letters, 45*, 102140. DOI: 10.1016/j.frl.2021.102140

Henkle, E., Igur, V., Karnik, S., & Velaga, S. (2024). Quantum Finance: Exploring Asset Management with QAOA.

Hentzen, J. K., Hoffmann, A., Dolan, R., & Pala, E. (2022). Artificial intelligence in customer-facing financial services: A systematic literature review and agenda for future research. *International Journal of Bank Marketing*, *40*(6), 1299–1336. DOI: 10.1108/IJBM-09-2021-0417

Hernandez, J. R. (2011). Good Value from Shared Values: A fraud and risk perspective.

Hernández, E., Öztürk, M., Sittón, I., & Rodríguez, S. (2019). Data protection on FinTech platforms. In Highlights of Practical Applications of Survivable Agents and Multi-Agent Systems. The PAAMS Collection: International Workshops of PAAMS 2019, Ávila, Spain, June 26–28, 2019 [Springer International Publishing]. *Proceedings*, *17*, 223–233.

He, W., Yan, G., & Da Xu, L. (2014). Developing vehicular data cloud services in the IoT environment. *IEEE Transactions on Industrial Informatics*, *10*(2), 1587–1595. DOI: 10.1109/TII.2014.2299233

Hewa, T., Ylianttila, M., & Liyanage, M.. (2020). Survey on Blockchain based smart contracts: Applications, opportunities and challenges. *Journal of Network and Computer Applications*.

Hilal, W., Gadsden, S. A., & Yawney, J. (2022). Financial fraud: A review of anomaly detection techniques and recent advances. *Expert Systems with Applications*, *193*, 116429. DOI: 10.1016/j.eswa.2021.116429

Hill, J. (2018). *Fintech and the remaking of financial institutions*. Academic Press.

Hilpisch, Y. (2020). *Artificial Intelligence in Finance*. O'Reilly Media.

Himeur, Y., Elnour, M., Fadli, F., Meskin, N., Petri, I., Rezgui, Y., & Amira, A. (2023). AI-big data analytics for building automation and management systems: A survey, actual challenges and future perspectives. *Artificial Intelligence Review*, *56*(6), 4929–5021.

Hira, T. K. (2009). *Personal finance: Past, present and future*. Networks Financial Institute Policy Brief.

Hirvonen, T. (2021). Behavioural finance in financial crises: the case of Covid-19.

Hoffmann, J., Bakhoum, M., & Beneke, F. (2018). Digital markets, mobile payments systems and development–Competition policy implications in developing countries in light of the EU experience. *Max Planck Institute for Innovation & Competition Research Paper*, (18-13)

Hofmann, J. S., Khalaf, E., Vishwanath, A., Berg, E., & Lee, J. Y. (2022). Fermionic Monte Carlo study of a realistic model of twisted bilayer graphene. *Physical Review X, 12*(1), 011061. DOI: 10.1103/PhysRevX.12.011061

Hopalı, E., Vayvay, Ö., Kalender, Z. T., Turhan, D., & Aysuna, C. (2022). How Do Mobile Wallets Improve Sustainability in Payment Services? A Comprehensive Literature Review. *Sustainability (Basel), 14*(24), 16541. Advance online publication. DOI: 10.3390/su142416541

Hougan, M. (2015). Robo-Advisers: What it means to you. *Journal of Financial Planning, 28*(2), 26.

Huang, A., & You, H. (2022). Artificial Intelligence in Financial Decision Making. *Handbook of Financial Decision Making, Forthcoming*.

Huang, W., & Zheng, Y. (2020). COVID-19: Structural changes in the relationship between investor sentiment and crude oil futures price. *Energy Research Letters, 1*(2).

Huang, M. H., Rust, R., & Maksimovic, V. (2019). The feeling economy: Managing in the next generation of artificial intelligence (AI). *California Management Review, 61*(4), 43–65.

Huang, W., Nakamori, Y., & Wang, S. Y. (2005). Forecasting stock market movement direction with support vector machine. *Computers & Operations Research, 32*(10), 2513–2522. DOI: 10.1016/j.cor.2004.03.016

Huang, Y. C., Backman, K. F., Backman, S. J., & Chang, L. L. (2016). Exploring the implications of virtual reality technology in tourism marketing: An integrated research framework. *International Journal of Tourism Research, 18*(2), 116–128. DOI: 10.1002/jtr.2038

Huang, Y., Wang, X., & Wang, X. (2020). Mobile payment in China: Practice and its effects. *Asian Economic Papers, 19*(3), 1–18. DOI: 10.1162/asep_a_00779

Hwang, H., & Park, H. I. (2023). The relationships of financial literacy with both financial behavior and financial well-being: Meta-analyses based on the selective literature review. *The Journal of Consumer Affairs, 57*(1), 222–244.

Illiashenko, P. (2017). Behavioral finance: History and foundations. *Visnyk of the National Bank of Ukraine*, (239), 28–54. DOI: 10.26531/vnbu2017.239.028

Iman, N. (2018). Is mobile payment still relevant in the fintech era? *Electronic Commerce Research and Applications*, *30*, 72–82. DOI: 10.1016/j.elerap.2018.05.009

Infosys, B. P. M. (2024). *Infosys BPM*. https://www.infosysbpm.com/

Iqbal, M., Sumantri, R., & Khoirunnisa, R. (2022). Acceleration of Financial Technology Growth in Islamic Banks as an Existence Effort to Face the Pandemic of COVID-19. *Al-Masraf: Jurnal Lembaga Keuangan dan Perbankan, 7*(2), 21-31

IRPAAI. (2024). *Institute for Robotic Process Automation & Artificial Intelligence*. https://irpaai.com/

Işık, C., Ongan, S., Islam, H., Pinzon, S., & Jabeen, G. (2024). Navigating sustainability: Unveiling the interconnected dynamics of ESG factors and SDGs in BRICS-11. *Sustainable Development, n/a*(n/a). https://doi.org/https://doi.org/10.1002/sd.2977

Iskandar, R. D. M., Maryanti, T., Jayaprawira, A. R., & Sari, S. N. (2022). Indonesian islamic banking fintech model strategy: Anp method. [ATT]. *Aptisi Transactions on Technopreneurship*, *4*(2), 142–152. DOI: 10.34306/att.v4i2.257

Ivančić, L., Suša Vugec, D., & Vukšić, V. (2019). Robotic process automation: Systematic literature review. In *Organizational Transformation and Managing Innovation in the Fourth Industrial Revolution*. Springer., DOI: 10.1007/978-3-030-30429-4_19

Ivanov, N., Li, C., Yan, Q., Sun, Z., Cao, Z., & Luo, X. (2023). Security threat mitigation for smart contracts: A comprehensive survey. *ACM Computing Surveys*, *55*(14s), 326. Advance online publication. DOI: 10.1145/3593293

Jacobi, R., & Brenner, E. (2018). How large corporations survive digitalization. *Digital marketplaces unleashed*, 83-97.

Jadhav, P., & Dongare, R. (2023). Robotic process automation (RPA) in business processes: Benefits and challenges. *International Journal of Advanced Research in Science, Communication and Technology, 3*(1). ISSN 2581-9429.

Jain, A., Agrawal, S., Goswami, S., Banga, S., Kumar, S., & Singh, N. (2020). Behavioural Finance Effect on Stock Price Trends During Covid-19 Pandemic. *Management Dynamics*, *20*(2), 6.

Jain, V., Balakrishnan, A., Beeram, D., Najana, M., & Chintale, P. (2024). Leveraging artificial intelligence for enhancing regulatory compliance in the financial sector. *International Journal of Computer Trends and Technology*, *72*(5), 124–140. DOI: 10.14445/22312803/IJCTT-V72I5P116

Jamil, S. (2021). From digital divide to digital inclusion: Challenges for wide-ranging digitalization in Pakistan. *Telecommunications Policy*, *45*(8), 102206.

Jan, N., Jain, V., Li, Z., Sattar, J., & Tongkachok, K. (2022). Post-COVID-19 investor psychology and individual investment decision: A moderating role of information availability. *Frontiers in Psychology, 13*, 846088. DOI: 10.3389/fpsyg.2022.846088 PMID: 36248582

Januszewski, A., Kujawski, J., & Buchalska-Sugajska, N. (2021). Benefits of and obstacles to RPA implementation in accounting firms. *Procedia Computer Science, 192*, 4672–4680. DOI: 10.1016/j.procs.2021.09.245

Jovanović, A., & Milosavljević, A. (2022). VoRtex Metaverse platform for gamified collaborative learning. *Electronics (Basel), 11*(3), 317. DOI: 10.3390/electronics11030317

Jünger, M., & Mietzner, M. (2020). Banking goes digital: The adoption of FinTech services by German households. *Finance Research Letters, 34*, 101260. DOI: 10.1016/j.frl.2019.08.008

Jung, T., Chung, N., & Leue, M. C. (2015). The determinants of recommendations to use augmented reality technologies: The case of a Korean theme park. *Tourism Management, 49*, 75–86. DOI: 10.1016/j.tourman.2015.02.013

Kahneman, D., & Tversky, A. (1979). On the interpretation of intuitive probability: A reply to Jonathan Cohen.

Kajol, K., Singh, R., & Paul, J. (2022). Adoption of digital financial transactions: A review of literature and future research agenda. *Technological Forecasting and Social Change, 184*, 121991.

Kamila, M. K., & Jasrotia, S. S. (2023). Ethical issues in the development of artificial intelligence: recognizing the risks. *International Journal of Ethics and Systems.*

Kamoune, A., & Ibenrissoul, N. (2022). Traditional versus Behavioral Finance Theory. *International Journal of Accounting, Finance, Auditing, Management and Economics, 3*(2-1), 282-294.

Kang, J. (2018). Mobile payment in Fintech environment: trends, security challenges, and services. *Human-centric Computing and Information sciences, 8*(1), 1-16

Kaplan, A., & Haenlein, M. (2019). Siri, Siri, in my hand: Who's the fairest in the land? On the interpretations, illustrations, and implications of artificial intelligence. *Business Horizons, 62*(1), 15–25. DOI: 10.1016/j.bushor.2018.08.004

Kapoor, A., Sindwani, R., Goel, M., & Shankar, A. (2022). Mobile wallet adoption intention amid COVID-19 pandemic outbreak: A novel conceptual framework. *Computers & Industrial Engineering*, *172*, 108646. DOI: 10.1016/j.cie.2022.108646 PMID: 36118531

Kapoor, S., & Prosad, J. M. (2017). Behavioural finance: A review. *Procedia Computer Science*, *122*, 50–54. DOI: 10.1016/j.procs.2017.11.340

Kapur, P. K., Sharma, H., Tandon, A., & Aggarwal, A. G. (2019). *Studying BHIM App Adoption using Bass Model: An Indian Perspective*. International Journal of Mathematical, Engineering and Management Sciences., DOI: 10.33889/IJMEMS.2020.5.1.011

Kar, A. K., & Kushwaha, A. K. (2021). Facilitators and barriers of artificial intelligence adoption in business–insights from opinions using big data analytics. *Information Systems Frontiers*, •••, 1–24.

Karolina. (2023). Advanced cryptographic techniques for secure Blockchain development. This manuscript is made available under the Nextrope user license. https://nextrope.com/

Karp, A., & Gaustad, G. (2022). Blockchain for sustainability: Enhancing accountability in carbon markets. *Sustainable Development*, *30*(3), 526–534. DOI: 10.1002/sd.2291

Karpoff, J. M. (2021). The future of financial fraud. *Journal of Corporate Finance*, *66*, 101694. DOI: 10.1016/j.jcorpfin.2020.101694

Katterbauer, K., Hassan, S. Y. E. D., & Cleenewerck, L. (2022). Financial cybercrime in the Islamic finance metaverse. *Journal of Metaverse*, *2*(2), 56–61. DOI: 10.57019/jmv.1108783

Kazachenok, O. P., Stankevich, G. V., Chubaeva, N. N., & Tyurina, Y. G. (2023). Economic and legal approaches to the humanization of FinTech in the economy of artificial intelligence through the integration of blockchain into ESG Finance. *Humanities & Social Sciences Communications*, *10*(1), 167. Advance online publication. DOI: 10.1057/s41599-023-01652-8

Kengatharan, L., & Kengatharan, N. (2014). The influence of behavioral factors in making investment decisions and performance: Study on investors of Colombo Stock Exchange, Sri Lanka. *Asian Journal of Finance & Accounting*, *6*(1), 1. DOI: 10.5296/ajfa.v6i1.4893

Khan, A., Khalid, W., Faisal, S., & Suliman Fadl Elseed, E. (2023). The future: Artificial intelligence's profound impact on accounting and society—Anticipating job market dynamics and evolving skill requirements for accountants. *Seybold Report*, *18*(11), 1596–1622.

Khanboubi, F., Boulmakoul, A., & Tabaa, M. (2019). Impact of digital trends using IoT on banking processes. *Procedia Computer Science*, *151*, 77–84. DOI: 10.1016/j.procs.2019.04.014

Khandelwal, K., & Upadhyay, A. K. (2021). Virtual reality interventions in developing and managing human resources. *Human Resource Development International*, *24*(2), 219–233. DOI: 10.1080/13678868.2019.1569920

Khan, S. N., Loukil, F., Ghedira-Guegan, C., Benkhelifa, E., & Bani-Hani, A. (2021). Blockchain smart contracts: Applications, challenges, and future trends. *Peer-to-Peer Networking and Applications*, *14*(5), 2901–2925. DOI: 10.1007/s12083-021-01127-0 PMID: 33897937

Kim, S., & Park, H. (2020). An Exploratory Study on the Factors Determining Acceptance of Blockchain-Based Financial Platform by Gender. *Journal of Digital Convergence*, *18*(3), 139–147.

Kishore, R. (2004). Theory of behavioural finance and its application to property market: A change in paradigm. *Australian Property Journal*, *38*(2), 105–110.

Kitsios, F., & Kamariotou, M. (2021). Artificial intelligence and business strategy towards digital transformation: A research agenda. *Sustainability (Basel)*, *13*(4), 2025. DOI: 10.3390/su13042025

Kołodziej, M. (2017). Virtual reality as the indicator of the modern banking. *Financial Sciences*. Nauki o finansach, (2 (31)).

Kombe, C., Sam, A., Ally, M., & Finne, A. (2019). Blockchain Technology in Sub-Saharan Africa: Where does it fit in Healthcare Systems: A case of Tanzania. *Journal of Health Informatics in Developing Countries*, 13.

Komulainen, H., Saraniemi, S., Ulkuniemi, P., & Ylilehto, M. (2018). End-customer value restructuring the financial service supply chain. *Marketing Intelligence & Planning*, *36*(6), 709–720. DOI: 10.1108/MIP-11-2017-0320

Königstorfer, F., & Thalmann, S. (2020a). Applications of Artificial Intelligence in commercial banks–A research agenda for behavioral finance. *Journal of Behavioral and Experimental Finance*, *27*, 100352. DOI: 10.1016/j.jbef.2020.100352

Koohang, A., Nord, J. H., Ooi, K. B., Tan, G. W. H., Al-Emran, M., Aw, E. C. X., Baabdullah, A. M., Buhalis, D., Cham, T.-H., Dennis, C., Dutot, V., Dwivedi, Y. K., Hughes, L., Mogaji, E., Pandey, N., Phau, I., Raman, R., Sharma, A., Sigala, M., & Wong, L. W. (2023). Shaping the metaverse into reality: A holistic multidisciplinary understanding of opportunities, challenges, and avenues for future investigation. *Journal of Computer Information Systems*, *63*(3), 735–765. DOI: 10.1080/08874417.2023.2165197

Kooli, C. (2023a). Chatbots in education and research: A critical examination of ethical implications and solutions. *Sustainability (Basel)*, *15*(7), 5614. DOI: 10.3390/su15075614

Kooli, C. (2023b). Artificial intelligence dissociative identity disorder (AIDIS): The dark side of ChatGPT. *QScience Connect*, *2023*(2), 2. DOI: 10.5339/connect.2023.2

Kozodoi, N., Jacob, J., & Lessmann, S. (2022). Fairness in credit scoring: Assessment, implementation and profit implications. *European Journal of Operational Research*, *297*(3), 1083–1094.

KPMG. (2024). *KPMG*. https://assets.kpmg.com/

Kreibich, N., & Hermwille, L. (2021). Transparency and credibility in the carbon markets: Blockchain applications and limitations. *Climate Policy*, *21*(7), 970–986. DOI: 10.1080/14693062.2021.1917685

Krichen, M. (2023). Strengthening the security of smart contracts through the power of artificial intelligence. *Computers*, *12*(107), 107. Advance online publication. DOI: 10.3390/computers12050107

Krichen, M., & Abdalzaher, M. S. (2024). Performance enhancement of artificial intelligence: A survey. *Journal of Network and Computer Applications*, •••, 104034.

Krollner, B., Vanstone, B. J., & Finnie, G. R. (2010, April). Financial time series forecasting with machine learning techniques: a survey. In *ESANN*.

Kshetri, N. (2016). Big data's role in expanding access to financial services in China. *International Journal of Information Management*, *36*(3), 297–308.

Kubilay, B., & Bayrakdaroglu, A. (2016). An empirical research on investor biases in financial decision-making, financial risk tolerance and financial personality. *International Journal of Financial Research*, *7*(2), 171–182. DOI: 10.5430/ijfr.v7n2p171

Kulkarni, N., & Bansal, S. (2023). Finance business process automation using RPA. *Journal of Economics & Management Research*, *4*(3), 1–5. DOI: 10.47363/JESMR/2022(4)220

Kumar, S., Akoglu, L., Chawla, N., Nagrecha, S., Naware, V. M., Faruquie, T., & McCormick, H. (2022b). KDD Workshop on Machine Learning in Finance. In Proceedings of the 28th ACM SIGKDD Conference on Knowledge Discovery and Data Mining (pp. 4882-4883).

Kumar, A., Dhingra, S., Batra, V., & Purohit, H. K. (2020). A Framework of Mobile Banking Adoption in India. *Journal of Open Innovation*, *6*(2), 40. Advance online publication. DOI: 10.3390/joitmc6020040

Kumar, A., Sharma, S., & Mahdavi, M. (2021). Machine learning (ML) technologies for digital credit scoring in rural finance: A literature review. *Risks*, *9*(11), 192. DOI: 10.3390/risks9110192

Kumar, D., Singh, R. K., Mishra, R., & Vlachos, I. (2023). Big data analytics in supply chain decarbonisation: A systematic literature review and future research directions. *International Journal of Production Research*, •••, 1–21.

Kumar, R., Singh, R., Kumar, K., Khan, S., & Corvello, V. (2023). How Does Perceived Risk and Trust Affect Mobile Banking Adoption? Empirical Evidence from India. *Sustainability (Basel)*, *15*(5), 4053. Advance online publication. DOI: 10.3390/su15054053

Kumar, S., Sharma, D., Rao, S., Lim, W. M., & Mangla, S. K. (2022a). Past, present, and future of sustainable finance: Insights from big data analytics through machine learning of scholarly research. *Annals of Operations Research*, •••, 1–44.

Kushwaha, A. K., Kumar, P., & Kar, A. K. (2021). What impacts customer experience for B2B enterprises on using AI-enabled chatbots? Insights from Big data analytics. *Industrial Marketing Management*, *98*, 207–221. DOI: 10.1016/j.indmarman.2021.08.011

Laidroo, L., Koroleva, E., Kliber, A., Rupeika-Apoga, R., & Grigaliuniene, Z. (2021). Business models of FinTechs – Difference in similarity? *Electronic Commerce Research and Applications*, *46*, 101034. https://doi.org/https://doi.org/10.1016/j.elerap.2021.101034. DOI: 10.1016/j.elerap.2021.101034

Lai, M. M., Low, K. L. T., & Lai, M. L. (2001). Are Malaysian investors rational? *The Journal of Psychology and Financial Markets*, *2*(4), 210–215. DOI: 10.1207/S15327760JPFM0204_5

Larkin, C., Drummond Otten, C., & Arvai, J. (2021). Paging Dr. JARVIS! Will people accept advice from artificial intelligence for consequential risk management decisions? *Journal of Risk Research*, *25*(4), 407–422. DOI: 10.1080/13669877.2021.1958047

Latif, M. N., & Ozcan, R. FIN-TECH adoption in Pakistan: mobile wallet service (MWS) over GDP causality evidence for pre and post COVID-19. Journal of Research & Reviews in Social Sciences Pakistan, 6 (1), 1999-2011

Lee, I. (2017). Big data: Dimensions, evolution, impacts, and challenges. *Business Horizons*, *60*(3), 293–303.

Lehenkari, M., & Perttunen, J. (2004). Holding onto the losers: Finish evidence. *Journal of Behavioral Finance*, *5*(2), 116–126. DOI: 10.1207/s15427579jpfm0502_5

Lei, X., Mohamad, U. H., Sarlan, A., Shutaywi, M., Daradkeh, Y. I., & Mohammed, H. O. (2022). Development of an intelligent information system for financial analysis depend on supervised machine learning algorithms. *Information Processing & Management*, *59*(5), 103036. DOI: 10.1016/j.ipm.2022.103036

Leke, C. A., & Marwala, T. (2019). *Deep learning and missing data in engineering systems*. Springer International Publishing. DOI: 10.1007/978-3-030-01180-2

Leong, P., & Sung, H. (2023). Predictive analytics and ESG risk management in decentralized finance. *Finance Research Letters*, *15*(2), 215–223. DOI: 10.1016/j.frl.2023.101298

Leukfeldt, E. R., Lavorgna, A., & Kleemans, E. R. (2017). Organised cybercrime or cybercrime that is organised? An assessment of the conceptualisation of financial cybercrime as organised crime. *European Journal on Criminal Policy and Research*, *23*(3), 287–300. DOI: 10.1007/s10610-016-9332-z

Liang, H., & Xue, Y. L. (2010). Understanding security behaviors in personal computer usage: A threat avoidance perspective. *Journal of the Association for Information Systems*, *11*(7), 1. DOI: 10.17705/1jais.00232

Liao, S. H. (2005). Technology management methodologies and applications: A literature review from 1995 to 2003. *Technovation*, *25*(4), 381–393. DOI: 10.1016/j.technovation.2003.08.002

Liao, Y., Rocha Loures, E., & Deschamps, F. (2018). Industrial internet of things: A systematic literature review and insights. *IEEE Internet of Things Journal*, *5*(6), 4515–4525. DOI: 10.1109/JIOT.2018.2834151

Li, B., Du, J., Yao, T., & Wang, Q. (2023). FinTech and corporate green innovation: An external attention perspective. *Finance Research Letters*, *58*, 104661. https://doi.org/https://doi.org/10.1016/j.frl.2023.104661. DOI: 10.1016/j.frl.2023.104661

Li, F. (2020). The digital transformation of business models in the creative industries: A holistic framework and emerging trends. *Technovation*, *92*, 102012. DOI: 10.1016/j.technovation.2017.12.004

Linden Lab. (2013). Infographic–10 Years of Second Life.

Liu, Z., & Li, X. (2024). The impact of bank fintech on ESG greenwashing. *Finance Research Letters*, *62*, 105199. Advance online publication. DOI: 10.1016/j.frl.2024.105199

Lo, A. W. (2017). Big Data and the Industrial Organization of Financial Markets. *Annual Review of Financial Economics*, *9*(1), 1–26.

Loizou, P., & French, N. (2012). Risk and uncertainty in development: A critical evaluation of using the Monte Carlo simulation method as a decision tool in real estate development projects. *Journal of Property Investment & Finance*, *30*(2), 198–210. DOI: 10.1108/14635781211206922

Luo, Y., & Van Assche, A. (2023). The rise of techno-geopolitical uncertainty: Implications of the United States CHIPS and Science Act. *Journal of International Business Studies*, *54*(8), 1–18. DOI: 10.1057/s41267-023-00620-3 PMID: 37359753

Maad, S., Garbaya, S., & Bouakaz, S. (2007). From virtual to augmented reality in financial trading: A CYBERII application. *Journal of Enterprise Information Management*, *21*(1), 71–80. DOI: 10.1108/17410390810842264

Macchiavello, E., & Siri, M. (2022). Sustainable Finance and Fintech: Can Technology Contribute to Achieving Environmental Goals? A Preliminary Assessment of "Green Fintech" and "Sustainable Digital Finance.". *European Company and Financial Law Review*, *19*(1), 128–174. Advance online publication. DOI: 10.1515/ecfr-2022-0005

Madakam, S., Holmukhe, R., & Jaiswal, D. (2019). The future digital workforce: Robotic process automation (RPA). *Journal of Information Systems and Technology Management*, *16*(e201916005). Advance online publication. DOI: 10.4301/S1807-1775201916001

Majchrzak, A., Markus, M. L., & Wareham, J. (2016). Designing for digital transformation. *Management Information Systems Quarterly*, *40*(2), 267–278. DOI: 10.25300/MISQ/2016/40:2.03

Malali, A. B., & Gopalakrishnan, S. (2020). Application of artificial intelligence and its powered technologies in the indian banking and financial industry: An overview. *IOSR Journal Of Humanities And Social Science*, *25*(4), 55–60.

Mandvikar, S. (2023). Indexing robotic process automation products. *International Journal of Computer Trends and Technology*, *71*(4), 52–56. DOI: 10.14445/22312803/IJCTT-V71I8P108

Manser Payne, E. H., Dahl, A. J., & Peltier, J. (2021). Digital servitization value co-creation framework for AI services: A research agenda for digital transformation in financial service ecosystems. *Journal of Research in Interactive Marketing*, *15*(2), 200–222. DOI: 10.1108/JRIM-12-2020-0252

Marella, S. T., & Parisa, H. S. K. (2020). *Introduction to quantum computing*. Quantum Computing and Communications.

Margiono, A. (2021). Digital transformation: Setting the pace. *The Journal of Business Strategy*, *42*(5), 315–322. DOI: 10.1108/JBS-11-2019-0215

Martins, N. C., Marques, B., Alves, J., Araújo, T., Dias, P., & Santos, B. S. (2022). Augmented reality situated visualization in decision-making. *Multimedia Tools and Applications*, *81*(11), 14749–14772. DOI: 10.1007/s11042-021-10971-4

Ma, X., & Lv, S. (2019). Financial credit risk prediction in internet finance driven by machine learning. *Neural Computing & Applications*, *31*, 8359–8367.

Mazurek, G., & Małagocka, K. (2019). Perception of privacy and data protection in the context of the development of artificial intelligence. *Journal of Management Analytics*, *6*(4), 344–364. DOI: 10.1080/23270012.2019.1671243

Mazur, M., Dang, M., & Vega, M. (2021). COVID-19 and the march 2020 stock market crash. Evidence from S&P1500. *Finance Research Letters*, *38*, 101690. DOI: 10.1016/j.frl.2020.101690 PMID: 32837377

McKinsey & Company. (2018–2023). *McKinsey & Company*. https://www.mckinsey.com/

Medium. (2024). *Medium*. https://medium.com/

Mehdiabadi, A., Tabatabeinasab, M., Spulbar, C., Karbassi Yazdi, A., & Birau, R. (2020). Are we ready for the challenge of Banks 4.0? Designing a roadmap for banking systems in Industry 4.0. *International Journal of Financial Studies*, *8*(2), 32. DOI: 10.3390/ijfs8020032

Mehrban, S., Nadeem, M. W., Hussain, M., Ahmed, M. M., Hakeem, O., Saqib, S., & Khan, M. A. (2020). Towards secure FinTech: A survey, taxonomy, and open research challenges. *IEEE Access : Practical Innovations, Open Solutions*, *8*, 23391–23406. DOI: 10.1109/ACCESS.2020.2970430

Meng, J., & Weng, X. (2018). Can prospect theory explain the disposition effect? A new perspective on reference points. *Management Science*, *64*(7), 3331–3351. DOI: 10.1287/mnsc.2016.2711

Mer, A., & Virdi, A. S. (2025). The Influence of Artificial Intelligence on Personal and Corporate Finance: A Comprehensive Literature Review with Prospects for Future Research. Financial Landscape Transformation: Technological Disruptions, 253-268.

Merello, P., Barbera, A., & De la Poza, E. (2023). Analysing the determinant factors of the sustainability profile of Fintech and Insurtech companies. *Journal of Cleaner Production*, *421*, 138437. Advance online publication. DOI: 10.1016/j.jclepro.2023.138437

Meylan, G., & Nastasi, P. (2020). Case study: Blockchain for carbon credits in Switzerland. *Energy Policy*, *146*, 111806. DOI: 10.1016/j.enpol.2020.111806

Michael, B., & Latkovska, T. (2021). The FinTech Dividend: How Much Money Is FinTech Likely to Mobilize for Sustainable Development? *Global Policy*, *12*(5), 677–688. Advance online publication. DOI: 10.1111/1758-5899.12994

Mio, C., Panfilo, S., & Blundo, B. (2020). Sustainable development goals and the strategic role of business: A systematic literature review. *Business Strategy and the Environment*, *29*(8), 3220–3245. Advance online publication. DOI: 10.1002/bse.2568

Miroudot, S. (2020). Reshaping the policy debate on the implications of COVID-19 for global supply chains. *Journal of International Business Policy*, *3*(4), 430–442. DOI: 10.1057/s42214-020-00074-6

Mishra, A. K., & Tyagi, A. K. Richa, & Patra, S. R. (2024). Introduction to Machine Learning and Artificial Intelligence in Banking and Finance. In Applications of Block Chain technology and Artificial Intelligence: Lead-ins in Banking, Finance, and Capital Market (pp. 239-290). Cham: Springer International Publishing.

Mitchell, T. (2023, May 22). *What We Know About Gen Z So Far | Pew Research Center*. Pew Research Center's Social & Demographic Trends Project. https://www.pewresearch.org/social-trends/2020/05/14/on-the-cusp-of-adulthood-and-facing-an-uncertain-future-what-we-know-about-gen-z-so-far-2/

Modgil, S., Gupta, S., Stekelorum, R., & Laguir, I. (2021). AI technologies and their impact on supply chain resilience during COVID-19. *International Journal of Physical Distribution & Logistics Management*, *52*(2), 130–149. DOI: 10.1108/IJPDLM-12-2020-0434

Mogaji, E., Soetan, T. O., & Kieu, T. A. (2020). The implications of artificial intelligence on the digital marketing of financial services to vulnerable customers. *Australasian Marketing Journal*, j-ausmj.

Mogaji, E., & Nguyen, N. P. (2022). Managers' understanding of artificial intelligence in relation to marketing financial services: Insights from a cross-country study. *International Journal of Bank Marketing*, *40*(6), 1272–1298.

Mogaji, E., Soetan, T. O., & Kieu, T. A. (2021). The implications of artificial intelligence on the digital marketing of financial services to vulnerable customers. *Australasian Marketing Journal*, *29*(3), 235–242. DOI: 10.1016/j.ausmj.2020.05.003

Mohamed, H., & Ali, H. (2018). Blockchain, Fintech, and Islamic Finance. In *Blockchain, Fintech, and Islamic Finance*. de Gruyter.

Mohamed, S., & Frank, L. (2024). Improved efficiency and reduced costs: The role of robotic process automation (RPA) in automating price adjustments.

Moher, D., Liberati, A., Tetzlaff, J., & Altman, D. G. (2010). Preferred reporting items for systematic reviews and meta-analyses: The PRISMA statement. *International Journal of Surgery*, *8*(5), 336–341. https://doi.org/https://doi.org/10.1016/j.ijsu.2010.02.007. DOI: 10.1016/j.ijsu.2010.02.007 PMID: 20171303

Mohieldin, M., Wahba, S., Gonzalez-Perez, M. A., & Shehata, M. (2023). How Businesses Can Accelerate and Scale-Up SDG Implementation by Incorporating ESG into Their Strategies. In *Business, Government and the SDGs*. DOI: 10.1007/978-3-031-11196-9_3

Montanez-Barrera, J. A., Willsch, D., Maldonado-Romo, A., & Michielsen, K. (2024). Unbalanced penalization: A new approach to encode inequality constraints of combinatorial problems for quantum optimization algorithms. *Quantum Science and Technology*, *9*(2), 025022. DOI: 10.1088/2058-9565/ad35e4

Moreira, S., Mamede, H. S., & Santos, A. (2023). Process automation using RPA – A literature review. *Procedia Computer Science*, *219*, 244–254. DOI: 10.1016/j.procs.2023.01.287

Morgan, J. P. (2020–2021). *J.P. Morgan*. https://www.jpmorgan.com/

Mori, M. (2021). AI-powered virtual assistants in the realms of banking and financial services. In *Virtual Assistant*. IntechOpen.

Moro-Visconti, R., Rambaud, S. C., & Pascual, J. L. (2020). Sustainability in FinTechs: An explanation through business model scalability and market valuation. *Sustainability (Basel), 12*(24), 10316. Advance online publication. DOI: 10.3390/su122410316

Mougayar, W. (2016). *The Business Blockchain: Promise, Practice, and the Application of the Next Internet Technology*. Wiley.

Mozumder, M. A. I., Theodore, A. T. P., Athar, A., & Kim, H. C. (2023, February). The metaverse applications for the finance industry, its challenges, and an approach for the metaverse finance industry. In *2023 25th International Conference on Advanced Communication Technology (ICACT)* (pp. 407-410). IEEE.

Mumtaza, Q. M. H., Nabillah, S. I., Amaliya, S., Rosabella, Y., & Hammad, J. A. (2020). Worldwide mobile wallet: A futuristic cashless system. *Bulletin of Social Informatics Theory and Application, 4*(2), 70–75. DOI: 10.31763/businta.v4i2.204

Munoko, I., Brown-Liburd, H. L., & Vasarhelyi, M. (2020). The ethical implications of using artificial intelligence in auditing. *Journal of Business Ethics, 167*(2), 209–234. DOI: 10.1007/s10551-019-04407-1

Mushafiq M, Sindhu M, Sohail M (2021) Financial performance under influence of credit risk in nonfinancial firms: evidence from Pakistan. J Econ Admin Sci 1026–4116

Mushafiq, M. (2021). Industry-level analysis of COVID-19's impact in emerging markets–evidence from Pakistan. *International Journal of Emerging Markets*, (ahead-of-print).

Mu, W., Liu, K., Tao, Y., & Ye, Y. (2023). Digital finance and corporate ESG. *Finance Research Letters, 51*, 103426. https://doi.org/https://doi.org/10.1016/j.frl.2022.103426. DOI: 10.1016/j.frl.2022.103426

Naimi-Sadigh, A., Asgari, T., & Rabiei, M. (2021). Digital transformation in the value chain disruption of banking services. *Journal of the Knowledge Economy*, •••, 1–31.

Neelam, K., & Bhattacharya, S. (2023). *The Role of Mobile Payment Apps in Inclusive Financial Growth. Australasian Accounting*. Business and Finance Journal., DOI: 10.14453/aabfj.v17i1.02

Negka, L. D., & Spathoulas, G. P. (2021). Blockchain state channels: A state of the art. *IEEE Access : Practical Innovations, Open Solutions, 9*, 160277–160298. Advance online publication. DOI: 10.1109/ACCESS.2021.3131419

Nestler, G. (2017). *The Derivative Condition: A Present Inquiry into the History of Futures* (Doctoral dissertation, Goldsmiths, University of London).

Newell, A. (1982). The knowledge level. *Artificial Intelligence*, *18*(1), 87–127. DOI: 10.1016/0004-3702(82)90012-1

Nezami, M., Tuli, K. R., & Dutta, S. (2022). Shareholder wealth implications of software firms' transition to cloud computing: A marketing perspective. *Journal of the Academy of Marketing Science*, *50*(3), 538–562. DOI: 10.1007/s11747-021-00818-7 PMID: 35079189

Ngoc, L. T. B. (2014). Behavior pattern of individual investors in stock market. *International Journal of Business and Management*, *9*(1), 1–16.

Nguyen, D. K., Sermpinis, G., & Stasinakis, C. (2023). Big data, artificial intelligence and machine learning: A transformative symbiosis in favour of financial technology. *European Financial Management*, *29*(2), 517–548.

Nicholls, J., Kuppa, A., & Le-Khac, N. A. (2021). Financial cybercrime: A comprehensive survey of deep learning approaches to tackle the evolving financial crime landscape. *IEEE Access : Practical Innovations, Open Solutions*, *9*, 163965–163986. DOI: 10.1109/ACCESS.2021.3134076

Njegovanović, A. (2018). Digital financial decision with a view of neuroplasticity/neurofinancy/neural networks.

Notteboom, T., Pallis, T., & Rodrigue, J. P. (2021). Disruptions and resilience in global container shipping and ports: The COVID-19 pandemic versus the 2008–2009 financial crisis. *Maritime Economics & Logistics*, *23*(2), 179–210. DOI: 10.1057/s41278-020-00180-5

O'hara, M. (2015). High frequency market microstructure. *Journal of Financial Economics*, *116*(2), 257–270. DOI: 10.1016/j.jfineco.2015.01.003

Oberlechner, T., & Osler, C. L. (2008). Overconfidence in currency markets. *Available atSSRN* 1108787.

Odean, T. (1998). Are investors reluctant to realize their losses? *The Journal of Finance*, *53*(5), 1775–1798. DOI: 10.1111/0022-1082.00072

Omarova, S. T. (2020). Dealing with disruption: Emerging approaches to fintech regulation. *Wash. UJL & Pol'y*, *61*, 25.

Orús, R., Mugel, S., & Lizaso, E. (2019). Quantum computing for finance: Overview and prospects. *Reviews in Physics*, *4*, 100028. DOI: 10.1016/j.revip.2019.100028

Osman, C.-C. (2019). Robotic process automation: Lessons learned from case studies. *Informações Econômicas, 23*(3), 66–71. DOI: 10.12948/issn14531305/23.4.2019.06

Owolabi, O. S., Uche, P. C., Adeniken, N. T., Tanoh, V., & Emi-Johnson, O. G. (2024). Quantum computing applications, challenges, and prospects in financial portfolio optimization. *World Journal of Advanced Research and Reviews, 22*(3), 014-022.

Oyeniyi, L., Ugochukwu, C., & Mhlongo, N.Lawrence Damilare OyeniyiChinonye Esther UgochukwuNoluthando Zamanjomane Mhlongo. (2024). Robotic process automation in routine accounting tasks: A review and efficiency analysis. *World Journal of Advanced Research and Reviews, 22*(2), 695–711. DOI: 10.30574/wjarr.2024.22.1.1156

Ozili, P. K. (2021). Big data and artificial intelligence for financial inclusion: benefits and issues. In *Artificial intelligence, fintech, and financial inclusion* (pp. 1–10). CRC Press.

Ozkan, M., & Ozkan, O. (2020). Financial evaluation of mental accounting.

Panos, G. A., & Wilson, J. O. (2020). Financial literacy and responsible finance in the FinTech era: Capabilities and challenges. *European Journal of Finance, 26*(4-5), 297–301.

Patrício, L., Costa, L., Varela, L., & Avila, P. (2023). Sustainable implementation of robotic process automation based on a multi-objective mathematical model. *Sustainability (Basel), 15*(18), 15045. DOI: 10.3390/su152015045

Penfold, P. (2009). Learning through the world of second life—A hospitality and tourism experience. *Journal of Teaching in Travel & Tourism, 8*(2-3), 139–160. DOI: 10.1080/15313220802634224

Peng, K., Li, M., Huang, H., Wang, C., Wan, S., & Choo, K. K. R. (2021). Security challenges and opportunities for smart contracts in internet of things: A survey. *IEEE Internet of Things Journal, 8*(15), 12004–12020. https://www.ieee.org/publications/rights/index.html. DOI: 10.1109/JIOT.2021.3074544

Perez, A. J., & Zeadally, S. (2022). Secure and privacy-preserving crowdsensing using smart contracts: Issues and solutions. This manuscript is made available under the Elsevier user license. https://www.elsevier.com/open-access/userlicense/1.0/

Phoon, K., & Koh, F. (2017). Robo-advisors and wealth management. *Journal of Alternative Investments, 20*(3), 79–94. DOI: 10.3905/jai.2018.20.3.079

Pistoia, M., Ahmad, S. F., Ajagekar, A., Buts, A., Chakrabarti, S., Herman, D., . . . Yalovetzky, R. (2021, November). Quantum machine learning for finance ICCAD special session paper. In *2021 IEEE/ACM international conference on computer aided design (ICCAD)* (pp. 1-9). IEEE. DOI: 10.1109/ICCAD51958.2021.9643469

Plous, S. (1993). *The psychology of judgment and decision making*. Mcgraw-Hill Book Company.

Pomerol, J. C. (1997). Artificial intelligence and human decision making. *European Journal of Operational Research, 99*(116), 3–25. DOI: 10.1016/S0377-2217(96)00378-5

Portmann, C., & Renner, R. (2022). Security in quantum cryptography. *Reviews of Modern Physics, 94*(2), 025008. DOI: 10.1103/RevModPhys.94.025008

Prete, A. L. (2022). Digital and financial literacy as determinants of digital payments and personal finance. *Economics Letters, 213*, 110378.

Pretz, K. (2013). The Next Evolution of the Internet. *[cited 2013 May 20]; available from*http://theinstitute.ieee.org/technology-focus/technology-topic/the-next-evolution-of-the-internet

Protocol, T. (2022). *Toucan's decentralized carbon market: Using blockchain to enhance transparency in carbon trading*. Retrieved from https://toucan.earth

Purba, J. T., Samuel, S., & Budiono, S. (2021). *Collaboration of digital payment usage decision in COVID-19 pandemic situation: Evidence from Indonesia*. International Journal of Data and Network Science., DOI: 10.5267/j.ijdns.2021.8.012

Puschmann, T., Hoffmann, C. H., & Khmarskyi, V. (2020). How green fintech can alleviate the impact of climate change—The case of Switzerland. *Sustainability (Basel), 12*(24), 10691. Advance online publication. DOI: 10.3390/su122410691

PwC Germany. (2019). *PwC*. https://www.pwc.de/

Qi, Y., & Xiao, J. (2018). Fintech: AI powers financial services to improve people's lives. *Communications of the ACM, 61*(11), 65–69. DOI: 10.1145/3239550

Quach, S., Thaichon, P., Martin, K. D., Weaven, S., & Palmatier, R. W. (2022). Digital technologies: Tensions in privacy and data. *Journal of the Academy of Marketing Science, 50*(6), 1299–1323. DOI: 10.1007/s11747-022-00845-y PMID: 35281634

Quddoos, M. U., Rafique, A., Kalim, U., & Sheikh, M. R. (2020). Impact of behavioral biases on investment performance in Pakistan: The moderating role of financial literacy. *Journal of Accounting and Finance in Emerging Economies, 6*(4), 1199–1205. DOI: 10.26710/jafee.v6i4.1512

Rabbani, M. R., Abdulla, Y., Basahr, A., Khan, S., & Moh'd Ali, M. A. (2020, November). Embracing of Fintech in Islamic Finance in the post COVID era. In *2020 international conference on decision aid sciences and application (DASA)* (pp. 1230-1234). IEEE DOI: 10.1109/DASA51403.2020.9317196

Ramelli, S., & Wagner, A. (2020). What the stock market tells us about the consequences of COVID-19. *Mitigating the COVID Economic Crisis: Act Fast and Do Whatever, 63*.

Ramphul, K., Ramphul, Y., Park, Y., Lohana, P., Dhillon, B. K., & Sombans, S. (2021). A comprehensive review and update on severe acute respiratory syndrome coronavirus 2 (SARS-CoV-2) and Coronavirus disease 2019 (COVID-19): What do we know now in 2021? *Archives of Medical Sciences. Atherosclerotic Diseases*, *6*(1), 5–13. DOI: 10.5114/amsad.2021.105065 PMID: 34027207

Rapal, H. (2024). Smart contracts and regulatory compliance: Navigating the legal landscape. This manuscript is made available under the Legitt user license. https://legittai.com/

Rashata, H. (2022). Investors' Behavior in the Pakistan Financial Market during the COVID-19 Pandemic. *Available atSSRN* 4013498. DOI: 10.2139/ssrn.4013498

Reis, L. (2022). How Can Compliance Steer Companies to Deliver on ESG Goals? In *The Palgrave Handbook of ESG and Corporate Governance*. DOI: 10.1007/978-3-030-99468-6_16

Renduchintala, T., Alfauri, H., Yang, Z., Pietro, R. D., & Jain, R. (2022). A survey of blockchain applications in the fintech sector. *Journal of Open Innovation*, *8*(4), 185. DOI: 10.3390/joitmc8040185

Ren, J. (2021). Research on financial investment decision based on artificial intelligence algorithm. *IEEE Sensors Journal*, *21*(22), 25190–25197. DOI: 10.1109/JSEN.2021.3104038

Ren, X., Zeng, G., & Zhao, Y. (2023). Digital finance and corporate ESG performance: Empirical evidence from listed companies in China. *Pacific-Basin Finance Journal*, *79*, 102019. https://doi.org/https://doi.org/10.1016/j.pacfin.2023.102019. DOI: 10.1016/j.pacfin.2023.102019

Riaz, S., Ahmed, R., Parkash, R., & Ahmad, M. J. (2020). Determinants of stock market investors' behavior in COVID-19: A study on the Pakistan Stock Exchange.

Ribeiro, J., Lima, R., Eckhardt, T., & Paiva, S. (2021). Robotic process automation and artificial intelligence in Industry 4.0: A literature review. *Procedia Computer Science*, *181*, 51–58. DOI: 10.1016/j.procs.2021.01.104

Ritter, J. R. (2003). Behavioral finance. *Pacific-Basin Finance Journal, 11*(4), 429–437. DOI: 10.1016/S0927-538X(03)00048-9

Rodgers, W., Murray, J. M., Stefanidis, A., Degbey, W. Y., & Tarba, S. Y. (2023). An artificial intelligence algorithmic approach to ethical decision-making in human resource management processes. *Human Resource Management Review, 33*(1), 100925. DOI: 10.1016/j.hrmr.2022.100925

Rodrigo, R. (2023). Impact of robotic process automation (RPA) implementation in banking sector of South Asian countries. DOI: 10.13140/RG.2.2.20867.27680

Rogers, E. M. (1995). *Diffusion of innovations* (4th ed.). New York Free Press.

Ross, J. W., Beath, C. M., & Sebastian, I. M. (2017). How to develop a great digital strategy. *MIT Sloan Management Review*, *58*(2), 7.

Roszkowska, P. (2020). Fintech in financial reporting and audit for fraud prevention and safeguarding equity investments. *Journal of Accounting & Organizational Change, Advance online publication.*

Roy, S., Arefin, S. R., & Mallik, A. (2023). How Volatility and Herding of the Stock Markets in the Oceania Region Influence Investors and Policymakers: A Sector-Wise Exploration in Pre and Post-COVID Period. *International Journal of Economics and Finance*, *15*(1), 24. DOI: 10.5539/ijef.v15n1p24

Ruiz-Real, J. L., Uribe-Toril, J., Torres, J. A., & De Pablo, J. (2021). Artificial intelligence in business and economics research: Trends and future. *Journal of Business Economics and Management*, *22*(1), 98–117. DOI: 10.3846/jbem.2020.13641

Rumiński, D., Maik, M., & Walczak, K. (2019). Visualizing Financial Stock Data within an Augmented Reality Trading Environment. *Acta Polytechnica Hungarica*, *16*(6), 223–239. DOI: 10.12700/APH.16.6.2019.6.14

Rutschi, C., & Dibbern, J. (2020). Towards a framework of implementing software robots: Transforming human-executed routines into machines. *The Data Base for Advances in Information Systems*, *51*(2), 104–128. DOI: 10.1145/3380799.3380808

Saba, I., Kouser, R., & Chaudhry, I. S. (2019). FinTech and Islamic finance-challenges and opportunities. *Review of Economics and Development Studies*, *5*(4), 581–890. DOI: 10.26710/reads.v5i4.887

Sabir, S. A., Mohammad, H. B., & Shahar, H. B. K. (2019). The role of overconfidence and past investment experience in herding behaviour with a moderating effect of financial literacy: Evidence from Pakistan stock exchange. *Asian Economic and Financial Review*, *9*(4), 480–490. DOI: 10.18488/journal.aefr.2019.94.480.490

Safdar, N. M., Banja, J. D., & Meltzer, C. C. (2020). Ethical considerations in artificial intelligence. *European Journal of Radiology*, *122*, 108768. DOI: 10.1016/j.ejrad.2019.108768 PMID: 31786504

Samuel, D. (1996). Investigation of ancient Egyptian baking and brewing methods by correlative microscopy. *Science*, *273*(5274), 488–490. DOI: 10.1126/science.273.5274.488 PMID: 8662535

Samuel, J. (2017). Information token driven machine learning for electronic markets: Performance effects in behavioral financial big data analytics. *JISTEM-Journal of Information Systems and Technology Management, 14*, 371-383.

Sang, Y., Xie, M., Bai, X., & Guo, F. (2024). Does natural resource dependence influence the impact of financial technologies on corporate ESG and digital governance in China's listed enterprises? *Resources Policy*, *91*, 104948. https://doi.org/https://doi.org/10.1016/j.resourpol.2024.104948. DOI: 10.1016/j.resourpol.2024.104948

Santos, F., Pereira, R., & Braga de Vasconcelos, J. (2019). Toward robotic process automation implementation: An end-to-end perspective. *Business Process Management Journal*, *26*(2), 405–420. Advance online publication. DOI: 10.1108/BPMJ-12-2018-0380

Sarika, P., & Vasantha, S. (2019). Impact of mobile wallets on cashless transaction. *Int. J. Recent Technol. Eng*, *7*(6), 1164–1171.

Saunders, M. N., Lewis, P., Thornhill, A., & Bristow, A. (2015). Understanding research philosophy and approaches to theory development. In: Saunders, Mark N. K.; Lewis, Philip and Thornhill, Adrian eds. Research Methods for Business Students. Harlow: Pearson Education, 122–161

Saunders, M., Lewis, P. & Thornhill, A. (2007). Research methods. Business Students 4th edition Pearson Education Limited, England, 1-268.

Saunders, M., Lewis, P., & Thornhill, A. (2007). Research methods. *Business Students 4th edition Pearson Education Limited, England, 6*(3), 1-268

Saunders, M. N. K., Lewis, P., Thornhill, A., & Bristow, A. (2015). *Understanding research philosophies and approaches: Research methods for business students.* Pearson.

Saunders, M. N., Lewis, P., Thornhill, A., & Bristow, A. (2015). Understanding research philosophy and approaches to theory development. In Saunders, M. N. K., Lewis, P., & Thornhill, A. (Eds.), *Research Methods for Business Students* (pp. 122–161). Pearson Education.

Saunders, M., Lewis, P., & Thornhill, A. (2007). *Research methods. Business Students* (4th ed.). Pearson Education Limited.

Sawwalakhe, R., Arora, S., & Singh, T. P. (2023). Opportunities and Challenges for Artificial Intelligence and Machine Learning Applications in the Finance Sector. Advanced Machine Learning Algorithms for Complex Financial Applications, 1-17.

Schommer, M., Richter, A., & Karna, A. (2019). Does the Diversification–Firm Performance Relationship Change Over Time? A Meta-Analytical Review. *Journal of Management Studies, 56*(1), 270–298. Advance online publication. DOI: 10.1111/joms.12393

Schroeder, K., Ajdadilish, B., Henkel, A. P., & Calero Valdez, A. (2020, April). Evaluation of a financial portfolio visualization using computer displays and mixed reality devices with domain experts. In *Proceedings of the 2020 CHI Conference on Human Factors in Computing Systems* (pp. 1-9). DOI: 10.1145/3313831.3376556

Seth, D., Gupta, M., & Singh, B. J. (2022). A Study to Analyse the Impact of Using the Metaverse in the Banking Industry to Augment Performance in a Competitive Environment. In *Applying Metalytics to Measure Customer Experience in the Metaverse* (pp. 9–16). IGI Global. DOI: 10.4018/978-1-6684-6133-4.ch002

Shankar, A., & Datta, B. K. (2018). Factors Affecting Mobile Payment Adoption Intention: An Indian Perspective. *Global Business Review, 19*(3_suppl), S72–S89. DOI: 10.1177/0972150918757870

Shanmuganathan, M. (2020). Behavioural finance in an era of artificial intelligence: Longitudinal case study of robo-advisors in investment decisions. *Journal of Behavioral and Experimental Finance, 27*, 100297. DOI: 10.1016/j.jbef.2020.100297

Shawat, R., Wassef, A., & Badawy, H. (2023). Artificial Intelligence in Financial Services: Advantages and Disadvantages. In Artificial Intelligence for Capital Markets (pp. 28-40). Chapman and Hall/CRC.

Shefrin, H., & Statman, M. (2011). Behavioral finance in the financial crisis: market efficiency, Minsky, and Keynes. *Santa Clara University, November.*

Shehab, A. R. (2021). Environmental, social and governance (ESG) considerations in real estate investments. Impact of environmental performance disclosure, activities and score on financial performance of SIIQ.

Shepherd, D. A., Williams, T. A., & Patzelt, H. (2015). Thinking about entrepreneurial decision making: Review and research agenda. *Journal of Management, 41*(1), 11–46. DOI: 10.1177/0149206314541153

Sheth, J. N., Jain, V., Roy, G., & Chakraborty, A. (2022). AI-driven banking services: The next frontier for a personalised experience in the emerging market. *International Journal of Bank Marketing*, *40*(6), 1248–1271.

Shiller, R. J. (2015). Irrational exuberance. In *Irrational exuberance*. Princeton university press.

Shofawati, A. (2019). The role of digital finance to strengthen financial inclusion and the growth of SME in Indonesia. *KnE Social Sciences*, 389-407.

Showkat, M., Nagina, R., Nori, U., Baba, M. A., & Shah, M. A. (2024). Empowering women in the digital age: Can digital financial services fulfil the promise of financial autonomy and gender equality in the attainment of Sustainable Development Goal 5? *Cogent Economics & Finance*, *12*(1), 2342459. DOI: 10.1080/23322039.2024.2342459

Siew Bee, T., & Ying, Y. K. (2021). An examination of determinants for e-wallet adoption in Malaysia: a combined approach. F1000Research. https://doi.org/DOI: 10.12688/f1000research.73402.1

Simon, H. A. (1947), Administrative Behavior, The Macmillan Company, New York, NY (2nd ed. published in 1957).

Singh, V., Chen, S. S., Singhania, M., Nanavati, B., & Gupta, A. (2022). How are reinforcement learning and deep learning algorithms used for big data based decision making in financial

Singh, S. (2012). Investor irrationality and self-defeating behavior: Insights from behavioral finance. *Journal of Global Business Management*, *8*(1), 116.

Siraji, M. (2019). Heuristics bias and investment performance: Does age matter? evidence from Colombo stock exchange. *Asian Journal of Economics. Business and Accounting*, *12*(4), 1–14.

Sochi, M. H. (2018). Behavioral factors influencing investment decision of the retail investors of Dhaka stock exchange: An empirical study. *Cost and Management*, *46*(1), 20–29.

Soegoto, E. S., Purna, S., & Sumitra, T. P. (2021). Mobile Payment Technology for Future Transaction. *Jurnal Ilmiah Sistem Informasi*, *1*(2), 86–92. DOI: 10.46306/sm.v1i2.11

Sohangir, S., Wang, D., Pomeranets, A., & Khoshgoftaar, T. M. (2018). Big Data: Deep Learning for financial sentiment analysis. *Journal of Big Data*, *5*(1), 1–25.

Sohrabi, C., Alsafi, Z., O'neill, N., Khan, M., Kerwan, A., Al-Jabir, A., Iosifidis, C., & Agha, R. (2020). World Health Organization declares global emergency: A review of the 2019 novel coronavirus (COVID-19). *International Journal of Surgery*, *76*, 71–76. DOI: 10.1016/j.ijsu.2020.02.034 PMID: 32112977

Song, L., & Zhou, Y. (2020). The COVID-19 pandemic and its impact on the global economy: What does it take to turn crisis into opportunity? *China & World Economy*, *28*(4), 1–25. DOI: 10.1111/cwe.12349

Soto-Acosta, P. (2020). COVID-19 pandemic: Shifting digital transformation to a high-speed gear. *Information Systems Management*, *37*(4), 260–266. DOI: 10.1080/10580530.2020.1814461

Sousa, M. J., & Rocha, Á. (2019). Digital learning: Developing skills for digital transformation of organizations. *Future Generation Computer Systems*, *91*, 327–334. DOI: 10.1016/j.future.2018.08.048

Šperka, R., & Halaška, M. (2023). The performance assessment framework (PPA-FR) for RPA implementation in a loan application process using process mining. *Information Systems and e-Business Management*, *21*(2), 277–321. DOI: 10.1007/s10257-022-00602-2

Srivastava, D. A. (2021). Central banking, financial stability and Macro-Prudential policy. *CAB Calling*, *44*(1&2).

Stewart, H., & Jürjens, J. (2018). Data security and consumer trust in FinTech innovation in Germany. *Information and Computer Security*, *26*(1), 109–128. DOI: 10.1108/ICS-06-2017-0039

Subrahmanyam, A. (2008). Behavioural finance: A review and synthesis. *European Financial Management*, *14*(1), 12–29. DOI: 10.1111/j.1468-036X.2007.00415.x

Su, K. W., Chen, S. C., Lin, P. H., & Hsieh, C. I. (2020). Evaluating the user interface and experience of VR in the electronic commerce environment: A hybrid approach. *Virtual Reality (Waltham Cross)*, *24*(2), 241–254. DOI: 10.1007/s10055-019-00394-w

Sumathi, N., & Jeyalakshmi, A. (2022). Implementing robotic process automation to improve operational efficiency in the health-care sector. *International Journal of Health Sciences*, *6*(S1), 9666–9672. Advance online publication. DOI: 10.53730/ijhs.v6nS1.7256

Sun, W., Dedahanov, A., Shin, H., & Li, W. (2021). Using extended complexity theory to test SMEs' adoption of Blockchain-based loan system. *PLoS One*, *16*(2), 16. DOI: 10.1371/journal.pone.0245964 PMID: 33544745

Suresh Babu, C. V. & Abhinaba Pal. (2023). Securing Decentralized Finance Through Blockchain Technologies. In R. Thanigaivelan, S. Kaliappan, & C. Jegadheesan (Eds.), *Cyber-Physical Systems and Supporting Technologies for Industrial Automation* (pp. 351-372). IGI Global. https://doi.org/DOI: 10.4018/978-1-6684-9267-3.ch020

Suresh Babu, C. V. & Sanjai Das (2023). Impact of Blockchain Technology on the Stock Market. In K. Mehta, R. Sharma, & P. Yu (Eds.), *Revolutionizing Financial Services and Markets Through FinTech and Blockchain* (pp. 44-59). IGI Global. https://doi.org/DOI: 10.4018/978-1-6684-8624-5.ch004

SureshBabu. C. V., Sudhir Manoharan., L., G. K., & V., S. K. (2024). Application of Support Vector Machine Algorithm in Automated Lending Protocols for Decentralized Finance Platforms. In L. Vardari & I. Qabrati (Eds.), Decentralized Finance and Tokenization in FinTech (pp. 1-20). IGI Global. https://doi.org/DOI: 10.4018/979-8-3693-3346-4.ch001

Suryono, R. R., Budi, I., & Purwandari, B. (2020). Challenges and trends of financial technology (Fintech): A systematic literature review. *Information (Basel)*, *11*(12), 590. DOI: 10.3390/info11120590

Svahn, F., Mathiassen, L., Lindgren, R., & Kane, G. C. (2017). Mastering the digital innovation challenge. *MIT Sloan Management Review*, *58*(3), 14.

Syed, M., & McLean, K. C. (2021). Disentangling paradigm and method can help bring qualitative research to post-positivist psychology and address the generalizability crisis. Behavioral &amp. *Brain Sciences*, *45*, 58–60. DOI: 10.1017/S0140525X21000431 PMID: 35139943

Talasila, S. D. (2024). AI-Driven Personal Finance Management: Revolutionizing Budgeting and Financial Planning. *International Research Journal of Engineering and Technology*, *11*(7), 397–400.

Tang, C. P., Huang, T. C. K., & Wang, S. T. (2018). The impact of Internet of things implementation on firm performance. *Telematics and Informatics*, *35*(7), 2038–2053. DOI: 10.1016/j.tele.2018.07.007

Tang, X., & Shi, Z. (2024). Automation and fraud detection in sustainable finance: The role of AI and DeFi smart contracts. *Computational Economics*, *49*(2), 456–470. DOI: 10.1007/s10614-023-09987-5

Tan, L., Chiang, T. C., Mason, J. R., & Nelling, E. (2008). Herding behavior in Chinese stock markets: An examination of A and B shares. *Pacific-Basin Finance Journal*, *16*(1-2), 61–77. DOI: 10.1016/j.pacfin.2007.04.004

Tapscott, D. (2010). Grown up digital. How the net generation is changing your world. *International Journal of Market Research, 52*(1), 139–140. DOI: 10.2501/S1470785310201119

Tapscott, D., & Tapscott, A. (2016). *Blockchain Revolution: How the Technology Behind Bitcoin Is Changing Money, Business, and the World*. Penguin.

Tawiah, B., & Keefe, M. O. C. (2022). Financing a corporate venture capital program. *Journal of Banking & Finance, 135*, 106364. DOI: 10.1016/j.jbankfin.2021.106364

Tetlock, P. C. (2007). Giving content to investor sentiment: The role of media in the stock market. *The Journal of Finance, 62*(3), 1139–1168. DOI: 10.1111/j.1540-6261.2007.01232.x

Tetlock, P. C. (2011). All the news that's fit to reprint: Do investors react to stale information? *Review of Financial Studies, 24*(5), 1481–1512. DOI: 10.1093/rfs/hhq141

Tetlock, P. C., Saar-Tsechansky, M., & Macskassy, S. (2008). More than words: Quantifying language to measure firms' fundamentals. *The Journal of Finance, 63*(3), 1437–1467. DOI: 10.1111/j.1540-6261.2008.01362.x

Thaler, R. H. (2015). *Misbehaving: The making of behavioral economics*. WW Norton & Company.

Thekkethil, M., Shukla, V., Beena, F., & Chopra, A. (2021). Robotic process automation in banking and finance sector for loan processing and fraud detection. In *2021 6th International Conference on Recent Innovations in Technology and Engineering (ICRITO)* (pp. 1–6). IEEE. DOI: 10.1109/ICRITO51393.2021.9596076

Thomson Reuters. (2014). Edited transcript: FB – Facebook M&A call to acquire oculus. In *Thomson Reuters Streetevents* (pp. 1–13). Thomson Reuters.

Thomson Reuters. (2022). *Thomson Reuters*. Retrieved May 18, 2024, from https://www.thomsonreuters.com/

Tian, J., Yu, L., Xue, R., Zhuang, S., & Shan, Y. (2022). Global low-carbon energy transition in the post-COVID-19 era. *Applied Energy, 307*, 118205. DOI: 10.1016/j.apenergy.2021.118205 PMID: 34840400

Ţiţan, A. G. (2015). The efficient market hypothesis: Review of specialized literature and empirical research. *Procedia Economics and Finance, 32*, 442–449. DOI: 10.1016/S2212-5671(15)01416-1

Tokic, D. (2018). BlackRock Robo-advisor 4.0: When artificial intelligence replaces human discretion. *Strategic Change, 27*(4), 285–290. DOI: 10.1002/jsc.2201

Torrente, M., Sousa, P., Hernández, R., Blanco, M., Calvo, V., Collazo, A., Guerreiro, G. R., Nuñez, B., Pimentão, J., Sánchez, J. C., Campos, M., Costabello, L., Novácek, V., Menasalvas, E., Vidal, M., & Provencio, M. (2022). An Artificial Intelligence-Based Tool for Data Analysis and Prognosis in Cancer Patients: Results from the Clarify Study. *Cancers (Basel), 14*(64041), 4041. DOI: 10.3390/cancers14164041 PMID: 36011034

Treacy, S., Adyanthaya, A., Kearny, C., Anand, J., O'Sullivan, K., & Xu, Y. (2023). From hype to reality: Navigating the challenges of RPA implementation. In *Proceedings of the 18th European Conference on Innovation and Entrepreneurship* (pp. 875–882). DOI: 10.34190/ecie.18.2.1721

Trippi, R. R., & Turban, E. (Eds.). (1992). *Neural networks in finance and investing: Using artificial intelligence to improve real world performance*. McGraw-Hill, Inc.

Trivedi, C., Rao, U., Parmar, K., Bhattacharya, P., & Tanwar, S.. (2024). A transformative shift towards Blockchain-based IoT environments: Consensus, smart contracts, and future directions. https://doi.org/DOI: 10.22541/au.170663514.49171896/v1

Trivers, R. (1991). Deceit^ ind Self-Deception The Relationship between Communication and Consciousness.

Tungsten Automation. (2023). *Tungsten Automation*. Retrieved May 21, 2024, from https://www.tungstenautomation.com/

Tvede, L. (1999). *The psychology of finance*. Wiley.

Tyagi, S., Reddy, G. C., Chandu, V., & Koteswararao, N.. (2022). Study of smart contracts. https://doi.org/DOI: 10.2139/ssrn.4376852

Uhl, M. W., & Rohner, P. (2018). Robo-advisors versus traditional investment advisors: An unequal game. *The Journal of Wealth Management, 21*(1), 44–50. DOI: 10.3905/jwm.2018.21.1.044

UiPath. (2021, 2022, 2023). *UiPath*. Retrieved May 20, 2024, from https://www.uipath.com/

Upadhyay, N., Upadhyay, S., Abed, S. S., & Dwivedi, Y. K. (2022). Consumer adoption of mobile payment services during COVID-19: Extending meta-UTAUT with perceived severity and self-efficacy. *International Journal of Bank Marketing, 40*(5), 960–991. Advance online publication. DOI: 10.1108/IJBM-06-2021-0262

Utama, A. N. B. (2023). Analysis of the Development of Financial Management Theory to Support Financial Research.

Vallino, J. (2002). *Introduction to augmented reality*. Rochester Institute of Technology.

Van Tulder, R., Rodrigues, S. B., Mirza, H., & Sexsmith, K. (2021). The UN's Sustainable Development Goals: Can multinational enterprises lead the Decade of Action? In *Journal of International Business Policy* (Vol. 4, Issue 1). DOI: 10.1057/s42214-020-00095-1

van Tulder, R. (2018). Business & The Sustainable Development Goals: A Framework for Effective Corporate Involvement. In *Rotterdam School of Management*. Erasmus University.

Venkatesh, V., & Davis, F. D. (2000). A theoretical extension of the technology acceptance model: Four longitudinal field studies. *Management Science*, *46*(2), 186–204. DOI: 10.1287/mnsc.46.2.186.11926

Venkatesh, V., Morris, M. G., Davis, G. B., & Davis, F. D. (2003). User acceptance of information technology: Toward a unified view. *Management Information Systems Quarterly*, *27*(3), 425–478. DOI: 10.2307/30036540

Venkatesh, V., Thong, J. Y., & Xu, X. (2016). Unified theory of acceptance and use of technology: A synthesis and the road ahead. *Journal of the Association for Information Systems*, *17*(5), 328–376. DOI: 10.17705/1jais.00428

Veuger, J. (2018). Trust in a viable real estate economy with disruption and blockchain. *Facilities*, *36*(1/2), 103–120. DOI: 10.1108/F-11-2017-0106

Vial, G. (2019). Understanding digital transformation: A review and a research agenda. *The Journal of Strategic Information Systems*, *28*(2), 118–144. DOI: 10.1016/j.jsis.2019.01.003

Vigliotti, M. G. (2021). What do we mean by smart contracts? Open challenges in smart contracts. *Frontiers in Blockchain*, *3*, 553671. DOI: 10.3389/fbloc.2020.553671

Vijai, C. (2019). Mobile wallet and its future in India. *Journal of Emerging Technologies and Innovative Research*, *6*(5), 574–580.

Vijai, C., Suriyalakshmi, S., & Elayaraja, M. (2020). The future of robotic process automation (RPA) in the banking sector for better customer experience. *Shanlax International Journal of Commerce*, *8*(3), 61–65. DOI: 10.34293/commerce.v8i2.1709

Villar, A., & Khan, N. (2021). Robotic process automation in banking industry: A case study on Deutsche Bank. *Journal of Banking and Financial Technology*, *5*(1). Advance online publication. DOI: 10.1007/s42786-021-00030-9

Vinayamoorthi, G., & Manickam, T. (2020). Consumer's Adoption of Digital Wallets With Special Reference to Bangalore City. *Management Science*, *8*(2), 108–113. DOI: 10.34293/management.v8i2.3429

Waheed, H., Ahmed, Z., Saleem, Q., Din, S. M. U., & Ahmed, B. (2020). The mediating role of risk perception in the relationship between financial literacy and investment decision. *International Journal of Innovation. Creativity and Change*, *14*(4), 112–131.

Waisi, M. (2020). Advantages and disadvantages of aI-based trading and investing versus traditional methods.

Wang, X., & Xu, F. (2022). The value of smart contract in trade finance. https://doi.org/DOI: 10.1287/msom.2022.1126

Wang, J., Cui, M., & Chang, L. (2023). Evaluating economic recovery by measuring the COVID-19 spillover impact on business practices: Evidence from Asian markets intermediaries. *Economic Change and Restructuring*, *56*(3), 1–22. DOI: 10.1007/s10644-023-09482-z

Wang, K. H., Kan, J. M., Jiang, C. F., & Su, C. W. (2022). Is geopolitical risk powerful enough to affect carbon dioxide emissions? Evidence from China. *Sustainability (Basel)*, *14*(13), 7867. DOI: 10.3390/su14137867

Wang, R., Mirza, N., Vasbieva, D. G., Abbas, Q., & Xiong, D. (2020). The nexus of carbon emissions, financial development, renewable energy consumption, and technological innovation: What should be the priorities in light of COP 21 Agreements? *Journal of Environmental Management*, *271*, 111027. Advance online publication. DOI: 10.1016/j.jenvman.2020.111027 PMID: 32778307

Ward, O., & Rochemont, S. (2019). Understanding central bank digital currencies (CBDC). *Institute and Faculty of Actuaries*, 1-52.

Watson, K., & White, S. (2022). Greenwashing in sustainable finance: A challenge for ESG compliance. *Journal of Business Ethics*, *180*(1), 87–98. DOI: 10.1007/s10551-021-04928-7

Waweru, N. M., Munyoki, E., & Uliana, E. (2008). The effects of behavioural factors in investment decision-making: a survey of institutional investors operating at the Nairobi Stock Exchange. *International Journal of business and emerging markets*, *1*(1), 24-41.

Weber, P., Carl, K. V., & Hinz, O. (2023). Applications of Explainable Artificial Intelligence in Finance—a systematic review of Finance, Information Systems, and Computer Science literature. Management Review Quarterly, 1-41.

Wen, S., Li, J., Huang, C., & Zhu, X. (2023). Extreme risk spillovers among traditional financial and FinTech institutions: A complex network perspective. *The Quarterly Review of Economics and Finance*, *88*, 190–202.

Williams, C. P. (2010). *Explorations in quantum computing*. Springer Science & Business Media.

Williams, P., & Hobson, J. P. (1995). Virtual reality and tourism: Fact or fantasy? *Tourism Management*, *16*(6), 423–427. DOI: 10.1016/0261-5177(95)00050-X

Wilson, J. O. S., & Molyneux, P. (Eds.). (2019). *The Oxford Handbook of Banking*. Oxford University Press.

Wójcik, D., & Ioannou, S. (2020). COVID-19 and finance: Market developments so far and potential impacts on the financial sector and centres. *Tijdschrift voor Economische en Sociale Geografie*, *111*(3), 387–400. DOI: 10.1111/tesg.12434 PMID: 32836484

World Health Organization. (2020). World health statistics 2020.

Wu, M., Subramaniam, G., Li, Z., & Gao, X. (2025). Using AI Technology to Enhance Data-Driven Decision-Making in the Financial Sector. Artificial Intelligence-Enabled Businesses: How to Develop Strategies for Innovation, 187-207.

Xiao, F., & Ke, J. (2021). Pricing, management and decision-making of financial markets with artificial intelligence: Introduction to the issue. *Financial Innovation*, *7*(1), 1–3. DOI: 10.1186/s40854-021-00302-9 PMID: 35024295

Xiao, J. J., & Porto, N. (2022). Financial capability and wellbeing of vulnerable consumers. *The Journal of Consumer Affairs*, *56*(2), 1004–1018.

Xie, B., Liu, H., Alghofaili, R., Zhang, Y., Jiang, Y., Lobo, F. D., Li, C., Li, W., Huang, H., Akdere, M., Mousas, C., & Yu, L. F. (2021). A review on virtual reality skill training applications. *Frontiers in Virtual Reality*, *2*, 645153. DOI: 10.3389/frvir.2021.645153

Xie, H., Li, Q., & Zhang, Y. (2023). AI-powered verification of carbon credits: Leveraging IoT and blockchain technologies. *Environmental Science & Technology*, *57*(3), 1212–1223. DOI: 10.1021/acs.est.2c05565

Xu, Z., Elomri, A., Kerbache, L., & El Omri, A. (2020). Impacts of COVID-19 on global supply chains: Facts and perspectives. *IEEE Engineering Management Review*, *48*(3), 153–166. DOI: 10.1109/EMR.2020.3018420

Yagol, P., Ramos, F., Trilles, S., Torres-Sospedra, J., & Perales, F. J. (2018). New trends in using augmented reality apps for smart city contexts. *ISPRS International Journal of Geo-Information*, *7*(12), 478. DOI: 10.3390/ijgi7120478

Yang, J., & Hui, N. (2024). How digital finance affects the sustainability of corporate green innovation. *Finance Research Letters*, *63*, 105314. https://doi.org/https://doi.org/10.1016/j.frl.2024.105314. DOI: 10.1016/j.frl.2024.105314

Yang, W., Wang, S., Sahri, N. M., Karie, N. M., Ahmed, M., & Valli, C. (2021). Biometrics for internet-of-things security: A review. *Sensors (Basel)*, *21*(18), 6163. DOI: 10.3390/s21186163 PMID: 34577370

Yao, M. (2024). RPA technology enables highly automated development of corporate financial accounting processes. *Applied Mathematics and Nonlinear Sciences*, *9*(1), 1–13. DOI: 10.2478/amns-2024-0541

Yarlagadda, R. T. (2018). The RPA and AI automation. *International Journal of Creative Research Thoughts (IJCRT), ISSN*, 2320-2882.

Yilmaz, N. K., & Hazar, H. B. (2019). The rise of internet of things (IoT) and its applications in finance and accounting. *PressAcademia Procedia*, *10*(1), 32–35. DOI: 10.17261/Pressacademia.2019.1139

Yovcheva, Z., Buhalis, D., & Gatzidis, C. (2012). Smartphone augmented reality applications for tourism. [ertr]. *Ereview of Tourism Research*, *10*(2), 63–66.

Yung, R., & Khoo-Lattimore, C. (2019). New realities: A systematic literature review on virtual reality and augmented reality in tourism research. *Current Issues in Tourism*, *22*(17), 2056–2081. DOI: 10.1080/13683500.2017.1417359

Zahera, S. A., & Bansal, R. (2018). Do investors exhibit behavioral biases in investment decision making? A systematic review. *Qualitative Research in Financial Markets*, *10*(2), 210–251. DOI: 10.1108/QRFM-04-2017-0028

Zaremba, A., & Demir, E. (2023). ChatGPT: Unlocking the future of NLP in finance. *Available atSSRN* 4323643.

Zarifis, A., & Cheng, X. (2022). A model of trust in Fintech and trust in Insurtech: How Artificial Intelligence and the context influence it. *Journal of Behavioral and Experimental Finance*, *36*, 100739.

Zengler, T. J., & Zheng, Z. (2020). Application of AI in Financial Services: Opportunities, Challenges, and Regulatory Implications. *Journal of Financial Regulation and Compliance*, *28*(3), 285–303. DOI: 10.1108/JFRC-02-2020-0022

Zetzsche, D. A., Buckley, R. P., & Arner, D. W. (2019). FinTech for Financial Inclusion: Driving Sustainable Growth. *Journal of Finance, first edit*(February).

Zhang, D. (2023). Can digital finance empowerment reduce extreme ESG hypocrisy resistance to improve green innovation? *Energy Economics*, *125*, 106756. Advance online publication. DOI: 10.1016/j.eneco.2023.106756

Zhao, M., & Shi, L. (2021). Carbon market transparency through AI-driven blockchain solutions. *Journal of Cleaner Production*, *280*, 124618. DOI: 10.1016/j.jclepro.2020.124618

Zheng, X. L., Zhu, M. Y., Li, Q. B., Chen, C. C., & Tan, Y. C. (2019). FinBrain: When finance meets AI 2.0. *Frontiers of Information Technology & Electronic Engineering*, *20*(7), 914–924.

Zheng, Z., Xie, S., Dai, H. N., Chen, W., Chen, X., Weng, J., & Imran, M.. (2019). An overview on smart contracts: Challenges, advances and platforms. https://arxiv.org/abs/1912.10370

Zhou, H., Fard, A. M., & Makanju, A. (2022). The State of Ethereum Smart Contracts Security: Vulnerabilities, Countermeasures, and Tool Support. *Journal of Cybersecurity and Privacy.*, *2022*(2), 358–378. DOI: 10.3390/jcp2020019

Zhou, X., Tang, X., & Zhang, R. (2020). Impact of green finance on economic development and environmental quality: A study based on provincial panel data from China. *Environmental Science and Pollution Research International*, *27*(16), 19915–19932. Advance online publication. DOI: 10.1007/s11356-020-08383-2 PMID: 32232752

Zhu, X., Song, B., Ni, Y., Ren, Y., Li, R., Zhu, X., ... & Li, R. (2016). Digital finance—from traditional finance to digital and internet finance. Business Trends in the Digital Era: Evolution of Theories and Applications, 161-190.

Zinovyeva, E., Reule, R. C. G., & Hardle, W. K., et al. (2021). Understanding smart contracts: Hype or hope.

About the Contributors

Muhammad Ali is an active academic and finance lecturer with significant teaching and banking sector experience. He has held prestigious teaching positions at various renowned institutions and holds advanced degrees, including an MBA and a PhD in Finance from reputable universities. Dr. Ali's teaching portfolio spans across critical areas such as Personal Finance, Bank Management, Business Finance, Behavioral Finance, Risk Management, Corporate Finance, and Islamic Banking. He has supervised numerous undergraduate and graduate students and possesses extensive research expertise in Green Finance, Corporate Finance, Financial Inclusion, Fintech, Behavioral Finance, and Islamic Banking. Dr. Ali is adept in working with primary and secondary datasets and proficient in statistical tools including E-views, STATA, Smart PLS, and SPSS. He has an impressive publication record, having authored multiple research articles and presented at international conferences. Dr. Ali is also experienced in organizing international conferences and workshops. His editorial roles are extensive, serving as Guest Editor for leading journals such as Energy Efficiency Journal (Springer), International Journal of Social Economics (Emerald), International Journal of Educational Management, and Journal of Agribusiness in Developing and Emerging Economies (Emerald). Additionally, he has edited notable books with Emerald Publishing and IGI Publishing on topics such as Green Finance, Financial Inclusion, Corporate Governance, and Sustainability. Dr. Ali currently holds various prominent editorial roles, including Associate Editor for the International Journal of Social Economics and Editor for the Arab Gulf Journal of Scientific Research. His dedication to bridging the gap between industry and academia is further highlighted by his role as an Advisory Board Member for Softech360 Sdn Bhd, where he contributes to sustainability projects. d2717957-227b-4108-ba7a-2d62faec8587)

Syed Ali Raza is a distinguished academician and researcher associated with a leading multidisciplinary university in Pakistan. As a Professor and Director of

Academics, Research & Publications, he has played a pivotal role in transforming the university into a research-oriented institution. His scholarly excellence in the fields of Accounting, Finance, Economics, and Business Management, has earned him recognition as one of Asia's Top 15 Scientists in Accounting and Finance and has consistently been recognized as one of the world's top 2% scientists in the field of Business & Management, according to the rankings compiled by Stanford University. His impactful research work, published in esteemed journals, has garnered over 8,500 citations. Under his leadership, the university has substantially increased its research output, with an annual count of 356 Scopus-indexed publications and a cumulative total of 1,349 publications in the past five years. This outstanding research has amassed a citation count of 15,439. Furthermore, Dr. Raza has successfully secured research funding amounting to approximately PKR Rs. 65 million. He has also been invited as a keynote speaker at multiple national and international conferences, seminars, and workshops. He is also the founder of 4 nationally recognized research journals and serves as an editor and reviewer for many reputed journals across the globe. Beyond research, Prof. Dr. Raza has implemented innovative strategies as an academic administrator. He has developed curriculum aligned with educational standards, implemented faculty development programs, and integrated technology into the learning environment. His vision for internationalization has led to partnerships with renowned universities, providing global learning opportunities. He is a visiting professor at Roma Tre University, Italy and an honorary visiting professor at UCSI University, Malaysia. He is an actively member of the Prime Minister of Pakistan's Ehsaas Program, serves on many academic committees, editorial boards, and professional organizations, and has received multiple awards for his exceptional achievements.

Chin Hong Puah is a Professor cum Chief Executive Officer at the UNIMAS Business School, Universiti Malaysia Sarawak (UNIMAS). He obtained his PhD degree majoring in Financial Economics. Puah has been actively involved in Financial Economics, Macroeconomics and Business Economics areas in the past 20 years. Until now, he has received more than 60 research grants and consultancy projects totaling amount more than RM12 million. He has supervised more than 100 postgraduate students at Master and PhD levels (including CMBA students). At present, he has published more than 140 refereed journal articles in various international journals. Based on his excellent performance, he had received some significant academic awards from UNIMAS which include Best Researcher Award, Young Researcher Award, Anugerah Ahli Akademik Harapan, Highest Impact Factor Journal Article Award (Social Sciences Category) and Best Teaching Award. In addition, he also received several Best Paper Awards and Gold Medal Awards in international conferences and research exhibitions..

***

Magelesh G is affiliated with St. Joseph's College of Engineering. Finance is his primary area of interest, and his work has been prominently featured in numerous esteemed journals, reflecting his significant contributions to the field. He has garnered respect and recognition from the academic community.

K. Balasubramanian is an Assistant Professor specializing in finance, in the department of management studies, Jain University, (Deemed to be University), Kochi Campus, bringing a wealth of expertise to the field. With a Doctorate in Entrepreneurial Finance. He has made significant contributions to the academic community. Drawing on three years of industrial experience and over 10 years of teaching experience. His areas of specialization are financial management, security analysis and portfolio management, Fintech and Risk management. He has published several research articles in scholarly research publications such as Scopus, UGC Care, InderScience etc., He offers a unique blend of practical and theoretical knowledge in the realm of finance. With a passion for research and a dedication to excellence in education, continues to inspire and empower students in their pursuit of financial knowledge and success.

M.Ganesan Alias Kanagaraj, Assistant Professor (Senior Grade), Department of Management Studies, Saveetha Engineering College has been in academics for 15 years and is passionate about teaching, research and learning. He has completed his Ph.D in Management in Manonmaniam Sundaranar University, Tirunelveli, Tamilnadu. His teaching interests focus on the areas of Accounting for Management, Security Analysis and Portfolio Management, Financial Management, International Trade Finance and Total Quality Management. He has participated over 15 FDPs, presented 15 research papers in International Conferences, 10 papers in national conferences, published 20 research papers in International Referred Journals.

Surenthran David is an Assistant Professor at St. Joseph's College of Engineering in Chennai, India. His academic contributions include publications in both Scopus and UGC CARE indexed journals, reflecting his active engagement in research and scholarly activities. In addition to his academic endeavors, he has also shared his expertise as a resource person in the field of Finance, contributing to the development and dissemination of knowledge in this crucial area.

Amudha R is an Associate Professor in School of Management, SASTRA Deemed To Be University, Thanjavur, Tamilnadu, India. She is a fellow member in Institute of Cost Accountants of India, Kolkata, India and a doctorate in the area of marketing from SASTRA Deemed To Be University. She has 34 years of academic experience and 20 years of research experience. She has published 85 research papers in Scopus indexed journals and more than 30 papers in national and international indexed peer referred journals. She has also published case studies in case centre organisation, UK and reputed journals. Her area of specialization is marketing, accounting and finance.

C.V. Suresh Babu is a pioneer in content development. A true entrepreneur, he founded Anniyappa Publications, a company that is highly active in publishing books related to Computer Science and Management. Dr. C.V. Suresh Babu has also ventured into SB Institute, a center for knowledge transfer. He holds a Ph.D. in Engineering Education from the National Institute of Technical Teachers Training & Research in Chennai, along with seven master's degrees in various disciplines such as Engineering, Computer Applications, Management, Commerce, Economics, Psychology, Law, and Education. Additionally, he has UGC-NET/SET qualifications in the fields of Computer Science, Management, Commerce, and Education. Currently, Dr. C.V. Suresh Babu is a Professor in the Department of Information Technology at the School of Computing Science, Hindustan Institute of Technology and Science (Hindustan University) in Padur, Chennai, Tamil Nadu, India.

Muhammad Nawaz Tunio is a Ph.D. in the Doctoral track Entrepreneurship, Innovation, and Economic Development, from Alpen Adria University, Klagenfurt, Austria on the government scholarship of Higher Education Commission of Pakistan. He was awarded a one-month young scientist research fellowship for Kent State University, Ohio, USA under the mentorship of Professor Robert D. Hisrich by the Alpen Adria University, Klagenfurt. He has few publications in the research areas of his interest. his research interest is entrepreneurship, self-employment, ICT, and youth. He has presented papers at international conferences and attended research workshops.

Index

A

B

C

D

E

F

H

I

M

www.ingramcontent.com/pod-product-compliance
Lightning Source LLC
LaVergne TN
LVHW081345300926
849161LV00008B/2072